The Cultural and Political
Environment of International Business

To all of the people who have opened windows
on the world for me by introducing me
to the cultures of their homelands, including

my wife Lydia and her family *(Switzerland);*
Daisy Kwoh *(China);* Keiko Ogihara Stadler *(Japan);*
Dr. Palamand S. Rao *(India);* Saiburee Tyocharoen *(Thailand);*
Izhar Bin Shaari *(Malaysia);* Mohammed Hussein *(Pakistan);*
Dora Araya-Sanchez *(Costa Rica);* Michael and Stassi Hannah *(Lebanon);*
Lorna Young *(England);* Paul Chang *(Taiwan);*
Kubilai Celebi *(Turkey);* Christine Tran *(Vietnam);*
Adeline Cheong *(Singapore);* Marlene King *(Trinidad-Tobago);*
Ndon Emah *(Nigeria);* Harry Vorn and family *(Netherlands);*
Pauline Kraus Karrels *(Germany);* Roar Kvernhusengen *(Norway);*
Lone Wittliff *(Sweden);* Sirkka Short *(Finland);*
Elaine Neukermans *(Belgium);* Mehdi Eshragh-Hedayat *(Iran);*
Isaac Almanza *(Mexico);* Frank Puskas *(Hungary);*
Antonio Navarro and family *(Spain);*
Francesco Adobati and family *(Italy);*
Jaime Valdivieso and family *(Chile);*
Emma Nipp Ramon *(Liechtenstein)*

and other students, friends and acquaintances
from other lands too numerous to mention.

The Cultural and Political Environment of International Business

A Guide for Business Professionals

by

Don Alan Evans

McFarland & Company, Inc., Publishers
Jefferson, North Carolina, and London

British Library Cataloguing-in-Publication data are available

Library of Congress Cataloguing-in-Publication Data

Evans, Don Alan.
    The cultural and political environment of international business :
a guide for business professionals / by Don Alan Evans.
    p.   cm.
    Includes bibliographical references and index.
    ISBN 0-89950-639-9 (lib. bdg. : 50# alk. paper) ∞
    1. International business enterprises—Social aspects.
    2. International business enterprises—Social aspects—Developing
countries.   I. Title.
    HD2755.5.E93   1991
    909.82'9—dc20   91-52754
                                                                  CIP

Manufactured in the United States of America

McFarland & Company, Inc., Publishers
  Box 611, Jefferson, North Carolina 28640

Contents

Preface vii
1. The Races of Humankind 1
2. Western Culture 14
3. Non-Western Cultures 39
4. Languages 59
5. Religions—Christianity 80
6. Non-Christian Religions 94
7. Other Cultural Considerations 117
8. Family, Gender and Marriage 147
9. The International State System 173
10. Governmental Systems 193
11. National Governments 209
12. Nomination and Election Systems 239
13. Nationality and Human Rights 266
14. Economic Systems 279
15. The Future 302
    Glossary 325
    Bibliography 335
    Index 343

Preface

American business education is admired throughout the world for the quality of its technical content. Holders of business degrees from American universities possess excellent knowledge of accounting, finance, economics, management and marketing, and attain a high degree of computer literacy.

Yet our students of international business learn little or nothing of foreign languages, cultures, religions, governments and politics.

It is not surprising that this should be so. Undergraduate curricula in schools of business are so crammed with courses providing basic general education, mathematical and communication skills, and technical business knowledge that few elective hours remain. The average student's elective courses don't strain the intellect but offer easy opportunities to earn good grades and improve grade point averages.

What little information American business students acquire about the outside world comes from texts on international management, economics, marketing or finance. They cover technical subject matter very well, but have little space to cover anything else.

My previous volume, *The Legal Environment of International Business* (1990), provides hard information on the legal systems of the world and the legal problems of international business.

The present work is in a sense a supplement to that one, providing information on the cultural, political, and economic systems of the world's nations. It consolidates information from several disciplines into one short volume — anthropology, linguistics, sociology, history, political science and economics.

In addition to my degree in law, I have been a student of history. I've spent many summer vacations in the company of my Swiss in-laws. My speaking and reading knowledge of French, German and the Swiss-German dialect has acquainted me well with life in Switzerland.

My knowledge of Mandarin Chinese and my fifteen months of U.S. Air Force service in the Orient have provided insight into the lives and thought processes of persons of Chinese culture.

The openness of graduate and undergraduate students from the four corners of the earth has enabled me to learn from, as well as teach, my academic charges. Without these precious personal contacts, my understanding of the world would be more limited.

I firmly believe that no one can claim a broad knowledge of the international business environment without exposure to the information contained in this volume.

The first eight chapters cover the cultural environment of business, beginning with the various human races of man in Chapter 1 and the major cultures of the world, which are covered in Chapters 2 and 3.

Chapter 4 proceeds to the subject of languages—the families of languages, how speakers of the various tongues are distributed in the world, dialects, writing systems and problems of language study.

Religion is the subject of Chapters 5 and 6. Covered here are the belief systems of the world's major religions, and the effects of these belief systems upon human cultures.

In Chapter 7 human attitudes toward time, social hierarchy, names, food and drink are discussed. Also covered are some unique peculiarities of other cultures such as the Oriental concept of *face*.

Chapter 8 closes the cultural section of the text with a discussion of varying human attitudes toward family, gender and marriage.

The remainder of the book deals with the world political environment. Chapter 9 discusses the origin of the European state system and its operation in today's world, and Chapter 10 contains an exposition of governmental systems and a discussion of how forms of government have changed throughout history.

Chapter 11 deals with contemporary forms of government, while Chapter 12 discusses the mechanisms by which officials are chosen in today's democracies. Chapter 13 covers the relationships between government and the governed.

Chapter 14 discusses the world's economic systems, pointing out that hostility toward the free market and its manifestations has been the rule throughout most of human history, and explaining why this has occurred.

The final chapter looks into the future, closing with a brief discussion of the current ecological crisis and the obstacles standing in the way of its resolution through the action of the free market.

Chapter 1

The Races of Humankind

In his book, *The Living Races of Man,* Carleton S. Coon divides humanity into five races. These are:

(1) Caucasoid, found originally in Europe, west Asia and the Indian subcontinent;

(2) Congoid, found in Africa south of the Sahara and north of the southernmost area of that continent;

(3) Mongoloid, found in east Asia and the Western Hemisphere;

(4) Australoid, found in Australia, the islands of the Pacific, and as small minorities in Indonesia, the Philippines and elsewhere in southeast Asia; and

(5) Capoid, found at the southern tip of Africa.

On the other hand Stanley M. Garn states in his book *Human Races* (second edition) that there exist nine major geographic races of humanity. These are:

(1) European, found in Europe and west Asia;

(2) Indian, found in the Indian subcontinent;

(3) African, found in Africa south of the Sahara;

(4) Asiatic, found in east and southeast Asia;

(5) Amerindian, found in the Western Hemisphere;

(6) Polynesian, found in Hawaii, Easter Island, Tahiti, New Zealand, and certain other Pacific islands;

(7) Micronesian, found on islands such as Palau and Yap in the Pacific;

(8) Melanesian, found on Pacific islands such as the Solomons, New Britain and New Guinea; and

(9) Australian, found in Australia.

Garn's European and Indian races seem to be branches of Coon's Caucasoids. Garn's African race seems to comprise Coon's Congoids. Garn's Asiatics and Amerindians seem to be branches of Coon's Mongoloids. Garn's Polynesians, Micronesians, Melanesians and Australians seem to be branches of Coon's Australoids.

Garn speaks also of identifiable large local races of humanity. Subdivisions of the European race are:

(1) Northwest European, originally inhabiting Scandinavia, Germany,

1

the British Isles and adjoining areas (mainly speakers of Germanic languages);

(2) Northeast European, inhabiting Poland, Russia and adjoining areas (speakers of some Slavic languages);

(3) Alpine, inhabiting the Alpine regions and the northern Balkan peninsula;

(4) Mediterranean, including south Europeans, north Africans and most west Asians (speakers of Romance languages, Greek and Arabic); and

(5) Iranian, including inhabitants of Asia Minor, Iran, Afghanistan and part of northern India.

Garn lists two local divisions of the Indian race:

(1) Hindu, living in northern India; and

(2) Dravidian, living in southern India.

Local divisions of the African race include:

(1) East African, inhabiting the area around the Horn of Africa (Ethiopia, Somalia, and parts of Kenya);

(2) Sudanese, found in the areas just south of the Sahara;

(3) Forest Negro, found in West Africa and Zaire; and

(4) Bantu, living in the area from just south of the Equator to the northern portions of the Republic of South Africa.

Local divisions of the Asiatic race include:

(1) Tibetan, inhabiting the mountainous areas of central Asia;

(2) North Chinese;

(3) Extreme Mongoloid, living in northeast Asia; and

(4) Southeast Asiatic (south Chinese, Vietnamese, Laotians and the like).

Lastly Garn mentions some small local races worthy of mention:

(1) Lapp, the herding peoples of far north Scandinavia and Russia;

(2) Negrito, the small dark people found in parts of Australia, Indonesia and the Philippines;

(3) Pygmy, the small jungle people of the African rain forests;

(4) Eskimo, the inhabitants of far northern North America;

(5) Ainu, the seemingly non–Asiatic aborigines of the Japanese island of Hokkaido; and

(6) Bushmen, Coon's Capoid race of southern Africa.

Before 1492 and the great migrations that came after, the human races were distributed as follows: Europeans occupied Europe, North Africa and western Asia. Indians occupied the Indian subcontinent. Africans occupied all of central and southern Africa except for most of the modern Republic of South Africa. Bushmen occupied southernmost Africa. Asiatics occupied southeastern and eastern Asia. Amerindians occupied all of the Western Hemisphere. Australians occupied Australia. The Pacific islands were inhabited by mainly the same peoples who inhabit them now.

Caucasoids vary considerably in appearance. Scandinavians are primarily people of pale skin, blue eyes and blond hair, while Latins tend to have darker skin, dark hair and dark eyes. Slavs—Czechs, Poles, Russians and the like—are primarily ash blond with gray eyes.

Conventional wisdom says that blue-eyed blonds exist only in the cool lands of the European north, but they can also be found in the Atlas Mountains of north Africa among the Berbers, who lived there before the Arabs came in the eighth century.

To a degree, Iranians, Arabs and Turks all resemble the Latin Europeans.

The dark skin and eyes of the typical north Indian may conceal a physical resemblance to the European—but place a person from Delhi alongside one from Oslo, Kinshasa and Tokyo and the kinship becomes clear enough.

Most, but not all, central and southern Africans share the physical features of the prototypical Congoid-Negroid. The Gambian and the Zambian, the Liberian and the Tanzanian, may appear to be brothers.

In the north and east, Caucasoids from the Mediterranean coast and the Arabian Peninsula have mingled their genes with the Congoids. The Ethiopian Amhara may be as dark as the Gambian, but his hair might be straight and his nose prominent. The Tutsi of Rwanda and Burundi, who migrated into their present home from the northeast around the fifteenth century, may have lighter skin than the typical African and stand much taller.

The Pygmies of the central African forests are dwarf Congoids whose skin is lighter than their taller brethren. They rarely intermarry with Congoids or anyone else, and seldom venture far away from their jungle homes.

South Indians who speak a Dravidian language will have almost black skin and black eyes, yet their hair and other facial features will resemble those of the Indo-European speaker to the north. In skin color but not otherwise they resemble the central Africans.

When one thinks of people of the Mongoloid race, one thinks of Japanese, Koreans or south Chinese. We don't realize that northern Chinese can grow tall, have very fair skin, and sport prominent noses. Laotians and Vietnamese aren't too different physically from south Chinese—Kampucheans, Thais and Burmese are darker.

Filipinos, Indonesians, and Malays are much darker than their northern cousins, but the epicanthic folds of their eyes identify them as Mongoloids. Their darker skins are attributable to a mixture of Australoid genes.

The purest Australoids are the Australian aborigines, the Papuans of New Guinea and the Melanesians of the Pacific islands from New Britain to Fiji.

The dwarf Australoids mentioned earlier are found in the Philippines (the Negritos) and elsewhere in southeast and south Asia.

Throughout the remote islands of the Pacific are human types found nowhere else. On the Hawaiian islands and in Tahiti and New Zealand live the Polynesians—brown-skinned people of handsome features (to Caucasoid eyes). On the Marshall, Caroline and other islands nearby are found the

Micronesians, who are darker and generally shorter than Polynesians. They are mixtures of Mongoloid and Australoid.

On the northernmost Japanese island, Hokkaido, live people of Caucasoid features. These Ainu inhabited most of Japan before the Mongoloid Japanese came and drove them steadily back into the cold northland.

Before the dawn of recorded history Mongoloid peoples found their way from Siberia to Alaska and from there wandered over the entire Western Hemisphere. Wherever Europeans set foot in the New World in the centuries after the fifteenth, they found Mongolians—the Amerind—here first.

Pre-1492 racial frontiers. The frontier between Caucasoid and Congoid was the Sahara Desert, the Red Sea and the east coast of Africa. Some Congoid genes had found their way into populations of North Africa and the Arabian Peninsula, while Caucasoid genes had penetrated populations in Ethiopia, Kenya, Tanzania and at the south edge of the Sahara.

The frontier between Caucasoid and Mongoloid began at approximately the present-day frontier between Bangladesh and Burma. It ran north from there to the foothills of the Himalayas, northwest to the vicinity of Kashmir, north along the western foothills of the Tien Shan mountain range to the plains of Siberia.

The great plain that stretches from the Tien Shan westward into Europe was a great battleground of Mongoloid and Caucasoid. Armies of Mongoloid nomads repeatedly swept across here, bringing terror and destruction into the heart of the Caucasoid homelands: the Huns in the fifth century, the Magyars in the ninth and tenth, and the Mongols in the thirteenth.

Between 1237 and 1240 the hordes of the Mongol prince Sabutai destroyed the principalities of Kievan Rus (in the present-day Ukraine) and swept into Hungary, Poland and eastern Germany. One division of their forces destroyed an army of Poles and Germans at Liegnitz in Silesia on April 9, 1241; two days later the other destroyed the army of the king of Hungary at Mohi. Central Europe lay wide open to them. Only the death of the great Mongol khan Ogadai in far-off central Asia spared it (Sabutai and his army returning to Mongolia to participate in the choice of a new Great Khan and never returning), but virtually all of Russia passed under Mongol domination. For almost two centuries Mongol genes filtered into the Russian population and Mongol ideas crept into Russian culture. The Mongol threat to eastern Europe did not end until 1380 when the Muscovite prince Dmitri Donskoi's army defeated the Mongols at Kulikovo. Even so, Mongol khans continued to rule in the Crimea and in the valleys of the Volga and the Don; only the western portion of present-day European Russia remained Caucasoid.

Congoid and Mongoloid met only on the island of Madagascar, off the east coast of Africa.

Congoid and Capoid met at the north edge of the Kalahari Desert of southern Africa.

Australoid encountered Mongoloid in the islands of what is now eastern Indonesia, and on other islands scattered throughout the southwest and south Pacific.

Nations and races. Europeans, Arabs, Turks, Iranians and Indians were (and still are) Caucasoids, the most numerous of the five races.

Chinese, Japanese, Mongols, Filipinos, Malays, Indonesians, Southeast Asians and Amerinds were (and still are) Mongoloids, the second most numerous race.

Most central Africans were (and still are) Congoid, the third most numerous race.

Australians, Papuans and Melanesians were Australoids, the fourth most numerous race. Papuans and Melanesians are still the dominant peoples on their islands but the Australian aborigines are now an insignificant part of Australia's population; most of the inhabitants of that nation-continent are now Caucasoid.

The original southern Africans were Capoid. Before 1492 they and the part–Negroid part–Capoid Hottentots were the dominant population group of the area.

Post-1492 migrations and population changes. Human migrations and conquests since 1492 have permanently changed the nature of the population of many areas of the globe. The most astounding changes have occurred in the Western Hemisphere, where Caucasoid colonists and the Congoid slaves they imported completely altered the demographic map.

Most of the people of the United States, Canada, Costa Rica, Brazil, Argentina, and Uruguay are Caucasoid, though the original inhabitants were Mongoloid. The English, Spanish and Portuguese conquerors either exterminated the native Amerinds or confined them to reservations.

In a few relatively remote Western Hemisphere nations the majority of the population is still pure Amerind. Among these are Guatemala, Ecuador, Paraguay and Bolivia. Peru too has many pure Amerinds in its population.

The large majority of the inhabitants of most other continental Western Hemisphere nations are mestizos—people of mixed European and Amerind background. Included here are Mexico; all of Central America except Costa Rica, Belize and Guatemala; and, in South America, Colombia, Venezuela and Chile.

With respect to the islands of the Caribbean the majority of Cubans and Puerto Ricans are Caucasoid, but there is a large Congoid minority on both islands. On Hispaniola Haiti is completely Congoid, while the Dominican Republic has a mestizo majority and Congoid minority. The population of most of the other islands (Jamaica, Barbados, Guadeloupe, Martinique, Dominica, Grenada and the others) contains a large Congoid majority. Here the European conquerors exterminated the native Amerinds and brought in African slaves to work the sugar plantations they established. During colonial times the population came to consist of huge numbers of slaves ruled by a small well-armed Caucasoid minority.

In Haiti the Caucasoids were exterminated in turn during the great slave rebellion of the 1790s. In the Dominican Republic and on most of the other islands a Caucasoid minority remained behind when independence was granted.

Belize is the only non-island nation in the Western Hemisphere with a Congoid majority.

In the island nation of Trinidad and Tobago, and in the nations of Suriname and Guyana on the South American mainland the population is primarily a mixture of Congoid and Asian Indian. Trinidad and Tobago is more Congoid than Indian, but in Guyana and Suriname the east Indians are the largest element of the population. The British brought large numbers of Indians to Trinidad and Guyana to do agricultural labor. The Dutch similarly brought Indonesians to Suriname.

The populations of Eastern Hemisphere lands have also changed recently due to migrations. When the Mongoloid nomads were ejected from the plains of European Russia and much of their north Asian domain in the sixteenth and seventeenth centuries, the struggle of Caucasoid and Mongoloid for dominion over the Siberian plain ended. Though many Mongoloids still live in Soviet Siberia, much of the population is now European Russian. A new frontier between Caucasoid and Mongoloid has been established between the Soviet Union on one hand and the Mongolian People's Republic and China on the other.

Into the lands that were later to become the Republic of South Africa, the Dutch intruded about 1650, at which time only primitive Hottentots and Bush people lived in the area around Cape Town. These people were either exterminated or driven into the wilds of the Kalahari and Namibian deserts. Later English colonists established themselves along the Indian Ocean in what later became the Natal Province. Here too there were few native inhabitants to dispute control of the land. Only later did the Zulu warrior bands come south into the lands of present-day South Africa. Still later, after the discoveries of gold and diamonds in the Orange Free State and Transvaal, huge numbers of blacks were brought south to do the physical labor of mining. Around the turn of the century large numbers of Indians immigrated to South Africa; they were the ancestors of the country's sizable Asian minority.

Mongoloids and Congoids have continued to mix genes on the island of Madagascar. Today Congoid elements narrowly predominate in the population, but the language is Asian.

The frontiers of several nations along the southern fringe of the Sahara have been drawn in such a way as to throw Caucasoids and Congoids together in the same country. In the Islamic Republic of Mauretania a Caucasoid Arab majority lords it over a small Congoid minority, while in Senegal to the south the reverse situation prevails.

In Chad a Congoid majority has in the past dominated a Caucasoid Arab minority. Since Colonel Muammar Khaddafi came to power in Libya to the north the Arabs have had access to modern weapons, and racially inspired civil war has wracked the country. Without French aid the Congoids would have long ago been overwhelmed.

A large Arab Caucasoid majority in Sudan has sought to totally dominate a smaller Congoid minority. Here too there has been bitter racial civil war. Though the majority granted limited home rule to the minority the war continues; the issues and consequences of the Sudanese conflict will be discussed later.

The island of Zanzibar, twenty miles off the coast of east Africa, has had a predominantly Caucasoid Arab population for centuries. A Congoid minority, originally slaves, worked the clove plantations of the island. Both the island and the neighboring mainland (with an overwhelmingly Congoid population) were British colonies. Independence came in 1961 when the mainland became the Republic of Tanganyika, and in 1963 when the island became the Sultanate of Zanzibar. In 1964 the Congoid minority on Zanzibar overthrew the Sultanate (massacring many Arabs in the process) and demanded union with Tanganyika. Later in 1964 the nations merged, forming the Republic of Tanzania. Since that time Caucasoids and Congoids have nervously coexisted side by side on the island, with little violence.

In Australia Caucasoid settlers have all but exterminated the Australoid aborigines. However, in the uncomfortable humidity of New Britain and the Solomons and in the remote mountain fastnesses of New Guinea the Australoid Papuans and Melanesians survive in large numbers.

In New Zealand Caucasoid colonists nearly exterminated the Polynesian Maori. In Hawaii Caucasoid Americans and Mongoloid Japanese have virtually displaced the Polynesian Hawaiians. In Tahiti Caucasoid diseases have decimated the Polynesian aborigines.

So far the native Micronesians have fared better; neither Caucasoids nor Mongoloids find the climate of islands like Saipan to their liking.

Non-racial Migrations and Population Changes

Many significant human migrations haven't involved the supplanting of one race by another, but have involved the supplanting and uprooting of nations and cultures.

The caste system of India apparently came into existence when light-skinned Indo-European conquerors imposed their rule upon dark-skinned Dravidians at the dawn of Indian history. Since that time the march and countermarch of conquerors have created a monumental racial intermixture in the subcontinent. Iranians, Afghans, Huns and Mongols have come here as conquerors; the genes of all remain in the bloodstream of the modern north Indian.

Mongoloid peoples have spilled over the crests of the Himalayas and occupy the high ground dominating the north Indian plain. The Nepalese, Bhutanese, Sikkimese and the Tibetans of Ladakh share the facial features of their cousins north of the great mountains.

In southeast Asia Chinese immigrants from the area around Canton began to appear six centuries ago. Since the native Malays, Vietnamese and Thais had no talent for or interest in economic activity, the Chinese colonists found an economic niche they could fill. Because they could come to southeast Asia, work hard and maybe become rich, the opportunities beckoned to their kinsmen. As a result, most of today's nations of this part of the world have substantial Chinese minorities. In fact, one southeast Asian nation—Singapore—has a population 76 percent of which is descended from these Chinese colonists.

In peninsular Malaysia three groups strive to peacefully coexist. The Chinese first came to the other lands of southeast Asia. During the nineteenth century the British colonial masters of the area imported Indians to work in the newly established rubber plantations. When they pulled out they left behind a land without a majority ethnic group. There were, and still are, more Malays in peninsular Malaysia than any other group, but Chinese and Indians together outnumber the Malays. So far the three antagonistic groups live in relative peace, and Malaysia is one of the more democratic nations in the area.

On the island of Ceylon—the present-day republic of Sri Lanka—British tea plantation owners brought in Tamil laborers from India. Northern Sri Lanka acquired a sizable Tamil population; the religious, linguistic and cultural incompatibility between them and the Sinhalese majority on the island has resulted in conflict which poisons the political and social life of the nation to this day.

Twenty-three hundred years ago the state of Nam Viet, inhabited by the ancestors of the Vietnamese, occupied the Red River valley of present-day Vietnam, along with much of present-day south China and Laos. North lay the growing Chinese empire, while to the south lay the kingdom the Chinese called Funan, whose inhabitants were ancestors of the Cambodians and the Chams.

In 111 B.C. Chinese armies occupied Nam Viet and annexed it to their empire. The northern inhabitants accepted Chinese rule and culture, becoming Chinese themselves. The people of the Red River valley also adopted much of Chinese culture but preserved their own language and social customs. Bitter resistance to the Chinese occupation flared repeatedly, resulting in cruel repression. At last, in A.D. 939 the Vietnamese expelled Chinese armies from the country and established independence.

By now Funan had evolved into two separate states—Champa along the coast of present-day southern Vietnam, and Cambodia, occupying the Mekong River valley. The inhabitants of the land were dark-skinned, Chams and Cambodians being near kin.

The history of Vietnam after that is the story of steady expansion southward by the Vietnamese at the expense of the Chams and Cambodians and occasional desperate struggles to preserve independence from the Chinese. There were massive Chinese invasions in 1284 and 1287 and total Chinese reconquest in 1407. By 1428, however, Vietnamese rebels had driven the Chinese out, never to return. By 1471 the empire of Champa had disappeared, and the light-skinned kin of the Chinese had become the major population group in all of present-day Vietnam except the Mekong delta and the Saigon area. The Cambodians were expelled from the vicinity of Saigon before 1700 and by 1757 Vietnamese ruled the whole country. This history created the bitter hostility between Vietnamese and Chinese on the one hand and Vietnamese and Cambodians (now Kampucheans) on the other which causes such difficulty in southeast Asia today.

Until the seventh century the only Arabic-speaking peoples on the face of the earth were in the Arabian Peninsula, or nearby. Because the prophet Mohammed converted the Arabs to his new faith of Islam and inspired them to carry it to the ends of the earth Arab armies marched out of their peninsula to Spain, Siberia, and the gates of China and India. As a result the Middle East and North Africa became Islamic in religion; the Zoroastrianism of Iran virtually vanished and the Christianity of Syria, Egypt and Africa's north shore was submerged. Arabic became, and remains today, the prevailing language from the western borders of Iran to the Atlantic coast of Morocco.

The inhabitants of Spain at the dawn of history were the Iberians, a Celtic people, kin of the Gauls and Britons. Carthaginian conquerors added the blood of the Middle East. The Roman victors over the Carthaginians contributed Latin European genes to the Spanish bloodline.

In the fourth and fifth centuries the Germanic Visigoths expelled the Romans, and blue-eyed blonds ruled the Iberian peninsula for two centuries.

In 711 the Muslims destroyed the power of the Visigoths in one battle and Spain became al-Andalus, one of the brightest jewels in Islam's crown. In 1212, however, the Castilians smashed an Islamic army at Las Navas de Tolosa and most of Spain reverted to Christian control. The last vestige of Islamic rule vanished when Granada surrendered to the armies of Ferdinand and Isabella in 1492. Present-day Spain is a prime example of a country in the blood of whose people courses the genes of many races, nations and cultures.

The lands of Asiatic Turkey were inhabited by Greeks up to the eleventh century. After the Turks overwhelmingly defeated the armies of the Byzantine Empire at Manzikert in 1071, Turkish colonists moved into the area. The Greeks either converted to Islam and adopted Turkish speech to conform to the new order, or they migrated westward to territories that were still Christian. Thus the ethnic character of Asia Minor changed forever.

Even England has known great changes in population and culture due to migration and conquest. Little is known of the pre–Celtic peoples who erected the amazing standing stones of Stonehenge. All we know for sure is that they were displaced by Celtic invaders during the first millennium B.C.

In 54 B.C. Julius Caesar's Roman army paid the island a visit, and a hundred years later the Romans returned to stay, for three centuries. Few Romans settled in far-off Britain, but some Latin genes did enter the population. The language and culture were altered permanently.

In the fifth century the Romans pulled out, and Germanic peoples from the Continent (primarily Angles and Saxons) flooded in. The Romanized Celts were driven westward into the hills of Wales, and England became Anglo-Saxon.

In the ninth century the Danes poured in, dominating the north-central part of the island for a time, as Scandinavian genes and cultural influence were added.

In 1066 came the last conquest, as the Normans (descendants of Viking conquerors of Normandy who had adopted French culture) overthrew the Anglo-Saxon kingdom. Since that landmark year French, Germanic, Scandinavian, Roman and Celtic influences fused together to produce modern England, the home of the colonists who have transformed so much of the earth in the last three centuries.

Lastly we must mention the exterminations and great migrations of the twentieth century which have altered demographic maps.

In the early 1920s the Greeks attempted to conquer western Asia Minor from the Turks and failed. The peace treaty allowed the Turks to expel most Greek residents of their country; the Greeks were permitted to expel their Turkish minority. The result was a massive exchange of populations which changed the demographic maps of both countries. (Turkey retains a small Greek minority concentrated in Istanbul; Greece retains a small Turkish minority in its Thracian borderlands.)

The Nazi holocaust changed the demographic map of eastern Europe by nearly exterminating the sizable Jewish minorities of Poland and the western Soviet Union.

In the late 1940s, after World War II, the boundaries of Poland were shifted westward and populations moved to conform to the new borders. What had been eastern Poland was incorporated into the Soviet Union. What had been eastern Germany was incorporated into Poland and the Soviet Union. Ethnic Poles were expelled from land that was now Soviet; ethnic Germans were expelled from land that was now Polish and Soviet. The Polish city of Lwow became Russian Lvov. German Koenigsberg became Soviet Kaliningrad. German Breslau became Polish Wroclaw. The results of a millennium of

German colonization of what had been eastern Germany were erased, as was the result of five hundred years of Polish colonization of what is now the western marches of the Soviet Union.

When the boundaries of Czechoslovakia were drawn after World War I, 3 million German Austrians who inhabited the mountainous Sudetenland were incorporated against their will into the new nation to give it a defensible frontier with Germany. Because Adolf Hitler desired to incorporate these German speakers into his Third Reich Czechoslovakia was dismembered in 1938 and wiped off the map a year later. When it was restored in 1945 the Czechoslovak government claimed revenge by expelling these Germans from the Sudetenland, pushing them across the frontier into Germany. Thus present-day Czechoslovakia has no significant German-speaking minority.

The influx of Jews into Palestine after World War II made possible the creation of the state of Israel. It caused large numbers of Palestinian Arabs to leave, changing the demographic map of the area and creating the Palestinian refugee problem that has threatened the peace of the Middle East ever since.

In British India over 75 percent of the population was Hindu; in large areas of the colony the population was overwhelmingly Hindu. However, in the northwest adjoining Iran and Afghanistan the population was overwhelmingly Muslim, as it was in parts of Bengal in the east. In a few other areas Hindus and Muslims lived side by side.

When the British abandoned the colony in 1947 it was partitioned into Hindu India and Muslim Pakistan. Muslims living in India were given the right to move to Pakistan; Hindus living in Pakistan were given the reciprocal right to migrate to India. In an immense population exchange Pakistan lost most of its Hindus while India lost most of its Muslims. During the migrations tens of thousands of persons of both religions were massacred — Muslims by Hindus in India and Hindus by Muslims in Pakistan.

The island of Taiwan was a part of the Chinese Empire before 1895. Its population was a mixture of the aborigines who had settled the island in prehistoric times and the colonists from China's Fukien Province (speakers of Fukienese) who had crossed the Taiwan Straits to settle the accessible parts of the island. As a result of Japan's victory over China in the Sino-Japanese War of 1894–95, the island became a colony of Japan. A few Japanese settled there and the islanders acquired some of the culture of the colonizing power.

In 1945 Taiwan was restored to China; the Chinese Nationalist government sent Mandarin speakers from north China to govern. When the Nationalists were driven from the Chinese mainland by the Communist armies of Mao Tse-Tung in 1949, hordes of northern Chinese refugees descended upon the island. The mainlanders, who considered themselves a privileged caste, dominated the government and armed forces and subjected the native Taiwanese to galling discrimination. As the refugees from the mainland have progressively died out, their children have opened more doors to the

Taiwanese, who have benefited greatly from the economic development of the island, and play a progressively larger role in its government. Eventually, perhaps, the mainlanders will be absorbed into the Taiwanese majority.

Before Bulgaria obtained independence in 1878, it was part of the Turkish Empire. Several hundred thousand ethnic Turks had settled there before independence and remained there afterward. In the late 1980s the Communist government of the country decided to rid it of this alien minority. Over 300,000 of these Bulgarian Turks have fled or been expelled across the Bulgar-Turkish frontier. (Since the fall of the Stalinist dictator Todor Zhivkov, Bulgaria has reversed its expulsion policy. Bulgars still have no love for Turks so relations between the two ethnic groups remain troubled.)

During the last thirty years a more subtle migration of peoples has slowly been changing the demographic maps of western Europe, Australia, the United States and even the Arabian Peninsula.

The great economic boom of the 1960s and early 1970s caused an immense labor shortage in the nations of western Europe; employers and governments sought to import workers from areas of high unemployment to supply the demand. Italians poured into Switzerland; Turks and Yugoslavs flooded into West Germany; North Africans came to France; Indians, Pakistanis and Africans sought jobs in Great Britain. Decolonization added to the influx; Great Britain, France and the Netherlands recognized residents of many of their ex-colonies as privileged immigrants to the mother country. When the boom faded into the recession of the late 1970s and early 1980s the West Europeans found that they couldn't simply expel their guest laborers. Not only did the possibility of expulsion raise grave questions about violation of human rights; the guests had in a sense acquired vested rights as hewers of wood and drawers of water. Natives of the host countries were no longer willing to do the unpleasant jobs they had so joyfully relinquished to their guests in the days of prosperity; the guest workers had become an essential part of the national economy.

In addition, large numbers of non–European refugees have settled in the countries of western Europe. Vietnamese, Kampucheans, Sri Lankan Tamils, Tibetans, Zaireans, Chileans and other fugitives from war and oppression have found welcome of sorts there.

The *Economist* estimated in its December 23, 1989, issue that 1.5 million Turks now reside in western Germany, and that 5 million North Africans now work in western Europe (a large number of them in France). In several western European countries from 10 percent to 15 percent of the population now consists of persons born abroad. Though some of these are fellow Europeans (Yugoslav guest workers, Hungarian and Polish refugees), many came from outside Europe.

Asians and Africans comprise 2.8 percent of the population of the United Kingdom, while 1 percent of the population of the Netherlands is non-

European and 1 percent of the French population consists of practicing Muslims, mostly north Africans. The unprecedented immigration has probably caused the racial homogeneity of West European populations to vanish forever.

Before 1973 Australia followed a "white only" immigration policy, welcoming English-speaking immigrants and admitting small numbers of non–English-speaking Caucasoid immigrants who possessed skills of value to the economy. In 1973 Australia changed over to a color-blind immigration policy, in part to improve relations with its Asian neighbors. As a result, 4 percent of the Australian population is now Asian and the percentage will continue to grow.

The United States too followed a policy of discouraging non-white immigration until 1965. Since then its policy has been color-blind; a large proportion of U.S. immigrants since the changeover has been Asian. Vietnamese communities have sprouted all over the country; in Los Angeles and a few other cities large Korean communities exist.

In addition the influx of lawful Cuban refugees and unlawful immigrants from Mexico is changing the demography of Florida and the Southwest. Miami has become in some respects an Hispanic city while the Hispanic population of Texas, Arizona and California grows rapidly. The United States is in the process of becoming, if it hasn't already become, a multi-racial, multi-lingual and multi-cultural nation.

The great oil boom in the lands of the Arabian Peninsula created an immense demand for labor in a very thinly populated part of the world. Asians and Africans have gone there in large numbers seeking economic betterment. Ten percent of the population of Saudi Arabia is Afro-Asian, most of it concentrated in the oil-producing areas. In the smaller oil-producing lands of the Arabian Peninsula, the newcomers are much more numerous. Twenty-eight percent of the population of Bahrein is non–Bahreini; 61 percent of that of Kuwait was non–Kuwaiti before the Iraqi invasion of 1990. Most extreme is the situation in the United Arab Emirates, where only 19 percent of the population consists of UAE citizens. Though the governments of these lands severely restrict the right of their guest workers to bring families with them and to remain in the country when their labor contracts expire, some manage to do both. In this part of the world the nature of the population is irrevocably changing.

The peoples of most of Earth's nations share an immense racial and ethnic diversity. As people of all races migrate to the far corners of planet Earth, the ethnic homogeneity of most human populations diminishes. Not only do we share our planet with persons of other races and cultures, gradually we are likewise sharing our nations.

Chapter 2
Western Culture

According to William H. McNeill's *The Rise of the West,* four great human cultures exist on planet Earth: Western, Middle Eastern, Indian and Chinese. Today one would add a fifth, the African. Though our Western culture to a great extent dominates the planet, we forget the existence of the others at our peril.

Our culture is the youngest of the five and certainly the most aggressive. It's also the most materialistic, the most technologically oriented, and the most individualistic.

Born in the primitive city-states of Homeric Greece, its early heroes battled each other before the walls of Troy a thousand years before Christ. It produced the determination that stopped the Persian invaders of the west at Marathon and Salamis. It early demonstrated diversity by producing on the one hand the democracy of Athens and on the other the grim militarism of Sparta and the tyrannies of Syracuse. It produced a congeries of disunited city-states that made themselves powers in the Mediterranean basin.

Because these small political units couldn't cooperate to preserve and extend their power, they lost it. The great Greek civil war—the Peloponnesian War between Athens and Sparta and their allies at the end of the fifth century B.C.—fatally weakened all participants. They finally lost their independence to Philip's kingdom of Macedonia a half-century later; most contributed troops to the disciplined phalanx of his son Alexander that smashed Persia and marched to the gates of India.

The spread of Greek culture and language into the lands of the Middle East caused its dilution by the ideas of the ancient cultures of Egypt, Mesopotamia and Persia. Thus was the groundwork laid for the half Western, half Eastern way of life of the later Byzantine Empire.

At this same time came expansion of the Roman Republic, a city-state governed by a complex constitution of checks and balances. Through a combination of iron discipline, clever military leadership and ruthless determination the armies of this small state subdued first all of Italy, then the western Mediterranean basin, and then the entire shoreline of the great inland sea. It was clear by as early as 100 B.C. that the city-state constitutional structure of

14

the Republic was inadequate for the governance of a huge empire. The ambitions of generals, the chaos of assassination and civil war, and the political genius of Octavian (later Caesar Augustus) caused it to evolve into the Principate, under which a mighty "first citizen" dominated the state while preserving republican institutions.

The peoples of the Roman Empire weren't culturally uniform. In the west, where Latin was the language of high culture, Greek and Roman ideas and ideals prevailed in their purity. In the east the amalgam of Levantine and Greek culture created by Alexander's conquests continued. During the first and second centuries of the Christian era the empire was governed according to western principles. Though madmen like Caligula and Nero behaved like oriental potentates solemn men like Hadrian and Marcus Aurelius ruled as responsible leaders of the state.

As time marched on eastern notions gained ground. After the death of Marcus Aurelius a century of governmental instability destroyed the Augustan system. By the time Diocletian restored order at the beginning of the fourth century the empire had become an absolute monarchy in many ways more akin to the Persia of Xerxes than to the Rome of Caesar Augustus.

A few years after Diocletian's death the Emperor Constantine imposed religious unity upon the realm by making Christianity, a Middle Eastern faith, the state religion. Thus a peculiar brand was placed upon the West.

Christianity, like so many other "miracle religions" of the time of the Roman Empire, preaches that our sojourn in this world is but a way station on the road to eternity. Our mission here is to live so that we'll be assured eternal heavenly bliss. It holds that this world is incurably evil and humanity is so corrupted by the sin of Adam that we can neither hope nor expect to live a godly life here.

The pessimistic St. Augustine wrote in the fifth century that no one may achieve salvation through his own efforts, that it can be attained only through the grace of God; those fortunate ones who attain it have been chosen by God before birth. For the huge majority who aren't among the elect, there's only misery in this world and the next.

Augustine's contemporary Pelagius presented the opposing argument that the world isn't inherently good or evil; neither is humanity, which has the mighty power of free will; we may choose between good and evil. We may achieve salvation through our own good acts if our willpower is strong enough. We may control our own destiny.

Pelagius lost the theological argument as the Augustinian view became Church doctrine. To Westerners of the fifth century it must have made sense; twice within fifty years Rome was sacked by armies of Germanic barbarians, and in 476 the last Western Roman emperor was deposed.

The conquerors accepted conversion to Christianity, preserving the culture's religious unity. The western branch of Christianity evolved into Roman

Catholicism, the one and only church of the West. Latin and Greek Christianity parted company, seemingly forever.

Thus the West's first flowering died under the primitive sandals of conquering German tribesmen, and its lands lay almost powerless and fallow during a Dark Age that lasted for half a millennium. There were times when it seemed that its culture would perish forever under the hooves of conquering Muslim horsemen, and that the culture of the Middle East would reign from England to the gates of India. At other times it seemed that what little remained of the old civilization would be chopped to splinters by Viking battle-axes or bled to death by Magyar arrows.

It was not to be. Through military prowess and a generous helping of luck the West survived.

The memories of the old political unity lived on. In 800 Charlemagne was crowned by the Pope as Holy Roman Emperor, but his reign dissolved into anarchy after his death. Two centuries later Otto I established the Saxon dynasty of Holy Roman Emperors, and the Empire returned to life. Had Pope and Emperor been willing to coexist in peace, with Pope supreme in matters religious and Emperor supreme in matters political the culture could have reacquired the unity of the waning days of the old Empire. This too was not to be.

Pope and Emperor were unwilling to coexist as equals. In the titanic power struggle of the eleventh, twelfth and thirteenth centuries the Popes broke the power of the Emperors and the dream of western political unity vanished. In turn the rising power of the kings of France and a power struggle within the Church (the Great Schism) broke the political might of the Popes in the fourteenth century. These events in a sense made possible the Protestant Reformation of the sixteenth century, which insured that the West would enter upon its time of power and glory in a state of political and religious anarchy.

It was during these grim centuries of the Dark and Middle Ages that our culture assumed its present form. Only by the cultivation of military virtue was Western Europe defended. The feudal organization of society emphasized duty, property and dynasty as westerners began to consider the betterment of conditions in this world to be of a higher priority than salvation in the next.

The groundwork was early laid for economic and technological change. From the sixth century forward Benedictine monasteries engaged in disciplined production of foodstuffs, making good use of the principle of division of labor. The newly devised manorial agriculture applied similar principles in the secular domain.

The invention of the horsecollar made it possible for a horse to develop more pulling power. The discovery of the moldboard plow enabled agriculturalists to cultivate for the first time the heavy soils of river valleys. Water mills and windmills harnessed mighty natural forces to the tasks of grinding grain and powering primitive machinery. During the twelfth century a remarkable economic rejuvenation began; and for the first time since the fall of Rome the wealth of the West appreciably increased.

In the year 1095 Pope Urban II urged Europeans to take up arms and drive the Muslims from the Holy Land. The response was overwhelming; for the first time people of the West took the offensive against the forces of Islam. Jerusalem fell to the Crusaders in 1099; Palestine and a part of Syria became in essence European colonies for a century. Though the Holy City was lost again in 1187, other Crusader states survived until almost the end of the thirteenth century. European curiosity about the rest of the world had been aroused.

Now Westerners such as Marco Polo began to travel across the vastness of Asia, bringing knowledge of India and China to Europe. Gunpowder, the compass and paper were adapted to widespread use. The invention of printing from movable type made practicable the cultivation of literacy on a large scale; the means of acquiring knowledge were for the first time available to large numbers of people.

Though Europeans didn't discover gunpowder, the compass, cheap paper or printing with movable type, they adapted these inventions to the cause of progress. With gunpowder weapons Europeans created powerful armies, superior to all but the most mighty non–European empires. With the compass they sailed fleets farther and with more certainty than had ever before been possible. With books printed by movable type on cheap paper they made knowledge available on an unprecedented scale.

Now began an intellectual revolution the like of which the world had never seen, continuing into today. Old certainties were questioned as Copernicus asserted that the earth was not the center of the universe and Luther questioned the religious authority of the Roman Catholic Church. Galileo's telescope opened the universe to human study, as Leeuwenhoek's microscope later did for the world too small for the human eye to see. The limitations upon the exercise of human curiosity began to fall as Europeans began to question the unquestionable and to think the unthinkable.

On the other hand military and economic developments caused Western culture to become the culture of the nation-state, in which the secular ruler could command the allegiance of all who resided within his domain. Its ideal was best expressed in the French statement, "Un roi, une foi, une loi." One king, one faith, one law within the state. Even after the Reformation, each nation-state had its one official faith. Only the French Revolution in 1789 ended the idea of religious uniformity.

But the notion of uniformity within the state survived into the twentieth century. In the 1920s Benito Mussolini expressed it thus: "Tutto nello stato, niente al fuori lo stato, nullo contro lo stato." Everything within the state, nothing outside the state, nothing against the state. In the Germany of the

1930s it was expressed more simply: "Ein volk, ein reich, ein fuehrer." One people, one country, one leader. An enduring tension arose between rulers seeking political and philosophical unity among their subjects and intellectuals seeking freedom to expand the frontiers of the human intellect.

During the fifteenth century Portuguese explorers probed the terra incognita of the coast of West Africa. In 1486 Bartholomew Diaz rounded the Cape of Good Hope; in 1498 Vasco da Gama rounded southern Africa and reached India. By 1550 Portuguese trading posts could be found along African and Asian coasts all the way from Morocco to Japan.

Meanwhile Christopher Columbus, an Italian sailing under the Spanish flag, discovered the New World. In 1494 Spain and Portugal agreed to divide the world between them by the Treaty of Tordesillas, Portugal claiming the Eastern Hemisphere (except for the Philippine Islands) and Spain the Western (except for Brazil). Spanish conquistadores destroyed the empires of the Aztecs in Mexico and the Incas of Peru; soon their dominions extended from Florida and California to the southern tip of South America.

These discoveries loosed a revolution of incalculable magnitude in Europe. A lightly settled Western Hemisphere (except for Mexico and Peru) beckoned to European adventurers. The gold plundered by the Conquistadores from the fallen Aztec and Inca empires swelled the coffers of the kings of Spain and increased the money supply of all Europe. The proceeds of the silver mines of Mexico continued the process.

The transplantation of American maize and potatoes to Europe laid the groundwork of an agricultural and nutritional revolution, increasing productivity and reducing the possibility of famine. Tobacco, coffee and sugar grown in America changed the living habits of the West.

The huge potential profit to be earned in trade with the Orient and in economic development of the Western Hemisphere led other Europeans to intrude upon the Spanish and Portuguese dominions. The Dutch expelled the Portuguese from Asia and established a permanent presence in Indonesia. Later the English and French ended Dutch influence elsewhere in Asia, the French emerging supreme in Indo-China and the English in India, Burma and Malaysia and southeast Asia.

The Spanish lost the Caribbean islands to the Dutch, French and English, but held on to their mainland possessions. Ultimately the French began expanding into the St. Lawrence Valley of Canada, while the English did the same along the east coast of what is now the United States.

The paradox of our culture became apparent to non–Westerners during these centuries, as soldiers and traders diligently sought the goods and the power of this world while the missionaries sought to save souls for the next. How could Western society produce both disciplined soldiers and loving otherworldly men of the cloth?

As more food became available in Western Europe the population began to grow and governments became more efficient and powerful. Royal armies and navies grew in size; the strong nation-states found it easier to enforce their wills outside their national frontiers.

Yet national governments remained quite weak by modern standards. Slow communications made the dissemination of governmental decrees a time-consuming business. Public records were still laboriously written out by hand. A respect for tradition restrained the power of even the most absolute kings. An almost universal exemption of the nobility and the Church from taxation limited the financial resources of the state. Special privileges granted to families, guilds, social classes, and towns and cities by former monarchs were in most lands scrupulously adhered to.

In the seventeenth century most national armies numbered less than 100,000 soldiers; only during the eighteenth century were powers like France able to field armies of 200,000. Universal military conscription was financially and technologically impossible; war was a matter for monarchs, statesmen and professional soldiers. The state was now affluent enough to be able to buy adequate weaponry although trained men and competent leadership remained in short supply. The idea was to find the great captain who could defeat superior enemy forces with a minimum of loss to his own.

During these centuries a few such leaders appeared: The English Duke of Marlborough and Oliver Cromwell, the Swedish kings Gustavus Adolphus and Charles XII, the Prussian king Frederick II (the Great), Prince Eugene of Savoy, the French marshals Turenne and de Saxe. These men and their armies were unmatched in the art of war.

Eighteenth-century England saw the stirrings of the Industrial Revolution as the steam engine was harnessed to industrial tasks, coal began to replace wood as an industrial fuel, and a network of canals created a cheaper, more efficient internal transportation system.

At the time of the French Revolution Europeans thoroughly dominated the Western Hemisphere. Trading posts dotted the coasts of Africa (though the interior of that continent was still marked "Terra Incognita" on European maps). In Asia too European trading posts were everywhere, though they didn't possess the military muscle as yet to destroy the power of Asia's great empires and middle-rank kingdoms.

The French Revolution brought permanent change to European culture. The soul-stirring revolutionary slogan, "Liberté! Egalité! Fraternité!" (Liberty! Equality! Brotherhood!) stirred human aspirations in many lands.

In the name of the people ancient privileges were swept away in France and in countries subjected to French domination. Legal and traditional obstacles, making it difficult for government to enforce its will, were eliminated.

The French Republic resorted to almost universal conscription to create armies to fight its numerous enemies, and in battle after battle French draftees took the measure of enemy professional soldiers. Napoleon turned this military force into a machine that subjected most of Europe; his genius as a great captain plus the quality of his armies made him virtually invincible.

The enemies of France were forced to resort to French methods to survive. When Napoleon sought to impose his brother Joseph upon the Spaniards as their king in 1808 the entire Spanish nation rose in revolt against him. Though the French smashed every regular Spanish army sent against them they could never suppress the guerrillas of the countryside; it required 200,000 men to hold Spain's cities and essential lines of communication—men Bonaparte desperately needed in other campaigns.

Six hundred thousand men of the Emperor's Grand Army marched into the fastnesses of Russia in June of 1812; only a handful straggled back into Germany in December. Nearly 500,000 men clashed on the battlefield of Leipzig in 1813; war had become the business of the nation in arms. Advancing age and disease sapped Napoleon's leadership skills; his errors plus his enemies' big battalions eventually cost him his throne and his empire.

The period between the fall of Napoleon and the beginning of World War I brought the great revolutions that transformed the West and made possible its domination of the Earth. The Industrial Revolution came to full flowering; factories sprang into existence all over Europe, mass producing countless varieties of relatively cheap capital and consumer goods.

The transportation revolution made the carrying of goods and people much cheaper, faster, and more reliable. The steamship liberated marine transport from dependence on wind and the muscle power of human oarsmen and made possible the construction of vessels of unprecedented size. The steam locomotive allowed for the first time large-scale, fast, cheap overland transportation. The internal combustion engine made possible the automobile and motor truck, liberating overland transportation from the constraint of the railway. The airplane lifted humanity for the first time into the third dimension, above the crowding and confusion of the highways and railways below.

The communication revolution increased the speed of messages at one fell swoop from the speed of a sailing ship or a galloping horse to the speed of light. The telegraph tied quick communication to wires using the dots and dashes of Morse code. The telephone opened the wires to the transmission of the human voice. The radio made possible the transmission of the human voice without the aid of wires. And with television pictures became transmissible through space without wires.

The industrial revolution spurred the agricultural revolution, causing an unprecedented increase in productivity. New machinery worked wonders. The cotton gin spurred an increase in cotton production, while the reaper and the threshing machine made possible the growth of more grain. With tractor-drawn plows more land could be cultivated and chemical fertilizers rejuvenated wornout soils.

There was also a revolution in the ability to get food to the market without spoilage. Canning had already come on the scene early in the nineteenth century and was later perfected. The railway and the steamship made possible fast long-distance transport of bulky food items. Refrigeration, however, provided the most important breakthrough—meat and dairy products could now be moved far and preserved for a long time without the trouble and expense of canning, salting or conversion into cheese.

The health care revolution combined with the agricultural revolution to lengthen human life and liberate people from the plague of germ-borne disease. Anesthesia made surgery more bearable. The discovery that microbes cause infectious disease opened the door to immunization while also emphasizing the importance of antisepsis—cleanliness—in health care. The invention of X-rays opened the door to viewing much of the human body without surgery.

The eighteenth century had witnessed an increase in the European birth rate. The nineteenth century agricultural and health care revolutions spectacularly lowered the culture's death rate. As a result, the population of many lands grew by leaps and bounds.

The ongoing intellectual revolution continued to saturate Western society with mind-boggling notions. Politically the American and French revolutions spread the notions that the only legitimate government is that which rules by the consent of the governed, and that all people have inalienable rights.

Adam Smith preached that human economies work best when human beings are free to produce, buy and sell as they will in an environment free of governmental interference. At the other extreme utopian Socialists condemned the market and the French anarchist Proudhon stated that "property is theft."

Karl Marx proclaimed his scientific socialism, telling the world that society would inevitably evolve into a classless utopia of economic equality and prosperity, governed by the maxim "From each according to his ability, to each according to his need."

Charles Darwin shook the religious beliefs of millions with his theory of evolution—that the earth's life forms were not created by a supernatural being but rather evolved from lower forms.

Sigmund Freud began his studies of the recesses of the human subconscious mind, proclaiming that our actions are often not subject to the direction of our reason but are commanded by unconscious drives and conditioning over which we have no control. Thus, we are not rationally responsible for much that we do.

The military revolution changed the nature and basis of national power by using new technology. With rapid-firing long-range breech-loading rifles, iron-clad steamships, more powerful artillery and telegraphic communications European armies were now superior to all others on earth. The Dutch completed the conquest of Indonesia; the French took Indo-China and much of north and west Africa; the British took India, Burma, Malaya and huge tracts of Africa. By 1900 over 60 percent of the land area of the world was under more or less direct rule by Europeans. The great European powers now kept hundreds of thousands of soldiers permanently under arms; the mobilization of reserve manpower could now create armies of millions.

The age of the great military captains ended; a minimally competent general commanding troops armed with modern weapons could shatter any non–European horde of spearmen or musketeers. The infrequent European wars of the nineteenth century produced no Marlboroughs or Gustavus Adolphuses, as the commanders who blundered the least emerged the victors.

Europeans ruled supreme. The Pelagian half of their cultural nature held this to be their earned, deserved triumph; it was the beginning of the march toward Utopia. But their Augustinian conscience cringed at the violence that had made the triumph possible, and wondered if some horrendous day of reckoning didn't lurk somewhere down the road.

It did. The Achilles heel of Western culture was the nation-state system and its accompanying international anarchy, combined with the radical political and economic notions unleashed by the intellectual revolution. The competition among the great powers for status and influence created the pre–World War I system of alliances; four decades of incompetent political and military leadership were to undo the accomplishments of four centuries.

Lack of restraint by a few statesmen in handling the crisis caused by the assassination of the Austrian Crown Prince Franz Ferdinand in June of 1914 dragged Europe into World War I. Western Europeans were now to repeat the experience of the city-states of classical Greece—but with much larger armies and more powerful weapons. The armies of 1914 marched off to battle in August as privates, generals, politicians and ordinary civilians expected glorious victory by Christmas, not a stalemate of trenches, barbed wire, machine guns and mud. No one expected the death of most of a generation in the shell holes of no-man's land.

There were no truly great captains. Though the Germans Hindenburg and Ludendorff humiliated the incompetently led armies of the Czar in the east and at last broke the deadlock of the trenches in the west, they failed to win a complete victory.

New weapons changed the nature of warfare. The machine gun slaughtered charging infantrymen by the tens of thousands. Poison gas asphyxiated thousands that the machine gun missed. The clumsy tank combined modern metallurgy and the internal combustion engine to create the first primitive land battleship.

Aircraft carried warfare into the third dimension; for the first time in centuries London civilians knew battle as German Zeppelin dirigibles and Gotha bombers hurdled the English Channel. The hidden submarine brought a new brutality to the sea, striking from the invisible depths to sink unsuspecting surface ships and cause death to crew and passengers.

Millions of soldiers and hundreds of thousands of civilians died as Europeans devastated their continent and virtually destroyed their own power. Germany destroyed the might of Russia, bled France white and nearly strangled the economy of England. Had the human and economic power of the United States not entered the war in 1917 Germany would have won, or at least imposed a compromise peace.

As it was England, France and Italy were winners; Russia (beaten by Germany), Austria-Hungary and Germany were losers. Austria-Hungary disintegrated, Russia became a Communist dictatorship and Germany plunged into a maelstrom of social upheaval and politico-economic dislocation. Resentfully the Germans watched and waited for a chance to claim revenge.

For the winners victory was an illusion: Italy suffered many of the ills of Germany and yielded itself to Mussolini's dictatorship, while England and France emerged from the carnage economically and spiritually weakened, fearful and to an extent demoralized.

Between the two wars Europeans invented the most repressive governmental system ever devised by the human mind — the totalitarian dictatorship. Though the winners of the war possessed the power to strangle these monstrous creations in their cradles (Lenin's Russia in 1919, Hitler's Germany in 1934) they lacked the will to do so.

France cowered behind the forts of the Maginot Line and Great Britain behind the moat of the Channel as they supinely watched Hitler create a new German Wehrmacht almost from scratch, equipped with the most up-to-date weaponry technology could devise. They watched him ally himself with Stalin's Russia and march into Poland in September of 1939.

Only then did they finally declare war.

It was almost too late. Though on paper French and British armaments were equal to those of the Germans, and though the German Wehrmacht wasn't equipped to fight a long war, the Anglo-French allies passively waited for their enemy to strike first.

Strike he did in May of 1940. Concentrated hordes of German tanks attacking in a totally unexpected place (the hilly forested Ardennes) overwhelmed a sluggish French defense; the confused and demoralized French Army was utterly defeated within six weeks while the British Army was driven from the Continent and lost much of its equipment. Only the moat of the English Channel spared Great Britain from invasion and occupation. Had Hitler not double-crossed his Soviet ally and invaded Russia in June of 1941 his hold on Europe might have become unbreakable. Even so, in August of 1942 Hitler's control stretched from the English Channel to the Volga River, and from the Arctic Ocean to the Mediterranean.

Never could Germany have conquered such an empire without the help of a few great captains such as Heinz Guderian, Erwin Rommel and Erich von Manstein. Germany's continental enemies produced no one to match them.

Great Britain alone could never have challenged Hitler's new empire but the German failure to end Russian resistance and Hitler's declaration of war against the United States made German defeat through attrition inevitable. Eighty million Germans stood no chance against 50 million Britons, 120 million Americans and 200 million Russians, backed by mighty economies, all bent upon German destruction. By the spring of 1943 Hitler's defeat was inevitable, but the struggle against impossible odds consumed two more years.

Though soldiers were spared asphyxiation from poison gas in Hitler's war and the military casualties of the belligerents were lighter than those of World War I, the horrors of the new war were greater. Fast-moving tanks added a new and terrifying mobility to land warfare; once the front had been broken the enemy could appear anywhere.

New and heavier aircraft, carrying bomb loads undreamed-of in 1918, spread death and destruction among civilians behind the front lines. Warsaw, Rotterdam, Coventry and London suffered massive destruction from the bombs carried by German twin-engine bombers. But British four-engine bombers claimed revenge in spades upon Cologne, Lubeck and Hamburg long before the fighting ended. By 1945 the combined bomber fleets of the British and Americans had reduced most German cities to wreckage.

German secret weapons introduced the warfare of the future. The Messerschmitt ME-262 jet fighter flew rings around Allied aircraft, but there were too few of them to turn the tide of the air war. The pilotless V-1 aircraft that pounded London from June of 1944 to virtually the end of the war were forerunners of today's cruise missile. The V-2 rockets that pounded London and Antwerp from above the atmosphere were the first ballistic rocketry used in war and the ancestors of today's intercontinental ballistic missiles. Fortunately for the Allies, these weapons appeared too late and in too small numbers to reverse the trend of the war.

Since Hitler fought to almost the last German to defend his power and his life he left much of the continent in ruins. There was no western European winner of World War II—only Great Britain of these belligerents escaped invasion, but her economy was totally exhausted. The Soviet Union and the United States provided the manpower and weaponry that crushed the Third Reich; in a sense the two outside winners divided Europe between them at the line of the Elbe River. Europeans had lost control of their continent.

During the next twenty years they also lost their colonies as Asians and Africans discovered the potential of "the war of the flea"—guerrilla warfare. French, English, Dutch and Portuguese encountered enemies they could beat in open battle every time, but who fled into the jungles to continue the fight tomorrow. Against these determined foes who never admitted defeat European will faltered. The fleas emerged triumphant; Europe was unwilling to pursue victory in endless bitter campaigns. The colonial empires vanished by 1965.

The political and cultural power of Western Europe has been negligible since this period, though its economic power remains great. Should the European community evolve into a United States of Western Europe, political unity will reign in the heartland of western culture for the first time in 1500 years. The dreams of the old Holy Roman Emperors will in a sense come true. Europe may once more take charge of its destiny.

Russia. Russia has always been to Westerners the "riddle wrapped in a mystery inside an enigma," as Sir Winston Churchill once so aptly described it. Is it a part of Western culture? Has it evolved a distinct culture of its own? Or is it a part of the culture of the Middle East or of the Orient?

The answer is debatable. Russia has developed in its own way to become a unique and powerful player upon the world's stage. We must have some understanding of it if we're to understand our business environment adequately.

How the gentle and unobtrusive Slavic peoples came to the lands of eastern Europe is a subject of great debate. It's sufficient for our purpose to say that a group of these people called Rus, living in the great plain of the Ukraine in the valley of the Dneiper River in the ninth century, asked the Swedes of the northland to come and rule them.

Thus Rurik and his followers moved south to accept the invitation and Kievan Rus stepped on to the stage of history. Many small principalities were established, the major one with its capital at the city of Kiev. To this place came the Christian missionaries from Constantinople who converted the Rus to Eastern Orthodox Christianity in 988.

For a few centuries Kievan Rus was a power to be reckoned with. At least once its armies marched to the Bosphorus to besiege Constantinople, subjecting much of the eastern Balkan Peninsula to its rule. Prince Sviatoslav broke the power of the Khazar Empire of the lower Volga valley. A thousand years ago Russians were asserting power in the areas they now master.

The civilization of Kiev slowly percolated northward from the Ukrainian plain into the forest lands of Russia. Up here towns like Moscow and Novgorod and Tver and Ryazan and Vladimir began to grow, pale moons reflecting the civilized sunshine of Kiev to the south.

Then came unmitigated disaster as the Mongol armies of Genghis Khan and his successors poured westward. Sabutai's horsemen came to Rus in 1237; by 1240 they had thoroughly sacked and plundered Kiev and the other cities of the Ukraine; Kievan Rus died, never to rise again.

To the north Moscow, burned by the invaders in 1238, accepted subjection to the Mongols, as did all other Russian towns. Only Novgorod, far enough west to have trade relationships with German towns on the Baltic, retained prosperity and relative independence.

Yet even here independence didn't come easy. Swedes and Germans cast longing eyes upon these forested lands; Prince Alexander Nevsky of Novgorod made himself a legend by defeating an army of Swedes on the banks of the Neva River and an army of German Teutonic Knights on the ice of Lake Peipus.

After the fall of Kiev to the Mongols, the Metropolitan of Russia, head of the Russian Orthodox Church, moved his headquarters from city to city as the various holders of the office desired. In 1326 Prince Ivan I of Moscow (called "Kalita," the Moneybag, for his skill at accumulating money and his unwillingness to spend it) convinced the Metropolitan to establish his permanent headquarters in Moscow. Thus, Moscow became in a sense the religious capital of the Russian lands.

Then, in 1327, Ivan obtained from the Mongols the right to collect their tribute from the lands of Moscow and from the neighboring principality of Vladimir. In return the Mongols allowed Ivan and his successors to use the title "Grand Prince" and recognized the Muscovites as their chief Russian vassals.

As Mongol power began to wane the strength of Moscow waxed. The Muscovite grand prince Dmitri led the army that won the first Russian victory over the Mongols, at Kulikovo on the Don River in 1380. As the fifteenth century dawned the fearful Asiatic power was beginning to fade in Russia.

Independent principalities dotted the north Russian woodlands—Tver, Ryazan, Pskov, and Vladimir. The rulers of Moscow nibbled away at their territory and independence, annexing one after another. It was soon clear that the city on the Moskva River was going to be the new center of Russian culture and political power.

In 1472 Prince Ivan III of Moscow took as his bride Princess Sophia Paleologus, niece of Constantine XI, last Emperor of the Byzantine Empire, who fell in battle against the Turks when they captured Constantinople in 1453. In 1480 he shook off all allegiance to the Mongols, declared that Moscow was the heir of the Byzantine Empire and took the title of Czar (Caesar) in regularization of his position. Russian churchmen proclaimed Moscow the new center of Christendom, the third Rome (as Constantinople had been the second).

By 1500 Moscow had united all of the independent Russian principalities under its rule; from now on there would be only one Russian state, and its ruler would be the Muscovite Czar. The major theme of Russian history—inexorable expansion in all directions—was set.

During the sixteenth century Czar Ivan IV (The Terrible) fought wars on all borders of his domains. To the east and southeast he won great victories, destroying the Muslim Emirate of Kazan and adding the entire valley of the

Volga to his empire. To the west he locked horns with Poland, coming off with little more than a draw. It became apparent that Russian expansion to the east would be relatively easy but expansion to the west would be very slow and difficult.

At the beginning of the seventeenth century the House of Rurik, the first dynasty of Czars, died out. The struggle for succession is called by Russian historians the "Time of Troubles," as civil war wracked the land and Poles and Swedes sought to manipulate things to their own benefits. For a short time a Polish garrison occupied the Kremlin and a Polish puppet sat on the Czar's throne. Eventually the foreigners were expelled and the Romanov dynasty called to power, the dynasty that would rule Holy Russia until the Revolution of 1917.

Now began the slow and inexorable occupation of Siberia. Now too, as Poland weakened, began the expansion to the south and west.

The Lithuanians had driven the Mongols from the lands Kievan Rus had once ruled; after the union of Poland and Lithuania in 1567 Kiev had fallen under Polish control. The Eastern Orthodox peasantry of the Ukraine hated Tartar Islam and Polish Roman Catholicism bitterly and impartially. When Russia began to intervene in this power struggle the natives welcomed it. Gradually both Tartar power and Polish power were broken and Kiev once more became Russian.

The power that blocked Russian access to the west was now Sweden. When Czar Peter (later to be called the Great) came to the throne, he assembled a huge army to brush the Swedes aside. It was summarily and humiliatingly smashed by them at Narva in 1700.

Peter now realized that if Russia was to acquire the military power to defeat a powerful Western state it would have to westernize. By the Czar's command government and the armed forces were modernized; Russia was dragged kicking and screaming into the eighteenth century. To show the earnestness of his desire to become a part of the west an entirely new capital city, St. Petersburg (now Leningrad), was built on the banks of the Neva River. Upon its completion the government moved there from Moscow.

Peter's successes provoked Swedish invasion resulting in the great Russian victory of Poltava in 1709, which destroyed Swedish pretensions of great power and informed the West that Russia was now to be reckoned with.

Under Czar Peter Vitus Bering discovered the strait that bears his name, and the great expanse of Alaska was claimed for the Czar.

Under Czarina Elizabeth Russian armies fought in central Europe during the Seven Years War, at one time briefly occupying Berlin. Later Catherine the Great cemented Russian control over the Ukraine and the Crimea, in 1781 pushing Russia's border all the way to the Black Sea and presiding over the partitions that wiped Poland from the map. By 1800 Russia's western borders were somewhere near where they are today.

Napoleon's disastrous march to Moscow in 1812 opened the door to Russian intervention in central Europe, as Russian troops participated in the occupation of Paris and the political settlement at the Congress of Vienna moved the Russian-Prussian frontier in Poland to less than two hundred miles from Berlin.

During the nineteenth century the borders of the present-day Soviet Union were rounded out. In lengthy bitter campaigns the independent Caucasian mountaineers were subjected to Russian rule, while the Armenians and Georgians happily accepted Russian annexation as the price of protection from the Islamic Turks. The Islamic khanates along the northern borders of Iran and Afghanistan were destroyed and annexed. China was forced to sign over huge tracts of almost uninhabited land along its northern frontier.

In other parts of the world the Russian frontiers ebbed and flowed. In about 1830 Russian adventurers built Fort Rossiya on the coast of California, a hundred miles north of San Francisco; the possibility existed that the Czar's domains would extend as far south as San Francisco Bay. British pressure and the distance of these remote lands from European Russia caused abandonment of this toehold, but the restored Russian fort (now called Fort Ross) can still be seen. Russia's North American adventures ended in 1867 when Czar Alexander II sold Alaska to the United States.

During the nineteenth century Russian armies invaded the Balkans several times in warfare against the Turks. In the Russo-Turkish War of 1877–78 the Turks were utterly defeated as Russian troops marched to the environs of Istanbul. The possibility dawned that the Turks could be expelled from Europe and that Istanbul would again become Constantinople, a Christian city, under Russian auspices.

However, the Great Powers of Europe refused to tolerate this and the Russians were forced to disgorge their conquests.

It was during the nineteenth century that Russia came to be known as "the prison-house of nations." Even then the Great Russians — the master race of the Czar's realm — comprised only a bare majority of its population.

From the time of Peter the Great until the end of the Tsarist Empire Russia was an exasperating mixture of east and west, Western enough to be able to overpower all non-western states who sought to resist it, but not Western enough to prevail in any lengthy power struggle with a Western country. Here its advantages were immense manpower and sheer land mass.

Never did the Russian military system produce a great captain such as the Duke of Marlborough. It never needed one. Russian armies crushed non–European enemies through technological superiority and took advantage of the blunders of European enemies to overwhelm them by superior numbers.

Russian intellectuals continued to preach that it was still the third Rome, destined to some day restore the unity of Christendom and to replace godless Western materialism with God-respecting Eastern Orthodoxy.

Industrialization proceeded at a great pace in the late nineteenth century, but bureaucratic inefficiency interfered with government operations, terrorism became so prevalent that the dreaded secret police (the Okhrana) were unable to effectively cope, military weakness became manifest in the Russo-Japanese War, and riot and revolt shook the throne in 1905.

The rickety empire almost suffered the fate of Austria-Hungary in World War I. Poor military leadership and lack of morale among the troops made military defeat at the hands of the Germans inevitable. Middle-class revolutionaries overthrew the Czar in March of 1917, only to be themselves overthrown by the Bolsheviks (Communists) in November. As Lenin's revolutionaries sought to fasten their grip upon the land another Time of Troubles dawned.

The victorious Germans occupied the Ukraine and other parts of western Russia, until forced out by the armistice terms imposed by the Western Allies in November 1918. White Russian armies sought to overthrow the Bolsheviks. American, British, French and Japanese troops trod Russian soil to aid the Whites. Many of the non–Russian nationalities of the empire tried to secede during the uproar.

At length the foreign governments lost the will to fight the Reds, withdrawing their troops. The Reds defeated the Whites and reincorporated most of the seceders into the Soviet Union. Only Finland and Poland permanently made good their separation; Lithuania, Latvia and Estonia remained free until 1940.

Stalin succeeded Lenin as the Soviet leader during the 1920s. The Moscow-run command economy that has held the fate of the Soviet peoples in its grasp for more than half a century is his creation. By fiat and immense expenditure of lives and money he created the heavy industry that turned the USSR into a superpower.

Stalin's alliance with Hitler in 1939 caused Hitler to attack Poland, precipitating World War II. Soviet gasoline in part fueled the German tanks that smashed the French and the German bombers that attacked London in 1940. Only Hitler's cynical double-cross of his ally in 1941 enrolled the Soviet Union among the Allies of World War II.

Now Stalin's investment in heavy industry paid off; the massive numbers of tanks and aircraft produced in Soviet factories helped to overwhelm the German legions on the eastern front in perhaps the greatest war of attrition of all times. Soviet commanders made use of German blunders plus huge quantities of men and machines to grind down Hitler and bleed him white; these were the tactics that brought the Red Army to the Elbe in May of 1945.

Now the Soviet Union was one of Earth's two superpowers. Post-war developments provided the nation with the equivalent of a colonial empire (the east European satellites) and an industrial complex which created and maintained the largest armed forces in the world.

Those who assumed power after the death of Stalin saw their nation surrounded by enemies. They remembered the catastrophe of the Mongol invasions of seven centuries ago. They remembered how the Tartars burned Moscow in 1571, they remembered the Poles in the Kremlin in 1612, they recalled the Swedish invasion of 1708–09, the French incursion of 1812, the interventions of 1918–20, and the incredible destruction and brutality of what they call the Great Patriotic War of 1941–45. Events like these must not happen again. The feet of foreign soldiers must never again tread the soil of Holy Russia. Hence their determination to hold on to the European satellites and to assure the existence of a pro–Soviet regime in Afghanistan (at the expense of fighting an endless guerrilla war).

Though some Westerners like to think that the Soviet Union technologically will always be the moon to the suns of western Europe and the United States, it's a mistake to adhere to such opinions. Though Soviet rocketry owes much to German science and Soviet nuclear physics much to successful espionage in the West, there have been noteworthy purely Soviet accomplishments.

The T-34 tank, a Soviet design, was better than any German tank of World War II, and was also superior to any comparable American or British model. The IL-2 Stormovik ground attack aircraft was one of the best of its kind in that war.

The first artificial earth satellite was the Soviet Sputnik; the first man in space was a Russian, as was the first woman. A Russian holds the record for spending the longest time in space. A Russian robot was the first man-made device to land upon the moon. Only Russians have landed a robot on the surface of Venus; what we know of conditions on the surface of that planet we know due to this accomplishment.

Before 1962, the Soviet Navy was a collection of second-rate ships. After the humiliation (as the Soviets perceived it) of the Cuban missile crisis, the leadership commanded the creation of a world-class fleet able to challenge American domination of the high seas. Within a decade the goal was in sight; by 1980 the Soviet Navy was the second-largest in the world, and still is.

To be sure, Soviet technological accomplishments in non-military areas are almost non-existent. The Soviet leadership has chosen to spend its relatively scarce resources on projects involving the military and space and leave the civilian economy to its own devices; thus, in non-military areas technological advance occurs only though importation from Japan or the West.

With Mikhail Gorbachev a new generation came to power. The Afghanistan venture has been abandoned; the Red Army is no more capable of winning the war of the flea than any other modern army. The satellites are in the process of peacefully liberating themselves; Gorbachev is willing to see them go. As the new leadership seeks to reform the creaking command economy in the interest of increased prosperity for average Soviet citizens and to allow more popular participation in public affairs, the non–Russian inhabitants of the "prison-house of nations" again sense an opportunity for liberation. What is happening will be discussed in a later chapter.

How fundamental a change will Gorbachev make in his country? How will the Soviet Union change, culturally and technologically? As of May 1991, it's far too early to tell.

The United States. Though Russia's membership in Western culture is open to question, that of the United States is absolutely certain. In a sense the United States *is* modern Western culture.

It began as a scattering of English outposts along the Atlantic seaboard of North America. The English motherland helped these to expand by acquiring Dutch New Amsterdam and the Swedish colonies along the Delaware, and by destroying French military power in Canada.

From the English point of view, the ungrateful colonists responded to this generosity with the Revolutionary War. Our ancestors won their war of independence against the English in a sense as the Vietnamese won their war against us two centuries later—by holding out long enough against overwhelming odds to destroy the will of the enemy to continue the fight.

The United States introduced to the world a new, unprecedented type of government in 1789: the presidential republic. The constitution that created it is still the supreme law of our land, and governments modeled upon it rule other lands all over the globe.

Even before the American Revolution it was clear that the English colonies were not developing into miniature Englands. Each acquired its own unique character, the fundamentalist Protestant colonies of New England, the cosmopolitan trading colonies of the center, the agricultural colonies of the south with their slavery-based economies. One, Pennsylvania, had so large a German-speaking population that it seriously considered making German an official language during the 1780s.

From the beginning American attitudes toward the outside world were ambivalent. New England traders sailed the seven seas before the Revolution, buying and selling wherever there was business to be done. Independence freed the American foreign trader from the interference of English Navigation Acts. The revolts of the Latin Americans from their Spanish and Portuguese masters opened vast new markets to Yankee aggressiveness.

Though in 1797 retiring President George Washington warned Americans not to get involved in foreign quarrels, anger and frustration at interference with our international trade prompted military retaliation. A bitter undeclared naval war with France raged during the late 1790s, ended only by Napoleon Bonaparte's moderation. When Tripolitan and Algerian pirates interfered with American merchant shipping in the Mediterranean, American naval squadrons sailed in 1803 and 1815 to deal with their depredations.

Similar resentments to a degree prompted the declaration of war upon

England in 1812. Three years later most Americans regretted that departure from the wise policy of our first president. The city of Washington lay in blackened ruins. British warships blockaded the nation's ports and foreign trade was ruined. Only English unwillingness to commit an army of several hundred thousand men to the conquest of the upstart ex-colonies saved the nation's independence.

Americans pulled in their horns politically, asserting international authority only in the Western Hemisphere with the proclamation of the Monroe Doctrine of 1823.

It's somewhat humbling to remember that the policy of preserving the independence of the states of Latin America was British as well as American. The United States could have done little to interfere with, say, a Spanish effort to reconquer Argentina. But since Britannia ruled the seas all through the nineteenth century, no continental nation cared to tangle with King William's or Queen Victoria's navy. It's fair to say that British naval power made possible the American isolation from European affairs that lasted for a century.

But the United States was not inactive in its foreign policy. Within 65 years after the gaining of independence the boundaries of the continental United States were rounded out by clever diplomacy and occasional aggressive war. American expansionists cast longing eyes upon lands outside the present-day United States; had the dice of diplomacy and war fallen differently our country could have grown much larger.

One of the reasons for the declaration of war against England in 1812 was the dream of annexing Canada. A noisy minority proposed the annexation of all of Mexico after our victory in the Mexican War. Others chanted "Fifty-four forty or fight!" during the American negotiations with Great Britain over the future of the Oregon country during the 1840s; had they attained their goal the Stars and Stripes would have flown over all of British Columbia. More than once the United States considered buying or conquering Cuba from Spain.

The United States navy co-operated with the British in trying to suppress the African slave trade during the 1840s and 50s, while United States warships forced Japan to open its ports to the world's traders in 1853.

Meanwhile, an almost empty continent, teeming with natural resources, beckoned to the American people. Americans devoted themselves to populating the land and pursuing the Industrial Revolution. The free market ideology of Adam Smith was given its head as unrestricted free enterprise built the nation.

As early as 1860, America contributed much to the burgeoning Industrial Revolution. To Eli Whitney the world owes the concept of the cotton gin, and of mass production of manufactured products with interchangeable parts. The steamboat was an American invention, as were the telegraph and the mechanical reaper. The petroleum industry was born in America, as the first producing oil well was brought into Pennsylvania in 1859.

Only once did the internal political consensus of our country break down and the result was the most bloody war in American history.

Only during the years 1861 to 1865 did some Americans — mostly the citizens of the would-be Confederate States of America — experience what many Europeans knew at least once per generation: the marching and counter-marching of great armies across the land, the plundering of farms and towns by hungry soldiers, the harshness of military government, and the grim reality of military defeat.

The Union's objective was total victory — the destruction of the Confederacy and the reunion of the United States. It began by seeking to checkmate the Rebels through maneuver without battle, but George B. McClellan couldn't bring it off. Ambrose Burnside and others tried charging head-on into Rebel artillery and rifle fire; that too failed. The war in Virginia was a stalemate until 1864, while Ulysses Grant defeated the Confederate generals in the West by taking advantage of their blunders.

When Grant became the Union Commander-in-Chief in 1864 he decided to fight a war of attrition; to keep the Rebels in constant battle and use superior Union manpower and weaponry to grind them down, allow no time for recovery and destroy their capacity to continue the war. This succeeded.

From 1865 forward Americans had to deal with a problem faced by no other people in exactly the same form — what to do with the millions of ex-slaves. When the slaves of the West Indies were freed by the British in 1837, they had comprised the overwhelming majority of the population of Jamaica, Barbados and the other sugar islands. It was inevitable that they or their descendants would one day rule their islands, as they now do. In the states of the former Confederacy the blacks were a slight majority here (as in South Carolina), an immense minority there (as in Louisiana) and a small minority elsewhere (as in Texas). Black and white lived intermingled all across the land. How would the races coexist in peace? How were the freed ex-slaves to survive? How were they to be made a part of the nation?

The United States needed a leader of the highest caliber to deal with that problem. Unfortunately the only person who might have qualified died of the bullet of John Wilkes Booth in April of 1865. Abraham Lincoln's successors couldn't handle it.

The majority of our ancestors were unwilling to receive the ex-slave as an equal; thus the regime of segregation and discrimination settled upon the land, not to be ended until the 1960s.

Meanwhile the immigration gates opened wide and hundreds of thousands from all of the world poured in; Irishmen fleeing the potato famine of the 1840s, Germans fleeing the suppression of the 1848 revolutions, Chinese coming to labor on the transcontinental railroads, Italians fleeing the poverty of their country from the 1870s on, Jews fleeing the pogroms of Russia, Mexicans seeking opportunity in the Rio Grande and Imperial valleys, and others.

More American inventions fueled the Industrial Revolution after the Civil War. Alexander Graham Bell contributed the telephone. Thomas Edison contributed the electric lightbulb, the phonograph and the movie projector. The Wright brothers contributed the airplane.

By the 1890s the United States was on the verge of becoming the world's greatest industrial producer. The U.S. had become a superpower in embryo, flexing its muscles in some of the far corners of the earth.

In 1865 an army of victorious Union troops marched to the Rio Grande to enforce the Monroe Doctrine against French occupiers of Mexico. The French took the hint and withdrew.

In 1872 the Grant administration negotiated a treaty with the Dominican Republic providing for the annexation of that country by the United States. This fell through because the United States Senate refused to ratify the treaty.

Because American seamen were injured in a riot in Valparaiso the United States threatened war against Chile in 1881. In 1892 American interests overthrew the monarchy in Hawaii; the new republican government at once negotiated a treaty of annexation to the United States. But again a territorial acquisition was blocked by refusal of the Senate to ratify. (When a new annexation treaty was presented to the Senate in 1898 during the Spanish-American War it was ratified at once.) In 1895 war with Great Britain threatened due to a boundary dispute between Great Britain's colony of British Guiana and Venezuela.

As a result of the Spanish-American War the U.S. acquired the Philippines, Guam and Puerto Rico. Like the older lands of Europe it had become a colonial power.

During the first seventeen years of the twentieth century American soldiers, sailors and marines fought in China to suppress the Boxer Rebellion, fought a bloody guerrilla war to suppress Filipino nationalists in our new Far Eastern colony, prevented the landing of Colombian troops in Panama to suppress that land's secession (opening the door to the construction of the Panama Canal), occupied Haiti and the Dominican Republic to prevent European powers from doing likewise, and occupied various points in Mexico to avenge insults to the American flag during that country's civil war.

The year 1917 was the critical year for the United States, for western Europe and for western culture. The first round of the great European Civil War (World War I) had lasted three years and the belligerents were exhausted. Unless one side or the other could acquire a new accretion of strength a compromise peace was inevitable.

Had the war ended in compromise, the old nineteenth-century European dominance might have continued. Kaisers might still reign in Berlin and Vienna, and czars in St. Petersburg. Lenin would have remained a refugee in Switzerland, and Hitler would have seen no future in politics. There might never have been totalitarian dictatorships. The butchery of World War II might have been avoided.

It wasn't to be. The United States forsook its isolationism and entered the war. Germany shipped Lenin from Switzerland to Russia, loosing the virus of Communism upon it and knocking it out of the war. Despite the limited successes of the German offensives of 1918 American manpower assured the Allies the ultimate victory. German revolutionaries deposed the Kaiser and made peace before the inevitable Allied invasion of Germany began.

It was the worst kind of peace. The empire of Austria-Hungary was destroyed but Germany was merely humiliated, neither dismembered nor forgiven. The seeds of World War II were planted.

America sought to return to isolationism between the wars, but it was impossible. The nation was a part of the world's power structure now whether it wanted to be or not.

Despite a burning desire on the part of most Americans to sit out World War II, it couldn't be done. American power decided the second round of the European Civil War as it had decided the first. The ultimate strategy of the United States in Western Europe was the strategy of Grant in Virginia in 1864 — engage the enemy, keep him engaged, and grind him to nothing with superior manpower resources and weaponry. Again it worked.

The victory was total. There was no revolution in Germany this time; Hitler and the Nazis fought to the bitter end. Most of the victors were scraping the bottom of their economic and manpower barrels when it was over.

Only the United States had come through it with its homeland and economic plant unscathed. The United States, the world's one and only nuclear power, dominated the planet whether it wanted to or not.

Had Americans shared the will to power of the continental European nations in their primes, they would have imposed a Pax Americana upon quarrelsome mankind and enforced it as did the Romans of old.

Had King Louis XIV of France or King Frederick the Great of Prussia had such power they would have exercised it without flinching. Had Great Britain's Sir Winston Churchill had it he probably would have exercised it, but been disturbed by twinges of conscience.

But for America to do it wasn't dreamed of; it's totally contrary to the American national character.

In us the inherent contradictions that have bedeviled our culture for a thousand years stand forth in sharp relief. Our economic and political dreams are centered upon this world. We want the best life possible for ourselves and our loved ones right here, now.

Our view of humanity is uncompromisingly Pelagian; humanity is inherently good and can accomplish anything through the exercise of sovereign will.

Many of us belieive in the Freudian notion that when people behave abnormally or irrationally they're subject to the pulls and tugs of psychic powers beyond their control; they're therefore not responsible for what they do. The aberrant should be treated gently.

Yet we can be persuaded that an enemy is the personification of absolute evil. Most of us never saw any good in the natives we fought for possession of the American land. The legends of the old West cast the bad guys in black hats as devils incarnate, while the good guys in white hats were the epitome of virtue. In the legends, the good guys always absolutely triumphed — justice was always done.

When confronted in war we will do everything necessary to destroy a powerful enemy. Union soldiers in the Civil War sang of hanging Jeff Davis to a sour apple tree, and devastated Georgia from Atlanta to the sea to teach the Confederacy that war against the Union didn't pay. In World War I we sought the destruction of the Austro-Hungarian Empire and the abdication of the German Kaiser; some of us would gladly have hanged Kaiser Wilhelm as a war criminal.

In World War II we participated in the utter destruction of the cities of our enemies from the air, including the smashing of helpless Dresden in February of 1945 and the incineration of tens of thousands of civilians in the firebombings of Tokyo and other Japanese cities later in that year.

U.S. submarines cut communications between Japan and its empire through the ruthless sinking of merchant ships without warning. The ultimate American acts of violence against the evil archfiends were the nuclear bombings of Hiroshima and Nagasaki. We finished the orgy by seeing to it that the surviving leaders of the enemy were indeed hanged as war criminals.

Today the American conscience cringes whenever these subjects are mentioned. How could a gentle Pelagian person cause such destruction? Does the pursuit of power, the pursuit of victory at all costs, lead to such inhumanity? Have the Augustinians always been right, that evil will dominate this world and that the best will commit the worst of it?

No! A thousand times no! cries a substantial body of American opinion. If the pursuit of power must inevitably cause such destruction, Americans must play no part in it. But the United States is a superpower whether we like it or not, is the reply. Superpowers must play the power game for that's the way the world operates.

Neither opinion dominates American society; both have influence within government and without. Therefore we have been fumbling and hesitant in the use of our power since 1945. Superpower status was in a sense thrust upon us. We dislike it, we fear it, we wish we could push it aside.

When the use of power can bring a favorable return with little cost, we exercise it (as in the American masterminding of the overthrow of the governments of Iran and Guatemala by CIA operations during the 1950s, the invasion of Grenada in the 1980s, or the deposition of Manuel Noriega of Panama in

1990). When exercise of power appears risky we back off (as during the Hungarian revolt against the Soviet Union in 1956, the Bay of Pigs operation in 1961, the erection of the Berlin Wall during that same year, the Soviet occupation of Czechoslovakia in 1968 and the Lebanon intervention in 1982).

We went to war in Korea in June of 1950 hoping for total victory. Douglas MacArthur seemed to have won it in the syle of the European great captains of the eighteenth century as a result of the landing at Inchon; the North Korean army was destroyed.

Then came the Chinese intervention and a new chapter in American warfare. For the first time ever we fought an enemy with superior manpower resources to ours, an enemy who could successfully use the tactics of attrition against us. No great captain can defeat China through brilliant maneuver and no army can bleed the Chinese to death through attrition. There was no way (other than through the great gamble of nuclear attack) to defeat the Chinese dragon. We had to fight for a draw; we could expect no better. That's what we got.

In Vietnam we fought for a draw from the beginning; the objective was not the destruction of North Vietnam but rather the preservation of the independence of South Vietnam. On the battlefields of that war our ferocity was great. American artillery and air bombardment pulverized many a South Vietnamese village, killing countless civilian non-combatants; napalm and cluster bombs added new dimensions to the horror of ground warfare in that country. Yet we spared North Vietnam the full horror of aerial warfare and kept most of our chemical weaponry under wraps (a restraint the Soviets did not practice in Afghanistan, nor the Iraqis in Kurdistan). Our voluntary restraint prevented a true war of attrition against North Vietnam; instead we fought the war of the flea in the south. As almost always happens, the flea broke our will to resist him by refusing to admit the possibility of defeat.

We faced a new sort of military confrontation in January 1991. When our military buildup in Saudi Arabia didn't cause the Iraqi occupiers of Kuwait to withdraw, Operation Desert Storm was unleashed. Within 40 days a substantial part of the Iraqi armed forces were destroyed and Kuwait was liberated. Casualties were low, but Saddam Hussein retains power in Iraq. Military victory was ours but did we win politically?

The desert confrontation was a painful business. We long for a world in which the international competition is economic rather than political and military; where nations follow a policy of "live and let live"; where the prosperous nations enjoy their riches while striving to help elevate others.

Until 1989 there was no sign that the dream was coming to pass. The Soviets seemed not to want such a world; all they knew, it seemed, was the inexorable drive to expand which has motivated Muscovites since the fourteenth century.

Now Mikhail Gorbachev may be turning his back upon that dynamic in the interest of promoting Soviet economic prosperity. Could the superpower competition be winding down?

The west Europeans would welcome such a world; but their sense of history warns them that the appearance could be an illusion. The United States welcomes it in the hope that peace will pay a gigantic economic dividend that will better the lives of all humanity; our less developed sense of history makes us more certain that there's no illusion. Common sense should warn us against too much euphoria.

Technologically, we have dominated the world. The world's first atomic and hydrogen bombs were American. We put the first men on the moon, and the first robot landing device on Mars. We sent the first spacecraft to photograph the mysteries of Jupiter, Saturn, Uranus and Neptune.

We pioneered in the areas of computer technology and commercial television broadcasting. In non-military technology, however, we face increased Japanese competition. Whether or not we can hold our own isn't yet clear.

In the cause of women's liberation and world population control we've scored noteworthy breakthroughs. We were the first nation to market birth control pills in large quantity, and the first major Western nation to legalize abortion on demand.

Economically, we dominated the world for a generation after World War II. The dollar was the most desired of world currencies, and the measure of the value of all others. The American gross national product was by far the greatest in the world, as was American per capita income. The best automobiles came from Detroit and the best movies came from Hollywood.

Since the early 1970s this has changed. The dollar is but one sort of hard currency; traders now often find more value in deutschmarks, yen and Swiss francs. The American gross national product remains the largest in the world, but per capita income now ranks nearer tenth than first among the world's nations. The best automobiles come from Japan and West Germany rather than from Detroit, most people believe.

Yet many of the world's movies still come from Hollywood. Most of the world's television viewers watch at least some American-made programs. One may buy American newspapers and magazines at most of the world's newsstands. One hears popular songs sung in American English on radio stations all over the world. American popular culture is everywhere.

While the nations formerly subjected to European colonial domination regained their formal political freedom, the power of Western culture hasn't abated. From American rock music to Soviet weapons, the artifacts and ideas of Western culture influence people everywhere.

Yet one can't say that Western culture is all there is. The other three major cultures continue to exist, struggling bravely and to a large extent successfully to preserve their identities.

Chapter 3
Non-Western Cultures

The Middle East

The Middle East is probably where human civilization began, yet its prevailing culture is one of the youngest on earth. Egypt, Assyria and Babylon took their turns at dominating this area and faded into oblivion. For the long pull, only two powers have survived.

The oldest but in a sense the weakest is the power of Iran, the Persia of old. During the 1970s the government of the Shah celebrated the 2,500th anniversary of the founding of the Persian Empire.

The Persians came upon the stage of history in a big way when they allied themselves with the Babylonians to capture Nineveh and destroy the empire of Assyria in 612 B.C.

By the middle of the next century the Persian Empire of Cyrus had come into being; in 529 B.C. Belshazzar, last king of Babylon, was warned of the power of Cyrus's armies, and his city and kingdom fell shortly thereafter. For awhile the entire Middle East was part of this Empire, which stretched from the Bosphorus to the gates of India and unsuccessfully tried to conquer the Greek city-states.

In 331 B.C. the disciplined phalanx of Alexander the Great destroyed the last army of King Darius III at Gaugamela. The empire fell and Macedonian kings dominated the area. Before long the Parthians drove Alexander's successors out of Iran and Mesopotamia, leaving Middle Eastern culture to flourish there once more, while Syria, Palestine and Egypt remained under Macedonian and later Roman dominion.

Early in the Christian era the Iranian Sassanid dynasty restored a mighty Persian Empire, which battled Romans and Byzantines for control of the Tigris-Euphrates valley. Finally, at the beginning of the seventh century, Byzantines and Persians exhausted each other in a long and bloody war.

It was at this juncture that the Prophet Mohammed began preaching the new religion of Islam in northern Arabia. Once he had united the Arabian peninsula under the banners of the new belief a revolutionary faith and power sprung upon the world.

Neither Persians nor Byzantines had the strength to resist the fanaticism of the Arab horsemen; the Byzantines were driven from Egypt, Palestine and Syria forever while the Sassanid Empire was utterly destroyed.

Briefly a gigantic Islamic Arab empire dominated the lands from the Pyrenees of western Europe to the Indus valley of India. Under the Umayyad caliphs its capital Damascus was a great center of the civilized world; under their successors the Abbasids the seat of government moved to the new city of Baghdad. In the reign of Haroun al-Raschid, the contemporary of Charlemagne, Arab power and glory reached their height.

The fervor of Islam has made the Middle Eastern culture what it is. The Arabs created the highest civilization west of India between the seventh and twelfth centuries, preserving much of the ancient knowledge that later fueled the European Renaissance. Arab scholars translated ancient Greek works into Arabic and later Europeans who had no way to acquire the Greek originals translated these into Latin and European vernaculars. Other Arab scholars explored the complexities of mathematics, laying the foundations of what we call algebra.

A Muslim commonwealth extended from Morocco to the borders of India. Within it Muslim travelers could come and go as they pleased, conversing in Arabic all the way. Muslim traders operated freely within this large area, carrying the products of Morocco to Iran and vice-versa.

Muslim traders did business far beyond the borders of the empire. They crossed the Sahara to the towns of the Sudan, established trading posts along the coast of east Africa as far south as present-day Tanzania and bought and sold as far east as Indonesia and China.

They knew the art of sailing the sea out of sight of land. Regular traffic plied across the Arabian Sea between the Arabian peninsula and India; Arab vessels regularly made the long journey from the Arabian peninsula to China. Legend holds that, at least once, an Arab vessel sailed south through the Indian Ocean to the south tip of Africa and ventured westward into the Atlantic. Finding nothing in that strange sea, it returned home. So far as is known, the feat was never repeated.

Arab fleets also sailed the Atlantic along the coasts of Morocco, Portugal and Spain. However, they probably never ventured far enough away from shore to discover the Madeira or Canary islands. No Arab ever dreamed the dream of Columbus.

Muslims more than once backed the rulers of Europe against the wall, threatening to occupy their lands and transform their cultures. After the conquest of Spain in A.D. 711, a Muslim army crossed the Pyrenees into France. It was stopped at Tours by a Frankish host led by Charles Martel; the experiment was never repeated. Seaborne Muslim raiders harassed the Italian coasts during the ninth century, more than once threatening Rome. The Mediterranean coast of France received similar treatment.

Though invincible Arab armies brought Islam to the Middle East and North Africa, Arab control over the empire was relatively short-lived.

The later Abbasid Caliphs began to import barbarian soldiery from beyond the borders of their empire. Most of these were Seljuk Turks from Central Asia. Gradually these people acquired political power and the Arab Caliphs became figureheads. The great Abbasid Empire disintegrated as Seljuk princelings assumed power in their stead.

Now Persia asserted its independence from its Arab conquerors. Though it remained Islamic, most of its people adopted the minority Shi'ite version of Islam; Iranian religion and government evolved differently from that of its western neighbors. Persia went its way in relatively obscure peace for several centuries.

Seljuk power was battered by the Crusaders and the Mongols. The Mamelukes of Egypt became the great power of the Middle East for awhile, establishing the unique military system that preserved Middle Eastern Islamic power until the nineteenth century. Instead of recruiting soldiery among their subjects, they acquired children from abroad to raise as slave soldiers, who were subjected to military training from an extremely early age. This military caste dominated the army and the state, allowing the Mameluke Sultans to be kings of the Middle Eastern hill for more than three centuries.

The military power of the Ottoman Turks (the last great Muslim power) became based upon the same system. A corps of slave soldiers, the Janissaries, became the elite of the Ottoman armies.

It hadn't always been so. The Ottoman (or Osmanli) Turks came upon the scene during the thirteenth century, one of the several Turkish tribes that wandered into the Middle East from Central Asia. They appeared in eastern Anatolia (Asia Minor) and soon carved out a territory for themselves. Since they were militarily superior to the other Turks in the area, they conquered most of the peninsula.

Then they crossed the Dardanelles into Europe, destroying the armies of Serbia in 1389 and those of Bulgaria in 1396; from that time on they were the major power in the Balkan peninsula. In 1453 they captured Constantinople and ended the Byzantine Empire, making the imperial city the capital of their own empire. In 1480 they landed at Taranto in Italy, throwing a scare into the powers of that peninsula, though they later withdrew.

In 1517 the Ottoman Turks occupied Jerusalem and by 1520 they'd smashed the Mameluke power, bringing the entire Middle East under their dominion. In 1526 they destroyed the army of Hungary; in 1529 they reached their high-water mark when they besieged Vienna. Much of the old Arab empire of Haroun-al-Raschid's day had been reestablished.

For 400 years thereafter Constantinople (later Istanbul) was the center of the Middle Eastern world. The Ottoman Sultan was the most powerful potentate in Islam, exercising more power as Caliph than had ever been concentrated in one place since Abbasid times. During the reign of Suleiman the Magnificent in the early sixteenth century (during whose reign Vienna was besieged) the Ottoman Empire was one of the world's great powers. After Suleiman's death began the long decline of Turkish power, though the Empire was to survive into the twentieth century. It was unable to adapt its military forces to the great revolution of the nineteenth century, meeting final defeat in the first World War.

In Persia the Mongol conquest established the empire of the Il-Khans which lasted for many years. Later native Persian dynasties assumed control; countless wars were fought between Ottoman Turks and Persians over the lands of Mesopotamia, Armenia and Kurdistan. Never did the Ottomans win control over Persia.

Once the original religious fervor of the Muslims faded, the nature of Middle Eastern statehood made it difficult for its societies to generate political and economic power. Here the state wasn't a patch of real estate together with all of its inhabitants, consisting instead of the believers in a religious faith.

Thus, where members of two or more faiths lived together side by side, there existed two or more intermingled states. Since the Muslim conquests, Jews, Christians and Muslims have coexisted together throughout the Middle East. The Jews were governed by their own religious leaders and lived subject to their own religious law, as did their neighbors the Christians and the Muslims.

For reasons that will be discussed in a later chapter, a truly religious Muslim regards secular government as somewhat illegitimate. The leader of a religious community should govern in accordance with the commands of the faith, but in the Islamic world political power has inevitably flowed from the point of the sword, not from the word of the Holy Qu'ran. Secular rulers have used their power primarily to gratify themselves and their followers. Thus social and political disunity were the norm in the Islamic world almost from the beginning. Only those closely associated with the secular rulers showed any loyalty to the government in power.

There is little orientation toward building a better world in the Islamic view. By following the precepts of the faith Muslims, like Christians, seek to assure their salvation and admission to Paradise. In the Holy Qu'ran God assures them that he has made the road to salvation easy by keeping the burden of religion light.

Yet this world and everything in it operate as God wills. Humans are but a pawn upon God's chessboard; God moves them as He chooses. God's purposes are unknown and unknowable. People may strive to follow the commands of their faith and do right, but God may for His own reasons cause good people to lose their resolve. He may curse good people with all manner of catastrophes, and He may reward evil ones with all manner of earthly goodies. If all will be set straight anywhere, it will be when the Last Trumpet sounds and all people stand before God for judgment. Thus, notions that are kin to Augustinian predestination shape the Islamic world view, without the leaven of Western Pelagianism.

The brilliant Muslim culture had passed its prime in the fourteenth century; only Turkish military prowess preserved it for awhile from European assault. When the European armies of the Industrial Revolution burst upon its heartlands four centuries later Muslims resisted valiantly but in most areas were overcome. It took the French several years to subdue bitter Algerian resistance in the 1830s; they met less resistance in Morocco and even less in Tunisia. The British crushed the Egyptians in one battle (Tell el-Kebir) in 1881 and established outposts at Aden and along the shores of the Persian Gulf. Only the Asiatic lands of the Ottoman Empire (Turkey, Syria, Palestine, Iraq and lands between), Persia and the desert fastnesses of the interior of Arabia escaped this fate.

Early in World War I German-led Turkish troops marched to the Suez Canal, fueling British determination to expel Turkey from the Middle East. A British invasion of Iraq failed in 1915, but by 1918 British troops occupied Jerusalem and Baghdad. At war's end the Turks had been driven back to the borders of their Anatolian homeland.

The British promised freedom to the Arabs of the Middle East to induce them to rise up against the Turks. Though Arabs rendered some assistance to the British offensives in Palestine and Iraq these promises were forgotten when the shooting stopped. According to the terms of the Anglo-French Sykes-Picot agreement Syria and Lebanon fell under French dominion while the British occupied Palestine (to which European Jewish immigrants began to come under the terms of the Balfour Declaration of 1917). Iraq and Jordan got nominal independence but remained under close British supervision and control. By the time World War II began pro–German sentiment was very strong among Arabs; had German troops reached the Nile valley, Syria and Mesopotamia during that war they'd have been welcomed as liberators.

After World War II ended the British and French lost their will to maintain dominion in the Middle East. All of the Arab lands attained full independence except for Palestine; there Israel sprang into existence and along with it, the Palestinian refugee problem.

Today two centers of Islam compete for dominance in this culture—the Arab centered upon the oil lands of the Arabian peninsula, and the Iranian centered upon the old Persian Empire.

Of the two the Arabs possess more power. Due to the location of so many valuable oil reserves in the Arabian peninsula and nearby, Saudi Arabia and its neighbors acquired for a time (the early 1970s) an economic leverage that could shake the foundations of Western economies. The advent of the world oil glut and low petroleum prices has weakened this leverage for the moment, but Arabs still retain immense financial power. Billions of Arab petrodollars circulate throughout the world, many of them on deposit in Western banks. Should the owners of these petrodollars decide to withdraw them, shock waves would again batter Western economies.

In addition, Arabs are investing huge sums in the West, acquiring significant economic stakes here.

So far, Arab political influence has been minimal. Though leaders like Gamal Abdel Nasser during the 1950s and 1960s and Muammar Khaddafi today have spoken of Arab political unification, the chances of this happening are virtually nil. Arabic speakers share one of the world's great religious and cultural heritages, but their political differences are irreconcilable.

The military powers of the Arab world have been Egypt, Syria, Iraq and Libya. Iraq and Libya have financed military expansion with oil revenues while Syria and Egypt have had to rely upon outside financial assistance. During the 1950s, 1960s and 1970s Egypt was the most powerful of this quartet; though its armies were badly beaten by the Israelis in 1956 and 1967 they won noteworthy victories against their Jewish enemy in 1973 before again succumbing to defeat. The fighting quality of the current Egyptian armed forces is a question mark.

Syria is Israel's most rabid enemy. Today its forces occupy most of Lebanon; Syria was a political ally of Iran during the Iran-Iraq War. Well-armed Syrian troops would be a match for any Arab enemy, and would give a good account of themselves against Israel or the West.

Libya has been armed to the teeth since the Khaddafi revolution of 1969 and remains so, although the quality of its troops is questionable.

The million-man armed forces of Iraq were the troublemakers of today's Middle East. Virtually all Arab governments were united in their desire to see Iraq expelled from Kuwait. The army that fought Iran to a draw through eight bloody years emerged from the 1991 Gulf War battered but not destroyed.

Since Mohammed's time Iran has been a "loner" in Middle Eastern affairs. During the early twentieth century it was a cipher in world politics, under British and Russian influence. The Russian influence ended after the Bolshevik Revolution, but the British influence remained due to the oilfields developed by the Anglo-Iranian Oil Company in the southwest corner of the country.

Reza Khan made himself Shah by military coup during the early 1920s. He followed a somewhat pro–German foreign policy during the early days of World War II. Shortly after the German invasion of the Soviet Union in 1941 Russian and British troops occupied the country, deposing Reza Shah and allowing his young son Mohammed Reza Shah to assume the throne.

The occupiers withdrew after the end of the war. The Shah showed no interest in governing as a clique of politicians ran the nation. The leftist Mohammed Mossadegh emerged as king of the hill, expropriating the Anglo-Iranian Oil Company and making too many pro–Soviet noises to suit the Americans and British. A CIA-sponsored coup removed him from office in 1953.

Shah Mohammed Reza Pahlavi now assumed power in his own behalf, retaining the expropriated oil company. He built the country into what seemed to be one of the political and economic giants of the Middle East, using the immense oil revenues for this purpose. Americans especially looked upon Iran as the stabilizing power in the area, equipping the Shah's armed forces with modern equipment. We cheered the Shah on as he sought social and economic reform Western-style through his White Revolution. Gradually his domestic policies generated such discontent within the country that the modernizing regime was swept away by the 1979 upheaval. White revolution was replaced by Muslim green.

The fundamentalist Shi'ite Islamic government established by the Ayatollah Khomeini has turned the nation into a fulminator of religiously inspired revolution throughout the Islamic world. However, Iran has neither the financial nor the political power of the Arabs. Iranian oil reserves and oil sales to the West don't come close to equaling those of the Arabs, while Iranian military power could obtain no better than a draw in the bloody Iran-Iraq War of the 1980s. Iranian-supported revolutionaries and terrorists have cost their enemies many lives and much money, but so far they've overthrown no governments and made very few friends.

The most powerful appeal of Middle Eastern culture is neither political, military nor economic, but the power of the religion that has made the culture what it is, Islam. The reason for this phenomenon will be discussed in the chapter on world religions.

Indian Culture

When ancient Babylon flourished in Mesopotamia, the great cities of Mohenjo-Daro and Harappa dominated the Indus Valley of what's now Pakistan. Here are the earliest centers of Indian civilization.

For reasons we don't understand, India and its culture faded into obscurity for several centuries. It came to life again in the pages of the great works of early Indian literature — the Rig Veda, the Ramayana and the Mahabharata. Here are the tales of how life might have been when Indo-Europeans swept into the subcontinent to assert their dominion over the Dravidians.

By the time of the birth of Gautama Siddhartha, the founder of Buddhism, a flourishing civilization had come into existence in the subcontinent. Within it two of the world's great religions, Hinduism and Buddhism, began to struggle for dominance, a battle won by Hinduism.

This durable faith created a civilization in which economic activity, government and politics took a back seat to religion, paying little attention to history or to thought of the future.

The boundaries of Indian territorial states have been as fluid as the movement of waves on a lake. Here too power has always flowed from the point of the sword; temporal rulers have ruled as much real estate as they could control militarily.

Since Hinduism views life in terms of eons (because of reincarnation), human events in this world are not important. How does what happened in Benares in 1423 matter when you consider the importance of the soul's struggle to achieve Nirvana? Thus detailed historical records are rare in India.

Hinduism is a tolerant religion, never seeking to impose itself by violence upon non-believers. Thus a variety of non–Hindu faiths have always existed in the subcontinent. As in the Middle East, the various faiths have constituted states within the state, each being governed by its own religious leaders in accordance with its own law.

India was a rich civilization because of its fertile soil, a temptation to the poorer peoples who sat outside the subcontinent looking in.

The Persians invaded the northwest in the fifth century B.C., and the armies of Alexander the Great followed in the fourth. Shortly thereafter Chandragupta Maurya created the first great native empire, which reached its apex under Asoka a half-century later. This Maurya Empire united most of the subcontinent for a short period, then fell into decline. An era of small warring states followed.

In the fourth century A.D. another Chandragupta created the Gupta Empire, the second and last great native territorial state. After a short period of glory this too declined, and foreign invaders began to tear at the rich, unmilitary subcontinent. The Kushans came, and then the White Huns. In the ninth century the first armies of Muslims knocked upon the door.

Still Indian culture was strong enough to expand its influence to the east. Though Indians never engaged in military conquest outside the subcontinent, Hindu kings at one time reigned in southeast Asia and on the islands of Indonesia.

By 1500 this Hindu influence had vanished, ousted from southeast Asia by Buddhism and from Indonesia and Malaysia by Islam.

Evidence of this Indian cultural presence can still be seen at the Buddhist ruins of Borobudur on Java and the great Hindu complex of Angkor Wat in Kampuchea. Only on the island of Bali in Indonesia does a remnant of Hindu culture survive outside of India.

In the eleventh century the Afghan hordes of Mahmud of Ghazni plundered north India; in the fifteenth came the Mongol armies of Timur-i-Leng, known to the West as Tamerlane. Then came the Moghuls, who established their great empire at Delhi in the sixteenth century.

In south India the great Hindu kingdom of Vijayanagar maintained its independence against the waves of Muslim fury for several centuries. At last, though, the power of the Moghuls proved irresistible. Vijayanagar fell in 1565, and Muslim power was supreme everywhere in India.

Already Portuguese and Spaniards were beginning to spread European influence in the area. In the seventeenth century the Dutch came, and in the eighteenth arrived the French and English. The Moghul power declined while English and French influence increased. As a result of the Napoleonic wars French influence was destroyed and England united India under its scepter, using armies of Indian soldiers led by English officers.

The English continued the practice of the Moghuls under which the various religious communities were states within the state, each led by its own religious leaders and governed to a large extent by its own law. English courts applied Hindu religious law within the Hindu community, Muslim law within the Muslim community, and the law of the numerous religious minorities within their populations.

In 1857 the soldiers of the Indian army rose in rebellion against their English officers, massacring English soldiers and civilians. The Sepoy Rebellion shook the English hold upon India to the core, causing the colonial government to make a supreme effort to suppress it. Western military technology and discipline triumphed; the rebels were defeated.

Now the English strove to modernize the subcontinent and to educate numbers of Indians in the European style. Unwittingly the foundations of modern Indian nationalism were thus laid. People from all over India, believers in diverse religions and speakers of diverse languages, united to work for the cause of Indian freedom. The struggle lasted for the better part of a century.

Indians were tied to the English during this period in a love-hate relationship. Few Indians voiced support for Germany or Turkey in World War I; the British army that drove the Turks from Iraq comprised many Indians.

Indian troops fought for Great Britain against the Japanese in World War II; many fell into Japanese hands as POWs in Hong Kong, Malaya and Burma. The anti–British nationalist Subhas Chandra Bose sought to organize a pro–Japanese Indian legion from these prisoners but the huge majority of them remained loyal to the British crown.

The most prominent leader of Indian nationalism was Mohandas Gandhi, known as the Mahatma. His policy of Satyagraha — massive nonviolent resistance — caught the British in a vise they couldn't escape. In all conscience they couldn't resist nonviolence with violence.

In 1947 the British threw in the towel and abandoned their Indian empire; the area regained political independence. The influence of Western nationalist notions insured that the more or less peaceful coexistence of Hindu and Muslim on the soil of the subcontinent couldn't continue. The Muslim minority was unwilling to entrust itself to Hindu majority rule, so the subcontinent was partitioned into Hindu India and Muslim Pakistan. Hindu political authority returned in the new Republic, and a unique culture again began to rule itself.

The great uniqueness of Indian culture is that it has never sought to force itself upon any people. It doesn't loudly preach its superiority to other cultures. Traditionally it hasn't even been too diligent about self-defense.

Surprisingly the democratic government established for the Republic on the departure of the English has survived for more than forty years. India is the second-largest country on Earth in terms of population, and is the world's largest democracy.

The nation has been neutral in the struggle between East and West; its leaders have spoken out loudly against international violence. Yet it maintains powerful armed forces. Though these were badly battered in fighting against Chinese troops along the borders of Tibet in 1962, they have beaten the armed forces of Pakistan on three occasions. The home of Hindu culture is now strong enough to defend itself against intruders.

Until now no power on earth has succeeded in destroying Hindu culture, or even seriously damaging it. In times of trouble it hunkers down and ignores the world as much as it can, going about its business and seeking to survive.

Chinese Culture

Of the world's five great cultures, the Western and the Chinese have the greatest affinity. Like Westerners, people of Chinese culture are oriented toward this world and keep meticulous historical records. Like Westerners, they are essentially materialists and consider their culture to be obviously superior.

Chung Kuo, the Chinese name for their land, means "the central country." Traditionally Chinese believed it to be the center of the civilized world. They believed that their Emperor, the Son of Heaven, was the emperor of all people.

There was civilization in China during the second millennium before Christ. Among the writings that have come down to us from those remote days is that unique Chinese oracle the I Ching—the Book of Changes. By the time of Confucius (the sixth century B.C.) fair-sized states competed for power and the Far Eastern culture bloomed.

From the beginning the culture has been oriented toward this world— especially toward the present and the past. The Golden Age of Man has come and gone; the sages of the past knew and understood more than we of the present can possibly learn for ourselves. If we today are to live any kind of decent life, we must study what the ancient sages wrote down for our benefit, and follow their precepts.

The time frame of the future is limited by the length of this life. There is no other. Everything in nature is basically good, including people. They have discovered the principles upon which sound living is based; if they only have the sense to recognize the wisdom of the sages all will be well.

The art of war flourished in this era. It was at this time that Sun Tsu wrote his eternal classic *The Art of War*. Its instructions on achievement of political and military victory without battle have been studied by competent Chinese generals for two millennia and fascinate would-be strategists, military and otherwise, throughout today's world.

During the third century B.C. the larger states began to absorb the smaller ones. Toward the end of the century the state of Ch'in emerged as supreme, swallowing all of its competitors. Its prince Shih Huang Ti made himself the first emperor of united China and erected the Great Wall to keep the northern barbarians out.

The Ch'in dynasty didn't long survive the death of its founder; its successor dynasty the Han brought China its first flowering. Han armies added south China and Vietnam to the empire and penetrated far west into central Asia, as trade opened with the Roman Empire. Roman coinage flowed eastward in exchange for Chinese silk.

The principle was quickly established that no dynasty of Emperors was entitled to rule the land forever. It came to be understood that the Emperor and his underlings ruled by the grace of the powers above but they had no mandate to remain in power eternally.

They owed it to their subjects to provide good government. As long as the land was at peace and prosperity prevailed the dynasty's government was virtuous and possessed the Mandate of Heaven. Therefore it would be treasonable and evil to try to change it. However, when famine stalked the land, outlaws created civil disorders and invaders plundered the virtuous, the government had become evil; the bad social conditions showed that it had lost the Mandate of Heaven and was ripe for replacement.

It was in times like these that adventurers would overthrow the reigning dynasty and replace it with one of their own. The old upper class would be destroyed, to be supplanted by a new one.

It was also established that an imperial bureaucracy chosen through merit would help the Emperor rule. The nature of this bureaucracy will be discussed in a later chapter.

The Han power declined before Rome weakened. Barbarians from beyond the Great Wall threatened the civilized Chinese north and the empire split into three warring states. Degeneracy and disunion plagued the land for several centuries.

Then came reunion under the Sui and a second great flowering under its successor the T'ang in the ninth century. Again the Chinese armies moved west into central Asia. Trade relations opened with the Islamic empires of the Middle East, and Chinese travelers visited India. Chinese culture spread into southeast Asia, Korea and Japan.

Then decline struck again. Internal disorder grew; Vietnam was lost. The T'ang were overthrown; the Sung ruled in their stead. This dynasty lost the north to the barbarian Kin but retained control in the south. A culture that admired art, literature and poetry held sway in the Sung lands for two centuries.

During the thirteenth century the irresistible Mongol hordes of Genghis Khan smashed the Kin and dominated north China, later moving south and destroying the Sung. For a century Mongol emperors of the Yuan dynasty ruled the reunited Empire from Peking.

It was during the reign of the greatest of these, Kublai Khan, that Marco Polo came to China and made the observations that later so fascinated Europeans. He wrote of Chinese paper, gunpowder, printing with wooden blocks and the circulation of paper money.

Under Kublai the Chinese embarked on their most audacious military ventures, invading Japan, Java and Burma. The expeditions to Japan and Java were disastrous, while the Burmese venture accomplished little.

In the fourteenth century the Chinese bestirred themselves and overthrew the Mongol domination. The last of the native Chinese dynasties, the Ming, took power in Peking.

By now the Chinese had harnessed gunpowder to military use. The oldest Chinese cannon we know the exact age of is dated 1356, though evidence exists that such weapons were used at least a century earlier. Never did these weapons play a major role in Chinese military operations, however, nor were they equal in quality to those from the West.

By now, too, the Chinese had discovered the compass and adapted it to use in ships sailing beyond sight of land. The Chinese junk of the period was as efficient a seagoing vessel as anything built in European shipyards. During the fifteenth century massive Chinese fleets of junks visited Indonesia, Malaysia, Sri Lanka, the mouth of the Persian Gulf and Africa. Chinese armies carried aboard these fleets conquered areas of Sri Lanka and Sumatra. The possibility beckoned of turning the Indian Ocean into a Chinese lake. There was no technological reason why Chinese vessels couldn't round the Cape of Good Hope into the Atlantic and sail north to Europe.

Chinese trade with Indonesia, Malaysia, India and the Islamic world expanded during this era. Had Chinese culture encouraged inquisitiveness as Western culture did—the desire to visit unknown places just because they were there—China may have reached the West before the West reached China.

It wasn't to be. When the Mongol tribesmen again began to threaten the North, the emperors ordered the cessation of these maritime explorations. Of what use would it be to control East Africa if the Mongols once more plundered Peking?

By the time European ships appeared in Chinese waters a century later there were no Chinese fleets to challenge them. The Portuguese were able to found their colony of Macao and Jesuit priests established a permanent presence in Peking.

The control of the Ming over the country began to slip in the seventeenth century. Out of the wild northeast swept new armies of barbarian conquerors, the Manchu. By the middle of the century the Ming had been overthrown and the last dynasty of emperors, the Manchu Ch'ing, came to power.

Under the Ch'ing the last imperial conquests in central Asia took place. Chinese armies were able to permanently break the power of Mongol nomads and again Chinese influence extended itself toward the shores of the Caspian.

Russian influence expanded along China's western and northern frontiers, while English and French seafarers appeared along the eastern coast. The most traumatic period of the land's history was beginning.

The Chinese had not always been militarily superior to foreigners; in the past barbarian conquerors had established imperial dynasties by the power of the sword. These had until now always ended up absorbing the superior culture of the conquered, becoming Chinese themselves.

But the Westerners were different, showing disrespect and even contempt for the ways of the Middle Kingdom. Furthermore the nineteenth-century military revolution had given them the capacity to force their will upon the Chinese.

In the 1840s the English forced China to lease them Hong Kong. In 1860 an Anglo-French army took Peking and subjected the country to great humiliation. At the same time the Russians forced China to cede huge tracts of unsettled land in the north and northeast by the 1858 Treaty of Aigun and the 1860 Treaty of Peking. Soon Vladivostok on the Pacific bloomed from a Chinese fishing village into a modern Russian city and powerful naval base. In 1894 the rising Asian power of Japan handily defeated the empire in war, and by 1900 China seemed to be on the verge of partition by its greedy neighbors and exploiters.

Chinese government had lost the capacity to exercise its authority within the Empire. During the 1850s and 1860s the T'aiping rebels occupied huge areas of central China and were subdued only by western-led, western-trained Chinese troops. In 1900 the anti-foreign Boxers seized control of the Peking area and were driven off only through the exertions of a multi-national army of Europeans, Japanese and Americans. Had China's would-be executioners not disagreed as to how the country should be put out of its misery it would have disappeared from the map early in the twentieth century.

As it was it barely survived. The Manchu empire, which had clearly lost the Mandate of Heaven, was overthrown by a domestic coup in 1912; at last China had rulers who knew that imitation of the West was essential to preserve the land's independence.

The new Republic had to battle internal disintegration and the greed of imperialist Japan. The Nationalist forces of Chiang Kai Shek brought unity of sorts to the land, as the domestic contenders for power were reduced to two: Chiang's Nationalists and Mao Tse-Tung's Communists. All-out war with Japan delayed the showdown. Only after the victorious Anglo-Americans destroyed Japanese power were the Chinese contenders able to settle their differences.

Mao's forces had effectively used the maxims of Sun Tsu to harass the Japanese; now they used them to utterly defeat the more numerous, better equipped Nationalists.

The Communist victory of 1949 once more brought unity and strong government to the country. Though Westerners feared that China was now to become a satellite of the Soviet Union, Mao Tse-Tung had no intention of allowing that to happen. By the end of the 1950s the traditional Chinese dislike of Russians had reasserted itself and the country set out to find its own way to Communism.

Though China has not become a world power on the level of the United States and the Soviet Union, it stands proudly independent as no nation's satellite. In terms of military personnel, its People's Liberation Army is the largest in the world. It conquered Tibet, fought the forces of the United States to a draw in Korea (1950–53), defeated the Indian Army along the borders of Tibet (1962), held its own in border clashes with Soviet forces in the north (1969) and gave Vietnamese forces a bloody nose (1979).

China and its culture, after a century of merciless pummeling, are still very much alive.

Japan. China illustrates one facet of Far Eastern culture — a solid assurance that its culture is superior to all others no matter what the rest of the world thinks, and a refusal to adopt more of other cultures than is needed to preserve its own. Japan illustrates another.

Japan has known only one dynasty of Emperors throughout its long history. The Emperor Akihito, latest of the line, claims to be a direct descendant of Jimmu Tenno, founder of the empire in the legendary past.

Almost from the beginning Japan has had a culture which glorifies violence and war. The existence of the one imperial dynasty was preserved only by converting the Emperor into a ceremonial figurehead, while heads of noble families battled each other for political power.

During the seventh century the nation deliberately adopted Chinese culture in wholesale, including Chinese writing, Chinese-style Mahayana Buddhist religion and Chinese Confucian philosophy. Yet the nation didn't turn into a pale reflection of China. Thirteen hundred years ago the Japanese illustrated for the first time their uncanny ability to adapt chosen portions of a foreign culture to their own purposes.

Japan knew a great cultural flowering from the seventh to the tenth century. The emperors and the country were dominated by the Fujiwara family, lovers of art and literature. As time passed, however, the powerful nobility of the outlying areas of the country progressively ignored the commands of the central government and Japan slipped into feudal anarchy.

The Fujiwara dominance ended, and other families (such as the Taira and the Minamoto) battled for supremacy. Ultimately the Minamoto triumphed and established the Shogunate. The Sei-I-Tai Shogun (Barbarian-Subduing General) was in theory the second most powerful person in the Empire, owing allegiance only to the Emperor. In practice he was a military dictator.

In 1204 the Hojo family assumed power, establishing the Regency. The Hojo Regents were in theory the third most powerful persons in the land, subordinate to both Emperor and Shogun. In practice, again, they ruled as dictators.

With the help of typhoons—the Kamikaze, or Divine Wind—a Hojo regent led the Japanese resistance that fought off the great Mongol invasions of 1274 and 1281.

Shortly thereafter the Regency was overthrown, and the Ashikaga family assumed power as Shoguns. During their weak rule feudal anarchy again prevailed. Only in the sixteenth century was this suppressed by a succession of three remarkable men.

Oda Nobunaga began the process of imposing powerful central government on the land, subjecting half of it to his personal rule before he was assassinated. Spanish and Portuguese sailors had visited his domains and demonstrated to him the virtues of Western gunpowder weapons. His military successes were due at least in part to the fact that his troops effectively used artillery and musketry against their opponents.

His successor Hideyoshi Toyotomi united the land enough to assemble a powerful army which invaded Korea, hoping it could go on and conquer China. The result was disastrous. Though the army defeated every force the Koreans could throw against it, Korean Admiral Yi Sun assembled the first fleet of ironclad warships seen in the world to defeat the Japanese fleet and cut off the army's communications with its homeland. Ultimately this army never made it out of Korea; most of it never saw Japan again.

Hideyoshi's successor Tokugawa Iyeyasu had to fight a fierce civil war against Hideyoshi's son to win the Shogunate. This war was marked by some remarkable sieges in which heavy artillery played a prominent role in the operations of both besiegers and besieged.

Ultimately the Tokugawa forces won, constructing the strong central government that isolated Japan from the world in the 1640s. Had the government not adopted this policy, it's possible that Japan would have become a Far Eastern power two centuries earlier than it actually did.

The army Hideyoshi sent to Korea was a splendid fighting force, but it was far too small to accomplish its objective. The Tokugawa forces that fought and won the civil war were if anything more effective.

Japanese junks were as large and seaworthy as Chinese junks; Japanese pirates launched repeated raids on the Chinese coast during the sixteenth century. The most noteworthy Japanese nautical accomplishment was the voyage made by two junks manned by Japanese crews from the coast of Japan to Acapulco in Mexico during the sixteenth century. Vessels and crewmen capable of such a journey could certainly have sailed to almost anywhere.

Ironically, the success of Roman Catholic missionaries in obtaining Japanese converts was a major reason for Japan's adoption of isolation. Though a large portion of the army Hideyoshi dispatched to Korea was Christian, and though these men fought as well as their non–Christian colleagues—Japan's governing circles nursed the gnawing thought that Japanese Christians were at heart subversive. If a Spanish army from the Philippines invaded Japan (which was in theory quite possible), would the Christians defend their country or join their Spanish co-religionists?

The Tokugawa government demanded that the Japanese Catholics renounce their faith. The majority refused to do so, resulting in a persecution more bloody than that of the early Christians by the Roman Emperors. Some of the Christian community responded by rising in rebellion and fortifying the Shimabara peninsula of Kyushu; it required a major military operation to storm the fortifications and suppress them. Most (but not all) of this Japanese Catholic community was wiped out. A small remnant remained intact, and still remains so, in and around the southern Japanese city of Nagasaki. One of the objectives the Tokugawa isolation sought to accomplish was to preserve the Japanese people from further subversion (as the government saw it) at the hands of Christian missionaries.

The Tokugawa Shogunate preserved Japan in splendid isolation until 1853 when the American warships of Matthew C. Perry forced it to admit the world again.

The Japanese saw how strong the West had become over a period of two centuries, and what Westerners were about in China. Their antique seventeenth-century cannon were no match for modern Western naval guns and could never hope to defeat Western forces bent on conquest.

The Shogunate was abolished in 1868, to be replaced by more efficient Western-style government. Then, through amazing effort Japan transformed itself from the poor backward country of 1853 into the modern land and naval power that humiliated China in 1894–95 and Russia in 1904–05, the Japanese Navy annihilating a powerful Russian fleet at Tsushima in one of the most complete naval victories of all time.

Japan acquired an empire by annexing Korea in 1910, and by joining with the Allies in World War I and seizing the widely scattered German islands of the Pacific. It intervened in the Russian Civil War in the hope of annexing parts of far eastern Siberia; only strong Western objections dissuaded it. During the 1930s Japan sought to subject China to its will.

By now Japan was a formidable state whose naval air force sank an American fleet at Pearl Harbor. The army Japan sent to British Malaya made a British force twice its size surrender at Singapore; another sent to Luzon drove a larger American-Filipino force into the Bataan peninsula, where it later surrendered.

Superior American intelligence and massive bad luck caused Japan to lose four aircraft carriers at the battle of Midway in June of 1942; this cost it naval supremacy in the Pacific and made its loss of the Pacific war inevitable. Yet it fought on for three terrible bloody years.

In Japanese military tradition surrender was disgraceful; the honorable soldier died where he stood rather than give up. Thus the Britons who surrendered at Singapore and the Americans who surrendered on Bataan were given horrendous treatment as prisoners of war—as miserable cowards who gave up while they still held weapons in their hands, they merited nothing better.

From Guadalcanal through Tarawa and Palau to Iwo Jima and Okinawa, the Japanese garrisons of the Pacific islands fought American invaders to the death. Hardly ever did able-bodied Japanese troops surrender. During the war's last year Japanese pilots volunteered by the hundreds to become Kamikaze—men who would seek to crash their aircraft on the decks of American warships and sell their lives for maximum damage to the enemy. It was futile. For the first and only time in its history Japan had to admit military defeat by a foreign power and become subject to foreign occupation.

In September of 1945 Japan's cities had been burned, its industry smashed, and hundreds of thousands of its people killed and injured. Yet it rose from the ashes like the phoenix and through a combination of Far Eastern discipline and intelligent use of Western technology transformed itself into a major world economy, second in production only to the United States.

Today the Japanese yen is one of the world's strongest currencies and Japan has become one of the great creditor nations. It may well become the financial center of the western Pacific and perhaps of the world.

If the Chinese could adapt Western technology to their own purposes as the Japanese have done, what might they not accomplish? We mustn't judge the culture of this part of the world just by its country of origin. In a sense its most successful exponent has been its greatest copier—Japan.

Vanished Cultures of the Past

Western tradition called Africa "darkest"—the part of the continent south of the Sahara being supposedly unblessed by civilization before the coming of Europeans.

The tradition was in error. In northern Sudan the civilized kingdoms of

Meroe and Axum flourished in the early part of the Christian era. Along the upper Niger the great empires of Ghana, and later Mali, and still later Songhai bloomed, the latter surviving until the end of the sixteenth century. This last great African empire was destroyed in 1591 by an army of Moroccan raiders who crossed the Sahara bent on plunder.

Farther south the empire of Kongo flourished near the river which bears its name. The Portuguese destroyed its power in the fifteenth and sixteenth centuries, reducing it to a satellite, later eliminating it altogether.

Still farther south civilized people built the city of Great Zimbabwe, center of a sizable empire that endured for several centuries. This declined to insignificance in the fifteenth century, the ruined city giving its name to a new nation in the 1970s.

On the east coast Arab and African culture fused in the trading cities of Malindi, Kilwa, Mombasa, Zanzibar and others. The marauding Portuguese destroyed the prosperity of these; they stagnated until they fell under German and British domination in the nineteenth century.

Other African cultures possessed the capacity to resist European conquest until well into modern times. The Zulus of southern Africa assembled one of the most formidable, highly disciplined military forces of all time in the middle of the nineteenth century, armed only with spears. No Africans could stand against them. When they wiped out a British detachment armed with rifles at Isandhlwana Britons felt the horror Americans later felt after Custer's men met their fate at Little Big Horn. It took a larger British force armed with the most modern weapons to finally defeat these black warriors.

The Muslim emirates of northern Nigeria fielded strong military forces that kept them independent until the beginning of the twentieth century. A powerful British military expedition was required to subdue them.

The kingdom of Dahomey was glad to do business with Westerners, acquiring military forces skilled in the use of Western firearms. Dahomey retained its independence until the middle of the nineteenth century, when it was conquered by a determined French Foreign Legion armed with repeating rifles.

Proud Ethiopia retained its independence until 1936, isolated by mountains from outside aggressors. The first and only European power to make a determined effort to conquer these highlands was Italy. The Italian expedition of 1896 encountered Ethiopians at Adowa, some of them armed with modern weapons, and was forced to surrender. The humiliation rankled in Italian breasts for nearly forty years.

In 1935 Benito Mussolini's Italy sought revenge. An Italian army equipped with machine guns, modern artillery and aircraft quickly overran the country (but not before using poison gas to overcome some stubborn resistance). Adowa was thus avenged, but the new Italian colony lasted for only five years. British troops drove the Italians out in 1941, during World War II.

Though Africa never bloomed as did Europe, the Middle East, India and

China, its past isn't utter darkness. One wonders what Africans might have accomplished on their own had outside forces not interfered.

Unknown cultures have left mighty reminders of their existence strewn about the New World. On the altiplano of Bolivia overlooking Lake Titicaca, 13,000 feet above sea level, stand the remains of Tiahuanaco. Who erected its great buildings and for what purpose remains a riddle.

To the north in Peru are the ruins of Sacsahuaman, which were old in the time of the Incas.

In Mexico are the ruins of Monte Alban and the giant human heads sculptured by the Olmecs; these too were old when the Aztecs flourished.

Three known great Amerindian civilizations bloomed in the Western Hemisphere before the coming of the Spanish conquistadores. Earliest was the Mayan of Yucatan, Belize and Guatemala. Its cities dotted the jungles of this area during the first millennium of the Christian era. Tourists are still amazed by the ruins of Chichen Itza and Palenque, and scholars are even more amazed by the mathematical and astronomical knowledge of these people; their calendar was as accurate as ours. Around the year 1000 the Maya began to abandon their cities and high culture; they were in terminal cultural decline when the Spaniards came and destroyed what was left of their civilization.

Before the arrival of Hernán Cortés Mexico City was known as Tenochtitlan and was the capital of the greatest empire of North America. The Aztec Empire ruled all of central Mexico and its millions of people lived in relative prosperity. Its riches tempted the Spanish army of Cortés to enter the valley of Mexico, and the gunpowder weapons of that army destroyed the empire and virtually enslaved its people. The blood of the subjects of Montezuma, last Emperor of the Aztecs, still flows through the veins of today's Mexicans. Cuauhtemoc, Montezuma's would-be successor and last leader of the Aztec peoples, is still revered as a hero in Mexican history.

In 1525 Peru plus much of Ecuador and Bolivia was part of the empire of the Incas. It's a source of wonder that a people who had no written language other than knots in long cords, and who didn't know the wheel as anything other than a toy, could have built the Inca roads and temples. The magnificent masonry in the buildings of old Cuzco and of Macchu Picchu has never been duplicated. The riches of this empire were an irresistible magnet to the army of Francisco Pizarro. This empire too fell to Spanish gunpowder weapons, but the Quechua language of many of its people remains an official language of Peru and elements of Inca culture survive on the high Altiplano.

Lesser Amerindian cultures put up stiff resistance to European conquerors. One thinks of the Araucanians, who stoutly defended their lands in Chile against Spanish intruders, or the Yaqui who battled Spaniards and Mexicans in the Mexican state of Sonora. In the United States the Iroquois Confederation defended its lands in New York State with skill and tenacity.

Five skillful American Indian leaders are worthy of mention here — Pontiac, whose confederation of tribes shook the British hold on western Pennsylvania and the upper Ohio Valley during the 1760s; Tecumseh, who obstructed the American occupation of northern Indiana just before the War of 1812 until his warriors were scattered by army troops at the battle of Tippecanoe; Osceola, whose Seminole warriors skillfully hindered American occupation of Florida; Sitting Bull, whose Sioux wiped out Custer's cavalry at Little Big Horn; and Geronimo, whose desertwise Apaches led the United States cavalry on a long-lasting chase through the mountains and deserts of Arizona and New Mexico.

How would the civilizations of the New World have developed had Europeans not burst upon the American scene when they did? The question will remain a fascinating riddle for as long as our culture survives.

Chapter 4
Languages

Some of the world's nations are linguistically homogeneous, the vast majority of the population speaking the same tongue. Examples are Sweden, Germany, Poland, Saudi Arabia, South Korea and Japan.

Other nations have two official languages, such as Canada (English and French), Belgium (French and Flemish), Finland (Finnish and Swedish), Peru (Spanish and Quechua), Paraguay (Spanish and Guarani), and Czechoslovakia (Czech and Slovak).

Still other nations are multi-lingual. Switzerland and Singapore each recognize four official languages (German, French, Italian and Romansch in Switzerland; English, Mandarin Chinese, Malay and Tamil in Singapore).

Each of the fifteen constituent republics of the Soviet Union has its own official language, while in some republics residents of autonomous regions use still other languages. India recognizes thirteen official languages, while in almost all African nations south of the Sahara several tongues are spoken.

Even in France, Spain and Italy sizeable linguistic minorities exist. In the Middle Ages two varieties of French were spoken: the Langue d'Oc in the south and the Langue d'Oil in the north. (oc was "yes" in the southern tongue, Oil was "yes" in the northern.) The Langue d'Oil developed into modern French. Many southern French people speak the modern descendant of the Langue d'Oc—Occitan (or, as some call it, Provencal).

In Alsace (which was a part of German-speaking Europe until the late seventeenth century) many natives still speak a dialect of German as their first tongue. In Corsica (which was part of the Italian-speaking world until the mid-eighteenth century) people grow up speaking an Italian dialect, as Napoleone Buonaparte did before he came to France and changed his name and language. In Brittany the descendants of Celtic immigrants from the British Isles speak Breton. In the eastern foothills of the Pyrenees Catalan is spoken, while in the southwest around Biarritz, people speak Basque. Around Dunkirk and along the Belgian frontier Flemish may be heard.

In Spain Castilian Spanish is the major language, but Catalan is heard in the northeast down to Valencia, Basque around San Sebastian and farther west, and Galician (a close relative of Portuguese) in the far northwest, due north of Portugal.

In Italy Sard is spoken on Sardinia, while German is an official language in the South Tyrol (the area south of the Brenner Pass, which was part of Austrian Tyrol before 1919) and French in the Val d'Aosta (east of Mont Blanc). Slovene is spoken near the Yugoslav frontier, Friulian and Ladin are spoken in some Alpine valleys, and the people of scattered southern villages speak dialects of Greek and Albanian.

Even in the Netherlands and Great Britain there's linguistic diversity. In the Dutch province of Friesland, north of the great dike across the mouth of the Zuyder Zee, Frisian is spoken — the closest relative of English on earth. (There are also a few thousand Frisian speakers farther north in Germany.) In Great Britain Scots Gaelic is spoken in the Scottish Highlands and on the Hebrides Islands off the west coast of Scotland, while in the hills of north Wales Welsh is widely spoken.

The patterns of human speech will vary from locality to locality. If the speech of Podunk is very similar but not quite identical to that of Funk's Thicket we speak of local variation. When the speech of Podunk is different enough from that of Funk's Thicket that it's somewhat difficult for people from one to understand people from the other, we may say that they speak different dialects. When the speech of Podunk is so different from that of Funk's Thicket that people from the two towns don't understand each other at all we say they speak different languages.

When are variations in a spoken language wide enough to constitute dialects? When do dialects differ enough to become separate languages? There are no hard and fast rules. The opinions of professional linguists differ.

Altogether over three thousand separate languages are spoken on earth. Kenneth Katzner in his work, *The Languages of the World,* divides these into eighteen families: (1) Indo-European; (2) Uralic; (3) Altaic; (4) Caucasian; (5) Dravidian; (6) Munda; (7) Sino-Tibetan; (8) Mon-Khmer; (9) Malayo-Polynesian; (10) Papuan; (11) Australian; (12) Paleo-Asiatic; (13) Eskimo-Aleut; (14) Niger-Congo; (15) Afro-Asiatic (Semitic-Hamitic); (16) Chari-Nile; (17) Khoisan; (18) Amerindian.

Katzner also speaks of "independent" languages that belong to no family, and of Pidgin and Creole languages. A Pidgin language is one composed of a few words from two or more languages (such as the Pidgin English composed of words from African languages and English used by Africans and English speakers in the days of the slave trade on the West African coast, or that composed of words from Chinese languages and English used by Chinese and English speakers in Chinese ports) used by speakers of mutually incomprehensible tongues to communicate with each other. It's always a second tongue, spoken in addition to the speaker's native language.

When a Pidgin is spoken long enough by enough persons to become a native language or dialect, it becomes a Creole. The Taki-Taki of Suriname, the Papiamento of the Netherlands Antilles and the Gulla spoken by the black inhabitants of the Georgia coastal islands are good examples of this phenomenon.

The family of languages most familiar to us is the Indo-European. Languages of this family are spoken from the British Isles to India, and in most former European colonies. Most Western Europeans speak languages belonging to three branches of this family — Germanic, Romance and Celtic.

The Germanic family is descended from the now-lost speech of the original Germanic immigrants to Europe. The two most prominent members of the family are German and English. Other members are Dutch, Flemish, Frisian, Yiddish, Letzeburgesch, Danish, Norwegian, Swedish, Icelandic, Faroese and Afrikaans.

English is the second most widely spoken language on earth, English speakers having carried it to every point where the English flag at one time flew. Afrikaans is the language of the ancestors of Dutch settlers at the southern tip of Africa, and is the most widely-spoken language of white South Africans. Dutch is spoken in the Netherlands Antilles and in Suriname as well as in the Netherlands. Flemish is the variety of Dutch spoken in northern Belgium.

German is the official language of three nations (Germany, Austria and Liechtenstein) and is the majority language of another (Switzerland). A number of German speakers are also found in Eastern Europe (in the Soviet Union and Romania particularly), in the Western Hemisphere (Brazil, Argentina, Canada and the United States primarily), and in Namibia (once the German colony of Southwest Africa).

Yiddish had its origin in a medieval German dialect, and is spoken by Jews of European origin all over the world. Letzeburgesch is the variant of German spoken in the Grand Duchy of Luxembourg. (Some linguists consider it to be merely a dialect of German and not a separate language.)

Other Germanic languages are spoken almost exclusively in their European cradles, though as mentioned earlier Swedish is an official language of Finland as well as the native tongue of most of Sweden's people.

The Romance languages are direct descendants of Latin, the language of the Roman Empire. The most prominent of these are Spanish, French, Portuguese and Italian. Other members of the group include Occitan, Catalan, Galician, Sard, Romanian, Moldavian, Romansch, Ladin, and Friulian.

Spanish is the language of the majority of Western Hemisphere nations, from Mexico south to Argentina and Chile. It's also the second most widely spoken language of the United States. French is spoken widely in former French colonies in Africa, and also in a few places in the Western Hemisphere (Haiti, Quebec, the French Caribbean Islands and French Guiana). The world's largest Portuguese-speaking nation is Brazil. Portuguese is also an official language of Portugal's former African colonies (Angola, Mozambique, the Cape Verde Islands and Guinea-Bissau). Italian is an official language only in Italy and the Swiss canton of Ticino, but it's still spoken by the ancestors of Italian immigrants in the U.S., Brazil, Argentina and other nations. Romanian is the official language of Romania. Moldavian is its very close relative, spoken in the neighboring Moldavian Socialist Republic of the Soviet Union. Romansch is a distant relative of Italian, spoken by some 50,000 persons in the canton of Graubunden, Switzerland; it's one of that nation's four official languages. Ladin and Friulian are spoken by small numbers of persons in the Italian Alps, while Sard is heard only on its Mediterranean island home. The homes of the other Romance tongues have already been mentioned.

No nation exists where a majority of the people speak a Celtic language. Members of the family include Irish Gaelic (an official language of Ireland and taught in Irish schools, but not the major language of most Irish people), Scots Gaelic, Welsh, and Breton. Speakers of these languages are almost always bilingual, being fluent in either English (in Ireland, Scotland and Wales) or French (in Brittany).

Most eastern Europeans speak languages belonging to the Slavic family. These are descended from the tongue of the original Slavic settlers of eastern Europe. The major language of the group is of course Great Russian (or simply Russian), the preferred official language of the Soviet Union. Other Slavic national languages include Polish, Bulgarian, Serbo-Croatian (the major language of Yugoslavia), Czech, and Slovak (both of which are official languages in Czechoslovakia). Slavic languages which are official languages of republics of the USSR include Ukrainian or Little Russian (the speech of natives of the Ukrainian Republic), and Byelorussian or White Russian (the language of natives of the Byelorussian Republic). Slovenian is the official speech of Slovenia, one of Yugoslavia's constituent republics; small numbers of Slovene speakers are also found in Italy and Austria. Macedonian is the official speech of Macedonia, another Yugoslav republic. A small minority in the German Federal Republic speak Lusatian (or Sorbic), the language of the original Slavic inhabitants of that part of the world.

Two members of the Baltic family of Indo-European languages are the official languages of republics of the USSR. These are Latvian and Lithuanian, spoken only in their land of origin.

Greek and Albanian are Indo-European languages not closely related to other families of the group or to each other. Greek speakers are found mainly in Greece, part of Cyprus, and in the Greek colony of the city of Istanbul (Turkey). Albanian speakers are found in Albania, extreme northwestern Greece and in the Yugoslav province of Kosovo. (There are almost as many Albanian speakers in Kosovo as in Albania itself.)

Two European national languages do not belong to the Indo-European family. These are Finnish and Hungarian, both of which belong to the Uralic family of languages.

Most Finnish speakers live in Finland, though a substantial number reside across the border in the Soviet Union. Before World War II a Karelo-Finnish Republic existed to give this linguistic minority the rights of Ukrainians or Byelorussians, but Stalin abolished it because some of its inhabitants showed excessive loyalty to the cause of Finland in World War II.

Hungarian speakers are found mainly in Hungary, though large numbers live in the Romanian province of Transylvania and the Yugoslav province of Vojvodina. A few are also found in Czechoslovakia.

Estonian, the official language of the Estonian republic of the Soviet Union, is a close relative of Finnish and is spoken only in its land of origin. Other Uralic languages are spoken in the European Soviet Union by small numbers of people, including Mordvin, Udmurt, Komi and Mari. Still more languages of this family are spoken in Siberia.

Basque, an independent language with no proven relatives, is spoken in extreme southwest France and northwest Spain.

In the tangled and remote peaks and valleys of the Caucasus Mountains languages of the Caucasian family are spoken. The major of these is Georgian, official language of the Georgian Republic of the USSR. Other important Caucasian languages, all spoken in that mountainous area of the USSR, are Chechen, Ingush, Kabardian, Adygei, Circassian and Avar.

In western Asia, languages belonging to three major families are spoken. In Turkey the national language is Turkish, a major member of the Turkish branch of the Altaic languages. (There are also Turkish speakers in Bulgaria, Greece and the northern part of Cyprus.) Other Turkish/Altaic languages are official languages of Soviet republics, including Azerbaijani, Kirghiz, Kazakh, Uzbek, and Turkmen. Other important Turkish/Altaic tongues of the USSR are Tatar, Chuvash and Bashkir (spoken in parts of European Russia) and Altai, Khakass and Yakut, spoken in Siberia. Another Turkish/Altaic tongue, Uighur, is spoken in remote Sinkiang, in the westernmost part of China.

South of Turkey the major language in western Asia is Arabic, of the Semitic branch of the Afro-Asiatic family. It's the official language of Syria, Iraq, Jordan, Lebanon and the nations of the Arabian peninsula and of nations of north Africa from Egypt to Morocco, including Mauretania and Sudan.

Arabic's relative, Hebrew, is the official language of Israel. Another relative, Maltese, is the official language of the Mediterranean island republic of Malta.

Elsewhere in west Asia Indo-European languages are spoken. The major one is Farsi (or Persian), the official language of Iran. Close relatives of Farsi are the Kurdish spoken in parts of Turkey, Iraq and Iran; the Pushto spoken in parts of Afghanistan, the Baluchi spoken in Iran's far southeast, the Tajik spoken in the Tadzhik Republic of the USSR and the Ossetian which is spoken in north Georgia and adjoining areas.

Armenian, official language of the Soviet Armenian Republic, is an Indo-European language without close major relatives.

On the Indian subcontinent Indo-European languages predominate. In Pakistan Urdu, Sindhi, and Punjabi are major tongues, all of which belong to the Indic branch of this family. Pushto is also spoken near the Afghan frontier, while Baluchi is spoken along the Indian Ocean near the Iranian frontier.

In Bangladesh Bengali, another member of the Indic group, is the major tongue.

In Sri Lanka Sinhalese, yet another member of this group, is the major language.

In the kingdom of Nepal Nepali, still another member of the Indic group, is the official language.

Romany, the tongue of the world's Gypsies, is yet another Indic language.

Nine of India's official thirteen languages are Indo-European of the Indic group, including Hindi, Bengali, Punjabi, Oriya, Marathi, Gujarati, Assamese, Kashmiri and Sanskrit. The other four belong to the Dravidian family — Kannada, Tamil, Telugu and Malayalam.

Minor Dravidian languages include the Brahui spoken in a small part of Pakistan, plus the Gondi, Tulu and Kui of India.

The Munda family of languages is also spoken in India by some 5 million persons. Santali is the major member of this family; others include Mundari, Ho, Savari and Korku.

In southeast Asia are found members of two large families of languages, the Sino-Tibetan and the Malayo-Polynesian. Burmese, Thai, and Lao are all Sino-Tibetan tongues. Malay, Indonesian and Tagalog (the major language of the Philippines) are Malayo-Polynesian. Khmer, the language of Kampuchea, belongs to the Mon-Khmer family. Its relative Mon is spoken along part of the Burmese coast and in a small part of Thailand.

In Indonesia many other Malayo-Polynesian languages are found, including Javanese, Sundanese, Madurese, Batak, and Minangkabau. In the Philippines are spoken still other languages of this family, including Visayan, Ilocano, and Pampangan.

Some linguists believe that Vietnamese is independent, unrelated to other languages; others classify it as Sino-Tibetan.

In terms of numbers of speakers the major language of the Far East is Mandarin, the official language of China and the language with the most speakers on earth. It's the tongue of most northern and western Chinese. In south China Cantonese is spoken. In Fukien Province on China's east coast and across the straits in Taiwan Fukienese is widely used, while in the Shanghai area many speak Wu. South and west of Canton Hakka is used in some areas, while on the island of Hainan is heard Hainanese. All of these belong to the Sino-Tibetan family.

North of China three more major languages are found, none of which are very closely related to each other. Japanese and Korean are independent, unrelated to each other or to other languages (though some linguists claim a relationship exists between Korean and the Altaic tongues, and others say there is a relationship between the rules of grammar of Korean and Japanese).

Mongolian, official tongue of the Mongolian People's Republic, is an Altaic tongue, as are its close relatives Buryat and Kalmyk, spoken mainly in parts of the USSR adjoining Mongolia.

In far eastern Siberia and on the Kamchatka peninsula are found speakers of Paleo-Asiatic languages. The major of these is Chukchi; the other worthy of mention is Koryak.

In Africa huge numbers of languages are spoken. In the Atlas Mountains of the north, near the Mediterranean coast, Berber languages (members of the Afro-Asiatic family) are heard. These include the Shluh, Tamazight and Riffian of Morocco, the Kabyle of Algeria, and the Tamashek of the Tuareg nomads of the southern Sahara Desert.

In Ethiopia several members of the Semitic family of Afro-Asiatic languages are found, including Amharic (the official language of the country), Tigrinya, Tigre and Harari. Languages of the Cushitic branch of the Afro-Asiatic family are also heard in Ethiopia, including Galla, Sidamo, Afar and others.

Somali, another Cushitic language, is the official language of Somalia and is also widely used in Ethiopia.

The African languages used south of the Sahara are divided into several related groups: the Nilo-Saharan, the Niger-Congo, and the Khoisanian.

Nilo-Saharan languages are spoken in Sudan, Kenya, Uganda, Mali, Niger, Zaire, Nigeria and Chad. They include the Hausa and Kanuri of Nigeria, the Songhai of Mali, the Djerma of Niger, the Sara of Chad, the Mangbetu of Zaire, the Nubian of the Sudan, the Luo of Kenya, and many others.

The most widely used African tongues belong to the Niger-Congo family. Of these the Bantu branch is by far the most important. Bantu languages are spoken almost everywhere from a line drawn across the continent from Kenya to Cameroon south to the Republic of South Africa.

The most important Bantu tongue is Swahili, official language of Tanzania. Others are the Kikuyu of Kenya, the Kongo and Lingala of Zaire, the Bemba of Zambia, the Shona of Zimbabwe, the Sotho of Lesotho, the Nyanja of Malawi, and the Zulu and Xhosa of the Republic of South Africa.

The Mande branch of the Niger-Congo family includes the Mande of Sierra Leone, the Kpelle of Liberia, the Bambara of Mali and the Malinke spoken in several countries of West Africa.

The West Atlantic branch includes Fulani, a major language of north

Nigeria and an important tongue of other sub–Saharan lands. It also includes Wolof, a major tongue of Senegal.

Languages of the Voltaic branch are common in West Africa, including the Mossi of Burkina Faso and the Dagombo of Ghana.

The Kwa branch includes two of the most widely spoken languages of Nigeria, Yoruba and Ibo. Also included are the Fon of Benin, the Ewe of Ghana and Togo, and many others.

The Adamawa-Eastern branch includes the Songo of the Central African Republic, among others.

Khoisanian languages are spoken in southernmost Africa and in Tanzania. The most important members of the family are Bushman and Hottentot. Hottentot is heard only in Namibia, while Bushman is used there and in the Republic of South Africa and Botswana. Sandawa and Hatsa are spoken by a few thousand people each in Tanzania.

On the island of Madagascar is spoken Malagasy, a member of the Malayo-Polynesian family.

The Australian languages are those of the aborigines of that continent. Less that 100,000 aborigines remain, who speak several hundred different tongues.

Papuan languages are spoken primarily on the island of New Guinea, but are also heard on New Britain and in the Solomons. There are over 500 of these.

On the Pacific islands east of the Papuan zone, three families of Malayo-Polynesian languages are heard, Melanesian, Micronesian and Polynesian. On each island or group of islands a separate language is spoken. The Chamorro of Guam is one of the more important Micronesian tongues. Fijian is spoken by more persons than any other Melanesian language. The Maori of New Zealand is the Polynesian tongue with the most speakers.

Polynesian languages span the widest area of the Pacific, heard all the way from New Zealand east to Easter Island, only 2,000 miles off the coast of Chile, and northeast to Hawaii.

Two languages belong to the Eskimo-Aleut family: the Eskimo spoken on Greenland and in the far north of Canada, and the Aleut spoken by the few remaining natives of Alaska's Aleutian Islands.

The Amerindian languages of the New World are numerous, but most have very few speakers. Two, however, have become national languages — the Quechua of Peru and the Guarani of Paraguay. Two others, Nahuatl and Maya, have numerous speakers in Mexico.

Dialects. Often the spoken form of a language will differ from the written form, and two or more widely varying forms of the spoken language will exist.

There are differences between the written English of the United States and that of England. These are matters of spelling and punctuation only.

("Center" is American, "centre" is English. "Tire" is American, "tyre" is English. "Neighbor" is American, "neighbour" is English. In quoted material the American language uses double quotes but in English only single quotes are used.) Except for such matters, the written form of English is almost identical everywhere it's used, though no official agency exists to specify what is standard. The spoken language will of course vary from place to place.

According to Albert C. Baugh and Thomas Cable in their work, *The History of the English Language,* eight distinct varieties of English are spoken in the United States. These are:

(1) Eastern New England—in Maine, Rhode Island, New Hampshire and eastern Massachusetts.

(2) New York City—in the Big Apple and its suburbs.

(3) Inland Northern—in Vermont, western Massachusetts, upstate New York and the upper Great Lakes states.

(4) North Midland—in south New Jersey, north Maryland, Delaware, south Pennsylvania, Ohio, Indiana and Illinois.

(5) South Midland—in most of West Virginia, mountainous Virginia and North Carolina, Kentucky, Tennessee, south Missouri, Arkansas and northeast Texas.

(6) Southern—lowland Virginia and North Carolina, South Carolina, Georgia, the Gulf Coast states and east Texas.

(7) General American—almost everywhere west of the Mississippi River, Missouri, Arkansas and east Texas.

(8) Black English—spoken by American blacks wherever they reside.

There's some debate as to whether these varieties are dialects or simple variations of the American dialect. Some consider that the Gulla spoken by the black inhabitants of the islands off the coast of South Carolina, Georgia and Florida is a true dialect; others consider the speech of isolated Ozark mountaineers in Arkansas to be another.

There are regional variations in the English spoken in England, but only in Scotland and northern Ireland are the variations great enough to be called dialects.

Canadian English is very similar to standard American, except for that spoken in Newfoundland and the Maritime Provinces. Australian and New Zealand English differ considerably from the European and North American variants and from each other.

India has developed a variety of English, uniform throughout the country.

In the Republic of South Africa yet another variety of English, influenced by Afrikaans and native African languages, exists. In the former British colonies of eastern and western Africa, amazing varieties of English dialects are found. In large countries such as Nigeria there may be as many English dialects as there are native African tongues.

The English spoken in the West Indies differs enough from the standard variety that some consider it to be a separate language, not merely a dialect.

In the Spanish-speaking world the written language is uniform. Though there are distinct differences between the spoken languages of Madrid, Mexico City and Buenos Aires citizens of the great Hispanic world have little trouble communicating.

The same is true of the Portuguese-speaking world. There's a difference between the tongues of Lisbon and Rio de Janeiro, but the Brazilian and the Portuguese will be able to communicate with no trouble.

In France the Académie Française supervises the evolution of the French language and determines (as much as any official body can) what is standard. The French-speaking world defers to the Académie in matters of the written language, though the spoken language varies from place to place. For instance, the French spoken in Quebec differs significantly from that spoken in France. Generally, however, the spoken language is very similar to the written.

In the German-speaking world dialects are much more common. Standard written German (Hochdeutsch, High German) is essentially the form of the language in which Martin Luther wrote his sixteenth century translation of the Bible. In some parts of the Federal Republic the spoken language approximates the written language; in other parts there are striking differences.

Along the North Sea coast many people speak Plattdeutsch (Low German), in some ways more closely related to Dutch than to High German. To the south in the Alps, Bavarian German is significantly different from High German.

In German Switzerland, High German is the written language. Newscasts on German language television are in High German (spoken with a distinctive Swiss accent). The people use their unique Swiss German dialects (Schwyzerduutsch) in everyday life, however. These are very difficult for Germans to understand and they vary tremendously from place to place throughout German Switzerland.

The speech of Basel, the big city that touches the frontiers of France and Germany, is similar to that of the Badeners across the border in Germany and the Alsatians over the frontier in France. The dialect of Zurich and the rest of eastern Switzerland is farther removed from that of Germany, while the dialects of Bern (particularly those of the Bernese Oberland, the mountain area south of the nation's capital) and of the German-speaking part of Valais sound like another language altogether.

Ordinary German Swiss strongly resist efforts to discourage the use of Schwyzerduutsch; these dialects are part of what makes German Swiss different from Germans and from each other.

In Austria too, dialects are widely used. The speech of Vorarlberg in the west is very similar to that of St. Gallen across the Rhine in Switzerland. That of Salzburg in the center is very similar to that used by the Bavarians, while that of Vienna has been influenced by the Slavic and Hungarian subjects of the old Hapsburg Empire.

T. F. Mitchell states in *Colloquial Arabic* that the dialects of that language used throughout the Arabic-speaking world are as disparate as Spanish, French and Italian. There are rather wide differences between the spoken idioms of Iraq, the Arabian peninsula, Egypt and Morocco.

One of the most widely known of these dialects is the Egyptian, because Egyptian films and sound recordings are so common throughout the Arabic-speaking region. There is, however, no "official" spoken Arabic—no dialect similar to the Hochdeutsch of the German-speaking world. (Written Arabic is uniform, however.)

Though three-fourths of all Chinese speak Mandarin as their native language, several dialects of the language exist. The person from Peking may have to strain a little in order to understand a person from Chengdu.

Since distinct dialects of English hardly exist in the United States, we Americans aren't aware of the communication problems dialects cause until we travel abroad. Then we learn about them the hard way.

The differences in vocabulary between American and British English are not great, but they can cause confusion. For instance, the hood of the American auto is the bonnet in England. The American auto trunk is the English boot. American gasoline is English petrol. The American freeway is the English motorway. The American divided highway is the English dual carriageway. The American elevator is the English lift. The American diaper is the English nappie. The American is fired from his job; the Englishman is sacked.

The uniqueness of Australian English is illustrated by the words of the first verse of the unofficial Australian national anthem, *Waltzing Matilda:*

Once a jolly swagman camped by a billabong
Under the shade of a koolibah tree.
And he sang as he watched and waited till his billy boiled,
"You'll come a waltzing, Matilda, with me."

A swagman is a tramp. A billabong is a country waterhole. The koolibah is an Australian species of tree, while a billy is a tin can the tramp uses to boil the water for his tea. Matilda is the swagman's blanket roll; he and she waltz together when he shoves off on his day's journey to wherever.

The other three verses of this remarkable song disclose many other items of unique Australian vocabulary.

Writing systems. Writing systems are another aspect of culture which can either bind or divide. The most commonly used script on earth is the Latin alphabet (the alphabet used by the Romans as modified by current users), in which English is written. All of the Germanic and Romance languages use this alphabet, as do the majority of the Slavic. Many of earth's non–Indo-European languages are also written in this alphabet, including Maltese, Turkish, Vietnamese, Malay, Indonesian and Tagalog.

Russian is written in the Cyrillic alphabet, as are Bulgarian, Ukrainian, Byelorussian, and some of the non–Slavic languages of the Soviet Union. In Yugoslavia, Serbo-Croatian may be written in either the Latin or Cyrillic script. In Serbia, which is Eastern Orthodox, the Cyrillic is used. In Croatia, which is Roman Catholic by religion, the Latin script is used.

Greek uses the Greek alphabet, a modernized version of the script used in the golden era of Greek history.

The Arabic alphabet is used in much of the Islamic world. The written Arabic language is uniform wherever used, varying to a greater or lesser degree from the dialects spoken by its users. Major languages other than Arabic which use this script include Farsi and Urdu.

The Hebrew alphabet is used to write Hebrew and Yiddish.

A unique feature of both the Arabic and Hebrew alphabets is that they seldom express vowel sounds. If English was written as Arabic is, "cow" would be written "cw," "black" would be "blck," and "president" would be "prsdnt." The word "caw" would also be written "cw," while "blck" could be "black" or "block." How would the reader know whether "cw" is "cow" or "caw"? Or whether "cp" is "cap," "cop" or "cup"?

The context of the sentence would provide the answer to the riddle. It requires much study for the Westerner to master the art of reading these two scripts, but many have done it.

An amazing variety of scripts is used to write other Asian languages. Armenian uses its own unique script, as does Georgian; the two don't resemble each other at all.

In India several of the national languages are written in Devanagari script. However, Punjabi is written in the Gurmukhi script. Each of the four Dravidian languages has its own unique writing system, as does Gujarati, Oriya, and Bengali.

In southeast Asia, Burmese, Thai, Lao and Khmer each use a unique script, while Malay, Indonesian, Vietnamese and Tagalog use the Latin alphabet.

The world's most unique writing system is found in the Far East: Chinese. This is the world's only ideographic writing system, in which each symbol represents an idea rather than a sound. In contrast to the rest of the world's writing systems, which contain less than fifty symbols, the Chinese system consists of tens of thousands. It's said that one who knows 1,200 of these symbols can read 90 percent of any writing. To be able to understand 95 percent, one must know 5,000 symbols.

This system is used to write all of the major languages of China, and is also the major component of written Japanese. An advantage of the system is this: though people from Peking would have trouble communicating orally in Canton because Mandarin and Cantonese are very dissimilar languages, they could communicate in writing and be instantly understood.

The Communist government of China has devised a system of writing Mandarin in the Latin alphabet—the Pinyin. In that system the name of the founder of the Communist Chinese state is written Mao Zedong. Pinyin isn't intended to supplant the characters, but it makes the language easier to learn. In Taiwan and other Chinese-speaking areas where Communism doesn't rule, Pinyin isn't used. Here the written language is as it has always been.

Chinese writing consists of pure "characters." The Japanese use a combination of Chinese characters (Kanji in Japanese) and the unique Japanese writing systems in which a symbol represents a sound. Japanese uses two syllabaries—the Katakana and the Hiragana—both of which are called Kana for short. Katakana is used in signs and much printed material; Hiragana is used in newspapers and in handwriting. It's possible to write Japanese in Kana alone, but the language gains precision with the use of the Kanji. It's impossible to write the language in Kanji alone because, unlike Chinese, Japanese uses word endings to express plurals, tense of verbs and the like; only the Kana can express these.

The Hangul script of Korea is also unique. It's an alphabet of vowels and consonants combined according to rigid rules to express syllables. Each syllable takes a form which resembles a Chinese character. The reader, knowing which letters are combined in the syllable, has no difficulty in understanding the writing. In North Korea the written language consists of pure Hangul, but in South Korea Hangul is sometimes combined with Chinese characters. Since many Korean words were borrowed from Chinese, the use of the characters is logical and understandable.

In the past any culture under Chinese influence would most likely write its language in Chinese characters. Vietnamese was formerly written in this way, as was Korean. The Vietnamese have completely abandoned the characters for the Latin alphabet; as mentioned above the Koreans are in the process of replacing the characters with Hangul. The Japanese on the other hand show no sign of giving up their unique combination of the native syllabary with Chinese characters.

Numbers were originally written with letters of the alphabet; thus Aleph, the first letter of the Hebrew alphabet, was also used as the symbol for one; Beth, the second letter, served as the symbol for two and so on. The ancient Greeks used the same principle in writing numbers.

The Romans replaced this method of writing numbers with the simpler yet more complex Roman numerals (I being one, II two, V five, X ten, and so forth). One could not very easily confuse numbers with text using that system, but it was hardly adaptable to solving arithmetic problems.

The system we use for writing numbers is a product of the Indian and Middle Eastern cultures. The Hebrew and Roman systems contained no zero; that concept is an Indian invention. The ten symbols used for writing our digits were devised by the Arabs, hence their generic name (Arabic numerals).

Virtually all of the world's writing systems now use Arabic numerals to express number; no superior system exists.

On learning languages. English speakers aren't among the world's great linguists. Our attitude toward non–English speakers seems to be, "If you want to talk to me, speak English — otherwise I'm not interested."

French speakers and Spanish speakers are likely to share our attitude. They may well have studied English in school, but they may not let the English speaker know that.

In the canton of Zurich, Switzerland, secondary school pupils (seventh, eighth and ninth graders) must study two foreign languages before completing the ninth grade. Most Zurchers speak the Zurich dialect of Schwyzerduutsch at home; this is the first language the children learn. Later they learn Hochdeutsch — High German — from watching television and still later in primary school as they begin to read. (In 1988 the voters of the canton of Zurich authorized the teaching of French beginning in the fifth grade rather than in the seventh, a practice already followed in some other German Swiss cantons.)

All secondary school pupils must take three years of French. For the second language they have the option of two years of either Italian or English.

In the Netherlands three foreign languages are required in some secondary schools. The native tongue is of course Dutch. In addition, the pupils study French, German and English.

Here the national television network screens foreign movies in the original language (which can be English, German or French), with Dutch subtitles. This is excellent supplemental education in these foreign languages.

The Swedish state radio broadcasts news in three languages — Swedish, German and English.

In Japan some public school pupils are required to take six years of English.

The effort foreign educational systems make to teach their pupils foreign languages makes American endeavor in this area pale by comparison. Of course one can say, "Ah, but Europe is different; speakers of so many languages are packed so closely together there."

This is true, but it doesn't explain Japanese educational policy. Japan is linguistically homogeneous, and since it's an island nation it has no land frontiers. Japanese could well say, "If you want to talk to me, speak Japanese — otherwise I'm not interested."

If they had had such an attitude, they'd have been unable to successfully invade so many of the world's markets. Part of their success has been caused by their desire to communicate with others and to learn from others.

In the Soviet Union too, many educated persons learn English. Senator Paul Simon of Illinois states, in his work *The Tongue-Tied American,* that there are more teachers of English in the USSR than there are students of Russian in the United States.

In a sense English is one of the world's simpler languages, containing more one-syllable words than do most other languages. The meaning of an English word in a sentence depends to a large extent upon where in the sentence it appears—you know which noun an adjective modifies because it's next door, or whether a noun is a subject or direct object because it comes before or after the verb. It's not a highly inflected language—there aren't elaborate conjugations of verbs to show person and tense, nor declensions of nouns to show case, nor declensions of adjectives to show case and gender.

Yet it can be very difficult because of its sometimes illogical spelling. What person unfamiliar with English pronunciation would know that you pronounce "phone" as if it were "fone," "rough" as if it were "ruff," "through" as if it were "thru," "thorough" as if it were "thoro," "cat" as if it were "kat," and "city" as if it were "sitty"?

Most older Americans with university educations made the acquaintance of inflected languages by studying Latin in high school. We learned about the conjugation of verbs with "amare"—to love—of which the present active indicative is conjugated so:

Amo   I love
Amas   You love
Amat   He loves
Amamus   We love
Amatis   You love
Amant   They love

Then we wrestled with the other five tenses (imperfect, future, perfect, past perfect and future perfect), the two voices (active and passive) and the two moods (indicative and subjunctive), along with other assorted forms.

We learned about declension of nouns through their five cases (nominative, genitive, dative, accusative, ablative), like "puella"—girl:

Puella   The girl
Puellae   Of the girl
Puellae   To the girl
Puellam   The girl (direct object)
Puella   From the girl
Puellae   The girls
Puellarum   Of the girls
Puellis   To the girls
Puellas   The girls (direct object)
Puellis   From the girls

We had to learn the gender of nouns (masculine, feminine, neuter) and the form of adjective to go with each gender, as with *"bonus"*—good:

Bonus—masculine
Bona—feminine
Bonum—neuter

There was also the complication of declining the adjective through the five cases. We then thanked our lucky stars that English has few of these complexities! However, English is one of the few in the world of which this is true.

German is now the most highly inflected Western European language. Its verbs must be conjugated and its nouns declined and their genders memorized. The best approach is to memorize the appropriate definite article along with the noun, as:

Der Stein—the stone (masculine).

Die Tulpe—the tulip (feminine).

Das Gold—the gold (neuter).

When you learn German adjectives you must learn the forms which go with nouns of the three genders. For an English speaker it's a ticklish, complex business, especially for one who has never before studied an inflected language.

Yet in a sense German is simpler than English. Once you learn how German vowels and consonants are pronounced, you have no doubt as to how a German word is pronounced. You need not play the guessing games the student of English must sometimes engage in, because all vowels and consonants are always pronounced the same way.

English speakers find Romance languages easier to learn than German. Though verb conjugations can be complex and aggravating, and though one must learn the gender of all nouns (though Romance nouns have no neuter gender—they're all either masculine or feminine), there are no declensions; a noun doesn't change its form when it changes its function in the sentence.

As with German, pronunciation is absolutely logical. English speakers have problems with some of the nasal tones of French, but otherwise pronunciation difficulties are minimal.

Few Americans bother to learn Slavic languages. The only one of worldwide importance is Russian, and in a way Russian is the most difficult of them to learn. The thought of mastering the Cyrillic alphabet is enough to scare off many a would-be scholar, and when you add to that happy thought the knowledge that Russian is so highly inflected as to make German relatively simple by comparison you have enough to discourage all but the most dedicated. (Nouns have more cases than in Latin, verb conjugations are more complex than in Latin, adjectives have more forms than in Latin.)

If you would understand Islam and Islamic culture, you must learn Arabic. For most English speakers the prospect is forbidding. Not only is the Arabic alphabet very different from ours—it looks at first glance like a child's scribbling—but the very structure of the language seems alien. In Indo-European languages the end of a word may change with tense or case or gender, but never the rest of the word (with the exception of those aggravating irregular verbs, adjectives and nouns you encounter in all languages!). In Arabic many more words seem irregular; it isn't the ending that changes with number or tense, it's the vowels in the middle of the words. The word seems to transform itself into something utterly different as it changes number or whatever.

Thus, "kursi" is chair, "karaasi" is chairs.

"Bint" is daughter, "banaat" is daughters.

"Kitaab" is book, "kutub" is books.

The changes in verb forms during conjugation are also unusual.

Yiktib	He writes
Tiktib	She writes
Tiktib	You (masculine) write
Tiktibi	You (feminine) write
Aktib	I write
Yiktibu	They write
Tiktibu	You (plural) write
Niktib	We write

Most Americans are so terrified by the sight of Chinese characters that they believe that language is the most difficult on earth. To be sure, the task of memorization one must undertake to be able to read Chinese is formidable. But the task of learning the spoken language is much simpler.

Chinese is not inflected. The position of a character in a sentence determines its meaning in the sentence; word order is everything. The sounds of the characters are transliterated into the Latin alphabet for the student of the spoken language. Once the student masters the sentence patterns of the spoken language the speaking and understanding come relatively easily.

The major difficulty with spoken Chinese is the system of tones. There are four of these in Mandarin, more in Fukienese and Cantonese. They are most difficult to explain in writing. The first is a steady high pitch. The second is rising, as if one were asking a question. The third is a very low pitch. The fourth is a falling, as we speak when stating facts. Because of the tones one may construct a sentence from repetitions of the same syllable. The phrase "Ma ma ma ma ma" sounds like a child's babbling in English, but if the syllables are spoken in the proper tones it means "Is Mama cursing the horse?" in Mandarin. (It's one of the coincidences of linguistics that "ma ma" in the proper tones means "mother" in Mandarin, just as it does in English. If the last syllable in a sentence is "ma," this signifies that the sentence is a question.)

Many syllables other than "ma" have widely varying meanings as their tones change. "Mai" in the third, low tone means "buy." "Mai" in the fourth, falling tone, means "sell." A combination of the two, "buy-sell," means "business." "Mai" in the second, rising tone means "to bury."

"Shui" in the third, low tone is "water." "Shui" in the fourth, falling tone is "sleep."

"Yao" in the first, high tone is one way of saying "one." "Yao" in the second, rising tone means to rock (a cradle, a boat, or whatever). "Yao" in the third tone means to bite. "Yao" in the fourth tone means "to want."

Mandarin has a clever way of combining syllables of opposite meanings to express concepts. I've already mentioned "mai-mai," buy-sell, meaning business. "Ta" in the fourth tone is "large." "Hsiao" in the third tone is "small." Combine these into "tahsiao," big-small, and you get "size." "Fuch'in" is the formal term for "Father." "Much'in" is the same for "Mother." "Fumu" means "Parents."

The task of learning Japanese is much more difficult than that of learning Chinese. The only thing simpler about spoken Japanese is that the language doesn't use tones. However, one must master a grammar of considerable complexity, and also the combination of "kanji" and "kana" that is the written language. In addition one must concern oneself with honorifics — one vocabulary is used to address social inferiors while another is used in conversation with social superiors.

You and thou. The English language is one of the world's most informal. There's but one word for "you" in modern English; to whomever you speak, you say "you."

William Shakespeare's English knew another second-person pronoun — the Biblical "thou." Our ancestors of 500 years ago addressed family members and children as "thou" and reserved the more formal "you" for strangers and social superiors.

In most other Indo-European languages there are still two words for "you"; the equivalent of "thou" used when speaking to family and friends and the equivalent of "you" used otherwise.

Thus in French you use "tu" in speaking to your brother, but you call your boss "vous." "Tu" is the "thou" in all of the Romance languages; the "you" is "usted" in Spanish, "lei" in Italian, and "o senhor" or "o senhora" in Portuguese, depending on the sex of the person addressed.

In German your spouse, parent, sibling or dog is "du," but your teacher, boss, mailman or the stranger on the street is "sie."

In Russian friends and relatives are "ti," strangers are "vi." Polish is more like Portuguese; friends and relatives are "ty" while strangers are "pan" or "pana," depending on the sex of the person addressed.

The adult stranger is always addressed formally in most Indo-European languages; it's presumptuous not to do otherwise.

Mandarin, like English, knows but one form of second-person pronoun. Everyone is addressed as "ni."

Japanese, on the other hand, has devised an elaborate vocabulary of honorifics for use in addressing others. Which words you use depends upon the other person's status and his or her relationship to you.

More about gender. English speakers may not be aware that English nouns have gender, but they do. The names of male living creatures are masculine, those of female living creatures are feminine, and those of non-living things are neuter (with the exception of ships and a few other inanimate objects, which are feminine). Gender shows in the use of third person personal pronouns—"he" of course being masculine, "she" feminine, and "it" neuter.

Since Romance languages have but two genders, nouns are either masculine or feminine and third-person pronouns are just two in number. This causes the Spanish speaker who's just begun learning English to say, "The car, he ran out of gas," and "The house, she burn down." "El automovil" is Spanish for the auto—masculine. "La casa" is the house—feminine.

As mentioned earlier, German has three genders, but the use of German third-person personal pronouns is odd to the English speaker. If I ask a German-speaking person where the table is, he'll answer, "Er ist dort." "He's over there." Table—"der Tisch"—is masculine in German. If I point to a tulip to state that it blooms, I'd say, "It's blooming," since tulip is neuter in English. The German speaker would say, "Sie blueht" (she blooms), since "die Tulpe" is feminine in German. If I'd say, "The young lady is beautiful," the German speaker may well answer, "Ja, es ist schoen." "Yes, it's beautiful." Young lady—"das Fraulein"—is neuter in German.

If I tell you that my dog, Duchess, is asleep, using the pronoun rather than the noun, I'd say, "She sleeps" (Duchess is obviously female). The German speaker would say, "Er schlaft" (he sleeps), unless he knows that Duchess is female. Dog—"der Hund"—is masculine in German. However, German also has a word for female canines—"die Hundin." If he thinks of Duchess as "die Hundin" rather than "der Hund," he'd say "Sie schlaft."

Chinese nouns have no gender—the third-person personal pronoun is always "t'a," whatever noun it substitutes for.

Numbers. One would think that number would be expressed the same in all languages. It is in the sense that numbers are almost always written in Arabic numerals, but the expression of number in words varies amazingly throughout the world. It isn't always expressed the same even in English.

In the United States, the figure 1,000,000,000 is expressed, "one billion." In Great Britain, this figure is "one milliard." If you say, "one billion" in Great Britain, you mean 1,000,000,000,000. In the United States this figure is "one trillion."

In English, one counts "nineteen, twenty, twenty-one, twenty-two." In German, the equivalent count is, "neunzehn, zwanzig, ein und zwanzig, zwei und zwanzig." (That is, nineteen, twenty, one and twenty, two and twenty). The number 38 is expressed in German "acht und dreissig" (eight and thirty). The number 21,153 is "ein und zwanzig tausend ein hundert drei und funfzig" (one and twenty thousand one hundred three and fifty).

In English, one counts "fifty, sixty, seventy, eighty, ninety." In French, the equivalent is "cinquante, soixante, soixante-dix, quatre-vingt, quatre-vingt-dix." The literal translation into English is, "fifty, sixty, sixty-ten, four twenties, four twenties ten." The number 75 in French is "soixante-quinze" (literally, sixty-fifteen). The number 99 in French is "quatre-vingt dix-neuf."

The number 83,492 is "quatre-vingt trois mil quatre cent quatre-vingt douze" (literally, four twenties three thousand, four hundred, four twenties twelve).

In Mandarin Chinese, "I" is one, "shih" is ten, "pai" is hundred, "ch'ien" is thousand, and "wan" is ten thousand. Thus, "I wan" is ten thousand. "I ch'ien wan" is a thousand ten thousands, or ten million. The number 32,457 would be expressed in Chinese, "San wan liang ch'ien ssu pai wu shih ch'i," or "three ten-thousand two thousand four hundred five tens seven."

In Hindi, the expression "lakh" means one hundred thousand. Thus, when an Indian speaks of "seventeen lakhs of rupees" he means one million seven hundred thousand Indian rupees (rupees being the monetary unit of India). In numerals the figure would be written 1,700,000.

Negotiating with foreigners. In a sense we Americans are fortunate that English is so widely spoken. It's an essential part of education in Japan, the Soviet Union, and much of Asia and Africa. It's a national language in nations like India and Nigeria because there are so many native languages that people from different parts of the country can't communicate in their own tongues. Most of the world's educated people, no matter where they obtained their education, have some familiarity with our language. Because of this much of the world has some understanding of us.

However, few foreigners have such a comprehensive command of English that they care to negotiate with Americans in our language. In conversations that really matter, they use their own language, speaking to us through an interpreter. In such negotiations, Americans are usually at a linguistic disadvantage.

Really competent interpreters must be truly bilingual; they should be equally at home in both languages of the negotiators. They should understand the idioms, colloquialisms and slang of both languages. They should be able to think in both languages. Few native Americans are bilingual by this definition; thus few of us are qualified to act as interpreters.

Thus, in most bilingual negotiations involving Americans in which interpreters are used the interpreter is either a native of the other party's country or a native of some third country.

Consider the typical American-Russian negotiation. The American has very little or no knowledge of Russian. The Russian has some knowledge of English, but not enough to negotiate in it. An interpreter is therefore necessary.

Almost certainly there will be no American about who is fluent in both English and Russian; the interpreter will almost inevitably be a Russian. In this situation the American is completely at the mercy of the Russian interpreter. He has no way of knowing whether the interpreter's translation of his remarks is accurate. Even if he has some knowledge of Russian he probably won't be familiar with its idioms and slang.

Since the Russian party to the negotiation has some knowledge of English the American is at a further disadvantage. When he responds to the translated remark of the Russian in English, the Russian will understand the gist of the reply. While the translator is translating, he'll have time to consider what his answer should be.

When the Russian responds in Russian the American will have little or no idea of what he says until the interpreter translates for him. Then our American will be expected to reply immediately, without taking time for reflection. The Russian may think before he talks without appearing rude or stupid; the American cannot do likewise.

Is it any wonder that we have problems in negotiating with foreigners? As a nation we'll always be at a disadvantage in our dealings with non–English speakers until we shed our unwillingness to learn other languages. If we persist in our attitude of, "Let them speak to me in English, otherwise I'm not interested," we'll never learn to understand other peoples. In the developing one world market of our planet, can we afford our linguistic complacency?

Chapter 5
Religions — Christianity

Christianity in General

Christianity claims more followers, one and one-half billion, than any other of Earth's religions. Though it is one of the cornerstones of Western civilization, it did not begin its existence as a Western religion. Some of its branches remain non–Western, and many of its believers are non–Western.

It was originally a religion of the Middle East, beginning on the soil of what is now Israel. Jesus himself was born to Jewish parents, and his original disciples were Jews. The Old Testament of the Christian Bible is as much Jewish holy scripture as it is Christian. The faith of Jesus might have been an obscure offshoot of Judaism had not the Apostle Paul decided to preach it to the Gentiles (non–Jews) of the Roman Empire and to eliminate some Jewish practices (such as male circumcision) to make it more attractive to them. Almost from the first Christianity attracted Gentile converts in large numbers.

For three centuries it existed as an opposition faith within the Roman Empire, sometimes persecuted by the Imperial government. As it grew doctrinal differences threatened to shatter it into an infinity of fragments. Ebionites and other Jewish Christians observed Jewish holy days and lived by Jewish dietary and other laws. Marcionites claimed that only a portion of our present New Testament was true Christian scripture; the Old Testament, being Jewish scripture, was irrelevant to true believers. Docetists insisted that Jesus had only appeared to die on the cross, because the Son of God could never in reality suffer such a hideous fate. Gnostics claimed that the secrets of the true knowledge of God may be discovered only by a small chosen elite of true believers and must be kept concealed from all others. Donatists believed that baptized mortal sinners cannot be forgiven and received back into the Church. Slowly a mainstream faith emerged that refused to accept these and other notions. Slowly a Christian orthodoxy took form that rejected Marcionism, Docetism, Gnosticism, Donatism and Christian Judaism.

Early in the fourth century the nature of the faith changed forever when the Emperor Constantine declared Christianity to be the official religion of the Roman Empire. At one bound the Church leaped from opposing the state to close association with it. Now the state, in the person of the Emperor, sought to force doctrinal unity upon the Church. At the Council of Nicaea the process of working out this unity began, although it ultimately caused the first official division of the faith.

In the latter half of the fourth century Christendom threatened to split asunder once again over the question of the nature of Jesus Christ. Was the Savior totally human, totally divine, or a combination of human and divine?

The Arians took the position that he was essentially human. Councils of the Church declared this notion to be heresy. Nevertheless, for several centuries Arian doctrines were followed by many believers in northern Europe — but without strong political backing this heresy had limited staying power. By the eighth century it had vanished.

The Monophysites held that Jesus was essentially divine, only appearing to be human. This doctrine was widely accepted in the Middle East of the fourth century, though various Church councils of the period declared it too to be heresy. It acquired sufficient support in Ethiopia and Egypt to survive there despite persecution at the hands of the Imperial government and the orthodox Christian church. Monophysites denied that councils of the orthodox Church had any authority over them; they established their own organizations and went their own way during the fifth century. Thus occurred the first permanent division of the Christian Church.

The orthodox view of the nature of Christ as hammered out in these early councils has continued to be church doctrine in both East and West to the present day. It is that the Savior is both human and divine and that God possesses three persons — Father, Son, and Holy Spirit.

Eastern and Western Christianity began to grow apart after the fall of the Western Roman Empire. Political control by governments over the Church in Western Europe weakened. Though the Emperors of the Eastern Roman Empire (better known as the Byzantine Empire) asserted a theoretical political power in the lands of Western Europe they lacked the military resources to make the claim stick. Greek became the language of the Eastern church, Latin that of the West. The Bishop of Rome claimed more and more authority in the West, but East denied that Rome was superior to any other church bishopric. Other aggravating differences arose; the split was finalized when East and West excommunicated each other in 1054. Thus occurred the second great split in Christendom.

East Europe was, and still is, divided by the historic boundary between the Western and Eastern Christian churches. The Poles, Czechs, Slovaks, Hungarians, Slovenians and Croatians were converted to Christianity by Roman Catholic missionaries from Rome; from the beginning Latin was the language of their churches: They began to write their native languages in the Latin alphabet and looked to Rome for religious and cultural inspiration. The Russians, Romanians, Bulgarians and Serbs were converted by Eastern missionaries from Constantinople. Old Church Slavonic, written in the Cyrillic alphabet, becamed the language of their churches; they began writing their native languages in the Cyrillic alphabet and looked to Constantinople for religious and cultural inspiration. This in part explains the traditional enmity of Russian and Pole, and the mutual dislike of the Serbs and Croats of Yugoslavia.

During the Middle Ages the Church of Rome imposed religious unity upon the area of Western civilization. Various dissident groups were disillusioned by the power-seeking and materialism of the Church hierarchy and tried to establish competing churches more faithful to the original teachings of Jesus Christ as they understood them. Waldensians preached the virtues of poverty. Albigensians denied the authority of the Pope and sought to revive some of the doctrines of the Gnostics. Hussites sought to establish a popular church for Czechs outside the authority of Rome. Brethren of the Free Spirit claimed that since people were created by God in his own image they are in part God and thus cannot sin; therefore people may do as they please.

Waldensians and Albigensians were virtually exterminated during the thirteenth century. The church authority sought to do the same to the Hussites; though it was able to burn John Hus, founder of the movement, at the stake in 1415 it was unable to suppress his church because these heretics developed remarkable military power. Hussite troops defeated several armies of German crusaders and the Hussite church survived in Bohemia until the 1620s when it became a victim of the early Catholic victories of the Thirty Years War. The Brethren of the Free Spirit never became numerous enough to threaten the established Church.

The invention of printing with movable type in 1476 for the first time allowed large numbers of Bibles to circulate among the people. This plus continuing Church materialism and political weakness laid the groundwork for the last and greatest split in Christendom — the Protestant Reformation.

Martin Luther's successful defiance of Papal authority opened the door to the splintering of Western Christendom. Luther led German-speaking Europe and Scandinavia out of the fold of Roman Catholicism. The powerful doctrines of John Calvin attracted Dutchmen, Frenchmen and English. The desire of England's Henry VIII to divorce his Spanish Queen, Catherine of Aragon, without Papal approval caused the birth of Anglican Christianity.

Once the unity of the medieval church was broken, more divisions of the faith appeared. John Knox created the Presbyterian Church of Scotland. Huldreich Zwingli established German Swiss Protestantism. Calvinism became the prevailing faith in the Netherlands during and after the Eighty Years War with Spain.

Because European rulers insisted upon religious unity within their domains, those Protestant denominations lacking strong political support had nowhere to call home. English Calvinists sailed to the New World and established their own home bases in the colonies of Massachusetts, Connecticut and Rhode Island. Other new denominations (such as Quakers, Amish, and Mennonites) rejected state and military service, incurring the hostility of most governments. Pennsylvania became a refuge for such people. John Wesley's eloquent presentation of his objections to the High-Church Anglicanism of eighteenth-century England created Methodism.

By the time of the American Revolution large numbers of dissenting Protestants thrived in the thirteen colonies; thus there was little opposition to the adoption of the First Amendment to the United States Constitution and its guarantee of religious freedom. In the benign intellectual climate of America Protestant denominations multiplied. Nowhere else do so many unique variants of Protestant Christianity flourish. So many are they, and so much success have they achieved, that Walter Martin entitled his book about them *The Kingdom of the Cults.*

The Mormon Church is the majority denomination in the state of Utah. This native American denomination believes that the most important scripture is the Book of Mormon, found in the form of a book of gold-leaf pages on an upstate New York hilltop by Joseph Smith during the 1820s. Mormonism holds that Jewish refugees from the Holy Land settled in America before the time of Christ, establishing a high culture here, and that Jesus Himself visited them here; the culture fell before the European discovery of America. Its traditional belief in the legitimacy of polygamy has involved its members in difficulty with the secular law on numerous occasions.

Jehovah's Witnesses owe no loyalty to any government. According to Walter Martin they hold that Jesus Christ returned to the earth in spirit in 1914 to prepare mankind for the end of the present age. Thus the Second Coming has already occurred; the Witnesses now await the Battle of Armageddon in which all present-day governments and cultures will perish. Eventually King Jesus will reign in the heavenly sphere with the assistance of 144,000 witnesses — all of whom will be members of this denomination.

Christian Science was founded by Mary Baker Eddy during the late nineteenth century. This belief holds that humans are spiritual beings and that the physical world is an illusion of the mind. Thus all of our experiences in this world are illusions, including our bouts with physical illness. It is thus possible to cure illness without the assistance of health science; one must merely convince the patient that the affliction isn't real.

Unitarian Universalists believe as do Jews and Muslims that God is one and indivisible. They also believe that humanity is inherently good, and that all people will achieve salvation.

Seventh-Day Adventists worship on Saturday. Many of them are vegetarians, adhering to strict dietary and moral codes. They claim that Sunday-worshipers bear the Mark of the Beast; thus relationships between Adventists and mainstream Christians are strained.

The Worldwide Church of God too teaches that the true Sabbath day is Saturday and celebrates the Jewish festivals of Passover, Hannukah and the like rather than the mainstream Christian Christmas and Easter (which they claim are elements of paganism introduced into the faith by political-minded heretics). Old and New Testaments are equally important parts of their Holy Scripture.

The Quakers, Mennonites and Amish still flourish in parts of the United States. The Amish particularly seek to preserve a way of life isolated from modern temptations—some still reject electricity, internal combustion engines and buttons on their clothing, using horse-drawn buggies for travel and oil lamps for light.

Some of the ancient heresies have returned to life. Some opponents of organized churches preach a new Gnosticism, that all believers must establish their own relationship with God in their own way. Once again one hears that people are part God and therefore cannot sin; thus we have carte-blanche to do as we please.

The varieties of Christianity are legion. Though some Christian idealists speak of reuniting the splintered Church, the odds favoring this are minimal. There has been diversity of doctrine within the faith from virtually the beginning. The various gulfs between the systems of belief seem too wide to bridge.

Protestant Christianity

There are over 400 million Protestants in today's world, comprising a bit less than one-third of all Christian believers. A wide variety of beliefs find shelter under the Protestant umbrella, both with respect to the authority of the Bible and to church organization.

Fundamentalists believe in essence that the Bible is the unadulterated Word of God and must be interpreted exactly as written. Thus, the world and all therein was created by God in six days, exactly as described in Genesis. Non-fundamentalists contend that some parts of scripture are not to be taken literally but must be interpreted allegorically.

Some denominations possess hierarchical organization similar to that of Roman Catholicism with appointed or elected bishops exercising authority over individual churches. Others have no bishops but possess regional or denomination-wide assemblies to enforce doctrinal uniformity. Still others give individual parish churches almost complete autonomy.

The major religious influence upon American culture has been that of Protestant Christianity. The historical American distaste for established churches caused many varieties of Protestantism to flourish here, giving rise to broad tolerance. The "life is real, life is earnest" Protestant ethic is a major part of our culture still, along with counterpart notions of the virtues of punctuality, hard work and the like. A hallmark of American Protestant culture is that humanity must never accept what is today as the ultimate good. However good it is now, tomorrow we can make it much better. We do wrong if we don't strive to make it better.

American Protestantism vests immense trust in the ability of the individual to build his or her own relationship to God, environment, government and fellow humans. In return this requires a high degree of social discipline. Moderately deviant ideas are tolerated; the radically deviant we have often greeted with hostility (though not so vehemently since the 1960s).

Though originally somewhat hostile to non–Protestants (the Native American party of the 1850s would virtually have forbidden the immigration of non–Protestants into the country; Alfred E. Smith, the Roman Catholic Democratic presidential nominee of 1928, was buried under an immense landslide in part because of his faith; Jews were subjected to social discrimination until the middle of the twentieth century) the culture has become more accepting. There are now more Roman Catholics in the United Statess than there are members of any single Protestant denomination.

Religious modernism has caused many mainstream Protestant denominations to abandon nineteenth-century fundamentalism and embrace the "Social Gospel" — organized religion as social and economic reformer. The old Augustinian notions of the faith of a century ago have given way to Pelagianism within these groups yet among the fundamentalist denominations Augustinian notions are still strong.

The parallel growth of secularism in America has eroded the old Protestant virtues. Our country today is a rather amazing amalgam of secular hedonism among some and sincere religious faith among others.

Those who oppose the expression of religion in life outside the Church have probably gained more political power here than anywhere else in the Protestant world. Nowhere else in the First World is religion more effectively banned from public schools and to a large degree from public life.

Yet, nowhere else in the First World is religion taken so seriously by so many; nowhere else has political activity by the faithful (Jerry Falwell's Moral Majority, Pat Robertson's presidential candidacy) drawn such enthusiastic support or stirred such intense opposition.

Germanic Europe too is mainly Protestant in faith. There established churches are the rule — Anglican in Great Britain, Lutheran in Scandinavia, Evangelical in the Protestant states of Germany. American style Protestant fundamentalism is rare, and formal religion seems to play a smaller role in people's lives. Few Protestant Europeans belong to non-official denominations, though those who take their Protestantism most seriously are likely to be "dissenters," as the English call Protestants other than Anglicans.

Though most public holidays in these lands are religious holidays (for instance, Pentecost is a major holiday in Germany and Switzerland) and most businesses close on Sunday and religious instruction is offered in the public schools of some nations, the social influence of the church is less than among us. John Ross Schroeder calls this part of the world "The north German plain of irreligion" (in his article entitled "Secular Europe" in the May-June 1988 edition of *Plain Truth* magazine, page 21) because so many north Europeans are professed non-believers and church attendance is so low.

Some of these nations have large Roman Catholic populations — there are states in the German Federal Republic and cantons in Switzerland with Roman Catholic majorities. Peaceful co-existence between Protestant and Catholic is the rule, though the wounds of the Reformation and of the wars of religion still fester slightly and the members of the two communities still eye each other with some suspicion and distrust. Protestant parents may still get upset when their children date Roman Catholics, and vice versa.

The "life is real, life is earnest" ethic is still strong in Switzerland and Germany; it is less so in Great Britain, the Netherlands and Scandinavia.

Roman Catholic Christianity

When one thinks of Roman Catholicism one might well think of the great square in front of St. Peter's in the Vatican crowded with tens of thousands as the Pope delivers a blessing. Or one thinks of majestic Notre Dame in Paris, or of the overwhelming majesty of Chartres Cathedral.

There are almost one billion Roman Catholic believers in the world; over 60 percent of all Christians are Roman Catholic. Latin Europeans are overwhelmingly Catholic. In this part of the world a more relaxed view of life prevails. People aren't so obsessed with economic concerns. Punctuality's not quite so important. Life moves at a slower pace. Italians talk about "la dolce vita" (the sweet life) and "dolce far niente" (sweet doing nothing). Roman Catholicism accepts the imperfection of humanity as given, and doesn't buy the notion that all change is good.

Sinful people may not have the capacity to define their relationships to what is by themselves. Some of us know more about these matters than others; one should follow the lead of authority. There's more receptiveness to the notion that we should do as the experts tell us.

On the other hand Latin Europe gives people more free rein to express their essential being. Free expression of emotion is tolerated to a degree some northerners find repugnant; people are more likely to wear their feelings on their sleeves. Personal individualism flowers brightly.

Sometimes this radicalism that exists in personal lives spills over into public affairs. Political parties of the extreme right and left obtain more votes in Latin democracies than in Germanic ones. Acts of political terrorism are more common.

Protestants are rare in Latin Europe. People who take their religion seriously are almost all Roman Catholics, but anticlericalism — opposition to the Church in public life — is a powerful force.

Yet on the other hand family feelings are stronger and divorce rates are lower. To many northerners, human warmth seems to blossom sweetly in the warm Mediterranean sun.

In considering the cultural influences of Roman Catholic Christianity, however, we must not stop here. The Roman Church has been the Christian church of authority par excellence. The Pope was the temporal ruler of Rome and adjoining territory until 1871. He still rules Vatican City, the smallest independent state on earth, as a theoretically absolute monarch.

From the time of the Reformation until the 1950s the Roman Church was dominated by conservative Italian prelates. Reformed itself by the zeal of the leaders of the sixteenth-century Counter-Reformation, it thereafter fought a stubborn delaying action against the intellectual, social and economic fermentation caused by the Enlightenment, the French Revolution, the Industrial Revolution and Marxism.

In 1864 Pope Pius IX issued his Syllabus of Errors, which condemned the separation of church and state and other social reforms of the mid-nineteenth century. In 1870 the First Vatican Council (Vatican I) proclaimed the doctrine of papal infallibility; when the Pope speaks "Ex Cathedra" for the church on matters of faith and morals he cannot be in error. In 1891 Pope Leo XIII issued the encyclical Rerum Novarum, condemning the growth of governmental and corporate power over the individual.

During World War I Pope Benedict XVI didn't take sides, but worked for a compromise peace. During the decades after the first war the Church feared more than anything the growth of Communism; thus it tried to do business as usual with the Italy of Mussolini and the Germany of Hitler. After the Communist seizure of eastern Europe in the late 1940s Catholic opposition to Communism became more emphatic until the advent of Pope John XXIII.

While this was happening the Church's center of gravity in a sense shifted away from Latin Europe. The immense growth of the population of Latin America caused South America to become the continent with the most believers. The moderate success of missionary efforts in Africa and Asia has caused an increase in the numbers of believers there, while American Catholics have increased their influence within the United States and in the Roman Church.

Traditional aspects of Catholicism have come under fire from many quarters. As already mentioned, anti-clericalism has become a strong political force in Latin Europe. North European secularism and hedonism have had their effect on the Catholics of Great Britain, the Netherlands and Germany, making some of them speak out in favor of abortion, ordination of women as priests and the like.

The Second Vatican Council of the early 1960s (Vatican II) made many reforms in the ancient Church, the most noteworthy being the abolition of the old Latin Mass (the Tridentine Mass) and its replacement with Mass celebrated in the language of the celebrants. Many high Church officials believe, however, that Vatican II didn't go nearly far enough with its reform efforts.

In reaction to the continuing grinding poverty of Latin America more and more Spanish- and Portuguese-speaking clergy of the region have adopted Liberation Theology — the notion that the main mission of the Church is the salvation of human bodies from the misery of poverty and disease through promotion of social revolution.

At the other extreme, the land of most fervent Catholic belief has become Slavic Poland. There the Church has become a focus of nationalist aspiration, a vehicle for the expression of Polish longing to be free of the incubus of Soviet-imposed Communism.

From the reign of Pope John XXIII (beginning in the late 1950s) the Church has made an effort to come to terms with these new forces. Before John's time the College of Cardinals usually contained a majority of Italians. Since then the membership of the College has been greatly expanded; prelates of all races from all over the globe now wear the red hat.

Today the first non–Italian Pope in four and a half centuries reigns in the Vatican. The Polish religious fervor of John Paul II has locked horns with the Latin American liberation theologians and the north European and North American secularists in a battle for the soul of the ancient Church.

The efforts of recent Popes to compromise with what they call Modernism has provoked a conservative reaction within the Church. The French Archbishop Marcel Lefebvre maintains a seminary in Econe, Switzerland, where he trains potential priests in the doctrines followed by the Church before John XXIII began the process of reform. In churches following his lead the Mass is still celebrated according to the old Latin ritual. He calls Pope John Paul II a heretic for compromising with modernism. In July of 1988 the Pope excommunicated the Archbishop for daring to consecrate bishops without papal consent. Thus the extreme right wing of Roman Catholicism has been cut off and cast adrift from the Church; but many of the Archbishop's French and German supporters will follow him wherever he leads. What the consequences of of this might be only time will tell.

For the first time in centuries there's serious talk of efforts to heal the millennia-long divisions of Christendom. Olive branches of sorts have been presented to both Protestant and Eastern Orthodox Christians. The Pope speaks often of his dream of a Europe united in Christianity stretching from the English Channel to the Urals.

In our revolutionary age the virus of change has penetrated even into the conservative corners of the Vatican. How the Roman Catholic Church will adapt no one can say, but the four centuries of conservatism since the Counter-Reformation have apparently ended.

Eastern Orthodox Christianity

One who thinks of Eastern Orthodoxy might call to mind the great onion-shaped domes of St. Basil's in Moscow's Kremlin, or the gigantic dome of Hagia Sophia in Istanbul.

But the Orthodox choirs no longer sing their melodious chants in St. Basil's and the only glory worshiped in today's Kremlin is that of the Soviet Union and of Marxism-Leninism, though this could soon change.

Nor do the choirs chant inside Hagia Sophia; it happened for the last time in 1453. The needlelike minarets at each corner of the building tell of its transformation during that year. Five times a day the Muezzin chants the Muslim call to prayer from here; at noon on Friday the faithful gather to hear the weekly sermon of the Imam.

There are now approximately 150 million Eastern Orthodox believers in the world, concentrated in eastern Europe and the Middle East. Should true freedom of religion be established in the Soviet Union this number could increase dramatically.

Distrust and sometimes hatred have poisoned the relationship between the Eastern and Western churches through the centuries. The objective of the Fourth Crusade was Orthodox Constantinople rather than Muslim Jerusalem. As a result of the capture and sack of the city by the Crusaders in 1204 western Catholic Emperors ruled there for the next fifty years. Westerners battled Byzantines and Turks for control of Greece for four centuries; the Orthodox Greeks loathed the Turkish Muslims and Western Catholics with equal intensity.

When Byzantine emperors in the fourteenth and fifteenth centuries proposed reunion of Eastern and Western churches in the face of the danger posed by the Turks and militant Islam to all of Christendom, Eastern churchmen refused to cooperate — better existence under the Islamic Turks than submission to the heretical Roman Catholics. Under the Turk the purity of the true faith would be preserved; in close association with the Pope who could tell what might transpire?

Claiming to be the center of Eastern Orthodoxy after the fall of the Byzantine Empire, the Russian Church became the largest and wealthiest in the Orthodox world. The Orthodox peasantry of the Ukraine and Byelorussia sided with Russia in its struggle with Roman Catholic Poland over these Russo-Polish borderlands, thus aiding Russian territorial expansion to the south and west.

During the nineteenth century Russia sought to cultivate a special relationship with the Orthodox non–Russian Slavs. It aided the Serbs in their struggles against Turkish domination and liberated Bulgaria from Turkish rule by winning the Russo-Turkish War of 1877–78. Its support for Serbia during the diplomatic crisis of July 1914 helped to assure that the Sarajevo assassination would become the cause of World War I.

Orthodox Serbs in Serbian uniform and Catholic Croats in Austrian uniform cursed each other in the same language as they tried to kill each other in the battles of that war. Their mutual hatred continued after they became Yugoslavs together in 1919, and still causes trouble today.

During most of the twentieth century virtually all Orthodox believers lived under governments that oppressed the faithful, as the early Christians were oppressed under the Roman Empire. Russia, home of more believers than any other land, has had a militantly atheist government since 1917. The Eastern Orthodox lands of east Europe have suffered the same fate since the late 1940s. However, the revolutionary changes of 1989 in eastern Europe may revive the independence and strength of the Church in those lands.

The believers of the Middle East are a minority in lands governed by Muslims, living as states within the Islamic society. Only in Greece and the Greek part of Cyprus do the Orthodox live in self-governed societies.

The Orthodox Church is not a monolithic organization as is the Roman Catholic Church. Timothy Ware states in his volume, *The Orthodox Church,* that the believing community is divided into four Patriarchates and eleven National Churches. The four Patriarchates are the ancient centers of Constantinople (Istanbul), Alexandria, Antioch and Jerusalem. The national churches are the Russian, Romanian, Greek, Serbian (Serbia is a constituent republic of Yugoslavia), Bulgarian, Georgian (Georgia is a soviet republic), Cypriot, Czech, Polish, Albanian, and Sinai. (The Sinai Church's members are numbered in the hundreds only; it's centered around the ancient monastery of St. Catherine in what's now Egypt.)

Eastern Orthodoxy has always been closely associated with national governments when it has been the dominant church of a nation. Never has there been a figure like the Roman Pope among the Orthodox who's claimed a power superior to that of national rulers. The national Emperor, Czar or King has been accepted as the head of the Church and has been allowed to wield great influence in Church affairs.

The hierarchy of the Russian Church has been closely supervised by the Kremlin atheists. It has cooperated with the government in order to minimize outside interference with its activities. In return the Church has been permitted to continue to exist without overt persecution, though only 10 to 20 percent of the Russian population attend services or otherwise participate in religious activity. Under Mikhail Gorbachev government interference with the Church is being reduced; it's possible that its influence upon the Russian people may grow.

Whether or not a similar situation will develop in Romania and Bulgaria is open to question; it depends in part on what sort of government succeeds the fallen dictatorships there. Since former Communists have won the 1990 elections in both countries the position of their national churches may not grow much stronger.

In Yugoslavia a more benign Communist regime allows the Serbian Church more independence.

In Muslim lands the Church has no association whatsoever with the state. Where Islam is the state religion Christians are second-class citizens without political power, though no Middle Eastern government actively persecutes the Orthodox at the moment.

In Greece the Church is the state Church. In Cyprus the former head of the Church, Archbishop Makarios, was also President of the Republic for as long as he lived.

The modern Eastern Orthodox Church engages in no power struggles either within itself or with outside forces. It strives merely to continue to exist and to modestly expand, knowing that the times favor no other course. Hopefully, believe the faithful, tomorrow will bring better times; the horizon appears brighter now than it has for most of a century.

The Eastern Orthodox tradition deplores materialism and change for the sake of change. It condemns the moral laxity of both Roman Catholics and Protestants for allowing non-religious considerations to shove aside the basic consideration of human life — people's relationship to God.

Eastern Orthodoxy claims to be the Christianity that's closest to that of the original Church. To it Roman Catholicism destroyed the essential unity of Christendom by the erroneous insistence that the Bishop of Rome was Christ's vicar on earth. To it Protestantism carried that destruction to disastrous lengths by reducing much of the Christian world to religious anarchy. Hopefully it might ultimately restore the Western heretics to the one true faith, though believers in eastern Orthodoxy no longer aggressively strive to accomplish that.

Some of the differences between Orthodoxy and Catholicism are the following. Orthodox priests may marry and divorce isn't a mortal sin. Since there are no pews in Orthodox churches, the faithful remain standing throughout the service. Instrumental music is forbidden; the hymns and chants are sung without any form of instrumental accompaniment. Leavened bread is used in the Communion ceremony, in contrast to the Roman Catholic insistence upon unleavened bread.

Though the Orthodox have never approved of the notions of Pelagius, they never accepted the dark pessimism of Augustine either. People are indeed sinners, but they are capable of bettering their spiritual lot through the exercise of willpower. On the other hand, Orthodox and Catholic agree that there can be no salvation outside the embrace of the Church.

Monophysite Christianity

The remnants of the most ancient form of unorthodox Christianity are still to be found in Africa and the Middle East.

From the beginning the orthodox persecuted the Monophysites, causing many of these believers to welcome the Arab Muslim conquerors of the Middle East as liberators during the seventh century.

Small groups of Monophysites still exist in Lebanon and elsewhere in southwest Asia. The majority of adherents are found in north Africa, however.

The one nation dominated by this belief since its conversion to Christianity is Ethiopia. Isolated in their mountain fastnesses, cut off from the rest of Christendom by militant Muslims, the Ethiopians have preserved their unique culture and gone their own way.

The Italian conquest of 1935 dragged this land into modern times. Post-World War II progress exposed the land to Marxism. The temporal power of the Ethiopian Church was ended by the accession to power of Colonel Mengistu's Marxist-Leninist regime. Should Mengistu's regime evolve into something permanent this living fossil Church may become extinct; however, since the Soviet Union has ceased its massive military assistance to Mengistu the days of his regime may be numbered. The Ethiopian Church may survive this latest danger as it has so many others.

In Egypt a Christian minority has doggedly survived thirteen centuries of Muslim rule. Approximatley 10 percent of all Egyptians belong to the Coptic Church, parent of the Ethiopian Church and the other major surviving Monophysite group. These Copts speak Arabic and are as loyal to their government as Muslim Egyptians. Because their Christianity is out of the Christian mainstream, they have little association with their fellow believers in the rest of the world. Their status as a state within the Egyptian state has served them well until now — but the rise of western-style nationalism in Egypt has somewhat impaired their position.

Can one be a good Egyptian if one isn't a Muslim? The question has been absurd until recent times. Today, it's being asked by more and more Egyptian nationalists.

On the west coast of India, in the state of Kerala, a few hundred thousand Malabar Christians survive. Legend states that this once autonomous Church was founded by the apostle Thomas in the first century A.D. It now uses a Syriac language ritual and is affiliated with the world's Monophysites, though its doctrines differ from those of the Ethiopian and Coptic Churches.

Nestorian Christianity

In the fifth century Nestorius preached that Jesus Christ was both human and divine — born as a human being but with a coexisting divine nature.

Because Nestorius refused to call Mary the Mother of God, and because he disagreed with orthodox authority on other theological points he was declared a heretic. Despite this he built a following in the eastern provinces of the Roman Empire which was persecuted by the Roman and Byzantine Emperors. To escape this most Nestorians migrated eastward into Persia, where they existed in peace under Zoroastrian and Muslim rule until the Mongol conquest of the thirteenth century.

Missionary activity by Nestorians extended all the way to China; at one time their churches could be found in small numbers everywhere from the Mediterranean to the Pacific. They were decimated by the Mongols during the thirteenth and fourteenth centuries. Today a small remnant, known as the Assyrian Church, exists in Iran, Iraq and Syria — independent of Roman Catholics, Eastern Orthodox and Monophysites.

Summary. Christians exist in large numbers on all of the world's inhabited continents. Most denominations seek converts; some succeed more than others. Fundamentalist Protestants enjoy widespread success: in Africa south of the Sahara, in Latin America, in the Far East, and even in Communist lands.

Though Roman Catholicism must struggle to hold its own in Latin America, its missionaries enjoy success in Africa and Asia. Eastern Orthodoxy wins small numbers of converts in the United States and Western Europe.

Chapter 6
Non-Christian Religions

Judaism

"Hear, O Israel! The Lord our God, the Lord is One!"

The Shema expresses the essence of Judaism. There is but one indivisible God—the Yahweh of what to the Christian is the Old Testament.

Another such statement is the saying of Rabbi Hillel that dates from the first century of the Christian era. When asked if he could summarize the Jewish law while standing on one foot, he said, "What is hateful to you, do not do unto your neighbor. All the rest of the Law is commentary."

In number of believers, Judaism is one of the world's minor faiths. There are approximately 18 million Jews in the world, more of them in North America than anywhere else.

For over two millennia Judaism was a culture and religious belief without a country. The Jewish Diaspora (dispersion) began when the Assyrians deported the since-lost Ten Tribes from what's now northern Israel in the eighth century B.C. It continued when Nebuchadnezzar carried off the Judeans to Babylon in 586 B.C. and was completed when the Romans expelled the remaining Jews from Palestine after the suppression of the Bar Kochba revolt in A.D. 135.

We don't think of Judaism as a proselytizing faith. However, Jews did on occasion actively seek converts to their belief, especially during the centuries before the birth of Christ and the early centuries of the Christian era. So numerous were Greek-speaking Jewish converts that the Old Testament was translated into Greek in the third or second century B.C. This Septuagint was the version of the Old Testament most familiar to the Apostle Paul and other early Christian writers. Many European Jews are descendants of these proselytes.

The most noteworthy Jewish missionary success occurred during the seventh or eighth century of the Christian era, when the Khan of the Khazars, the people who then controlled the lower Volga valley of what's now the Soviet Union, accepted Judaism for himself and his subjects. The result was the creation of the most powerful Jewish state of all time and what Arthur Koestler called The Thirteenth Tribe of Israel in his book on the subject, *The Thirteenth Tribe.*

Khazar power was broken by the Russian Prince Sviatoslav in the tenth century and what remained of Khazar independence by the Mongols in the thirteenth. Khazar Jews were scattered over the length and breadth of eastern Europe by these events; this thirteenth tribe contributed much to the large Jewish population of the area from then on.

By the time the Western Roman Empire fell there were Jewish communities all over Roman Europe and the Middle East, continuing to exist into modern times.

Those Jews who lived in lands conquered by the armies of Islam fared reasonably well. Though they were second-class citizens they normally weren't subject to persecution and were allowed wide privileges of self-government. The Jewish inhabitants of Islamic Spain added much to its high civilization.

Those who lived among Christians fared somewhat worse. They suffered overt discrimination and occasional massacre (as happened to German Jews at the hands of Christian Crusader armies marching off to liberate the Holy Land from the Muslims in 1096).

However, Christians granted them the state-within-a-state status that they enjoyed in Islamic lands. They lived under their own law and customs, not being expected to do as their Christian neighbors did. Since Jews enjoyed a higher level of culture than their neighbors throughout the Dark and Middle Ages, they were happy enough to live separate from them.

They also on occasion suffered expulsion; King Edward I ejected England's Jews in 1290, and Ferdinand and Isabella deported those of Spain in 1492. More than once German and Italian states did likewise. At the other end of Europe, Czar Ivan the Terrible of Russia decreed that all Jews residing in his domains should be drowned.

Only one European nation did not follow policies hostile toward Jews; Poland became a sort of magnet attracting both western and eastern Jewry. Before the eighteenth-century partitions erased Poland from Europe's map it had a larger Jewish population than any other state.

By the time of the Renaissance the Jews who had lived in the Iberian peninsula and scattered into western Europe and the countries of the Mediterranean basin had become known as Sephardim and looked upon themselves as the most cultured, advanced members of the world's Jewish community. Their brethren whose ancestors had never lived in Iberia became known as the Ashkenazim.

By the time of the Industrial Revolution West European Sephardic Jews had become more or less accepted members of their national communities. The Jewish states within the state were abolished at the time of the French Revolution and their inhabitants became full citizens of the nation-state they shared with their Christian neighbors.

After the Congress of Vienna settled the Napoleonic Wars, most of old Poland lay within the boundaries of Russia; thus the Polish Jews became subjects of the Czars. Here the ancient hostility of Christians toward the Ashkenazic Jews still reigned. The Czar's Jewish subjects were confined to the former Polish parts of western Russia (called "the Pale") where they were subject to burdensome discrimination and occasionally to random massacre—the Pogrom.

Some of these Ashkenazim forsook their Russian homeland and emigrated—many to the United States, many to central Europe (Austria-Hungary and Germany). The sight of these eastern Jews on the streets of Vienna, clad in their strange caftans, planted in the mind of the then poor semi-vagrant Adolf Hitler the seed of his pathological hatred for these people. What Germans considered to be their bad manners made them less than welcome in the Kaiser's Empire.

This anti–Jewish hysteria rose to national power in Hitler's Third Reich, as one of Europe's most civilized peoples sought to eradicate Jewry from the face of the earth. It's ironic that before Russian hatred of Jews triggered the emigrations of the nineteenth century the states of Germany had become among the most tolerant of people of this faith.

Hitler's Holocaust and its aftermath made possible the rebirth of Israel in 1948. Since that year Jews have once more had a country to call their own.

The creators of Israel were European Jews. The political tensions caused by the existence of the new state called to the attention of Israelis and the world colonies of non–European Jews that had existed for centuries. Most of these lived in Islamic countries; their comfortable coexistence with Muslims was suddenly shattered by Arab-Israeli political hostility.

Urbanized Jews from Iraq and culturally primitive Jews from Yemen and Morocco joined their European brethren in Israel.

Most astounding among the newcomers were the Falasha—the black Jews of Ethiopia—until very recently unknown to most of their co-religionists.

For those who associate the religious faith with the nation, Judaism calls forth visions of the Wailing Wall in old Jerusalem, of the green kibbutzim of the Negev and Galilee, and of the tanks and aircraft that battered Israel's enemies in 1967 and 1973.

For those who don't, there's the vision of the Jewish doctor who treated you when you were a child, and of the synagogue in the other part of town.

Judaism's in a sense an integral part of Christian culture, in that the Old Testament is as much Jewish holy scripture as it is Christian. Yet the Jewish Passover, Yom Kippur and Hannukah holidays seem as foreign to the Christian as the Muslim fast of Ramadan.

To the Jew Christmas and Easter, the Sunday rest day, and the concept of the Trinity are equally alien, for to the Jew Jesus Christ was not the Son of

God or the Messiah, the Sunday rest day is a Christian import from ancient paganism, and God is but One, never Three in One.

The Messiah who will lead God's people to better things is yet to come, though on occasion the world's Jews have been galvanized by the appearance of persons claiming Messiahhood. The last such, Shabbatai Zevi, was proclaimed as Messiah in Gaza, Palestine, in 1665.

Paul Johnson, in his work *A History of the Jews,* explains how Shabbatai Zevi's claim was publicized throughout the Jewish world by Nathan of Gaza, and how believers everywhere were excited about this apparent fulfillment of ancient prophecy. When the would-be Messiah sought to visit Istanbul in 1666, he was taken prisoner by Turkish authorities. Since they deemed him a danger to the peace of the Sultan's realm (because of the large number of Jews within the Ottoman Empire) they proposed to keep him incarcerated. Eventually they offered him an unpleasant choice—conversion to Islam or death. Shabbatai Zevi chose life and conversion, which the Turks promptly announced to the world. The weak-willed Messiah's followers, disillusioned, returned to reality; never again has a would-be Messiah so galvanized the world's Jewry.

Only in Israel do believers in Judaism rule, but in that country reigns a conception of nationhood, not necessarily one of formal religion. Israel is a modern secular state; religious belief has not been incorporated into the law (though most economic activity ceases at sundown on Friday and Jewish dietary law is observed within the Israeli armed forces).

However, the Promised Land of the Old Testament has been restored to God's Chosen People. The Babylonian Captivity has ended. Never must the land be lost again. Never must the people be subject to another Holocaust, without a square foot of soil on which to call refuge.

Judaism has not suffered the fundamental divisions of most religious faiths. To be sure, there are Orthodox, Conservative and Reformed Jewish congregations. The Orthodox strictly observe the Law of the faith and conduct their worship services in Hebrew. They associate as little as possible with Gentiles and emphasize their Jewishness. They have their own political party in Israel which seeks to make the land into a religious state once again. Their services are conducted in synagogues; they never speak of the local place of worship as a temple. They look forward to the day when God's great temple (originally built by Solomon and later twice destroyed) will be rebuilt in Jerusalem.

The most orthodox of the orthodox are the Hasidim. They seek to preserve Judaism in its pure ancient form, making no concessions to modernity. Other Orthodox Jews are willing to compromise just a little with the changes history wreaks.

At the opposite pole Reformed Jews conduct their worship services in temples in the language of the country where they reside. They have sunk roots in the countries where they reside and few of them forsake their land of birth to return to Israel. They tend to believe in the separation of religion and the state.

Conservatives occupy a middle ground, mingling with Gentiles more than the orthodox, but observing the old Law more strictly than the Reformed. Reconstructionists seek to adapt Judaism to modern conditions while giving up as little as possible of the old traditions; other conservatives claim the old faith needs no real reconstruction.

Judaism's continued existence, and the passionate desire of its believers to preserve the existence of Israel, make it a powerful influence on the Middle East and on the world.

Islam

The Arabic word Islam means "Submission." The essence of Islam is submission to the will of God, the Merciful, the Compassionate.

When we think of Islam we visualize the dome of the mosque in the distance, with four minarets at its corners pointing to the cloudless desert sky. We hear the Muezzin singing his call to prayer, and we see the faithful prostrating themselves on the prayer rugs, heads pointed toward Mecca, as they comply.

In terms of the number of believers, Islam is the second-largest of the world's religions. Most of its almost 900 million followers live in Asia and Africa.

Like the Jew, the Muslim believes that God is one and indivisible. Like the Christian, the Muslim believes that Jesus was born of the Virgin Mary, destined by God to perform wondrous works. But unlike the Christian, the Muslim believes that Jesus was but a mortal man, the second most holy of God's prophets. He was not the Son of God, nor was he crucified, nor did he rise from the dead. Unlike both Jew and Christian, Muslims believe that, in the seventh century A.D., God sent his last and greatest Prophet, Mohammed, to make his final and ultimate revelation to humanity. This revelation is found in the Holy Qu'ran, and ultimately all people must and will accept and revere it. It's the duty of the true believer to make the good news known everywhere.

They are doing so. The minarets of mosques point to the cloudy skies of England. Islamic books and magazines grace the shelves of American bookshops. In Europe, the Western Hemisphere, sub–Saharan Africa and the Far East Islamic missionaries labor, and their labors slowly bear fruit. The number of believers steadily grows.

In North Africa, the Middle East, much of the Indian subcontinent and south Asia Islam is the prevailing religion. Though it and Judaism are the closest existing relatives of Christianity Islam has created a cultural environment many Westerners find alien.

There are five pillars of Islam. These are:

(1) To repeat and believe the Shehada: "There is no God but God, and Mohammed is his Prophet."

(2) To utter the required prayers (Salah). True believers must pray five times a day — early morning, noon, mid-afternoon, sunset, and evening. They must also attend the mosque at noon on Friday and participate in prayer there. They must also participate in the two annual Eeds, festivals of prayer. One of these is the Festival of Fast-Breaking, at the end of the fast month of Ramadan, and the other is at the time of return from the pilgrimage to Mecca.

(3) To observe the required fast (Sawm). This occurs during the Muslim month of Ramadan. During this month one must not eat during daylight, and ideally confine one's intake of food to two light meals — one just before dawn and the other just after sunset.

(4) To give the required alms (Zakah). True believers should give 2.5 percent of their net worth as alms each year. To give more than this isn't mandatory, but it is most praiseworthy.

(5) To make the pilgrimage to Mecca (Hajj) at least once in a lifetime.

Muslims are forbidden to eat pork and to drink alcohol. Regardless of conflicts with work schedules, Muslims are expected to pray when required and attend the weekly service at the local mosque at noon on Friday. (Otherwise, Friday is not a day of rest as is the Jewish Sabbath or the Christian Sunday.)

Traditionally the Muslim male may have up to four wives, and may divorce his spouse or spouses at will.

Women are segregated. Their duties are deemed to be those of wives and mothers and they must not mingle with men socially.

The human body must not be portrayed in any way, shape or form. Thus much Islamic art is expressed in the portrayal of geometric forms, or in calligraphy.

The perception of Muslim by Christian and of Christian by Muslim is clouded by more than a millennium of violent history. The believers of the two faiths have been bitter enemies. Europeans lived with the possibility of Muslim invasion and depredation from the time of the Muslim conquest of Spain in 711 to the breaking of the last Turkish siege of Vienna in 1683 and the final suppression of the pirates of North Africa in the early nineteenth century.

Muslims suffered the invasion of the Middle East by the Crusaders from the eleventh to the thirteenth centuries, the plundering of their outposts in East Africa and on the Arabian Sea by the Portuguese in the sixteenth century, and ultimately the military conquest of virtually all of their lands by European armies in the nineteenth and twentieth centuries.

Since the European Renaissance and Reformation didn't touch the Islamic world Muslim religious faith hasn't eroded as has Christian faith. Average Muslims still believe that their faith and culture are superior, despite current Western economic and military power. Seldom is a Muslim converted to another religious belief; often are believers in other faiths (including Christianity) converted to Islam.

Evidence of Islamic hostility to the West is everywhere. There was the effort by Arab-dominated OPEC to hold Western economies for ransom during the oil crisis of the 1970s. There was, and still is, the hostility of the Islamic world toward Israel and its supporters. There is the support given anti–Western terrorists by the governments of Iran and Libya. Most recently, there was the massive support for Saddam Hussein by the Arab man in the street.

All true believers divide the world into two parts — the Dar ul-Islam and the Dar ul-Harb — the Land of Islam and the Land of War. That which becomes part of Dar ul-Islam should remain so. Continuous effort must be made to incorporate the Dar ul-Harb into the lands of the true faith.

Or, to put it another way, what is ours remains ours. What is yours we'll try to make ours. Of course, parts of Dar ul-Islam have been lost over the centuries, such as Spain, eastern and southern Russia, and Palestine.

But the faithful agree that never should they allow a situation to come into being where Muslims must take orders from non–Muslims. Thus, it's bad for Muslims to be ruled by non–Muslims, and for Muslims to be dependent on non–Muslims politically, economically, or in any other way. It's therefore a ticklish business for Westerners to deal with Muslims. We find it most difficult to accommodate their sensitivities.

Yet, our culture has more in common with the Islamic than many of us realize. The Qu'ran, the holy scripture of Islam, commands the faithful to work hard during this life; God disapproves of laziness. It orders believers to live up to their contracts and not to commit fraud against others. It approves of the faithful accumulating property.

It doesn't oppose private ownership of property as such, though one must always realize that the true owner of all things on earth is God. If we become rich in this life, it's not by our doing; we have what we have as God's tenant. Therefore we must use what we have for God's glory and the benefit of our fellow humans.

The Qu'ran imposes the duty on all believers to care for the poor, the unfortunate, widows and orphans. In a sense the Islamic equivalent of the Christian tithe is the Zakat, which is levied by law in Saudi Arabia and a few other Islamic lands; in the others payment of it is a private matter.

Traditional Islam condemns capitalism and the free market economy for promoting selfishness and materialism, and for not properly caring for the needy. It condemns socialism and communism for their atheism, and for not allowing people who work to keep and enjoy the fruit of their labors.

Sunni Islam. There are two major branches of Islam, the Sunni and the Shi'a. The Sunni is the orthodox branch; over 80 percent of all Muslims belong to it.

The division between Sunni and Shi'a was originally an argument over whether any believing Muslim should be eligible to be Caliph—Commander of the Faithful—or whether this post should be reserved to persons who are direct descendants of the Prophet. The Sunni take the former position, the Shi'a the latter.

The prophet Mohammed had no son. When he died his cousin Ali, who was married to the prophet's favorite daughter Fatima, claimed the right to succeed as leader of the faithful. Since Arab tradition didn't recognize any hereditary right to tribal leadership, the close advisors of the old leader had the power to choose a successor. The Muslim community followed this custom.

The advisors rejected Ali's claim, choosing instead the prophet's close friend Abu Bakr as the first Caliph. Abu Bakr soon died and was succeeded by Umar, who was assassinated by an unhappy slave. Umar's successor was Uthman, who gave his relatives high posts in the administration of the conquered territories of the new empire. Malcontents assassinated Uthman, and Ali was chosen as the fourth Caliph. Ali made little effort to run down and punish the assassins of Uthman, which deeply offended Kharijite fundamentalists who in turn assassinated Ali.

Sunni and Shi'a agree in revering these four men as the "rightly guided Caliphs," worthy successors of the prophet as the leader of the faithful.

Now there was a power struggle between Ali's son Hassan and Muawiya, son-in-law of the prophet, who was married to the prophet's widow Aisha. Muawiya bribed Hassan to accept him as Caliph; Hassan afterward lived a comfortable life of leisure. Later legend says that Mauwiya got rid of his still-potentially dangerous rival by having him poisoned.

Now Husain, brother of Hassan and son of Ali, claimed the right to rule the world of Islam. He was quiet until Muawiya died. The old Caliph appointed his son Yazid as his successor. There was a final struggle between Yazid and Husain. Most Muslims sided with Yazid. In the final battle Husain and a handful of supporters fought Yazid's gigantic army at Kerbala in Iraq; Husain died a martyr's death in battle. The site of his death is one of the holiest of Shi'ite shrines.

To the Sunni, the triumph of Yazid was the triumph of legitimacy. The dynasty that began with Muawiya was the legitimate successor of the rightly guided caliphs.

This Ummayad dynasty was eventually overthrown, to be succeeded by the Abbasid. Ultimately political power within Islam became fragmented; one who claimed the title Caliph could no longer exercise political power over more than a small portion of the faithful.

Since this fragmentation has come to pass, the true legitimacy of Islamic governments has ended. The rightly guided Caliphs made the Qu'ran the cornerstone of their government. But no longer is this done. Power flows from the point of the sword; the rulers seek personal power and personal enrichment rather than the glory of God. One must accept this state of affairs as God's will. It's better to collaborate with the state and have order than to challenge the state and produce anarchy.

There is no ecclesiastical organization in Sunni Islam, and no clergy as we understand the term. Those who have made it their life work to study the writings of the Faith—the Ulama—are very highly respected. Such men are invited to preach the sermons at the mosque on Friday. In theory, however, any true believer may lead the service.

It amazes Westerners to no end that Sunni Islam can survive and grow without formal organization. The fact that it does so illustrates the strength of the believers' faith.

Shi'ite Islam. The supporters of Ali, Hassan and Husain became the Shi'a, no longer contesting for the Caliphate. They left that office to the power-seekers, claiming that the true leaders of Islam are those descendants of the prophet who head his family. The true leader has the title of Imam, the first of which was Ali, the second Hassan, and the third Husain.

According to the orthodox Shi'a, eleven Imams have lived and died. The twelfth, Mohammed al Muntazar, infant son of the eleventh Imam, went into occultation in A.D. 873 and still lives in that state. He has hidden himself away from the wicked world and awaits the appointed time to reveal himself and restore legitimate leadership to the faithful. This Twelfth Imam, called the Hidden Imam or Mahdi, fills a position in Shi'a belief somewhat similar to the Messiah in Jewish belief; he is the redeemer who will bring triumph to the faithful and justice to the world.

Occasionally a charismatic leader has appeared among Muslims and proclaimed himself to be the long-awaited Mahdi. In 1881 Mohammed Ahmed proclaimed this to the Arabs of the Sudan, raising large armies of fanatical faithful that took control of the land. His troops besieged a British army in Khartoum in 1885. British rifles, field artillery and Western military discipline couldn't stop the Muslims from storming the place; the British commander, General Charles "Chinese" Gordon, died beside his men.

Before the British could organize to claim revenge Mohammed Ahmed died, but his successors sought to keep his movement alive. They did until an army of British avengers marched south from Egypt twelve years later.

The fanatical Mahdist cavalry charged the British lines at Omdurman in 1898, just as they'd done at Khartoum, but now General Kitchener's troops had machine guns. The screeching horsemen were mown down by the hundreds. Mahdist military power was destroyed, Gordon was avenged, and thousands of martyred Islamic believers found instant admission to Paradise.

The mainstream Shi'ites are known as the Twelver Shi'a. Twelver Shiism has been the prevailing belief in Iran for centuries; the rulers of that country have been of that persuasion for many years. The majority of Iraqis are also Twelver Shi'ites, though they've never controlled the Iranian government.

Twelver Shi'a believe that it's their fate to be dominated by unbelievers — either Sunni Muslims or non-Muslims. They will always suffer at the hands of these oppressors until the true Mahdi appears and brings liberation. The more militant among them believe that struggle against the oppressor is a necessity, and that martyrdom — death in the righteous cause — earns one certain admission to Paradise.

Thus the true believer doesn't mind driving the auto with bomb underneath to the nests of the enemy and setting it off with himself inside. What matters the death of one believer if a dozen enemies are sent to Hell? Thus the fanatical Basij militiamen of Iran charged the Iraqi machine guns during the Iran-Iraq War in the thousands and were decimated. Thus the Hezbollah terrorists kill themselves and their chosen enemies by the dozen to this day.

The Shi'a celebrate the anniversary of Husain's death at Kerbala as a major festival. Flagellants march through the streets of Shi'ite cities beating themselves with chains to show their willingness to bear the pains of martyrdom.

Shi'a Islam recognizes a form of clergy. At the holy city of Qom in Iran hundreds of young men study the fundamentals of the faith in what Westerners would call seminaries. Those whose learning earns great respect among the faithful acquire the title of Ayatollah. The Ayatollahs of Iran have high prestige, and have on occasion exercised political power.

The Ayatollah Ruhollah Khomeini achieved unprecedented power, in a sense serving as combined emperor and pope in his country. So far his successor, Ayatollah Ali Khamenei, has not been able to exercise such power.

Minor Shi'a sects are found elsewhere in the Islamic world. The Zaidi or Fivers who dominate North Yemen claim that Zaid, a grandson of Husain, was the fifth Imam and that the true Imams of the faith are his descendants. (Twelvers refuse to recognize Zaid as a true Imam.) Originally they believed in political activism, thousands achieving martyrdom for their efforts. But modern Zaidi are more quietist.

Zaidi Imams ruled North Yemen as absolute monarchs until 1962. In that year the last was overthrown by a military coup, but his supporters bitterly resisted the new republican government. Saudi Arabia supported the Imamate cause with money and weaponry while Gamal Abdal Nasser sent Egyptian troops to support the republic. A bloody civil war raged until Egypt's defeat by Israel in the Six Day War of 1967 caused Nasser to withdraw his troops; without Egyptian support the republicans couldn't achieve total victory and the war ended in compromise. The Imamate was not restored, but its supporters now participate in the government of the republic. Now that the states of North and South Yemen have merged, the political power of the Zaidi may be further reduced.

The Ismaili or Seveners believe that Ismail was the seventh Imam, another claim that Twelvers don't accept. In the eleventh century at the Iranian fortress of Alamut, one of the most notable Ismaili leaders, Hassan Sabah, founded an order of fanatics. These were called by some the Hashishim, because they supposedly intoxicated themselves on hashish—marijuana. We know them better as the Assassins; they assumed the duty to kill public figures who were hostile to the true faith. The appointed assassins, high on drugs, were fearless in carrying out their assignments. More often than not they were killed at the site of their triumphs. They died willingly in the belief that they had earned immediate admission to Paradise.

For over a century the Assassins terrorized public figures in the Islamic world and among the Crusaders. Finally they were wiped out by the Mongol army of Hulagu Khan, the thirteenth-century destroyer of most of the Muslim principalities in the Middle East.

Ismailis have been peaceful citizens ever since. Today they're found mainly in Pakistan and India, doing the bidding of their Imam the Aga Khan.

The Alawites, who live in northern Syria, regard Ali very highly; some non–Alawites accuse members of this community of worshipping Ali as God, making them non–Muslims. Most Alawites deny this charge. The President of Syria, Hafiz al-Assad, is an Alawi. Some of his countrymen publicly doubted Assad's qualification to hold the office because the Syrian Constitution requires that the national President be a Muslim. In order to assure the nation that he truly is Muslim, Assad repeated the Shehada in public, thus quieting some of his critics. Though Assad's fellow believers are a minority in Syria they dominate the government of that country because the President hesitates to entrust non–Alawites with high governmental posts.

The Druzes are found in the country near Mount Hermon (where the borders of Syria, Lebanon and Israel join) and are a political force to be reckoned with. They worship Hakim, an insane tenth-century Egyptian sultan who declared himself to be God. This makes them non–Muslim in many orthodox eyes.

The Kharijites, who assassinated Ali, were for a long time a strong third force in Islam. They believed that sinners cannot be good Muslims, and thus excommunicated such from the ranks of the faithful. Neither Sunni nor Shi'a have ever believed this, both groups being willing to forgive the repentant backslider. Today the small remnant of this group are known as Ibadis, and are most numerous in the sultanate of Oman.

Mention must also be made of the Sufis. These are the Islamic mystics. Both Sunni and Shi'a believe that the Muslim establishes contact with God by following the prescribed rituals (repeating prayers at prescribed times and the like), and that one may not maintain rapport with the Almighty without doing this. The Sufi believes that people may establish contact with God in their own way without necessarily performing prescribed ritual. Sufis are organized into orders; each order imposes its own rules and discipline upon its members. These differ considerably from order to order.

Sufis are generally accepted as good Muslims, though their otherworldly approach to religion is unusual in such a pragmatic faith as Islam.

Thus, Islam is no more a united faith than is Christianity. Yet the various sects of Islam seemingly share more common ground than do the immense variety of Protestant denominations in Christendom.

The biggest obstacle to understanding between Westerners and Muslims, aside from the millennium of unpleasantness between us, is the insistence of both sides upon emphasis on our differences, rather than likenesses.

Baha'i. The Baha'i faith is an offshoot of Islam that originated in Iran. During the early nineteenth century Mirza Ali Mohammed preached a new doctrine to Iranians. He called himself the Bab, the Gate through which Mankind would learn of the coming of a new religious order, to be founded by a Promised One who would soon make himself known. The Iranian government found this message subversive and had the Bab executed in 1850.

In a sense the Bab played the role of John the Baptist to the coming Promised one. In 1863 Mirza Husain Ali announced himself as the one who would fulfill the Bab's prophecy, calling himself Baha'ullah. His message was that all of the great religions of the world have a common origin. Before Baha'ullah came upon the scene there had been eight great prophets of God: Moses, Jesus, Mohammed, Zoroaster, Buddha, Confucius, Krishna, and Lao Tse. He, Baha'ullah, was the ninth and last.

In order to avoid the Bab's fate he preached his doctrine outside Iran. He met with some success, dying a natural death in 1892 and leaving behind a flourishing organization. Since the faith regards the teachings and scriptures of the religions created by the first eight prophets as equally valid (as modified by the doctrines of Baha'ullah), it establishes a powerful spiritual base for asserting the oneness of humanity.

There are more than six million believers in this faith, scattered over the world. Many are found here in the United States; the Baha'i temple in Wilmette, Illinois, is one of the interesting architectural landmarks of the Chicago metropolitan area.

The faith has come upon hard times in Iran, the land of its origin. For a century or more the Shahs let these rather harmless heretics exist in peace, but the Ayatollah Khomeini was intolerant of dissenters. Iranian Baha'is have been subjected to ruthless persecution; it's unknown how many true believers remain in that country.

The faith slowly grows outside Iran, but it is and will remain one of Earth's minor religions.

Black Muslims. According to the eighth edition of Frank S. Mead's *Handbook of Religious Denominations in the United States* (as revised by Samuel S. Hill) the American Black Muslim movement was founded by Timothy Drew (Noble Drew Ali) sometime before 1920. Virtually all members and followers of the movement are young black men. They follow the practices of Islam in almost all respects, differing from the parent faith in that they seek the establishment of an independent black nation within the boundaries of the United States. So far orthodox Muslims have refused to recognize them as legitimate members of the Islamic community.

Religions of India

Hinduism. When Westerners think of Hinduism, they may imagine the hundreds of believers immersing themselves in the waters of the Ganges River at the holy city of Benares. Or, less charitably, they may call to mind the vision of bony sacred cows wandering along the streets of crowded cities among equally bony and undernourished children.

Hinduism is the major religion of India, and in terms of number of believers is the third-largest of the world's faiths. There are nearly 700 million believers, the majority of whom live in India.

Though at one time the cultural influence of the faith extended to Cambodia and Indonesia, this is no longer true. The only place where Hinduism of a sort is practiced outside India by non–Indians today is on the Indonesian island of Bali.

It's probably the oldest existing religion on the planet, and the only major religion whose founder(s) are unknown.

The worldview of Hinduism has largely shaped Indian culture. Hindus believe in the transmigration of souls. We don't live just one life upon the earth; we are bound to the wheel of Samsara for an almost endless series of lives. This series of births and deaths will continue until we acquire enough merit (Moksha) to be released from the wheel. When this finally happens we reach Nirvana; we become one with the Universe and acquire eternal peace.

During each incarnation we acquire Karma from our acts. The better a life we lead, the more good Karma we acquire; the worse we lead the more bad Karma we acquire. The sort of life we lead in each birth depends on the Karma we bring with us from former lives.

If I'm leading a life of poverty and misery, this is because I've done evil in previous incarnations and am in a sense being punished. If I'm rich, handsome and healthy I've done good in prior lives and am being rewarded.

The major consequence of this system of belief is that people see little point in striving to better one's station in this life. If my present misery is due to my bad conduct in past lives, all I can do is try to accumulate some merit in this one so I'll live better the next time around. The way to accumulate merit is by proper performance of religious ritual (Samskara) and of moral duty (Dharma). Economic activity is of no particular value (except to insure physical survival).

Some Hindus believe that animals have souls, and that persons who have accumulated much bad Karma can be reborn as animals. Thus, some true believers must not kill animals (because you might be killing a reincarnation of an ancestor) and must certainly not eat animals. (Other Hindus, however, do eat animal foods. The one food taboo common to virtually all Hindus is the refusal to eat beef.)

An immense variety of beliefs and rituals coexist in Hinduism. The Eternal manifests himself to humanity in many aspects. In his role as Creator he manifests himself as Brahma, but that isn't his only role. He also manifests himself as Vishnu the preserver, and as Shiva the destroyer. But the Eternal does not manifest himself only in male aspects. Goddesses—female aspects of the Eternal—also play a large role in the faith.

One can't begin to describe the breadth and depth of Hindu beliefs and practices in a page or two. It's been said that the soul of India is unfathomable for a Westerner.

There are many Hindu cults devoted to the worship of one of the manifestations of the Eternal. The major ones are devoted to Vishnu, Shiva and Sakti—the latter being the female aspect (or one of them) of Brahma. Each of these three manifests itself in many forms to the believer.

Thus Vishnu has appeared on earth as the dwarf Vamana, the hero Rama, the great lover and hero Krishna, and in seven other incarnations. His consort Lakshmi is a bringer of good luck, among other things.

Among the aspects of Shiva are Nataraja, Lord of the Dance; Mahakala the Remover, Lord of Death; and Pasupati, Lord of Animals. His consort Sakti (or Ambika, the Great Mother) is the third object of worship by many Hindu cults.

The cults of Sakti are thought to be Indian survivals of the ancient Mother Goddess cults that existed all across the Middle East in ancient times. Her manifestations include Mahadevi the great Goddess, Parvati the ideal woman, Durga who rides a lion and combats demons, and Kali, who according to some cults must be worshiped with the blood of sacrificed animals.

When the British came to India they were revolted by the practices of the Thuggee or Thugs, a Kali cult that commanded its devotees to do ritual murder. This was stamped out after a struggle; but the cults of Kali remain among the most bloody-minded of the Hindu groups, still practicing animal sacrifice. These are exceptional; the huge majority of Hindu cults preach non-violence to living things.

Such religion doesn't cultivate military and economic virtues. For the last thousand years—until 1947—most of India has lived under the dominion of foreigners. First there were the Muslim conquerors from Iran and Afghanistan, and later the British.

The rulers of the new republic of India have tried to foster nationalism to go along with the ancient religion. They've striven mightily to impose modern ideas upon the people of the country to bring about economic development and alleviate the terrible poverty of the land. But ancient traditions stand in the way.

The ability of the old faith to withstand cultural shocks seems to be unlimited. Neither Muslim conquest nor British colonial dominion nor native modernism put much of a dent in it. Evidently Hinduism will survive as long as India itself.

Hare Krishna. Several religious systems based upon Hindu beliefs have taken root in the West during the twentieth century. One of the most noteworthy is the Hare Krishna movement, more accurately called the International Society for Krishna Consciousness (Iskcon). Kenneth Boa, in his work *Cults, World Religion and You,* says though most Hindus believe that Krishna is one of the aspects of Vishnu the Preserver, Iskcon holds that in truth Vishnu is an aspect of Krishna, the Supreme God.

It is a part of the Caitanya sect of Krishna worship, founded by Caitanya Mahaprabu in Bengal in the early sixteenth century and transplanted into the West during the 1960s. Caitanya is still highly revered by Hare Krishnas as the founder of the faith.

The concepts of Samsara and Karma play a central role in Iskcon belief. The faithful earn good Karma by following a life of monastic discipline, living according to a rigid schedule. Initiates wear Indian clothing, follow a vegetarian diet, and are forbidden all alcohol and stimulants. Marriage is frowned upon; sex is permitted only with one's spouse, solely for procreation purposes.

Contact with the outside world is severely limited. Generally members venture out into the world only in groups, in order to sell items produced within the temple and the sect's religious literature, or to solicit monetary contributions.

Many young Westerners who find the materialism and moral corruption of our culture disgusting have found the allure of this movement irresistible.

Jainism. For the person who knows anything at all of this Indian faith, the name conjures up the vision of a man slowly walking down the street carrying a broom, meticulously sweeping the path he will tread. Jains believe that even insects have souls, and that persons may be reborn as insects. Thus the true believer must never accidentally kill an insect or any other animal; destruction of life is evil unless absolutely necessary.

Good Jains are thus uncompromising vegetarians. They cannot practice agriculture, because the farmer inevitably kills insects. They are town or city dwellers, earning their keep as skilled crafts people or merchants.

The faith was founded by Mahavira in the fifth century B.C. It has stubbornly maintained its existence since, though its members have never been numerous. There are now some five million, virtually all of whom reside in India.

Sikhism. Most Americans have encountered men with dark hair and dark eyes who have long black beards and wrap their apparently very long hair in colorful turbans. These are Sikhs, members of one of the most important of India's minority religious faiths.

Sikhism was founded in the fifteenth century (1499) by Guru Nanak as a sort of hybrid between Islam and Hinduism. Guru Nanak appointed Guru Angad as his successor; Angad appointed Guru Amar Das as his. For two centuries each Guru appointed his successor; each of these men had to strive mightily against efforts by the Islamic rulers of north India to exterminate the new religion. In response the Sikhs cultivated the military arts in order to defend themselves. They developed a fierce devotion to their Khalsa—the Sikh community. This almost fanatical loyalty still exists and helps to explain recent events in India.

The tenth Guru—Gobind Singh—declined to appoint a successor. In place of a human Guru he decided that members of the faith should revere their holy scripture as leader. Thus the holy book of the faith became known as the Guru Granth Sahib. Copies of it are treated with the reverence one would show to a respected saint.

Male Sikhs must never cut their hair or beards and must wear trousers of a specified type. Upon reaching adulthood they're given a sacred dagger which they must carry at all times, a sacred comb they must carry at all times, and a sacred bracelet which they must wear at all times. It's a virtue to be proficient with weapons. Sikhs served in large numbers in the British Indian Army, and are numerous in the contemporary Indian army.

Male Sikhs include the word Singh—Lion—as part of their names, while female Sikhs include Kaur—Princess—as part of theirs. Women are greatly respected, and have higher status than in the other religious communities of India.

Sikhs believe in one formless God. Their headquarters are found in the great Golden Temple in the Indian city of Amritsar. Not too long ago a faction of well-armed Sikhs led by Sant Jarnail Singh Bhindranwale took possession of the Golden Temple and used it as a military headquarters for the commission of terrorist acts against Hindus and other Sikhs because the Indian federal government refused to yield to certain of Bhindranwale's demands and portions of the Sikh community refused to support him. Units of the Indian army moved into Amritsar and stormed the Temple to put an end to this disorder; Bhindranwale and many of his followers died in the bitter fighting (not to mention some of the attacking Indian troops).

Sikhs regarded this attack on their temple as a great sacrilege. As a consequence many of them who had never supported Bhindranwale were outraged. One result was that an angry Sikh security guard assassinated Prime Minister Indira Gandhi because she'd authorized the storming operation.

There has been great tension between Sikhs and Hindus ever since. Efforts by the new prime minister, Rajiv Gandhi, to resolve them weren't completely successful. Sikh political activists supported the opposition coalition that defeated Gandhi in the election of 1989. The new government has done a better job of reducing these tensions.

Presently there are some 16 million Sikhs in the world, most of whom live in India.

Parsees. Those who know of this faith have visions of the tall flat-topped towers near Bombay where Parsee dead are exposed to the elements. To true believers in this faith it's equally wrong to bury the dead, or to cremate them.

These people are the remnant of what was once one of the world's great religions — Zoroastrianism.

Zoroaster (or Zarathustra) founded the faith in Iran in the sixth century B.C. It became the national faith of the Achaemenid Empire, whose kings tried to subdue Greece in the fifth century B.C. and were in turn subdued by Alexander the Great two centuries later. It continued to be the faith of Iran until the Muslim conquest of the seventh century.

Its holy scripture teaches that the Universe is the scene of eternal struggle between Good and Evil. Ahura Mazda the Creator fathered two powerful spirits, Ormuzd, protagonist of good, and Ahriman, protagonist of evil. Both have the powers of gods and manipulate the universe and everything in it to get the better of the enemy.

Humanity is not under the domination of either spirit. It's up to people to decide whether to do good and help Ormuzd, or to do evil and help Ahriman. The world is neither good nor evil; it's what humanity makes of it.

It's the mission of humanity to line up on the side of Ormuzd in the struggle, and to resist the temptations of Ahriman. Ultimately the Good will win the struggle, of course, but that consummation is to happen far into the future.

The faith of Zoroaster originated the idea of the eternal struggle between Good and Evil, personified in supernatural spirits, for dominance over the Universe and its intelligent life. The later Iranian prophet Mani refined this dualism in his faith (Manicheanism) which became influential in the Roman Empire of the second, third and fourth centuries.

Such dualism seeped into Christianity in the Gnosticism of this period, and became one of the cornerstones of the Albigensian (Cathar) heresy of the eleventh and twelfth centuries.

Though Zoroastrian and Manichean dualism have vanished from the popular religious beliefs of our time, their shadow remains. It may well be that the notion of the ambitious fallen angel Lucifer — Satan the Devil, Prince of Evil, eternal adversary of Jesus Christ — entered Christianity from Zoroastrianism via Judaism.

Zoroastrianism has almost died out in its homeland (the small remnant of true believers has been savagely persecuted by the government of Ayatollah Khomeini) as well as everywhere else in the world. The survival of the belief in India is noteworthy because its adherents are among the most wealthy and successful businesspeople in the country. Less than a half-million believers remain, virtually all living in the vicinity of Bombay.

Since Parsees believe that your life is what you make it, they pay much more attention to economic matters than do Hindus. Their belief makes it possible to pursue wealth for the sake of wealth, as Islam doesn't.

Buddhism

The Western view of the Buddhist may be the vision of the begging monk on the street, with the graceful spire of the pagoda pointing skyward in the background. Or perhaps it is the Zen master relentlessly harassing his pupil, driving him forward in his search for the lightning stroke of Satori.

Buddhism is the fourth-largest of the world's religions, with somewhat more than 300 million believers, found mostly in southern and far eastern Asia. Buddhism is an offshoot of Hinduism, born in India in the sixth century B.C. Its founder Gautama Siddhartha lived at about the same time as Zoroaster and Mahavira.

Born a prince, he became depressed at the sight of the human poverty and misery that surrounded him. Unable to do much about it as a prince, he abandoned title, wealth and family to wander the world seeking the solution to the problem. While sitting under a tree meditating, the answer came to him. He announced to the world the Four Noble Truths and the Noble Eightfold Path.

The Four Noble Truths are:

(1) All of life is suffering.

(2) The cause of suffering is unfulfilled wrong desire.

(3) The cure for suffering is elimination of wrong desire.

(4) Wrong desire may be eliminated by following the Noble Eightfold Path.

Wrong desire is essentially wanting things for oneself—putting comfort in this world above acquiring merit for the next life.

The Noble Eightfold Path consists of:

(1) Right Belief—acceptance of the Four Noble Truths.

(2) Right Thought—freedom from lust, ill will, cruelty, and untruthfulness.

(3) Right Speech—don't lie, boast, or curse.

(4) Right Action—don't kill, steal, or engage in sexual misconduct.

(5) Right Means of Livelihood—avoid luxury and don't make a living by doing violence to living creatures.

(6) Right Exertion—avoid the evil and promote the good.

(7) Right Remembrance—the body and this life are transitory and loathsome.

(8) Right Meditation—try to achieve purity of thought, which is thought free of all sensation.

The original Buddhism was thus a moral philosophy.

As a variant of Hinduism its adherents also believed (and still believe) in the transmigration of souls and the final liberation from the endless cycle of death and rebirth in Nirvana. They too believe that one's status in this life depends upon the Karma one brings forward from prior lives. Buddhism thus discouraged economic activity as did Hinduism.

It began to acquire the trappings of religion. Missionaries propagated it throughout India and carried it to Sri Lanka, Burma and the rest of Southeast Asia. Asoka, the greatest Emperor of the Maurya Empire, was a Buddhist; for a short time Buddhism made a bid to become India's dominant faith.

Later more daring missionaries found their way past the Himalayas and carried the faith into the Far East—China, Japan, and Korea. At the same time it began to die out in its land of origin.

Today few Buddhists are to be found in India. The centers of the religion are in southeast Asia and the Far East. The original form of the faith still exists in Sri Lanka, Burma and Thailand. It survives to an extent in Kampuchea and Laos.

The Theravada (or Hinayana) Buddhism emphasizes asceticism and isolation from the world. Since the world stimulates our wrong desires and therefore our suffering, one must have as little to do with it as possible. The true believers of these lands therefore do as the faith commands, striving to accumulate merit for the next life while not worrying too much about the affairs of this world.

A fairly close relative is the Tantric Buddhism of Tibet and Mongolia. When one thinks of this school, one envisions the great Potala of Lhasa and the horde of monks formerly resided nearby. It's based upon mysticism, upon secret knowledge handed down from guru to chela, master to aspirant. The aspirant learns the uses of mantras (magic chants), yantras (magic symbols) and mudras (ritual gestures).

The great man of Tantric Buddhism is the Dalai Lama, who in effect ruled Tibet before the Chinese conquest of 1950. Theoretically the Dalai Lama never dies; the moment the living Lama ceases to breathe his successor is born somewhere. Thus upon the death of the old Lama a thorough search is carried on throughout the Buddhist world to find the new incarnation.

The current Dalai Lama fled from Tibet in 1959 and has lived for many years in India as a refugee from the Chinese conquerors. Though the burden of Chinese repression has lightened in Tibet, believers must make do as they can under less than optimal conditions.

Theravada asceticism and Tantric mysticism didn't go over very well among the more worldly Chinese and Japanese. Forms of Buddhism were devised in the cold North that were more compatible with the character of the potential new converts.

The Pure Land, Zen and Nichiren Shoshu sects of Buddhism are variants of Mahayana Buddhism, now the most numerous sect of this religion.

Mahayana Buddhism has adopted the notion of the Bodhisattva. If you live an exceptionally devout life on this earth, you'll not only earn your own way into Nirvana but you'll also acquire the capacity to pass merit on to others and pave their way thence.

Believers in Pure Land Buddhism say that one may escape the wheel of Samsara in one lifetime by repeating, as often as possible, the phrase O Mi T'o Fo (if they're Chinese) or Amida Buddha (if they're Japanese). Both are a shortened form of the name of Amitabha, one of the noted Bodhisattvas. By repeating his name one induces Amitabha to dispense his merit to the petitioner so that when the believer dies the soul will be transmitted to the pure land, where there's eternal peace and plenty and the soul becomes one with Amitabha and the Universe.

The Jodo Chinshu form of Buddhism found in the United States is a variant of Pure Land.

According to Zen (Japanese) or Ch'an (Chinese) Buddhism the way to escape the wheel of Samsara is through enlightenment. One attains enlightenment through meditation on Koans—paradoxical or nonsensical riddles. (An example: Everyone knows the sound of two hands clapping. What is the sound of one hand clapping?)

The best time to do this meditating (Zazen) is while one is alone sitting in a ritually prescribed position. One must not do this for many hours of the day; it's best to spend most of one's time on manual tasks. Meditation without accompanying work isn't effective.

Enlightenment doesn't come through any logical process. It strikes like the sudden bolt of lightning. When one has achieved Satori (the Japanese term for this enlightenment) the meditation has served its purpose.

There are two schools of Zen, the Rinzai and the Soto. Rinzai masters mercilessly harass their pupils, believing that they will achieve Satori only if subjected to relentless pressure. The Soto believe in the efficacy of solitary Zazen; the novices are spared the psychic violence of Rinzai.

Nichiren Shoshu Buddhism was founded by Nichiren Daishonin in Japan, when he submitted to the Regent of the country in the year 1260 his work, the *Rissho Ankoku Ron (On the Securing of the Peace of the Land Through the Propagation of the True Buddhism)*. There are, according to Richard Causton in his work *Nichiren Shoshu Buddhism*, four obligations of the true believer. These are:

(1) Faith

(2) Practice for self
(3) Practice for others
(4) Study

Faith consists of cultivating the determination to achieve enlightenment through practice.

Practice for self consists of performing the Gongyo twice a day. This ritual, performed before the Gohonzon (the scroll given to new members of the faith) consists of reciting aloud two chapters of the Buddha's Lotus Sutra, the nearest thing to holy scripture the faith possesses, and chanting the phrase Nam Myoho Renge Kyo "to your heart's content." This Japanese phrase Causton translates, "I devote my life to the mystic law of the Lotus Sutra."

Practice for others consists of seeking to acquaint them with the blessings of Nichiren Shoshu Buddhism, and seeking to make the world a better place in which to live by conquering one's evil impulses and encouraging others to conquer theirs.

Study consists of mastering the commandments of the Lotus Sutra and the wisdom of Nichiren Daishonin's commentaries upon them. Thus Nichiren Buddhists are activists. The chant of Nam Myoho Renge Kyo isn't a plea to a Bodhisattva for salvation; it's a method of strengthening the soul for the battle to seek converts to the faith and to make the world a better place.

Nichiren Shoshu Buddhists participate in Japanese electoral politics as a political party—the Komeito (Clean Government Party). It is presently the third-largest political grouping in the Japanese House of Representatives. It has never participated in government, though it's a part of the opposition coalition controlling the House of Councillors, the upper house of Japan's parliament.

The Komeito would probably have become part of the governing coalition had the opposition deprived Japan's Liberal Democrats of their majority in the House of Representatives in the February 1990 elections. However, the Liberal Democrats held on to their House of Representatives majority while Komeito lost several of its seats (though it remained the third-largest party in the land).

The major organization of this sect is the Soka Gakkai (Value-Creating Academic Society is how Trevor Ling translates the term in his work *A History of Religion East and West*). It has numerous members in Japan and has established organizations of converts in many nations outside Japan (including Great Britain and the United States). These groups provide support to their members and to proselytizing efforts.

Thus the variants of Mahayana Buddhism have to a large extent made peace with this world, preaching a doctrine whereby people can strive to make this life better in economic terms while at the same time accumulating merit for the next life.

Far Eastern Religions

Confucianism. Confucianism generally calls forth a vision of a sharp-eyed gray-haired wispy-bearded Chinese sage looking out over an orderly obedient world. It's really erroneous to mention Confucianism in the context of religion; it is rather a philosophical system.

Kung Fu Tse (Confucius is the Latinized form of his name) lived during the sixth century B.C. over two centuries before China became a nation. In his writings he created a blueprint for an orderly society, based upon a pervasive concept of duty. There are five basic human relationships:

(1) Father-Son
(2) Elder Brother-Younger Brother
(3) Husband-Wife
(4) Ruler-Subject
(5) Friend-Friend

Each of these relationships involves the performance of duty on both sides. The superior human being is expected to perform these duties without compulsion. If all people behave as civilized persons carrying out their obligations to the state, society and other human beings, there will be little need for law or for the use of force by some people against others. Society will need no activist government.

This world view became the cornerstone of Chinese society and culture shortly after the establishment of the united empire and still greatly influences non–Communist Chinese societies and nations of Chinese culture wherever in the world they're located.

Taoism. The vision Taoism inspires is that of the dreamy-eyed man sitting on a rock and watching the world go by, without a care in the world. This is the one native Chinese religion that has some influence on earth.

The founder is known only as Lao Tze, "The Old One." Tradition says he's the author of the holy scripture of the faith—the Tao Te Ching—"The Book of the Way."

If humanity is to find peace in the world, it must follow the Tao—the Way. The Way is essentially the path of least resistance. Water, says the Tao Te Ching, is one of the most powerless of substances. It won't stand up and fight you. You strike it and it doesn't resist you. You block its flow and it sneakily finds a way to get around you.

Yet, it always strives mightily to reach the sea, and eventually it gets there. It always attains its objective. Its way of getting what it wants is the best way.

Thus, if someone or some thing obstructs the path ahead, don't fight them. There's got to be a way around. Strive diligently to find it—and, when you've found it, move on. This way you eventually get what you want without adding to the world's score of strife and injury.

Originally Taoism was a gentle faith of nonviolence. It's now acquired a gloss of mysticism and magical practices, but it's very much alive as a belief system in the non–Communist parts of the Chinese world.

Shinto

When the knowledgeable think of Shinto they may think of one of those unique Japanese paintings of the cloud-draped mountain with the odd-shaped pine trees in the foreground, and perhaps a cloak-wrapped monk walking past.

Shinto is the Japanese pronunciation of the Chinese characters Shen — spirit — and Tao — way or road. Thus the literal meaning of the term is "Way of the Spirits."

The native Japanese religion, Shinto is still a powerful influence in its native land.

To the Japanese everything, animate and inanimate, has its kami or spirit. Trees and mountains have kami, as do the gods that created heaven and earth and the ancestors of the worshiper. If people will live in harmony with their surroundings they must live in harmony with this multitude of kami. Shinto provides the mechanism for doing this.

This explains why the seemingly so urbanized Japanese still retain their love of nature. Shinto preserves urban people's contact with mountains and trees and wind and rain.

The kami command that worshipers keep their environment free from physical pollution. This helps to explain why Japanese strive very hard to keep their immediate surroundings clean.

Some Westerners believe that Shinto commands Japanese to worship their Emperor as a god. This was not a part of the belief in the beginning, and never was until Shinto became the Japanese state religion in 1882. As a part of the effort of Japanese militarists to indoctrinate their people in the necessity of fighting to create a powerful empire, the notion of the divine Emperor was grafted onto the faith and remained a part of it until the surrender of 1945. Shortly thereafter the Emperor Hirohito announced to his subjects that he was not a god, and never had been one.

Thus the ancient Japanese faith reverted to its original form, in which it still exerts great influence.

Summary. Those Americans who consider religious faith to be irrelevant and old-fashioned superstition should be aware of the fact that many people around the world disagree.

Earthly religion is found in many dissimilar packages, but those who must deal with the faithful will find their task much more fruitful if they make an effort to understand the faith.

Chapter 7

Other Cultural Considerations

Calendars and holidays. Most of the world uses the Western Gregorian calendar to measure months and years. This fact is another indication of how Western culture has come to dominate some aspects of the life of our planet.

Two celestial rhythms have been used as the basis for most human calendars: the four annual seasons (the revolution of the earth around the sun) and the phases of the moon (the revolution of the moon around the earth). The time span from new moon to new moon covers 28 or 29 days, roughly a month. The time span from summer solstice (the longest day of the year) to summer solstice is 365 + days, or one year.

The difficulty for calendar-construction purposes is that twelve lunar cycles pass in approximately 354 days, not 365. The solar year does not equal a number of complete lunar months.

The Egyptians used a solar calendar. They calculated that the solar year is 365 days long, so they devised a calendar of twelve 30-day months and added five festival days at the end (not a part of any month) to balance things out. Since the solar year is 365 + days long, however, this calendar lost synchronization with the seasons.

The original Roman calendar consisted of four 31-day months, seven 29-day months and one 28-day month (February). Since this added up to only 355 days, they added a thirteenth month of 22 or 23 days every second year. By Julius Caesar's time this calendar was out of synchonization with the seasons.

Caesar put into effect the Julian calendar in 46 B.C. This calendar was almost identical to ours; it contained our four 30-day months, seven 31-day months, and 28-day February. It sought to keep pace with the seasons by adding a 366th day (February 29) to every fourth year (leap year).

The Julian year was a bit too long. By the sixteenth century the calendar was again out of sync with the seasons. In 1582 Pope Gregory XIII put into effect in the Roman Catholic world the Gregorian calendar; it dropped ten days out of that year (the day after October 4 was October 15) and made all years ending in 00 non-leap years except years divisible by 400. Protestant Europe and Russia at first refused to abide by Gregory's decree. Protestant Ger-

117

many and the Dutch Republic adopted the new calendar in 1698. The English (and their colonies) went along in 1751; Russia remained on the Julian calendar until after Lenin's revolution, changing in 1918. (Thus, though the Soviets celebrate the anniversary of Lenin's revolution on November 7, their history books still call it the October Revolution because it happened on October 25, 1917, of the Julian calendar, in effect at the time.)

As mentioned above, most of the world now measures days, months and years by the Gregorian calendar.

The Islamic peoples, however, don't bother to make the lunar calendar equate to the solar year. Their year consists of simply the 12 lunar months of 28 or 29 days each. The month begins with the rising of the new moon; thus the Islamic day begins at sunset. The Islamic year is approximately 354 days long, roughly 12 days shorter than the Western year.

The Jews and Chinese also use the lunar calendar. However, they add intercalary (extra) days and months on occasion so that the calendar always matches the annual seasons.

National holidays of course vary from country to country. The French holiday is July 14, the day the Bastille fell to the Paris mob in 1789. The Swiss holiday is August 1, the day the cantons of Uri, Schwyz and Unterwalden formed the first Swiss union in 1291.

May 1 — May Day — is Labor Day in most of Europe. December 26, Boxing Day in England and St. Stephen's Day on the Continent, is just as much a holiday as Christmas. January 2, St. Berchtold's Day on the Continent, is as much a holiday as New Year's.

In some countries Christmas gifts are exchanged on December 6, St. Nicholas' Day. In others the magic day is January 6 — Dreikonigstag — the day of the Three Kings.

Mardi Gras — Fat Tuesday — is a day for revelling in many cities in addition to New Orleans. The Carnaval of Rio de Janeiro makes the festival of New Orleans almost insignificant by comparison. In German-speaking lands the evening before Ash Wednesday is called Fassnacht; in Basel and other cities people don masks and fancy costumes and perform pranks they wouldn't dare atTtempt on the other 364 days of the year.

The first month of the Jewish year is Tishri, which begins in September or October of our calendar. The Jewish New Year, Rosh Hashanah, is celebrated on the first and second of Tishri.

The beginning of the Chinese lunar year triggers four days of celebration. The date of the New Year is the day of the first new moon between the Gregorian dates of January 21 and February 19.

The first month of the Islamic calendar is Muharram, which currently begins in August of the Gregorian year. The most important individual day of observance is the tenth of Dhul-al-Hijja, last month of the year, called Id al-Adha, Feast of the Sacrifice. This day is the high point of the annual pilgrimage to Mecca. The ninth month of the Islamic calendar is Ramadan, during which (as mentioned earlier) the true believer must fast between daybreak and dark.

Clock time. Ancient people knew nothing of the precise measurements of time that we take for granted. The Romans divided the day and the night into an equal number of hours, but since they had no precise way of measuring them the length of the hour varied with the season; in winter night hours were longer than day hours and in summer the reverse was the case.

Benedictine monks were the first Westerners to invent the schedule — the notion that on a certain hour of a day one must perform a specified activity. They were the originators of modern time discipline.

They also invented the first mechanical clocks to enable themselves to better abide by their schedules. Eventually the clock emerged from behind monastery walls in the thirteenth and fourteenth centuries to begin the subjection of lay people to its dominion. In the fourteenth and fifteenth centuries it measured hours only, large clock towers announcing their passage by clanging bells. Then the bells began to announce the passage of quarter-hours. By the seventeenth century clocks were measuring minutes; by the eighteenth century the second hand had made its appearance.

By 1800 each of the world's localities had its own time. Before the days of fast travel and communication it didn't much matter if New York and Philadelphia time didn't coincide to the second. But with the coming of the railway, telegraph and telephone non-uniform time was a hindrance to commercial activity.

National governments began to take steps to impose time uniformity throughout their domains; Great Britain imposed one uniform time throughout the United Kingdom, while the United States created the familiar Eastern, Central, Mountain and Pacific time zones in 1883.

Finally, in 1884, an international conference created the present planetary uniform time zones, assuring that when it's noon in London it's 7 A.M. in New York and 3 P.M. in Moscow.

Governmental tinkerers in a sense still tamper with the uniformity of the world's time. Many nations and parts of nations move their clocks ahead an hour in the spring to create daylight savings time (or summer time, as some Europeans call it) in order to give working folks an extra hour of daylight after the end of the daily chores, moving it back again in early autumn. Since some nations don't follow this custom, and since those who do don't change their clocks on the same day, there exists a bit of time confusion during summer.

The times of astronomical events (such as the annual equinoxes and solstices) are stated in almanacs in Greenwich Mean Time (the clock time at the Greenwich Observatory in England). The GMT day begins at midnight London time even though it's only 7 P.M. in New York City at that hour.

Time attitudes. With accurate clocks and watches our culture has been able to harness time—or perhaps it's made it possible for time to harness us!

The efficiency expert uses a stopwatch to time assemblyline operations in the factory. If there's a way to insert and tighten a screw in 30 seconds, that's better than a method which does it in 40, since more screws may be inserted per day using the faster method.

With ultra-modern time-measuring devices we now time Olympic ski racers to the hundredth of a second, and luge racers to the thousandth. The most minute fraction of a second counts. Thus in the 1972 Winter Olympics in Sapporo, Japan, Danielle Debernard of France finished the two runs of the women's slalom in 1:31.26 (one minute thirty-one and twenty-six one hundredths of a second). Barbara Cochran of the United States did it in 1:31.24, taking home the gold medal. For lack of two one hundredths of a second Debernard had to settle for the silver.

The dawning age of the computer has carried precise time measurement much farther; the time needed for computers to perform their tasks is measured in nanoseconds (billionths of a second). In such a timeframe the amount of time required to snap one's fingers (a half-second) consumes the immense quantity of 500 million nanoseconds.

We insist upon beginning our work day at eight or nine in the morning and ending it at five in the evening. In the interest of this efficient beginning and ending we create huge traffic jams in our cities because so many workers have to get into and out of a small area in a short time. We resent the hours spent breathing exhaust fumes while we wait for autos stacked up ahead to get moving. But we accept the essential waste of private time so that our public time—the time we spend working—is used efficiently.

This attitude toward time is uniquely Western. In some respects Americans are the most time-conscious of the world's people. Americans were the first to use assembly lines in large-scale manufacturing operations. It was an American, Frederick J. Taylor, who was the first efficiency expert. Many American employers allow employees only 45 minutes for lunch because it's inefficient to allot more time for lunch than is required to eat.

In so many aspects of our culture time is precious—time is not to be wasted—time is money!

European attitudes toward time are similar to ours, but not identical. We Americans don't particularly like it when someone is five minutes late for an appointment, but we're more accepting of it now than we were 20 years ago. To a German or a German Swiss, being five minutes late is inexcusable.

When American planes and buses depart a few minutes late we don't mind too much. But if the Swiss train is scheduled to leave the Zurich railway station at 12:06 P.M. it leaves at 12:06, not at 12:07.

Many European businesses close for lunch at 12:00 noon and reopen at

2 P.M. North Europeans still like to eat the day's big meal at noon; they want the time to enjoy it and to rest for awhile afterward.

In Spain the lunch hour is even longer; the siesta may last for three hours. Shops may then remain open into the evening hours to make up for it.

Americans criticize this custom because it's inefficient and wasteful of time. Some Europeans are also critical; in larger European cities American lunch hours are becoming the vogue.

In industrialized areas of non–Western culture such as Japan, Taiwan and Singapore Western time discipline has become part of the culture to a degree. Otherwise, high industrialization seems almost impossible.

It wasn't until the onset of the Industrial Revolution and the factory method of production that the huge majority of Westerners were subjected to modern time discipline. Adults reared on farms who came to the city to work in factories never mastered it; they wouldn't give up their habit of working at their own pace and taking breaks when it pleased them. The second generation of such workers were subjected to time discipline as children; from then on the new order was an integral part of our culture.

In areas of non–Western culture people don't view time as we do. Lack of punctuality isn't a vice; if you show up for an appointment somewhere around the time for which it was made that's good enough. Or if the job's finished somewhere near the time you promised that's sufficient.

The non–Western sense of time is attuned to the natural cycles of nature. The non–Westerner's time frame may well be the alternation of day and night, and the changing of the seasons. These changes impose severe discipline upon work schedules, especially for those involved in agriculture. Non-Westerners may work just as hard or harder than Westerners, but they're very likely not to do it according to a rigid schedule measured in hours, minutes and seconds.

It is as difficult to accustom Third World peoples to the rigid commands of the timeclock as it was to accustom Westerners to it a century and a half ago.

The majority of the world's people aren't future-oriented as we are. They live in the present and let the future take care of itself. One of the most difficult tasks of a Western manager operating in a non–Western culture is to indoctrinate the natives with a sense of Western time. Such discipline often doesn't come easy.

Education. Education of children in public schools is another earth-shaking invention of Western culture. Throughout most of human history educating children has been a family responsibility. It's consisted mainly of teaching the children the culture of the social group and the skills necessary for survival.

Reading and writing haven't been essential elements of education until recently. One may learn social customs without reading about them or writing them down, and literacy isn't necessary to work successfully with one's hands.

Throughout most of history only the elite learned to read and write, because only those who kept records or dealt in ideas needed such skills. Besides, in the absence of cheap paper and printing from movable type all written material was handwritten and therefore very scarce and expensive.

To be sure, universities have existed since the Middle Ages in Europe. Here one could study law, medicine, theology, mathematics or other learned subjects. Similar institutions existed in the Islamic world, such as Al-Azhar in Cairo. There pious Muslims could study the doctrines of Islamic religion and law. In China children with intellectual potential were encouraged to study the classical works of the culture, and those who passed the periodic government examinations on these obtained admission to the mandarinate.

The inventions of cheap paper and printing from movable type caused the literacy explosion within the Western world of the late fifteenth century. From then on written material has been abundant and relatively cheap. As a culture we became fascinated with abstract ideas; as the Industrial Revolution gained speed more and more economic activity came to involve reading and writing. We've now progressed so far in this direction that illiterates—those who can't read and write—have trouble finding an economic niche in society.

Universal literacy is essential to the development of a modern economy. Therefore all developed nations have public education systems under which several years of education are mandatory for all children, and additional years are available to those qualified to benefit by it.

Originally American and European educational systems were very similar. Both were designed to teach the teachable as much as they could learn in the shortest possible time.

However, during the twentieth century the systems began to grow apart. Americans increased the number of years of compulsory education while Europeans lagged behind. Americans strove to make university education available to the maximum number of qualified people; Europeans continued to reserve it for a small elite. Americans began to make training in ways of earning a living part of public education, but Europeans continued to feel that this wasn't a legitimate part of the public education process.

Americans insisted upon maximum pedagogical equality in the classroom, even if this meant holding back the talented for the benefit of the average or untalented. Europeans resisted this trend. Americans pioneered the concept that the main purpose of public education is life adjustment—training in getting along in society—not necessarily the absorption of academic knowledge. Europeans felt that life adjustment is the task of parents, not schools. Americans made competitive athletics an immense part of their educational program while Europeans did not.

Only in one area do the Swiss and some other Europeans stoop to education in life adjustment. After the completion of their nine years of compulsory education young women are strongly encouraged to undertake a year of study in a special school for learning the skills of homemaking. Here they are introduced to the rudiments of cooking and baking, washing and ironing, sewing and mending. Here too they get very basic sex education with no admixture of Freud; the various consequences of indulgence are described with clinical accuracy. The course is topped off with indoctrination in the skills of motherhood—how to hold a child in your arms, how to feed it, how to dress it when you take it out into the world. (This sort of life adjustment isn't of interest to most American educators. Many Europeans wax indignant over the ways American mothers mishandle their young children in public.)

In the United States the usual academic progression is six years of primary school, three years of middle school (or junior high school), and three years of high school. Everyone spends a year in a "grade" and in many areas automatically passes on to the next regardless of academic progress. One enters the first grade at age six and usually must remain in school until age 16 or longer (meaning in essence 10 years of school for all). Immense pressure is brought to bear on pupils not to drop out at age 16, because the economy offers little employment opportunity to those lacking education. The pupil graduates from high school at age 17 or 18, perhaps with a marketable blue-collar job skill, or perhaps not.

Americans desiring further education (which they'll need to get good entry jobs in a skilled trade or profession) will attend a vocational school, junior college, or university. It takes four years at the university to earn a bachelor's degree, but even this is inadequate education for some professions. In that case, several more years of education are needed to acquire a master's degree or a doctorate. Whether the American wishes to be a primary school teacher, a business manager, an engineer, a scientist or a theologian he or she will need a high school diploma plus a university degree(s).

In the average Swiss canton everyone attends primary school for six years, as in the United States. The program is strictly academic, without life adjustment leavening or organized athletics. The pupils learn as much in these six years as Americans learn in eight. After graduation from there three possibilities exist. The most talented may enter the Gymnasium, an elite school offering a very challenging academic program to prepare pupils for university study.

The moderately talented go on to the Secondary school for three years, entering a program that emphasizes foreign languages, science, mathematics and the like intended to prepare graduates to enter white-collar apprenticeship programs or the less-demanding higher education programs.

The rest go on to the Realschule, which offers a none too demanding basic program for pupils intending to enter blue-collar apprenticeship programs.

Compulsory public education ends after the ninth grade. The graduates, most 15 years of age, aren't equipped to enter the economy other than as apprentices or unskilled laborers.

Realschule graduates mostly enter blue-collar apprenticeship programs. The Secondary graduates, corresponding basically to American high school graduates, mainly enter white-collar apprenticeship programs (for retail management trainees, bank management trainees and the like) or go on to higher education programs.

They might enter the Gymnasium at a higher level if they're thinking of going on to a university. Other possibilities are technical high schools which train engineers and the like, or seminaries which train public school teachers.

Apprenticeship programs are generally three or four years in length. The apprentices earn small salaries while learning a job skill from the bottom up, partly through on-the-job training and partly through practical classroom instruction. Upon graduation they're qualified for entry-level positions in their trades. Thus they become productive members of society at age 20 or thereabouts.

The potential schoolteachers leaving the seminary and the potential engineers leaving the high school are prepared to enter on-the-job training programs in their professions.

The Gymnasium graduate knows as much as the holder of an American bachelor's degree when upon graduation at age 18; the Matura is the equivalent of the American BA.

When Gymnasium graduates go on to a university they're doing the equivalent of American graduate-level work. They'll study law, medicine, science or one of the liberal arts and will emerge with a doctorate at about age 22.

The European system trains people to be economically productive sooner, but that's all. (That's all it should do, most Europeans say.) American students come out of their system with more social skills; they're at ease with other people, they probably know how to dance and how to drive an automobile. In terms of academic knowledge they're likely to lag behind Europeans of their age; they may well be functionally illiterate.

Though many Americans learned skilled trades through apprenticeships a century ago, such programs have become relatively rare in our country today. Child labor laws close many jobs to persons under the age of 18 because of potential danger. Trade unions may disapprove of programs over which they have no control. Minimum wage laws require the payment of uneconomically high wages to apprentices. Our system dispenses training in blue-collar skills mostly through the public schools (vocational-training programs in high schools, community colleges or public technical institutes), expensive private trade schools or on-the-job training by employers. Hence the often-heard American lament that there are too few really skilled plumbers, auto mechanics and the like in our country.

Far more Americans attend universities than do Europeans. However, the academic level of most material taught at the undergraduate level in our country is that of the European Gymnasium. American students put together a degree as a person assembles a jigsaw puzzle; he or she fits together courses and credit hours according to the prescribed pattern for an academic major. They do this by attending classes and passing examinations in each course. They're graded in each of these courses, and a grade-point average is the measure of progress and precocity as a student. Advisors shepherd students through every step of the process, since American university administrators and parents assume that students lack the intelligence to navigate through the academic maze on their own. Their academic transcripts will show a grade-point average figured to four or five decimal places; somehow Americans figure that it makes a difference whether the graduate's GPA is 3.0007 or 2.9999.

European university students know that to acquire a degree they must pass examinations on certain bodies of knowledge. They may acquire the information to pass these tests by attending lectures or by studying under tutors or through reading or whatever. It's their responsibility to know what they must learn; it's their responsibility to learn it; it's their responsibility to take the comprehensive examinations at the end of the academic preparation and to pass them. It's assumed that they have the maturity to accomplish all this on their own, without anyone in authority holding their hand.

Graduates from Oxford University in England have no grade-point average; they simply graduate with honor, high second, low second, or third. The high second is above average but not an honor student; the low second is somewhat below average; the third may have barely passed the exams. However, the British don't concern themselves about different gradations of high seconds; they're concerned with the program from which candidates graduated and the disciplines in which they passed their examinations.

There are fewer universities in Europe because their function in the educational scheme of things is narrower; the student bodies of these universities are usually small by American standards.

In some European states education beyond the secondary-school level isn't at public expense. As a result the cost of advanced education discourages some talented young people from pursuing it. In others the state will pay for as much education as the student can absorb; here lack of money is no barrier to a higher education.

The Japanese system is in a sense a hybrid American-European-Chinese system. It's European in the sense that it's totally academic, with no room for life-adjustment. It's American in the sense that large numbers of Japanese (relatively speaking) attend universities. It's Chinese in the sense that it emphasizes rote memorization over problem-solving, as did the ancient Chinese examinations by which members of the mandarinate were chosen.

It's more intensive than even most West European systems. The Japanese pupil attends school 240 days per year (in contrast to the usual American 180).

Admission to higher levels of the system depends upon passing very difficult examinations; the Japanese student attending an academic high school may spend many evening hours attending extra cram courses to prepare for the university entrance exams. Such courses are supposed to aid in the memorization of the huge numbers of facts that one must know in order to pass these exams.

Those who score highest will achieve admission to one of Japan's elite universities (such as the University of Tokyo). Those who score somewhat lower will qualify for admission to one of the country's secondary institutions of higher learning. Some will not qualify for admission to any university, and will thus not be able to obtain the credential necessary to obtain prestigious, well-paying employment.

Japanese university life isn't as strenuous and competitive as is that in high school. Students who apply themselves moderately will graduate. Only those with degrees from Tokyo University and other elite institutions will be hired by top-level Japanese corporations; graduates from secondary institutions must settle for less-promising employment.

Pupils who don't attend academic high school will go to a vocational high school instead. Here they will learn a valuable job skill on the most up-to-date equipment. Many of these graduates are hired by employers before graduation; thus they graduate immediately from school into the workaday world.

The Soviet Union too emphasizes academics. The talented are assisted to obtain as much education as they can absorb. Large numbers of Russians too (comparatively speaking) attend universities. The monetary worries of Soviet university students are minimal since the state pays all the costs and provides some pocket money to boot.

In underdeveloped countries governments find it difficult to obtain the money and trained manpower to establish systems of comprehensive public education. It's one thing to set up and maintain schools in the cities but it's quite another to do so in the hinterlands. The basic struggle to raise the national literacy rate can be a difficult one.

Secondary schools may exist only in larger cities; in poorer Third World nations universities may not exist at all. Where they do exist their graduates may have difficulty finding a place in the nation's economy.

In the more advanced Third World countries universities serve the same purposes as they do in Europe, offering education in law and the liberal arts. Medical schools are small where they exist at all, because the cost of equipping and maintaining them is high. The science faculties are apt to be small and ill-equipped for the same reason.

Political activism is relatively rare among American university students for three reasons: academic duties take up much time; many American students hold down part- or full-time jobs; and organized social activities consume so much time and energy.

European students are more likely to get involved in politics because organized social activities are rare to non-existent and because they tend to take more interest in public affairs. Third-world students are the same.

In many underdeveloped countries the national economy doesn't develop well-paying jobs for all university graduates; the students may know very well that they'll have to struggle to find a place in the economic sun. They'll feel that this state of affairs is unjust, and they may well want to rearrange things to create more places for themselves. Under-employed intellectuals are too often the tinder in which the fire of revolutionary movements begins to blaze.

Where there isn't much industrialization, facilities for training people in marketable blue-collar skills will be minimal.

The nation must in essence pull itself up by its bootstraps in creating an educational system. Alien investors in the economies of such countries may help by providing basic education and job skill training to natives. Government may later require that the aliens train natives to assume more responsible positions within the organization; those so trained may then be able to assist government in establishing more advanced educational programs.

In the interest of national stability, the number of educated people in the nation shouldn't run too far ahead of the capacity of the national economy to absorb them.

It seems that only nations of highest development, such as the United States, can afford educational systems emphasizing life adjustment and education in social graces. Only nations as prosperous as the U.S. tolerate public schools which turn out the percentage of functional illiterates ours do. Only the U.S. feels that it can afford to spend so much on public education for such relatively meager academic return.

Without national prosperity wealth and leisure don't exist for such things as enjoyment of athletics, social dancing and public-financed driver education; thus Third World educational systems develop along European lines.

Social hierarchy. Americans take pride in what we call our classless society. It doesn't matter who your parents are, runs our classical wisdom; if you have what it takes to get ahead, you can do it in America. The road to the top is open to all with talent.

Of course this isn't 100 percent true; it does matter who your parents are. There are more doors open to the sons and daughters of rich parents. Money speaks loudly in America, as it does everywhere. Rockefellers, Fords and Mellons are as respected here as are dukes and counts abroad.

Still, Americans are among the most informal of the world's peoples. Here we call the boss, the doctor and the lawyer by their first names. Employers and employees mingle at company picnics and enjoy life's good things together. People from all stations of life rub shoulders in all kinds of places.

In situations where one person has authority over another, American conventional wisdom says that it's better to persuade than to command. If possible, we convince subordinates to do what we require instead of flatly ordering them to do it. It's better to make them obey because they want to, rather than because they must.

The English language in a sense assists our informality; we address all others as "you." Despite this, the English are among the most class-conscious of Westerners. The boss is always "Mister Jones," and seldom do employers and employees associate socially. All people in authority have titles, and must be addressed by them.

The continued existence of titled nobility insures a stratification of English society that Americans find rather repulsive, and there are gradations of social class that don't depend upon nobility at all.

In German your boss will always be "Herr Schmidt," never "Hans." The doctor is always Herr Doktor, and his wife Frau Doktor; inevitably the wife takes the professional title of her husband.

Even in democratic Switzerland all people in authority have titles and must be addressed by them. Such relatively insignificant people as the postmaster and the police officer must be accorded great respect because they're government employees.

All over Europe it matters very much who your parents are when you seek to advance in the world. Careers are to an extent open to talent; but the child of the lawyer has a great advantage over the child of the assembly-line worker. The door from lower class to upper is open, but very narrow. It's difficult to force your way through, but possible.

In Europe it's still acceptable for those in authority to use the manners of the Prussian Feldwaibel — senior army sergeant. The master may well still command the apprentice to do a task and complain loudly if it isn't done. If you don't scream at your underlings they may forget who's boss! However, the role of persuasion is growing in Europe as the role of command is diminishing. The Dutch Army is completely unionized, for instance; if the private feels that a sergeant's order is unreasonable, the private might complain to the union steward about it.

Since Americans tend to think of each other as social equals, we're apt to resent rather bitterly having to accept orders from another. "Who's she to be ordering me around?" we're apt to ask ourselves.

In Czarist Russia class barriers were very high. Those who held high positions in government were mostly titled nobles. Economic development came late; possession of money was only beginning to create status at the time of Lenin's revolution. It was very difficult for the children of workers or farmers to rise.

The Russian Communists like to boast that they changed this; that in Soviet society class differences have disappeared and that the talent of the individual is all that matters. Only to an extent is this true.

The Soviet system does give breaks to the deserving children of workers and peasants; Mikhail Gorbachev's father was an agricultural worker. Many others holding high positions in the state have risen from humble origins. However, the system has created a new ruling class of great privilege—the Nomenklatura. Parents of this class strive with might and main to pass on their status to their children; more often than not, they succeed.

Ancient Chinese society too was stratified into classes, but one unique factor, the mandarinate, kept the stratification from being permanent. The mandarinate was the class of bureaucrats who governed the realm on behalf of the Emperor. It was recruited from all classes by written examination. Any Chinese male could qualify for a post in the bureaucracy by passing a written examination on his knowledge of the classic literature of the nation. The son of the poorest farmer could take part. Families would make great economic sacrifices to permit talented sons to study the classics; the honor to son and family was immense if he passed the exam. Once one became a mandarin, the possibility existed of rising to the point of being able to advise the Emperor on government policy.

The power of the mandarinate was broken by the revolution of 1912; power passed into the hands of people who controlled guns or money. The Communist revolution in turn destroyed the power of these.

Under Chairman Mao the Chinese system strove hard to minimize class distinctions. All but the mightiest were compelled to do manual labor for a part of every year, so that they'd not forget what it was like to be one of the toilers. This has been abolished; the mighty can better serve the people by performing their usual work 12 months a year.

In Japan those who controlled armies—the Daimyo or territorial lords—and those who wielded weapons—the Samurai—were the elite of the state, along with the nobles who served the Emperor. Moneyed men broke into the charmed circle during the Tokugawa period.

The Samurai lost their privileged position during the period of modernization, as did the Daimyo; professional military men and a moneyed elite ran things until after World War II.

Now the moneyed families are most important, but possession of a university degree provides admittance into the lower levels of the corridors of power. The excellence and openness of the Japanese educational system give opportunity to the talented.

Indian society was at one time organized into the tightest class system on earth. Traditional Indian culture divided people into five castes:

(1) Brahmins—originally priests.

(2) Kshatriya—originally warriors.

(3) Vaisya—originally merchants.

(4) Sudra—originally laborers.

(5) Harijan (a term devised by Mahatma Gandhi)—people of no caste—the Untouchables.

It's thought that the system was imposed by the Indo-Europeans upon the conquered Dravidians at the dawn of Indian culture. The rank order of the castes gives an idea of the values of the society.

Each caste was divided into many sub-castes, each of which made its living in a specified way. No member was allowed to marry outside his or her sub-caste, nor could one make a living in any way not authorized to sub-caste members.

The penalty for violating caste rules was loss of caste—expulsion. This turned the person into an Untouchable, fit only to do the most degraded work of the society.

The only way to escape the straitjacket of the caste system was to accept conversion to another religion. This is why many Hindu Indians accepted conversion to Islam or to Sikhism.

The government of independent India outlawed the caste system and made discrimination on the basis of caste illegal. However, you can't necessarily change such a deeply embedded culture by enacting law; the system is still engraved upon Hindu hearts. Caste still matters in India.

Though Islam prides itself upon the equality it accords its believers, class distinctions are common in Islamic countries. Who your parents are is most important. In addition, non-Muslims occupy positions of legal and social inferiority in these lands.

Class distinctions exist also in Africa. Here they can be based upon intratribal differences; some tribes recognize something akin to European nobility among their members. They may also be based upon tribal membership or ancestry.

Thus, in Kenya members of the Kikuyu and Luo tribes dominate the government; therefore these are given preference for government positions. In Zambia the Bemba tribe holds a similarly powerful position, while the Shona dominate Zimbabwe.

In the Hispanic world class distinctions are strong. A fairly small elite circle has run the economies and politics of most Latin American lands and will probably continue to do so, barring Marxist-Leninist revolution.

Distasteful as social hierarchy is to so many Americans, it's a fact of life to be dealt with abroad.

Personal names. The names by which people are known tell us something about human cultures. It wasn't too many centuries ago that Western people were known only by their given names—family names are a relatively recent invention in our culture.

The most common English family name is Johnson, which simply means "son of John." Seven hundred years ago Peter, the son of John, would have been known as Peter Johnson. Peter's son Edward, grandson of John, would have been known as Edward Peterson. The Norman conquerors of England brought another patronymic; Thomas the illegitimate son of William was known as Thomas Fitzwilliam. The patronymic would of course identify the person's father, but it wouldn't serve to identify his more remote ancestors. Thus government required that persons adopt family names.

Many English family names are derived from patronymics like those mentioned above (Robertson, Williamson, Fitzwalter, Fitzjames). Others derive from common adjectives (Long, Short, Black, Brown, White, Green). Others derive from places (York, Chester, Bristol). Still others derive from names of animals (Sparrow, Roebuck, Hawke, Bullock).

Upon marriage the English-speaking wife takes the name of her husband; thus when Mary Brown marries Sam Johnson she becomes Mary Johnson. Nowadays she may still call herself Mary Brown if she wishes, or she might choose to be known as Mary Brown Johnson. If she uses both surnames, her maiden name comes before her husband's family name.

English-speaking parents generally bestow two given names upon their children—a first name and a middle name. Usually the middle name is ignored, or only the initial is used. Sometimes the person chooses to be known by the middle name only, or by the initial of the first name followed by the middle name.

In England a person might bear two or more surnames. When a surname is about to die out for lack of male sons of its last holder, the husband of a daughter of the last holder might adopt it. Thus, Mary Londoner has no brothers and her father is the last known bearer of the Londoner name. Mary marries Thomas Barry Kent. Thomas may adopt the Londoner name to keep it alive, calling himself Thomas Barry Kent Londoner. Their son Walter Donald will call himself Walter Donald Kent Londoner, thus assuring that the Londoner name survives for at least one more generation.

Most Western family names are derived from the same sources as the English. The English Taylor has its equivalent in Italian Sarto, German Schneider and Hungarian Szabo. English Cook has its equivalent in German Koch and Dutch and Danish Kok. English Carpenter has its equivalents in French Charpentier, German Schreiner, and Dutch Timmerman. English Butcher equals French Boucher and German Fleischer. English Baker equals French Boulanger, German Baecker, Dutch Bakker, and Hungarian Pek. English Miller equals French Meunier and German Mueller. English Smith equals German Schmidt, French Lefevre, Italian Ferrari, and Polish Kowalski.

Some Scottish and Irish surnames may reflect membership in a clan (O'Brien, McGuire, MacGregor). These are among the most ancient family names of our culture.

Jewish names originally consisted of a given name and a patronymic. Thus, the author of the apocryphal biblical book of Ecclesiasticus is known to us as Jesus ben Sirach—Jesus, the son of Sirach. In German-speaking lands, various governments assigned family names to their Jewish subjects 200 years ago and earlier; many of these family names (Edelstein, Rosenblum, Grunbaum and the like) aren't uncommon in the United States. Most of us are totally unaware of the picturesque English translations of these surnames (precious stone, roseblossom, green tree). Other families were assigned more unpleasant surnames, such as Schmutz (dirt), Staub (dust), Eselkopf (donkey head), or Schwanz (tail). Most of these have gone out of use, but one still encounters them occasionally.

Some French, Spanish, Italian or Portuguese surnames are prefaced by the syllable "de," as Charles de Gaulle or Alcide de Gasperi (the first premier of postwar Italy). A century ago the particle indicated nobility in French or Spanish; now it no longer does so. The German particle "von" served the same purpose.

In Dutch and Flemish one finds a similar particle, "van." This never indicated nobility; it simply meant "of" (as "de" and "von" also do today).

Spanish-speaking men sometimes use the surnames of both their father and mother. Thus, Gustavo Morales marries Angelina Salinas, and they become parents of a son, Pablo Esteban. Pablo may well call himself Pablo Esteban Morales Salinas. If one is to omit one of the surnames, it must be the last. Angelina, mother of Pablo, may be known as Angelina Salinas de Morales, indicating that her family name is Salinas and she's married to a Morales.

In German-speaking lands, families are listed in the telephone directory by the husband's surname followed by the wife's surname. Thus, if Hans Schmid is married to Heidi Kraus, the listing will read, "Schmid-Kraus, Hans + Heidi," followed by the trade or profession of Hans and the family address. A letter mailed to Heidi would be addressed to "Frau Heidi Schmid-Kraus," and one to Hans would be addressed to "Herr Hans Schmid-Kraus."

Russian names consist of the given name, the patronymic, and the surname. Thus, the formal name of the president of the Soviet Union is Mikhail Sergeevich Gorbachev—Mikhail, son of Sergei Gorbachev. Lenin's true name was Vladimir Ilych Ulyanov—Vladimir, son of Ilya Ulyanov. All surnames have masculine and feminine forms; males use the masculine form, females the feminine. The feminine form of a Russian surname almost always ends in "a," thus the wife of Mikhail Gorbachev is Raisa Gorbacheva.

Though the patronymic isn't used in all Slavic nations the feminine ending of women's surnames is universal. Thus, if the tennis star Martina Navratilova had a twin brother Martin, he would be called Martin Navratilov.

In Iceland family names have not yet been adopted. Peter son of Sven would still be called Peter Svenson; Helga daughter of Johan would be called Helga Johansdottir.

Arabic names, like Jewish names, originally consisted of a given name and a patronymic; thus Abraham son of Yazid would be known as Ibrahim ibn Yazid. A name could consist of a given name plus a string of patronymics, such as Gamal ibn Suleiman ibn Daoud ibn Yusuf ibn Jakub (Gamal son of

Solomon son of David son of Joseph son of Jacob). Female names also contain patronymics, as Aisha bint Suleiman (Aisha daughter of Solomon).

In earlier times an Arab could adopt a personal name to indicate the name of a son, such as Abu Habib—father of Habib. Nowadays the phrase Abu is simply a sort of honorific.

Most Arabs now use family names. Often the prefix "al" (the) is used before the family name, as in Anwar al-Sadat, the late president of Egypt, or Hafiz al-Assad, the current president of Syria. The president of Iraq was originally known as Saddam Hussein al-Takriti, but family names have now been abolished in Iraq.

In the Far East, the surname was traditionally written and spoken before given names. Thus, the surname of the founder of the People's Republic of China is Mao (Mao Tse Tung).

Chinese personal names almost always consist of three characters—a one-character surname and two one-character given names. Very few Chinese characters are used as surnames. Mandarin speakers talk of the "lao pai hsing" the old hundred surnames. Actually the hundreds of millions of Chinese use about 500 surnames. Traditionally persons with the same surname could not marry, because they were almost certainly blood relatives.

Koreans and Vietnamese also use one-syllable surnames. Koreans adhere to the Chinese custom (the surname of South Korea's president Roh Tae Woo is Roh, that of North Korea's leader Kim Il Sung is Kim). Until recently Vietnamese did likewise (Ho Chi Minh's surname was Ho). However, Ho's brilliant general Vo Nguyen Giap's family name was Giap, not Vo. The surname of South Vietnam's last vice-president, Nguyen Cao Ky, was Ky.

Japanese names are multi-syllabic. Until the end of World War II Japanese followed the Chinese custom of speaking and writing the surname first; thus the name of the founder of the Tokugawa Shogunate is often written Tokugawa Iyeyasu, as it was in the seventeenth century. In some books the name of the planner of the Japanese attack on Pearl Harbor is written Yamamoto Isoroku, as it was in 1941. Now, however, Japanese write and speak their names as we do—surname last.

Personal habits. The huge majority of human beings are right-handed. There was thought to be something wrong—even devilish—about the "southpaw." In Latin, right is dextra while left is sinistra—from dextra comes the English word dexterity, implying skill and virtue; from sinistra comes the English word sinister, implying potential evil. At one time those born left-handed were forced to become right-handed.

In the United States we now allow left-handers to be themselves, as do most European societies. However, in the Middle East and elsewhere one always eats with the right hand and uses the left to perform essential operations in the toilet. It is deemed unclean to touch food at the table with the left hand.

Americans and north Europeans stand relatively far apart while talking to each other; they resent being crowded. Japanese stand farther apart than Westerners, while Latins and Arabs like to stand close together and will often touch each other during an animated conversation. We generally find Latins and Arabs far too brash and intimate; they find us cold and distant.

Americans and north Europeans greet and part with a handshake; closer body contact is unacceptable. Japanese and other Orientals may settle for a formal bow, without body contact at all. Latins may enthusiastically embrace (the Spanish abrazo), while Slavs and Arabs may kiss on the lips. (President Jimmy Carter surprised some Americans when he and Leonid Brezhnev exchanged kisses at the end of a summit conference. The President wasn't expressing love for his Soviet counterpart; he was simply taking leave Russian-style.) Here again, we find the non–Western far too intimate; the non–Westerner finds us cold and unaffectionate.

Westerners more often than not do business at arm's length. We don't expect to be friends with our counterparts; we're not all that interested in their personal lives. Latins and Orientals on the other hand hesitate to make deals involving large sums of money with total strangers. They don't necessarily want to be friends with their associates, but they want to know them as human beings and to feel comfortable around them.

Thus, in Western — non–Western negotiations the non–Westerner may want to spend large quantities of time getting acquainted. The Westerner may feel this is an unconscionable waste of valuable time; when are we going to knock off the bull and get down to business? It pays to proceed at the non–Westerner's slow pace.

Americans and north Europeans communicate face to face almost solely in words. We pay little attention to hand gestures and body language. In contrast Latins and Arabs may talk as much with hands and bodies as they do with voices. And the context in which words are used means much to the non–Westerner. How and under what conditions words are spoken means as much as the words themselves. The subtleties of non–European interpersonal communication are often lost upon Westerners; the non–Westerner finds us cold and dense while we find the non–Westerner rather slippery.

Those who would do business successfully in Latin America must be perceived by their counterparts as "simpatico," persons who comprehend the nuances of the area's culture. The average American, or North European can't measure up.

Americans are quite likely to give gifts to acquaintances or potential business customers on impulse or as a way of building good will; there aren't many occasions when we regard the giving of a gift as mandatory. We also aren't likely to expect any sort of valuable response (though perhaps we hope for it).

Europeans on the other hand are likely to get involved in complex mental bookkeeping in this matter of gifts. When Herr Schmidt invites Herr Kraus and his family over for dinner, Herr Kraus must bring Herr Schmidt a gift to show his appreciation. Furthermore, Herr Kraus must return the invitation within a reasonable time. When Herr Schmidt accepts, he must bring Herr Kraus an appropriate gift. The debits and credits created by these exchanges of hospitality and gifts must be kept in balance.

Orientals may take this one step farther, feeling that they must return more than they were given in response.

Tips and bribes. In the United States, one tips the waiter or bartender. It's assumed that these persons will earn a large portion of their income from tips; it's lawful for an American employer to pay waiters only 60 percent of the mandated minimum wage because they'll earn the rest in this way. Good manners command that one tip at least 15 percent for good service.

In most of Western Europe, on the other hand, a 15 percent service charge is added to the restaurant check in lieu of a tip. The customer need pay no gratuity directly to the waiter, though some people tip anyway.

Outside Europe the custom on tipping will vary from country to country. In many lands of Asia, Africa and Latin America one is expected to pay virtually all providers of services, even including government employees. Without such palm-greasing life may be very difficult.

In addition it may be next to impossible to enter into contracts with public or private entities in some of these countries without paying off one's opposite number in some way. Our culture and legal system condition us to regard bribery as reprehensible; some foreigners don't view the matter as we do.

To follow foreign custom with respect to commercial bribery may involve doing business abroad in violation of American criminal law; the Foreign Corrupt Practices Act forbids a wide variety of such conduct.

Eating habits. Many Americans regard cooking as a chore to be done as quickly and simply as possible (or just avoided), and some of us feel the same about eating. We're not likely to be upset if the meal's luke-warm rather than piping hot, or if the vegetables are too mushy. If the food isn't as good as we'd anticipated, or our eyes were bigger than our stomachs we leave what we don't want on our plates and think nothing of it. Hamburgers or pizza are perfectly acceptable lunches to us.

Many Europeans on the other hand regard cooking as an art form and eating as one of life's great pleasures. Everything that's heated should be served piping hot, cooked exactly right (neither overdone nor underdone), and seasoned just so. The meal should begin with a bowl of hot soup and meats and vegetables are served with tasty sauces. Ideally the day's big meal should be accompanied by wine, and no one sips the wine until everyone at the table has touched his glass to the glass of everyone else. (To sip the wine without first "making Prosit" is inexcusable bad manners.) Whatever is served is eaten; it's an insult for host or chef to leave uneaten food on the plate.

Americans habitually eat their hamburger, pizza or fried chicken by hand without intervention of knife or fork; Europeans are much less likely to dispense with silverware and consider many of us disgracefully lacking in table manners.

American and west European cuisines are similar, though there are differences. Some of us look at English kidney pie with jaundiced eyes, and have no desire whatsoever to sample French escargots (snails). We bitterly denounce our European cousins because they can't cook a steak American-style. Europeans detest American bread because it's so spongy, without crust or body. They also denounce American cheese as flavorless and claim we have no talent for brewing tea, beer, or much of anything else in between.

Most Americans look upon the idea of eating horsemeat with disgust. Some Europeans like it, though it isn't considered "haute cuisine." Few of us would care to dine on goat flesh, but some southern Europeans eat it regularly.

When Americans encounter non–Western cuisine they have greater problems. People influenced by Chinese culture are very likely to eat with chopsticks rather than knives and forks; first efforts to use these implements can be unforgettable (and sometimes embarrassing) learning experiences.

The cuisine itself sometimes provides culture shock; there are restaurants in the Orient where one of the specialties of the house is dog or even snake. Squid, octopus and similar seafood are valued highly. The odors of Vietnamese fish sauce and Korean kimchee aren't soon forgotten, but Japanese sukiyaki and tempura leave pleasant memories in the minds of many Westerners.

In the Arab world one may be invited to eat rice or couscous from a common platter with the bare right hand, along with, perhaps, such a delicacy as sheep eyes. No pork is found on Islamic menus; the hog is an unclean animal to Muslims. One must be careful not to touch any food or containers with the left hand; here especially is the left hand deemed unclean.

Americans and Europeans shudder at the thought of eating insects. But in other parts of the world creatures such as locusts, giant spiders, giant water bugs, termite larvae and the like are considered delicacies.

Beverages. The taste of the world's peoples with respect to non-alcoholic and alcoholic beverages varies considerably from country to country.

Americans are among the few peoples of the world who serve and drink water with meals. Traditionally this wasn't done elsewhere because of the danger of contracting illness from polluted water. Though European tap water is generally as pure as the American variety, the custom of drinking water with meals hasn't caught on there. (On the other hand, bottled mineral water is a quite popular European beverage.)

Coffee and tea are the most popular non-alcoholic beverages. Americans, most Latin Americans, most Western Europeans, Arabs, and other Middle Easterners prefer coffee to tea. Americans generally brew weaker coffee than do Europeans; few Europeans drink it black. The very strong espresso coffee is popular among Latin Europeans and grows in popularity farther north. Many like to "season" the brew with cream, sugar and a shot of an appropriate alcoholic beverage.

The English, Russians, Indians and peoples of the Far East prefer tea to coffee. In the Far East varieties of green tea are very popular; in the West black tea is preferred.

In some parts of southern Latin America, yerba mate (a native tea-like brew) is preferred to both tea and coffee.

American-style soft drinks such as Coca-Cola and Pepsi are popular almost everywhere on earth.

Alcoholic beverages are found in most lands. Beer and wine are the preferred light beverages. Traditionally, Americans drink beer rather than wine, though wine consumption has grown rapidly in the United States in recent years. English tastes run to beer (and its close relative ale) and the sweet fortified wines such as sherry and port. France is the home of many of the world's quality table wines.

Germany produces both excellent beer and wine; Bavarians prefer beer to wine, while Rhinelanders have the opposing preference. Swiss and Austrians prefer wine, as do Latin Europeans.

Sake, the Japanese rice wine, is a traditional beverage in that country. Modern Japanese also enjoy beer; they choose from several quality brands.

The peoples of the world produce many varieties of hard liquor. Most typically American, it seems, is bourbon whisky. Scotland and Ireland produce their own whiskies. The English enjoy rum and gin with gusto, as do the Dutch and Belgians. French brandies are the best in the world. German-speaking Swiss love to lace their coffee with kirschwasser, a cherry brandy. Germans enjoy their schnapps, and Scandinavians their aquavit. Italians have grappa, Greeks ouzo, and the various southern Slavs their slivovitz. Russians and Poles love vodka. Non-Europeans produce other varieties of distilled alcoholic beverages, such as Mexican tequila.

The only part of the world where alcoholic beverages are scarce to non-existent is the Middle East, because consumption of alcohol is forbidden by the Qu'ran. In strict Islamic nations such as Saudi Arabia and Iran the production, importation and sale of alcoholic beverages are strictly forbidden. In modern nations such as Egypt such beverages are available to those who seek them.

With respect to drink too, human preferences vary widely.

Dress. Western clothing styles have become almost universal on our planet. During the twentieth century the suit and tie have become the accepted dress for the businessman, while the skirt and blouse or woman's suit has become the same for businesswomen.

Western clothing styles have changed radically over the last two centuries. Four hundred years ago men adorned themselves in Elizabethan doublet and hose; 200 years later waistcoat, hose and wigs were "in." The early nineteenth century brought in the ancestors of our modern suits and ties.

Women were smothered in ankle-length dresses, multiple petticoats and corsets until the turn of the twentieth century, though the low-cut garb worn by some ladies of the court of Louis XVI of France would have been deemed scandalous by the matrons of Queen Victoria's time.

Traditional Western clothing has covered most of the body rather tightly, for two reasons. First, the cold north European climate makes loose garments like the ancient Roman toga very impractical. Second, the Christian taboo against undue exposure of the human body—particularly the female human body—has mandated voluminous clothing.

As Western culture has become secularized, however, this has changed. The coat and tie becomes less and less "de rigueur" for Western men, particularly Americans. Casual trousers with opennecked sport shirts are acceptable male dress for many occasions.

The changes in female attire have been much more radical. The ankle-length skirts began to go out early in the twentieth century; skirts sported by the "flappers" of the 1920s were as short (if not shorter) than those accepted by the more liberated but more conservative ladies of the 1950s. After World War II slacks and pant suits came in, and it became more and more acceptable for women to be seen in public in shorts.

Today the Christian taboo against exposure of the female body seems on the way to extinction. Western clothing styles, both male and female, are becoming more and more informal.

In most other modernized cultures, the more conservative Western styles of fifty years ago remain in place. Latin American, Asian and African businessmen still wear the coat and tie. Conservative women still wear the skirt and blouse.

Traditional non–Western garb still remains in use in some places. The Japanese man is still likely to shed coat and tie and don the comfortable kimono when he relaxes in the evening. The Indian woman is still likely to wear the colorful sari instead of the skirt and blouse. The Iranian woman is required by law to muffle herself in the chedor when she ventures forth.

Arab men may still greet those with whom they do business clad in the traditional burnoose, while the Chinese might be wearing the characterless, egalitarian Mao jacket.

Though conservative Western garb is acceptable almost everywhere, the modern revealing sort (particularly female) may not be.

Values. What is this life all about? Each human culture to an extent has its own distinct answer.

The original answer of Christian culture to the question was the salvation of the soul. The Protestant work ethic decreed that this could be brought about by faith and hard work. The secularization of the culture and the coming of the Industrial Revolution have changed that to a degree.

History demonstrates that any culture, such as ours, in which buying and selling consume much of the people's energy will be materialistic, centering around money and that which money will buy.

Traditionally we spoke of giving an honest day's work for an honest dollar. One must work in order to survive, and one must work as hard and competently as one can to earn a day's pay. To value leisure over work was a sign of laziness, and laziness was one of the most heinous of secular sins. The best measure of the value of a person was the size of his or her bank account.

The nature of Westeren materialism has changed somewhat during the twentieth century. Many of us no longer see virtue in work for the sake of work. Leisure has become something to be treasured and struggled for.

However, we haven't evolved to the point of valuing leisure for leisure's sake. Leisure is of little value unless we have the material means to enjoy it to the utmost—by traveling to remote lands, or eating the best food, skiing at the best resorts, or whatever.

Whether the American lives by the old rule that the purpose of life is to get rich, or by the new that the purpose of life is to create a situation where one may revel in luxurious leisure, the name of the game is to acquire money. Money is the fuel that keeps a culture like ours running; that truth is so obvious to us that few question it.

The values of Western materialists aren't identical. The American prefers many material luxuries and a load of debt to fewer luxuries and a large bank account; the German or German Swiss prefers the large bank account to the unpaid-for luxuries. The German word for debt is schuld; the word indicating guilt of a crime is also schuld. Thus convicted criminals are schuldig of crime; debtors are also spoken of as schuldig; in a sense they're guilty of an immoral act. Before the days of abundant consumer credit Americans too regarded heavy loads of debt as immoral; now we regard them as quite normal. As American life styles spread through Europe there are fewer believers in the ancient virtue of freedom from debt.

In the United States the individual with an overload of debt may escape the burden through bankruptcy; American bankruptcy grants debtors a discharge from their debts. Few other nations allow access to bankruptcy to persons other than businessmen or practitioners of a profession; those who go through the process lose their assets to their creditors and are still liable for debts not paid in full.

It doesn't bother Americans that their credit card transactions and canceled checks provide a detailed picture of their financial life to any government agency or credit bureau interested; rural French people on the other hand may well do all of their business in cash and stash the excess bank notes under a mattress because their financial affairs are nobody else's business.

Western culture emphasizes individualism—the right to express one's personality. The mode of expression will vary from place to place within the culture.

In a few ways American social discipline is more stringent than European. In the United States the speed limit on most highways is 55 miles per hour; on some German autobahnen there's no speed limit at all.

We outlaw the sale of alcoholic beverages in some areas; in Europe such are available almost anywhere during normal business hours.

Americans aren't too likely to be upset by slow drivers on freeways; Europeans blink their lights, lean on their horns and make other protestations when encountering such.

On the other hand European exams for driver's licenses are more stringent than ours. The European convicted of drunk driving will lose his license for a spell; Americans so convicted may get by with a fine because it's so difficult to live without driving here (though our laws are being tightened).

Periodically, European automobiles are thoroughly inspected for mechanical and structural soundness; they may be banned from the highway because of rusty fenders or the like. Americans in some states may drive rust heaps which emit exhaust smoke in clouds as long as brakes, headlights and the like are in good order.

In many respects American culture says, "Do your thing, right now, and don't worry if it bothers someone else."

Western European culture so often commands: "Before you do it, consider — if you do it what will other people think of you and your family?"

Thus, the American cuts across the campus lawn if that's the shortest way from here to there; the European goes the long way around on the walk.

The American tosses the empty beverage can out of his car window when he's drained it; the European keeps it in the car until he can dispose of it in a litter container.

Americans see nothing wrong with washing the car or mowing the lawn on Sunday; to Europeans this is contrary to the spirit of the day of rest.

Some Americans listen to music on the radio, CD player or tape deck with volume at full blast when others are nearby; most Europeans keep the volume low under such circumstances out of respect for others.

The European parent, teacher and apprentice master train their charges to know what the boss needs before he asks for it; thus the American woman working alongside a European may well find her colleague placing a required wrench in her hand before she realizes she needs it.

On the other hand, when the European is the boss this sort of dialogue might occur:

BOSS: Where's a screwdriver? Can't you see I need a screwdriver?
WORKER: I didn't know. Why didn't you ask for it?
BOSS: I shouldn't have to ask for it. You should know what I need without my asking!

Whether Americans devote much effort to home beautification depends on their personal interests. Some of us do; more of us don't. To the north European a house is a showplace; well-kept flowers bloom in the yard and in windowboxes around the house. On the other hand the Latin European's house generally presents bare walls to the public; flowers and the like are found in the courtyard for the edification of family and guests only.

Most Americans don't approve of bare female breasts in television commercials or magazine ads. They appear regularly on the European tube; total nudity appears in some print-media ads.

American baseball is incomprehensible and boring to most Europeans (just as English cricket is to us); there just isn't enough action. Until very recently they've felt the same about American football although the World League of American Football (WLAF), with franchises in London, Frankfurt and Barcelona, opened its first season in the spring of 1991. Almost all European sports fans love soccer; that's real football! Though cheering sections American-style don't exist, the fans take things quite seriously. When the home team is victimized by bad officiating, or the visitors win, riots can result.

Ice hockey is as popular in Europe as it is here, but European play is gentlemanly by our standards. The heavy body contact that's part of the American and Canadian game is frowned upon. Americans and Canadians try to win through brute force rather than finesse; that's not real hockey, say our trans-Atlantic cousins!

Marathon bicycle races are most popular in Europe; in the Tour de France hordes of riders need more than two weeks to pedal through the whole country in stages of about 100 miles per day. Other such noteworthy competitions are the Giro d'Italia and the Tour de Suisse. The winners are considered great heroes.

Alpine skiing is one of the most popular European winter sports; aficionados follow the World Cup point standings in the various events the way Americans watch the National and American League baseball standings.

There is a great difference between Europeans and Americans in their attitude toward victory. Ask American participants in tomorrow's competition how they'll perform and they're likely to say, "We're all psyched up for it. We're going to win." Ask European participants the same question and they're likely to say, "We're prepared and we'll do our best." It's bad form for Europeans to predict victory.

Legalistic and bureaucratic restrictions bother all Westerners up to a point; all sometimes have a go at trying to beat the system. German speakers and Scandinavians seem to be the most system-abiding. English speakers respect the system less, Americans less than their cousins. (American universities may teach one thing better than any other: how to learn to deal with — and sometimes beat — bureaucratic systems.) To the more anarchic Latins the system is something to be challenged and beaten if possible; some French-men and Italians feel that those who obey the income tax laws are stupid fools.

Notions on proper treatment of animals vary throughout Western cul-ture. Many Americans denounce the Spanish bullfight as the ultimate in cruelty toward animals; north Europeans claim the American rodeo is just as in-humane. Some Americans condemn English steeplechase horse racing because so many horses and riders fall after failing to make a jump; some English peo-ple as roundly denounce American dog racing. Americans make little effort to regulate the use of animals for laboratory experiments; by contrast, Swiss animal lovers initiate amendments to their federal constitution to abolish the practice (sometimes obtaining over 30 percent of the popular vote in favor) while British animal liberationists conduct terrorist campaigns against organi-zations engaged in animal vivisection.

The official values of the Second World are also materialistic. Since Com-munism holds that religion is the opium of the masses there's no room for spiritual values in the official calculus. Communist true believers do their best to make themselves into the ideal Soviet — the human creature who will work for the sake of society without asking anything in return.

The name of the game isn't supposed to be the acquisition of personal wealth; it's the increasing of production so that, theoretically, everyone will have more material things to enjoy.

Communist true believers are becoming rare creatures, however. Sup-porters of the system seek economic security and personal material well-being, while opponents seek personal freedom.

Sport plays a most important role in many Second World nations. The absence of a private sector in the economies of these lands blurs the distinction between the amateur athlete and the professional. Without privately owned teams professionalism as the West knows it can't exist. That makes all athletes in these lands amateurs, doesn't it? Communist governments say so. World sports organizations agree.

Second World athletes are therefore almost always career amateurs. They still compete in the Olympics when their Western counterparts have long since "turned pro" and begun earning big money or stopped competing. They win more than their share of gold medals too, because of their long experience in international competition.

In tennis, however, Soviet athletes compete as professionals among pro-fessionals. For a time in 1989 Natalia Zvareva was the third-ranked female ten-nis player of the world. When she reached the finals at Wimbledon in 1988 she earned a huge reward (though she lost the championship match to the West German Steffi Graf 6-0, 6-0). She was obligated to turn over her winnings to the Soviet Tennis Federation, which made her very unhappy. The Soviet system indeed provides rewards for athletic prowess, but they don't take the form of the immense quantities of money available to top Western professionals.

The best Soviet ice hockey teams regularly defeat teams of National Hockey League all-stars, the best professionals in the world. Yet they compete in the Olympics against American college all-stars. No wonder the Soviets have won every Olympic gold medal in hockey but two since 1956!

The Soviets also produce the best gymnasts (both male and female), weightlifters, figure-skating pairs and cross-country skiers on earth.

The German Democratic Republic, with a population of 16 million, won more Olympic gold medals per citizen than any nation on earth. With Prussian discipline its system strove to develop every bit of athletic talent in the population. East German bobsledders, female speed skaters and female swimmers were the best in the world (and as of now still are). However, with the end of Communist rule in East Germany popular discontent with the privileges given to athletes made itself felt. The East German system for identifying and developing athletic talent may be drastically modified now that the Germanies are reunited.

Russians and other east Europeans seem to view bureaucratic systems as Latin Europeans do—as a challenge to be beaten. Alexander Solzhenitsyn has written that Russians need an authoritarian government to preserve order in their country. The average Russian, says Solzhenitsyn, is an anarchist who would ignore the rights of others if allowed to do so.

Would the average American or west European be different?

Confucianism has made social conformists of the Chinese, Japanese and Koreans. To depart from the norm is inexcusable and unthinkable; the living of a virtuous life has been the primary value of Chinese culture for centuries. Western-style individualism is almost incomprehensible among the Chinese.

Non-Communist Chinese value hard work and its material rewards, as do Japanese and Koreans. Since they are oriented toward this world, a broad swath of materialism runs through their cultures. The free-market economy suits their way of life; this is in part why the economies of Japan, South Korea, Taiwan and Singapore enjoy such high productivity. Yet the living standards of these people don't match their productivity; conspicuous consumption is foreign to their styles of life. They save more of their income than do any other peoples on earth.

Western sports have caught on in Japan to a degree. Baseball is one of the major sports of the land; the country has a major professional league. Some of the star players are American imports; so far few Japanese pros have been able to come to the United States and make names for themselves here. American football has Japanese devotees and sports such as Alpine skiing and gymnastics are also popular in the Land of the Rising Sun.

Sumo wrestling is one of the most noteworthy native Japanese sports, in which gigantic 300-plus-pound wrestlers clash in ritualized physical combat.

Individual martial arts such as judo and tae kwon do are popular throughout the Far East. Korean boxers have done very well in recent summer Olympics.

There are two aspects of Far Eastern value systems that Westerners have difficulty understanding. First is face—respect in the eyes of the community. When Orientals are made to look incompetent or stupid in the eyes of others they have lost face; this is the most humiliating fate they can suffer. Their self-esteem may be shattered. Thus Orientals will never announce in advance that they will accomplish this or that. Not to do what they boasted that they would do is to lose face.

To fail an examination is to lose face.

To openly admit failure is to openly admit loss of face.

To reprimand an employee in public is to cause him to lose face.

To many Orientals the only way to expiate loss of face is by committing suicide. To the traditional Japanese Samurai the way to do this was by the gruesome ritual of seppuku (or hara kiri). Today this extremely painful ritual is seldom performed; the famed Japanese novelist Yukio Mishima made headlines all over the world when he ended his life this way in protest against changes in Japanese culture. Nevertheless, the suicide rate in Japan remains high.

The second is the Japanese concept of "on." Ruth Benedict describes it in *The Chrysanthemum and the Sword* as follows: You owe on to everyone who helps you in any way. Children owe on to their parents—employees owe on to their employers—the citizen owes on to the state. On imposes an especially sacred duty upon you; it's the strongest of all existing Japanese obligations.

If you borrow money from a bank, you have the legal obligation to repay it. This isn't an on, however, because the bargain is only a business transaction with nothing personal involved. If a person lends you money in a non-business transaction, however, you have not only a legal obligation to repay but also a very strong moral obligation. If you have two loan obligations coming due— one to the bank and one to your next-door neighbor—and you have the funds to pay only one of them, you'd be expected to pay the neighbor and make the bank wait. You owe the neighbor an on; it's mandatory that you discharge it.

If you help someone you're not socially obligated to help, an on is forced upon this person, who's now obligated to help you when you need help until the obligation is discharged.

Thus, if you rush to aid a pedestrian who's been run over by an auto, you force a big obligation upon him. If you save his life, he must consider himself deeply indebted to you for as long as he lives. He must forever be in contact with you, so that he can help you when you need help.

The ordinary Japanese owes on obligations to many people purely and simply because we can't live without accepting favors from others. No one wants more such obligations. The general rule is, "You don't want ons forced upon you, so don't force them upon others."

For this reason Orientals are very reluctant to help strangers. The burden that can be imposed on the other could be overpowering. One shouldn't be subjected to that without informed consent.

Orientals are among the most polite people on earth. It is extremely bad manners to openly contradict another person. Thus, when a non–Oriental is guilty of a severe breach of good manners (like not removing street shoes before entering a Japanese home) the host or hostess won't breathe a word about this faux pas, even if they're very upset about it. The Westerner learns of this embarrassing error later from a third party.

During long conversations between Westerners and Orientals the Chinese or Japanese may respond to a long Western oration with a simple "yes." Though the Westerner may think this signifies agreement by the Oriental, it generally doesn't. Such a "yes" simply means, "I heard you." To misinterpret it as an affirmative response could cause difficulty.

In the Islamic world the faith encourages hard work and the accumulation of wealth, but tending toward buying and selling rather than large-scale wealth production. The sharp and shifty Levantine merchant is the character who comes to mind when we consider the economic activity of the people of these parts.

Muslims view the world through somewhat fatalistic glasses, because to them riches and well-being are the gift of God, not the deserved reward of virtue. They're well aware of the fact that the virtuous person may live in poverty while the sinner amasses huge wealth. That's why they'll end every statement of intent with the word inshallah — "God willing." If God isn't willing, it won't happen, even to the most virtuous.

One must, in short, live a good life here on earth without any expectation of material or spiritual reward. If God chooses to impose trials and tribulations rather than blessings, so be it — all will be set straight at the Last Judgment and thereafter.

Hinduism emphasizes the accumulation of good Karma in this life, so that the next life will be better and the soul will take a few more steps toward Nirvana. It doesn't emphasize economic activity, but one of the ancient Hindu castes is that of merchants. Those who belong to this caste are obligated to devote their lives to buying and selling. Indian merchants are noted for their sagacity not only at home but everywhere in the world where Indians have emigrated. Success, again, isn't the reward of virtue, since much depends on the Karma carried over from prior lives. But to be a smart merchant accumulates good Karma, which is what life is all about.

Otherworldly Theravada Buddhism is anything but materialistic; Burmese, Thais and Sinhalese aren't that much attached to the things of this world. Malaysians and Indonesians, though believers in Islam, adhere to many of their old customs emphasizing non-material values. Thus immigrant Chinese have come to dominate many aspects of the economic life of these nations, causing grave social and political problems.

Most sub–Saharan Africans belonged to subsistence economies prior to independence. Many still live at subsistence level. Paid employment on a contract basis remains foreign to them. Material values Western-style haven't yet become part of their psychic makeup. Western time discipline may not yet exist among some of them.

Thus, in many parts of the world people still ask themselves, "Is it worth making ourselves slaves of the clock and of money just so we can acquire more Western baubles?" If economic development is to occur in these areas we must get the people to answer affirmatively. Should we press them to do so?

Conclusion. One cannot fully understand Hispanic culture without understanding the mystique of the bullfight. One can't understand the psychic makeup of Hindus without taking into account their respect for astrologers and astrology. One can't understand fully the Chinese without understanding their love for the art of fengshui (geomancy)—the locating of buildings in places that are compatible with the pulls and tugs of the forces of nature. And unless we comprehend the emotions that caused the kamikaze pilots to volunteer to die for their Emperor we won't totally understand the Japanese.

Human nature being what it is, no two of us may completely understand each other even if we share a common culture. And it's much more difficult when we don't. Still, if we mean to do business with each other we must make the effort.

Chapter 8
Family, Gender and Marriage

Family. The nuclear family—husband, wife and children—is the basic social building-block of nearly all human cultures. It's the institution responsible for rearing and training children, and regularizing relations between the sexes.

Coexisting alongside it is the kinship group, the association of persons related by blood to each other. This has determined the basic identity of human beings in many cultures, because membership in it determines the family name of the individual.

Human beings cannot exist without the actions of others. Their genetic makeup is determined by genes provided by parents. Their family names in most cultures are provided by the father. Their given name is provided by parents, or other adults. Their personality is shaped by the adults rearing them; without such nurture they couldn't survive to adulthood.

In most human cultures throughout history it's been accepted that the individual person is nothing without family. For the average person, survival as a lone human atom was very difficult to impossible; it was the family group against the world.

Thus association with others in close quarters was inevitable. Life was lived under the eternal scrutiny of relatives. There was little personal living space; privacy was scarce to non-existent. Unless one had a dominant personality one lived under the rule of others.

The majority of humanity has accepted, and still accepts, these arrangements. In the family there are fellowship and security; in the family one belongs.

In primitive cultures it's next to impossible for the individual to escape the bounds of family. Only the very powerful personality can live an individual life amid a swarm of relatives, defying the demands of others.

Most individuals, conditioned from childhood to obey the commands of the family elders, do what they're told and sometimes resent it.

Civilization, by increasing wealth and human mobility, encourages individualism. Towns and cities allowed such anonymity.

In medieval Germany city dwellers asserted, "Stadtluft macht frei." City air makes one free. The phrase literally meant that life in the city freed the peasant from obligations to the feudal landlord—but it also meant that the young man who came to town to seek his fortune freed himself from the commands of his father and other relatives.

When a culture encourages individualism—the right of a person to live his life as he sees fit, as free as possible from the commands of others—it creates a tension between individual and family.

Where the social encouragement of individualism is still weak the family retains much of its power but the sense of suffering and oppression felt by its members increases. When social encouragement of individualism is strong the very structure of family is threatened because its members are less willing to tolerate perceived oppression.

Western Protestant culture has exalted the individual more than any other human culture. In many respects the culture of the United States has carried this farther than any other.

We Americans have taken seriously the preachments of Freudian psychology that the family is the source of most human maladjustment and unhappiness. Though most members of our culture pay at least lip service to the commandment "Honor thy father and thy mother" many of us have ambivalent feelings about it. The experience of growing up, like every human experience, brands our psyches with a load of memories, pleasant and unpleasant.

Since human nature prefers counting curses to counting blessings, we so often remember the unpleasant forever—the times we were unjustly punished, the times Mom and Dad refused to understand, the times one of our siblings was preferred over us. Since the luck of the genetic draw doesn't guarantee that parents and children will be personally compatible, times of misunderstanding are inevitable.

When society operates on the premise that "Gemeinnutz geht vor Eigennutz" (the good of the group takes precedence over the good of the individual), people accept the ancient commandment as immutable law, unpleasant though it might be. Though the 50-year-old son resents his 75-year-old father treating him as if he were still a child, he may well treat his 25-year-old son the same way. (Dad should know by now that I'm not a child any more, but that immature son of mine doesn't know which end is up yet! When is he going to grow up?)

Americans turn that old German phrase around; with us, it's "Eigennutz geht vor Gemeinnutz" (the good of the individual takes precedence over the good of the group). "I'm free and 18; nobody, but nobody, is telling me what to do any more!"

The marriage of Americans to people or organizations is very often a marriage of convenience. When the relationship no longer serves the purpose for which it was created we tend to end it, for our own individual well-being is for many of us the be-all and end-all of our existence.

As a nation we have arranged things so that husbands and wives need not stay married if they don't choose to do so. It's been suggested that we go a step farther, allowing minor children to divorce their parents when there's incompatibility between them (two states, Utah and Iowa, allow children to seek judicial separation from parents). Some American parents (and parents of other nationalities) go beyond that, unofficially divorcing children and spouses by abandoning them.

More and more aged Americans who are unable to live alone are now in nursing homes because their children either can't or won't care for them themselves. "I'm doing my duty to society by caring for my children," say these people. "You can't expect me to care for my parents too! Life's too short!" Some American legislative enactments and court decisions have specified that children are not legally obligated to support their parents.

Most non–Western and some Western cultures still stick to the old tradition which holds that children are essentially the property of their parents. They are to be seen, not heard. They must be socialized and trained to fit into their communities. Human nature being what it is, children must be subjected to discipline to force them to learn and to conform. Europeans speak of breaking the child's will, of following a long-term policy of forcing the child to follow parental commands without question. Only the self-disciplined human being who will subordinate his desires to the wishes of his superiors is fit to function as an independent adult, runs the ideology.

The obligation of children to honor (and in the majority of cultures obey) their parents continues as long as the parents live. Furthermore the obligation to support in case of need rests upon the young as well as the old; just as parents support their children when they're too young to care for themselves, children should support their parents when they're too old to be self-sufficient. The family tie cannot and must not be dissolved by anything short of death.

Most human cultures further assert that age has and should have privileges. The older one grows, the wiser he becomes. One learns only through experience; the most valuable experience is that obtained from coping with life. (Throughout most of human history change has happened so slowly that the lessons of experience seemed to stay valid forever. Unfortunately change has a bad habit of sometimes making the lessons of experience outdated and obsolete. Change occurs so fast in the modern West that we often feel that the elderly themselves are outdated and obsolete.)

A society can afford to institutionalize individualism only when there's sufficient material prosperity to both allow the able-bodied person to survive on his own and for the state or charitable organizations to provide care for the disabled. Throughout most of human history poverty forbade that. In the majority of today's cultures this is still the case.

The weakness of the family in our country is illustrated by several facts. The American divorce rate is the highest in the world; the United States has more single-parent families than any other nation; there are more teenage pregnancies among Americans than among other nationalities.

In most of Western Europe family ties remain stronger than in the United States; children live at home with their parents longer (in part because housing is scarcer and more expensive), and they're more willing to take in and care for aging or disabled parents (though cheap housing for the able-bodied elderly is more abundant than in America).

On the other hand more young couples live together without being married than in America (again in part due to the scarcity and expensiveness of housing), and in some nations more children are born to unwed mothers twenty years of age or older than in our country.

In the Soviet Union married couples are likely to welcome the company of a widowed mother; she's very useful as a babysitter while the young mother works and shops.

In the Third World families are apt to stick together because it's too expensive and too risky for members to strike out on their own. Scarcity of housing and jobs lengthens the odds against success.

Most underdeveloped countries have no national social-security systems, and there aren't enough private employers of any size to provide many private pensions. The ambition of most people is to find a government job for self or family member. Only government employment is relatively secure and offers pensions on retirement. The presence of such employment within the family or kin group makes it easier to care for the elderly and disabled members.

The ancient notion that you're lost without family, that family makes you what you are in society—that it's us (family) against them (outsiders)—is still very much alive over most of the earth's surface. If you've lost your family, you yourself may well be lost.

Foreigners working in a strange country and strange economy—be they Mexicans in the United States, Yugoslavs in Switzerland, Malawians in South Africa or Pakistanis in Saudi Arabia—are very likely to send home a large percentage of pay to help support relatives.

A person given some authority within a Third World organization may well attempt to find jobs for as many of his relatives as possible. Nepotism may be nothing more than a nuisance to us, but to members of other cultures it is a social duty.

Women's place. Men and women are human beings, but because of their biological differences they have hardly ever been treated equally. Even in the most primitive hunter-gatherer societies one of the sexes, women, held a superior position simply because the plant foods gathered by women provided more for the table than the animal foods hunted by men.

Economic progress is believed by many to have diluted or destroyed the social position of women. This is true only to an extent. Horticultural societies, where most food is produced through cultivation of garden plots, have more often than not been dominated by women because they did most of the gardening. Herder societies on the other hand have inevitably been male-dominated because male strength and aggressiveness are needed to control the herds. Agricultural societies dependent on largescale cultivation of grain and the like are most often male-dominated since heavy labor is required to cultivate such fields.

Since most modern civilized societies are dominated by men, we tend to think that it has always been so. Mariette Nowak points out in her work, *Eve's Rib,* that this isn't true. From ancient Egypt to Sumeria to Crete to Sparta, women were considered to be at least the equal of men, if not their superiors. The polytheistic religions of these cultures emphasized this state of affairs as people worshiped a pantheon of deities, both male and female.

Pride of place in many of these pantheons was held by goddesses — Isis in Egypt, Inanna in Sumeria, Ishtar in Babylon, Ashtoreth in the pagan Canaan of the Old Testament. It is unknown what caused the patriarchal revolution in the civilizations of old, but by the time of Homeric Greece (1000 B.C.) Zeus had become the king of the gods, while his consort Hera held an inferior position. Helen and the other heroines of Homer's epic poems, though strong characters, had little influence on the outcome of the Trojan War. By the time democracy blossomed in Athens, woman was so inferior that she wasn't deemed a citizen.

Jewish Yahweh was the God of the first civilized monotheistic religion and a herald of the coming patriarchal revolution — Yahweh of course being uncompromisingly male. Though female leaders of Israelite tribes are described in the Old Testament book of Judges (Deborah for one), the monarchy founded by Saul was ruled by kings. The few queens who came on the scene (such as Jezebel and Athaliah of Israel) were pagans and enemies of the male Yahweh; most met unpleasant ends.

The Ahura Mazda, Ormuzd and Ahriman of Zoroastrianism are all male, as are Mithras and Sol Invictus who competed with the God of Christianity for religious domination of the Roman Empire. During the 500 years of the West Roman Empire not even one Empress ascended the throne of Caesar.

Under early Roman law all members of a family, men and women, were under the domination of the paterfamilias, the "father of the family," who in theory ruled wife and kinfolk with an iron hand. His wife and other members of the family were virtually his property, to do with as he pleased. So comprehensive was his authority that he could kill his children if he wished.

The power of this patriarch steadily diminished, until in the early centuries of the Christian era, when a prevailing irreligion and economic prosperity created a cultural environment similar to our own, woman acquired a legal position in Roman law not very different from that of her modern sisters. She could own property, make contracts, sue and be sued, and divorce her husband at will (but never dream of becoming Empress in her own right).

After Christianity became the state religion of the Empire the position of woman in the Roman world began to decline. The preachments in the epistles of Paul about the subordinate position of woman found their way into both culture and law. (In the Byzantine Empire, however, powerful women made their presence felt despite the Church.)

Among the German and Celtic barbarians of northern Europe on the other hand woman's status was generally high. Queen Boudicca (Boadicea) led a very bloody revolt of the English Celts against the Roman occupiers of Britain in the first century, briefly jeopardizing the Roman hold on the southern part of the British island. German queens and queen mothers often wielded influence in the barbarian kingdoms that replaced the West Roman empire. There's evidence that a female once reigned as Pope; John VIII (who reigned during the ninth century) may well have been an Englishwoman named Joan.

Western feudalism reduced woman to almost the status of a piece of property during the Middle Ages. Perpetuation of the family dynasty was the feudal noble's obsession.

Included in the Western concept of dynasty was a most rigid concept of legitimacy of children. Only a child of a couple who were married to each other could inherit dynastic property. An illegitimate son was filius nullius—no son at all.

The chastity of the noble wife had to be preserved at all costs, because the child of a married woman was assumed to be that of her husband and it would be disaster for the heir to the lord of the manor not to carry the incumbent lord's genes!

But the unchastity of the noble husband was of no consequence. His flinging of wild oats could damage no one else's dynasty unless someone else's noble wife erred; when that happened it was by definition her fault!

Divorce did not exist, but the Church was very obliging about annulling infertile marriages. For better or for worse, the dynasty had to survive.

A strain of Western thought, of some influence since Christianity had become a state religion, held that the only truly virtuous woman is the perpetual virgin who renounces marriage, motherhood and all relations with men. The prototypical such woman of course was Mary, mother of Jesus (and Mother of God, as the Ave Maria insists), who early became an object of Catholic adoration. The life of the convent was the best (and practically the only) life for women who wanted to follow her example.

In theory the truly virtuous man too would renounce marriage, fatherhood and relationships with women, taking up the life of the monastery. Men who chose to become monks were sworn to celibacy from the beginnings of the Church; priests were permitted to marry until the eleventh century.

A variation upon this view of woman crept into Western thought through the warm Provencal culture of southern France in the twelfth and thirteenth centuries. Here wandering minstrels composed and sang ballads of romantic love before willing audiences, ballads hinting that all women are semi-divine objects of worship, not just the ultra-virtuous who retire to the convent.

They created (or, as some say, resurrected) the legend of King Arthur of Britain, his Knights of the Round Table, and the quest for the Holy Grail. In those distant days, the legend insisted, some men respected women as persons, not just as a means of continuing a dynasty. Some even worshipped their loved ones almost as divinities, loving them from a distance, knowing that the relationship between them could never be other than spiritual. The loves of Tristan for Iseult and of Lancelot for Guinevere still exemplify that kind of romance.

This notion that woman should be placed upon a pedestal and in a sense worshipped (or at least romantically cherished) by men has been a unique part of our culture ever since, coloring our view of woman (not to mention our expectations of marriage).

The right of woman to inherit (and thereby cause family property to pass into the hands of other dynasties) was of necessity severely limited. France and many other continental European domains adopted the Salic Law, under which a woman could never become a reigning monarch.

In eastern Christianity, however, women enjoyed much higher status. The Empress Theodora, wife of Emperor Justinian (who reigned as Byzantine emperor during the sixth century) exercised much authority due to her strong personality. At the end of the eighth century Irene, widow of Emperor Leo IV, deposed her son Constantine VI and assumed the title of Emperor (not Empress!). Charlemagne, ruler of most of western Europe, thought of marrying her and thus reuniting the Roman Empire of old. Irene's death brought this scheme to an end.

In the early years of the eleventh century the two sisters of the deceased Emperor Romanus Argyrus, Zoe and Theodora, were the powers behind the throne for two decades. Theodora finally assumed the title of Byzantine Empress in 1025 at the age of 74, only to die a year later. She was the last female ruler of Byzantium, but women were held in high regard there until the Empire fell to the Turks in 1453.

Though there were no reigning queens of note in the western Europe of the Middle Ages, two remarkable women demonstrated by their careers that they could move and shake their worlds. Eleanor of Aquitaine was heiress to the Duchy of Aquitaine (in what's now southwest France) in the mid-twelfth century. She was married to King Louis VII of France at a young age. A spirited woman, she wasn't one to take orders from her royal lord and master. It's said that she loved riding horses, and on occasion donned the armor of a knight. She organized a paramilitary group of horsewomen, who accompanied her husband to the Holy Land during the Second Crusade (though there's no record of them seeing action against the Muslim enemy there). Louis got tired of her independence and obtained from the Vatican an annulment of his marriage (because he and Eleanor were distant cousins).

Eleanor then married Prince Henry of England, who soon ascended the throne of that realm as Henry II. For awhile she influenced the government of the state as his wife. She bore him three sons and then turned against him. She encouraged her sons to plot against him; the eldest, Henry, died while in revolt against his father. The other two became English kings: Richard I (the Lion-Hearted, the great crusader) and John I, who was forced by the English nobility to sign the Magna Charta, the first significant limitation upon the power of English kings.

The other was in a sense a living exemplar of the ideal Christian woman who rejects men, motherhood and marriage — the celebrated Joan of Arc. In 1429 France was about to be overwhelmed by the English and Burgundians in the Hundred Years' War. The devout teenager Joan claimed that she heard angelic voices commanding her to go to the King and rouse resistance against the English. Her charismatic manner gave her the power to sway thousands; French armies gained inspiration from her, driving off the English besiegers of Orleans and winning other victories.

In 1430 Joan fell into the hands of the Burgundians, who sold her to the English. The English induced the Roman Catholic Church to charge her with witchcraft. She was tried, convicted, and burned at the stake in 1431.

From that time on, the memory of Joan's deeds has stirred French souls. She was later canonized as a saint by the Church which had condemned her; she holds a unique position in the history of Western womanhood.

As commerce expanded in western Europe during the later Middle Ages the status of middle-class women rose. The merchants of that period conducted family-owned businesses. While the husband was on the road attending fairs and buying inventory his wife held the fort at home, managing the "headquarters." In order to do this she had to have the same legal authority as her mate; this the law provided. The merchant wife could make contracts, sign bills of exchange, and sue and be sued. She was in all respects her husband's partner.

In England the position of woman was paradoxical. The single woman had the legal capacity of a man, except that she couldn't normally hold a title of nobility. She could however become queen if she was the closest relative of the deceased monarch and had no living brother. Between 1540 and 1720 three queens sat upon England's throne, and all three placed their stamp upon the nation's development. Mary I's effort to reverse the effects of the English Reformation and restore Catholicism as the state religion had an opposite effect, earning her the epithet "Bloody" and insuring ultimate Protestant victory. Elizabeth I presided over one of England's golden ages while Anne ruled during the final defeat of Louis XIV's effort to establish French domination of Europe.

Once the Englishwoman married, there was a radical change. The situation of the English married couple was, "Husband and wife are one, and the husband is the one." Upon marriage the English husband became the owner of his wife's property other than land. The wife retained legal ownership of her land, but if she became a mother her husband acquired a right of curtesy that would prevent her from selling or otherwise disposing of the land while she lived and the child was growing up.

The married Englishwoman couldn't make contracts, sue or be sued. Her property (other than land) would go to her husband's heirs upon his death. Only at that time would she regain control of her land. (If she died before her lord and master, her land would go to her heirs, subject to the husband's right of curtesy if any.)

The only interest a married woman got in her husband's property was the right of dower in a third of his land; this gave her the right to use the chosen third for as long as she lived, after which it reverted to his heirs. His income earned during the marriage was all his.

The continental European husband was also likely to control all of his spouse's property during marriage, but it didn't become his. His earnings were very likely to be half hers; the notion of marital community property was prevalent on the Continent in those days.

Not all European states obeyed the Salic Law and excluded women from thrones. Several remarkable ladies put their stamp upon the history of their nations as they occupied thrones—Isabella of Castile who inspired the war that wiped out Spanish Islam and who financed the first expedition of Columbus to the New World; Maria Theresa of Austria who began the modernization of the ramshackle empire she inherited from her father; and Catherine the Great, the German princess who deposed her husband from the throne of Russia, seized it for herself, and made herself the most powerful Czarina ever to rule the land of the Bear.

In colonial America woman's status was the same as in England. Only in the mid-nineteenth century did married women's property acts give wives the right to retain control of their property on marriage, the right to make contracts, and the right to sue and be sued, though the earnings of a husband continued to be, and still are in most of the United States, all his. (The earnings of the wife were, and still are, all hers.)

In the parts of the United States where the influence of continental European law was strong (Louisiana, Texas, the Southwest, and California) the notion of community property was adopted—the earnings of the husband belonging half to the wife, and vice versa. In these states it was the mid-twentieth century when married women acquired the unlimited right to make contracts.

Only near the end of the nineteenth century did American women acquire the right to become licensed members of the learned professions. The right to vote and hold public office didn't become universal until the addition of the Nineteenth Amendment to the Constitution in 1920.

The niche of woman in society is unique in Western Protestant culture. We now tend to believe that woman should be able to fulfill herself in society as man does, through earning high pay in a skilled profession. The wife should have as much right to make a career for herself outside the home as her husband does.

The number of middle-level female business executives grows slowly, though few women have risen to the highest levels of corporate hierarchies. The number of female professionals (doctors, lawyers and the like) is on the increase.

Sandra Day O'Connor is the first woman to become an associate justice of the United States Supreme Court.

Patricia M. Wald serves as Chief Judge of the United States Court of Appeals for the District of Columbia. A total of 14 women sit on the benches of the various Federal Courts of Appeal (out of a total of 144 judges).

Female politicians aren't too numerous in the United States. No woman has ever been nominated for president by a major party. Only one has ever been nominated for vice president—Geraldine Ferraro by the Democratic Party in 1984.

One woman has served in the cabinet of President Bush—Secretary of Transportation Elizabeth Dole. Carla Hills serves in a near–cabinet level position as United States Trade Representative. There are two female United States senators, Nancy Kassebaum of Kansas and Barbara Mikulski of Maryland.

Three women served as state governors until January 1991: Rose Mofford in Arizona, Kay Orr in Nebraska and Madeline Kunin in Vermont. Mofford and Kunin didn't run for re-election, while Orr was unseated in November of 1990. There is now only one female governor in our country, Ann Richards of Texas.

As of now, American voters are less favorably inclined toward female politicians than voters of many other democratic nations.

There are still unanswered legal questions in the United States as to the extent of woman's liberation from the dominion of man. It's accepted in our country that a woman may terminate a pregnancy through abortion on demand. May she do this if her husband objects? Some states say yes, others say no.

Is it legally possible for a husband to rape his wife? Traditionally, the common law said no. Some state courts and legislatures now say yes.

Can a father force his children to bear his surname if his wife (their mother) objects? The common law emphatically said yes, but a few states now say no.

Only in Scandinavia do cultural attitudes on the place of woman in society resemble those in America. In fact, women's liberation has proceeded farther there than it has here; in Sweden, for instance, the housewife is entitled to three weeks of vacation away from husband and children, paid for at state expense.

Women's liberation in Europe is somewhat different from that in the U.S. The feminist movers and shakers of America want to arrange things so that women can be independent of man and family. Many of them want to make it possible for woman to enjoy a career without the burden of husband and children, and look down upon their sisters who desire domesticity.

The feminists of Europe generally don't seek that sort of liberation. They want a work environment conducive to career, husband and children without any factor unduly interfering with any other. The thrust of women's lib in Europe is toward social arrangements that make it as easy as possible for woman to be both worker and mother.

Thus, European welfare states are much more generous than ours in providing benefits for working mothers, such as paid maternity leave. (The European Community is considering making 14 weeks of paid maternity leave per childbirth mandatory.)

In some of Western Europe south of Scandinavia, though, the notion that women should receive equal pay for equal work hasn't yet been accepted. Nor has the notion that men and women should compete for advancement in the workplace; female business executives are less numerous in Europe than in the United States.

On the other hand female politicians seem to be more acceptable in Western Europe than in the United States. The prime minister of Norway is female, as was that of Great Britain until very recently. Until last year a woman held a seat in the Swiss Bundesrat, the seven-person executive council of the nation. A female prime minister has just taken office in France.

The most feminine of this trio, the Swiss Elizabeth Kopp, was forced to resign her Bundesrat seat in disgrace. Her husband was a director of a financial corporation allegedly engaged in laundering money brought into Switzerland by questionable characters in order to make it look legitimate.

Frau Kopp was appointed as the head of the Swiss Federal Department of Justice, a position roughly equivalent to that of U.S. Attorney-General. She was in charge of Federal law enforcement, and of drafting changes in the national Criminal Code.

Since Swiss public opinion is somewhat hostile to money launderers (it gives the country a bad name abroad) Frau Kopp was in charge of whatever action might be taken against them. As a good wife should (as some would say), she kept her husband informed of the government's law enforcement plans while not objecting to his company's line of business. Herr Kopp and his colleagues benefited greatly from this high-level inside information.

When this became public the Swiss media spoke of the "little Watergate" that had occurred. The unfortunate (or at least unwise) woman had to resign; the Swiss authorities brought criminal charges against her, but she was acquitted by the courts.

Had Geraldine Ferraro been elected vice president of the United States in 1984, she might have had similar problems because of her husband's business activities.

The other three ladies are hard-headed independent personalities. Norway's prime minister, Gro Harlem Brundtland, is very outspoken on world and national environmental issues; her statements sometimes offend business interests and foreign governments. She is leader of Norway's largest political party (the Labor Party).

Margaret Thatcher of Great Britain is loved by few residents of the United Kingdom, though she is respected by many. She supervised the war against Argentina over the Falkland Islands with diligence and stubbornly resisted efforts by Continental members of the European Community to establish a Community-wide monetary system.

Edith Cresson replaced Nichel Rocard as French prime minister in May of 1991. All three of these ladies are married; all of their husbands are politically invisible.

The president of Iceland is a divorcee, Vigdis Finnbogadottir. Though she exercises little governmental authority, her moral influence is considerable.

In Israel the sexes in theory share almost complete equality; here women are subject to military conscription. Here too a strong-willed independent woman served for a spell as premier—Golda Meir (who prosecuted the Yom Kippur War against the Egyptians and Syrians). However, the ancient concept of men's work and women's work dies hard. On Israeli kibbutzim (cooperative farms) men do the heavy work in the fields while women work in the kitchen and care for young children.

In the Second World men and women are in theory equal, though the practice is otherwise. Most married Russian women hold jobs because a man can't earn enough alone to support a family. However, the burden of child care and housekeeping falls primarily upon the woman of the house because the average Russian man considers it beneath his dignity to get involved in such activities. There are many female lawyers and doctors, though there are few industrial managers and even fewer important female functionaries in the Communist Party of the Soviet Union or in the governments of the Soviet Union and its constituent republics. Those posts the society holds in highest esteem are in practice reserved for men. (The lady prime minister of Lithuania, Kazimiera Prunskiene, is currently the major exception to this rule.)

In many non–Western cultures attitudes toward women are very different from ours. Even among us an almost-concealed stratum of thought fears woman as the witch who can befuddle the brain of right-thinking man with her femininity and cause him to forget his duties to God, society and family.

Such a view of woman still plays a large role in other cultures. Conventional wisdom holds that to allow women and men to mix freely will create chaos, because women are constitutionally incapable of handling such freedom responsibly. Allow one man and one woman to be alone together and the outcome is inevitable, because she'll be unable to control herself in such a situation. (It's strange that the inevitable is always supposed to happen because the woman can't control herself, not vice versa!)

Therefore the sexes must be segregated, and the alluring irresponsible female witches must be kept under the control of their menfolk — fathers and brothers before they marry, husbands afterward.

The penetration of Western ideas into these cultures has begun to dilute such notions, but the old ways of thought persist.

Since most Islamic societies are but a few years removed from polygamy and the harem, the cultural position of woman remains low. To be sure women may wear Western dress and go about unveiled in Egypt, Tunisia, Algeria and some other Islamic lands, but they hold no positions of importance in most. (In fact, unveiled women in lands such as Lebanon run the risk of being attacked by gangs of fundamentalist men. A favorite ploy of such gangs is to throw acid into the faces of these "immoral" ladies so that they'll want to wear veils in the future.)

In Egypt there are female entertainers and professional persons, as there are in Tunisia. In Algeria women and men share a theoretical equality which comes closer to reality than in most Islamic countries. In Colonel Khaddafi's Libya female military units exist (women are subject to military conscription there); despite the Colonel's statements that he is restoring traditional Islam in that country the position of woman is relatively high.

Female politicians are almost non-existent in the Islamic world. The only noteworthy ones are Begum Khalidazia of Bangladesh and Benaein Bhutto of Pakistan. Zia became prime minister of Bangladesh after her party won parliamentary elections in early 1991. Bhutto leads the major opposition party of Pakistan.

In Iran women must wear the chedor, the body-concealing Islamic dress, and in the lands of the Arabian peninsula they are for the most part veiled and segregated as of old.

Believers in Islam say that this state of affairs is best for woman. In 1987 this author met a young English female convert to Islam at the cashier's cage of an Islamic bookstore in London and asked her why she'd become a Muslim.

Her answer was that Christianity and Western culture exploit woman, while Islamic culture cherishes and protects her. The so-called freedom of woman in the West is an illusion. Woman needs man to be complete in both East and West. In the West woman is obligated to try to ensnare man through the lure of the flesh — a slender figure, a becoming hairdo, skillfully applied makeup, clothing that tantalizingly reveals yet conceals, and an outgoing personality.

The Western woman who lacks the beauty and perceived charm of a Miss Universe candidate feels useless and inferior; how can she be lovable if she doesn't measure up?

The young woman related that she'd had a morbid fear of losing her attractiveness by gaining weight; she'd starved herself to avoid this and as a result spent six weeks in a hospital recovering from the ill effects. Perhaps her fears were abnormal, but this fear of gaining weight and losing beauty causes psychic problems for many young Western women.

Why must Western culture evaluate woman that way? she asked. It's all physical, with no spiritual content, and degrading to all women. Moreover, Western man has no respect for or sense of responsibility toward woman. She is simply attractive and useful to him; a mere living doll.

The result is a relationship based solely on physical attraction. When this fades the relationship is very likely to end and the woman finds herself single again, older, less beautiful, probably with children to care for, with no more security at the end than she'd had at the beginning.

Islam doesn't permit this degradation, she continued; the concealment of the female body insures it. Islam values woman as woman, not as a mere bundle of physical charm. The true-believing Muslim owes his wife the duty of care and support; even when a Muslim marriage ends the ex-husband is obligated to support ex-wife and children. Since Muslims take their religion seriously the true believer won't ignore these duties.

(Of course, our culture too holds that the ethical man owes his wife care and support, but many Westerners don't perform this duty. The author's English friend considered Muslims to be more ethical than Westerners.)

It's a valid point of view, though those who see the world through Western spectacles have trouble accepting it.

The position of woman in India is marginally higher than in Islam. Hinduism recognizes female aspects of God, and some of the heroines of the ancient Indian epics were ladies of strong character. Indian states have occasionally been ruled by women; one of the more noteworthy such rulers was Lakshmi Bai who became the Rani of Jhansi on the death of her husband during the late 1850s.

She was ruling her state when the Sepoy Rebellion began in 1857. The Rani lent the support of her state to the rebels, and actually led her armies against the British. They captured the sizable city of Gwalior from the forces of Queen Victoria; a large British army marched to recover it. The Rani refused to surrender the place; the British resorted to a siege. Ultimately they stormed the place and she died in battle against them.

When one considers the life of Lakshmi Bai it's not quite so remarkable that Indira Gandhi became prime minister of the Republic. In some ways she had the high spirit of the Rani. She wasn't afraid to make enemies; because she wasn't a compromiser one of them hated her enough to kill her.

Sri Lanka also has had female prime ministers, though Buddhism is another faith which generally condemns woman to inferiority. Burma is another Buddhist land which has produced a charismatic lady politician, Aung San Suu Kyi, one of the leaders of the popular movement that overthrew the 26-year-old Burmese socialist dictatorship in 1988. Probably the most popular leader among the rebels, she opposed the new authoritarian government of the State Law and Order Restoration Council. The generals who ran the new government put her under house arrest and refused to let her run for a seat in the National Assembly, which was elected on May 29, 1990. Thinking it had the opposition cowed and demoralized, the government allowed a free election; the National League for Democracy, Suu Kyi's party, won 80 percent of the seats in the National Assembly. If the generals let the result stand, Suu Kyi may yet play a role in Burma's government. (This will not happen. As of May 1991, Suu Kyi is still under house arrest and the generals show no signs of giving up their power.)

Chinese culture too is fundamentally masculine. There was never a Chinese Empress, though a woman, Tzu Hsi, dominated the Imperial Government from 1862 until her death in 1908. She was a concubine of the Emperor Hsien Feng, who named her son T'ung Chih as his successor. When the Emperor died his heir was a minor. Tzu Hsi was named regent, and through the power of this post manipulated Emperors and ran the nation as long as she lived. The lady could have made herself Empress in her own right, but as a believing Confucian refused to do so.

Communism has in theory brought equality to the women of China, Vietnam and Kampuchea, but the women of Taiwan, South Korea and Singapore are still somewhat subject to the rules of the old culture.

Before Japan adopted Confucianism and other aspects of Chinese culture in the seventh century, powerful empresses sometimes sat upon the Japanese throne. Legend has it that one of them, Jingo, set out to (and did) conquer southern Korea for a spell.

After the seventh century, and up to modern times, such Japanese women that have had any political power have exercised it from behind the scenes.

Today more and more Japanese women are entering the workforce, but Japanese employers still believe that women will make unreliable employees. They reason that a woman will be likely to quit soon and become a wife and mother. Few Japanese women have attained any prominence, though this state of affairs is changing.

Japanese housewives have led an immense wave of protest against a three percent consumption tax imposed by the Liberal Democratic government. They have also made known in no uncertain terms their displeasure with male politicians who take under-the-table payoffs from special interest groups and engage in expensive extramarital affairs. Their repudiation of the Liberal

Democrats in the July 1988 elections to the House of Councillors cost the Liberal Democrats their majority there.

The leader of the Japan Socialist Party, second-largest party in the land, is now Takako Doi. She is the first female leader of a major party in Japanese history and stood to become prime minister had the Liberal Democrats lost their majority in the House of Representatives in the election of February 1990. (The Liberal Democratic government survived with a somewhat reduced parliamentary majority.)

In Hispanic countries the traditional machismo of the culture still condemns woman to inferiority, though two very charismatic females have risen to positions of fame—Eva Perón in Argentina in the 1950s and President Corazon Aquino of the Philippines. Three more ladies served as presidents in Latin America during the last two decades—Isabel Perón in Argentina, Lidia Gueiler Tejada in Bolivia, and Ertha Pascal-Trouillot in Haiti. The first two were removed from office by military coups. Madame Pascal-Trouillot yielded her position to Jean-Bertrand Aristice, her freely elected successor.

The other is Violetta Chamorro who was unexpectedly elected president of Nicaragua, defeating leftist Daniel Ortega in the most free Nicaraguan election in decades. She assumed office on April 25, 1990.

The Caribbean area also boasts a lady prime minister. Eugenia Charles has headed the government of Dominica for ten years; her party retained its parliamentary majority in the May 1990 election on the island.

Mariette Nowak argues in *Eve's Rib* that Westerners have sometimes lowered woman's position. Among the Iroquois and some other Indian tribes of North America, women enjoyed a political influence equal to men before the Europeans came. European refusal to recognize the power of native women plus the military conquest of the tribes destroyed this female influence.

Among the Balonda, Ekoi, Ibo, Yoruba and Tuareg of Africa women have enjoyed a privileged position. Contact with Europeans has destroyed this position among the Balonda and Ekoi, but Ibo and Yoruba women still have equality and great influence in their societies. The Tuareg of the Sahara Desert operate one of the few truly matriarchal societies left on Earth; among them, women are the superior sex.

Though Indonesia is in theory a Muslim nation, women in certain parts of that island land still enjoy great privilege that dates back to the pre–Muslim era. The Muslim missionaries who brought Islam to this part of the world in the fifteenth and later centuries were unable to force Middle Eastern ideas of female inferiority onto the Javanese, Sundanese and certain other Indonesian ethnic groups.

Marriage and children. The biological destiny of the female of a species is motherhood, our own species included. In virtually all human cultures motherhood occurs within the framework of marriage.

In most Western cultures monogamy—the marriage of one man to one woman—has been and still is the norm. So prevalent is it that we forget (or are unaware) that other forms of marriage exist.

Among certain tribes in India group marriage, the marriage of several men to several women, existed until very recently. The husbands were generally brothers; the wives were likely to be unrelated.

In the foothills of the Himalayas, Tibet, the Marquesas Islands and a few other places polyandry—the marriage of one woman to several men—has existed. Again, the husbands were very likely to be brothers, but not always. In the Marquesas Islands a middle-aged or elderly affluent man would marry a young beautiful wife and then allow her to marry other young men who would become part of the household.

Polygyny (or polygamy, as it's more loosely called), the marriage of one man to several women, has been the most common type of plural marriage. It's mentioned in the Old Testament, and has continued to be common in the Middle East until modern times. Even today it's found in the Arabian peninsula, parts of Africa, parts of Asia, and among fundamentalist Mormons in the western United States.

In societies that are theoretically monogamous, the institution of concubinage may make possible a de facto polygyny. The concubine is the long-term mistress of her paramour. She has a lower status than a wife, but a much higher status than a participant in a casual affair. More important, her offspring enjoy a sort of legitimacy.

In traditional Chinese culture the sterile wife was in a most uncomfortable position. Her husband could legitimately divorce her due to her problem, and her chances of finding another husband would be nil. Lacking property or affluent relatives, her situation would become grim if her marriage ended.

The best solution was for her to encourage her husband to take a concubine. She would enjoy superior status to the newcomer but if the concubine could bear sons they would be counted legitimate and continue the husband's family name.

Though the Qu'ran limits the Muslim male to four wives, there are no limits upon the number of concubines he may accumulate. The Turkish sultans of old numbered their concubines in the hundreds. The son of a favored concubine would often succeed his father upon the throne.

Though the Western preoccupation with dynasty caused our culture to insist upon a theoretically pure monogamous marriage regime, unmodified by concubinage, the elite have always enjoyed the privilege of serial monogamy. Powerful male personages have always been able to legally terminate an inconvenient marriage in order to contract another.

In our era of easy divorce, both sexes now enjoy this privilege. Westerners in general and Americans in particular may enjoy an unlimited number of spouses during a lifetime, so long as one contracts the marriages one at a time and ends the last before beginning the next.

During the centuries before the coming of modern medicine it was woman's fate and duty to mother as many children as possible during her fertile years. The enterprise was dangerous for both mother and child. Delivery complications and lack of knowledge of antisepsis caused many a mother to die in childbirth, while childhood disease carried off many a baby during its first year of life. Some who survived the first year didn't make it to adulthood. The very high death rate made a higher birth rate a biological necessity.

Mothers of the middle and lower classes worked long hours alongside their husbands during their childbearing years and after. They might do heavy physical labor alongside their mates until the pains of childbirth began, and they'd return to their work as soon as possible after giving birth.

The notion of the married woman being only a housewife and mother didn't come upon the scene in Western culture until the time of the Industrial Revolution. Our ancestors of a century ago looked upon the middle-class housewife-mother as a liberated woman; liberated from the toil of hard work in the cause of family survival, fortunate to have a husband who could support her in relative leisure. (Western working-class women didn't achieve this sort of liberation until well into the twentieth century.)

The expansion of educational opportunities for women—particularly American women—opened up new possibilities at mid-century. For the first time women could dream of professional careers, of the independence and relative affluence of the educated.

To many the career of housewife-mother no longer seemed liberating, but the exact opposite: oppressive and stifling. Are you truly free if you must ask your husband for pocket-money and account to him for every penny you spend? At the same time the legal developments of no-fault divorce and abortion on demand, plus the pharmaceutical development of near-perfect birth control, offered woman liberation from the biological and legal constraints of millennia of human history.

One of the objectives of American feminism has been to make marriage and motherhood optional for women. In theory they have always been optional, but in practice the spinster has been an object of ridicule and pity (unless she chose to join a cloistered order of Roman Catholic nuns), condemned to live in relative penury because the economy provided no niche for the working woman to earn a wage comparable to the working man's. The childless wife was either pitied or denounced as utterly selfish.

In essence this feminist objective has been attained. Most of American society no longer frowns upon the unmarried woman or the childless wife. Moreover the unmarried American woman may have an intimate relationship with a man without marriage; society and the law no longer object to unmarried couples taking up housekeeping together. (In a few states the law permits the female partner in such relationships to collect "palimony" when things break up.)

In Western Europe a similar situation prevails. Divorce isn't quite so easily obtained there, but more couples take up housekeeping without bothering to marry than is the case here. Though abortion on demand isn't the law everywhere, most European women live close to a country where it is.

Whatever happened to the notion of romantic love planted within the culture by the troubadours? It's been written about and sung about and mooned over for centuries—poems, plays, operas and novels have belabored the theme of the impossible love. Sometimes the supposedly impossible becomes possible, poor star-crossed lovers overcome all obstacles and at last marry, the tale ends, "and they lived happily ever after."

From the medieval era until modern times, romantic love for most individuals was a dream. Most marriages were either arranged by family for dynastic or financial reasons or were marriages of necessity to insure personal survival or economic security. Only with the relative prosperity created by the Industrial Revolution and the loosening of family ties that accompanied it could most think of choosing a spouse for purely romantic reasons. Only then did marriage for love become something like universal.

In the bad old days of arranged marriages it sometimes actually came to pass that "they lived happily ever after." In the modern era of marriage for love it more often happened. In neither era did it happen as often as we like to think.

The German word for honeymoon well expresses the unreality of romance for the long haul—"Flitterwochen." Literally translated it means "butterfly weeks." The married couple eventually must come to terms with the aggravating nitty-gritty of modern life; "graue Alltag"—gray everyday—sets in. The partners get to truly know each other. They learn of incompatibilities they'd never dreamed existed. Romance dies in the cold gray light of human frailty.

In the old days most accepted the end of romance, accepted a far less than perfect domestic situation, and pulled together to do what was expected of married folks because law and custom decreed that marriage was "for better or worse, 'til death do us part."

Today the cultural revolution of the last thirty years has turned this situation on its head. There's no need for lovers to play the roles of Tristan and Iseult or of Lancelot and Guinevere today; a couple infatuated with each other very often proceed to make the ultimate human acquaintance without undue delay, even if both are already married. The mystery that used to create romance is dispelled at once. One might think this would lead to more realistic, stable marriages.

It all too often doesn't. Partners may happily live together without marriage for years, marry, and divorce within a few months. Most hip Westerners feel that the notion of marriage "for better or worse, 'til death do us part" is as out of date as the stagecoach. A better statement of Western expectations may well be, "for better or worse, so long as this relationship pleases me." When marriage interferes with the desire of one of the partners to do his or her thing (as living together without marriage seemingly doesn't), the response is to end it and regain that precious individual freedom.

As stated earlier, the drive toward unlimited individualism—the right of every adult to live unburdened by the demands of others—has proceeded farther in our part of the world than in any other.

One of the consequences has been a drastic lowering of the birthrate in much of the First World. When most people earned their living from agriculture large families were beneficial because children were assets; the more children there were the more unpaid labor Dad had on hand to help with the chores. In the early days of the Industrial Revolution before the enactment of child labor laws children still were to an extent economic assets; as soon as they were old enough to work (six years of age or so) they could be found jobs in the factories or wherever to bring in money and increase the family income.

In industrialized societies children are now a decided economic liability; it costs large sums to feed, clothe and educate them. Besides, extreme individualists in Western society claim that they infringe upon adult freedoms— how can you do your personal thing when there are young ones to be cared for?

The American birthrate is marginally higher than that of the countries of northern Europe, but much of that is accounted for by the fact that the birthrates of American blacks and Hispanics are relatively high.

Birthrates in Latin Europe are higher than in the north. Roman Catholic hostility to abortion and birth control plus the fact that Latin societies value children more highly than north European ones account for the difference.

In Communist Europe a housing shortage makes it virtually impossible for a single person of anything but highest status to find living space. You generally either live with your parents or with some other person.

Most women marry, but divorce is available practically on demand. Abortion too is available on demand, so no woman need accept the burden of motherhood involuntarily.

Birthrates in Eastern Europe and in the Baltic and Slavic parts of the Soviet Union are extremely low, lower even than in northwestern Europe. Many eastern European women undergo several abortions during their reproductive years.

In Japan, where spinsterhood is still frowned upon, the huge majority of women marry. The availability of abortion keeps the number of children low. The fact that over 100 million Japanese are crammed into a mountainous chain of islands with the land area of the state of California provides strong incentive to limit family size and population growth.

In China government is striving to put a brake upon population growth. There are already over one billion Chinese; nearly 20 percent of the living members of our species reside in the People's Republic of China. Therefore it's government policy to encourage couples to delay marriage until they're established economically and to limit each family to one child. This single child is in theory entitled to many government benefits, including free education as far as the child's talents will permit. Multi-child families are entitled to no such benefits; in fact, the mother pregnant with a second child may be compelled to undergo abortion.

In the underdeveloped parts of the first two worlds and in most of the third people — both male and female — look upon the situation I've described with shock and in some cases horror.

The freedom of the unmarried Western woman to associate with males and to choose her own spouse is degrading, they say; marriage is too important a relationship to be entered into simply on the basis of physical attraction. The notion that one can find lasting happiness in a marriage based upon romantic love is a dangerous illusion. Human affections are too fickle and seldom last.

To say that woman can find happiness in a marriage with no or few children is another dangerous illusion. Male and female are too fundamentally different to have any long-term relationship that's emotionally satisfying. The only people with whom woman may have satisfying relationships in a marriage are her children; only they are truly hers.

We Westerners have therefore condemned woman to uselessness and unhappiness by trying to deprive her of her primary reason for existence — mothering.

These arguments appeal most cogently to the uneducated women of the Third World and to most of the men. As Third World women become more educated and sniff more of the seductive breezes of Western individualism and independence, they suspect that there is much more to life than mothering. As the levels of employment and education increase among the women of a Third World nation the birth rate begins to fall. Though Third World traditionalists of both genders fight stubborn delaying actions against foes of the old order the cause of female liberation moves forward.

Westerners tend to view with dismay some aspects of old-fashioned marriage Third World–style.

We're all somewhat familiar with the double standard applied to male-female relationships in the Latin world (and until very recently in our own). Because of the objections of the Roman Catholic Church, divorce is difficult or impossible in some Latin countries. The married woman who strays from faithfulness to her husband is condemned and perhaps punished, while the married man is allowed his flings and admired for his machismo.

The Muslim woman in the traditional culture is the dependent of either her father or her husband; independence with neither family nor husband to give her orders isn't a viable option in lands such as Saudi Arabia. The rigid segregation to which women are subjected in the traditional culture makes independence physically and psychologically impossible in any case.

In backward parts of Egypt, the Arabian peninsula and Africa the ancient custom of female circumcision still prevails. It's necessary to mutilate the genital organs of girls, runs the culture's ancient wisdom, to better enable them to control their desires when they become women. Thus they'll be less likely to bewitch men with their charms and will be content to be obedient wives and mothers.

The Muslim wife's best course of action in most of Dar-ul-Islam is to put up with her husband's doings, come whatever. The culture does permit the remarriage of widows, however; in fact, one of the major arguments in favor of polygyny advanced by Islamic traditionalists is that the institution provides a place for widows by making it easier for them to find another husband.

The state of wives is low in Indian culture also. Female circumcision never took root in India, but traditional Hinduism forbids remarriage of widows. For the Hindu wife to lose her husband can be unadulterated catastrophe unless she's wealthy enough to support herself or her family's able to support her.

Before the British came to India the respectable widow was expected to commit sati (or suttee); to allow herself to be burned alive on the fire that cremated her husband's body. She was thought to owe this to herself and to the soul of her husband because bad Karma carried over from her previous lives had caused the misfortune of her husband's death; it was all her fault. (Apparently no one suggested that a wife might suffer premature death due to her husband's bad Karma.)

The British outlawed the practice; it naturally remains outlawed in independent India. Yet the status of the widow in the traditional culture remains so low that to some the painful death of suttee may be preferable to the long life of poverty and misery that will be her lot if she keeps on living.

The wives of Indian Muslims have it marginally better than those of Hindus. And Sikh wives enjoy an exalted status compared to that of their non–Sikh sisters.

Among traditional Chinese the wife's position is stronger, though her position as a woman was physically miserable before the beginning of the twentieth century. Middle and upper class Chinese women were condemned to lives of pain and physical disability before then by the custom of foot-binding.

The old culture held that the smaller a woman's foot was, the more desirable she was. Therefore the feet of female children were very tightly bound at age six or thereabouts so that they couldn't develop normally. The child therefore grew up in constant pain, a physical cripple.

The compensation for this was that the middle and upper class Chinese wife wasn't expected to do any sort of work; her husband could afford to hire servants. If he was virtuous he treated her as Confucian ethics prescribed — with affection, respect and generosity — and she lived a life of affluent leisure.

Among the lower classes there was no money to hire servants, so the feet of farm girls weren't bound. They had to grow up strong and healthy to help their husbands with the hard physical labor of the homestead.

Among the Japanese the position of the wife was always strong, and has grown stronger. There was no mutilation of female children and no stringent discrimination against widows. To be sure the virtuous Japanese wife has been (and still is) expected to obey her husband in most things; but with respect to domestic arrangements he is more likely to obey her. In household matters she rules.

In parts of Indonesia, as previously mentioned, wives have a high standing.

In Africa the wife's status varies widely from tribe to tribe. Traditionally some tribes practiced polygyny, and in remote areas may still do so. Female circumcision still occurs in remote areas. Other tribes practice various sorts of mutilation of female children (and perhaps male children too). Still others (such as the Ibo and Yoruba) accord woman a relatively high status. Except among matriarchal peoples like the Tuareg of the Sahara, though, no African culture grants the married woman more power than ours.

Arranged marriages are very common in most of the Third World, and in some less developed parts of the Second and First. Since most human cultures are patrilocal—the wife takes her husband's family name and actually becomes a part of his family—there are property considerations to be taken into account when children marry. These considerations will vary from culture to culture.

The French anthropologist Germaine Tillion describes much of Mediterranean society as "The Republic of Cousins" in her book of the same name. These are all patrilocal cultures in which women are permitted to inherit property from deceased husbands or blood relatives.

Land is the major asset of many families in these cultures; a great objective of family leaders is to make sure that the homestead remains intact.

Thus, a family courts disaster by allowing a daughter to marry outside the family. She, as a child, has a right to inherit a portion of the homestead from her parents. If, after inheriting, she dies without children her husband will inherit some or all of her estate. If she dies with children these, who bear her husband's name, will inherit. If either misfortune happens her portion of the family homestead will pass into the hands of another family.

To prevent this catastrophe, daughters are generally required to marry someone within the family, preferably a son of a father's brother (a first cousin). Though all human cultures forbid incestuous marriages (marriages between very close blood relatives) first-cousin wedlock is generally outside the prohibition and lawful. A few cultures carry this one step farther and allow marriages between uncles and nieces. Informal betrothal arrangements may be made when children are very young; engaged cousins grow up together knowing they'll eventually marry.

There's not much romance in such arrangements, but at least the newlyweds are well acquainted!

These are endogamous cultures, where husband and wife come from the same community. Many cultures are exogamous, where husband and wife must come from different families. Here arise other problems.

In some cultures, like the Indian, a daughter is a distinct liability because of the dowry she must furnish her husband and his family when she becomes a bride. A family may have to save and scrimp for years to assemble a suitable marriage portion. A major part of the interfamily negotiations to arrange a suitable marriage involves the amount of dowry that will be required.

Sometimes the parents of an Indian daughter cheat on dowry arrangements (actually, or perhaps only in the eyes of the husband or his family) in a way that can't be detected before the wedding. The result can be a most bitter and acrimonious inter-family dispute.

The husband and his family sometimes resolve such a dispute in modern India by dousing the wife with kerosene and setting her ablaze. The unfortunate "accident" ends the marriage but allows the husband to keep the deceased's dowry (if any was paid). Theoretically, of course, it also leaves the culprit(s) open to a charge of murder; most often society accepts the fiction that it was an accident and life goes on. The husband may then seek another wife and, hopefully, a more affluent and honorable father-in-law and a larger dowry.

In other cultures a daughter is a valuable asset, because her husband-to-be must buy her from her parents. A young unmarried man must work hard and save his money in order to acquire enough of a nest egg to afford a suitable bride.

In such cultures young girls are well-trained in the skills necessary to please a husband; if the groom decides his blushing bride wasn't worth the price he paid for her he may rescind his purchase contract (by sending the lady home to Mother) and getting his money back.

That's the point of the lyrics of a West Indian popular song, part of the refrain of which runs,

"Pack she back to she ma!"

Marriage brokers are commonly used as go-betweens in the arrangement of weddings in these cultures.

Child marriage was very common in traditional India; couples could be betrothed when both were but three years old. Girls under the age of 10 could be married to men of over 50. Thus teenage widows weren't uncommon; they were either forced to commit suttee before knowing what marriage was all about or condemned to misery because of the prohibition against widow remarriage. Child marriage has been outlawed in India but the custom nevertheless continues to exist.

The same custom was common in Dar-ul-Islam and in tribal Africa. It has been outlawed by legislation in Egypt, Tunisia and most other Islamic lands but still exists in the remote fringe areas of these cultures.

The main purpose of marriage throughout most of the world remains reproduction, and boys are still the more valuable children. The barren wife is next to worthless, and the wife who bears nothing but daughters not much less. Since most human cultures are patrilocal sons are necessary to continue the family blood-line. A daughter is ultimately the asset of her husband's family, not her own; when her family must assemble a dowry to get her married off she's a sizable liability to her father!

The ancient cultural wisdom that sons are preferable to daughters still prevails in some Far Eastern countries that have bestowed liberty upon their women. In China the large majority of families prefer that the one child allowed them by law be male. Thus the Chinese mother may well abort a daughter (abortion being quite legal) in order to keep alive the possibility of bearing a son. If the one permitted child is a daughter the husband's family name will die out, an unacceptable possibility.

In South Korea there are no legal limits on the number of children, but members of the rapidly growing middle class prefer small families. Since abortion is available on demand, many traditionalists want the first child to be a son. The wife will abort a daughter hoping for a son on the next try. Once a son is born a daughter might be acceptable as a second child.

As a result, a large majority of very young children are male in both of these countries. If the trend continues there will be a shortage of wives for these boys when they mature. An unprecedented social problem will arise.

Divorce in the Third World is unlikely to occur for the reasons it does among us; most of the world's people would consider our reasons for it trivial. Most believe that romantic love is a form of temporary insanity, and that it's ridiculous to expect a marriage to generate and nurture such feelings. That Westerners end marriages because of incompatibility between husband and wife is proof to many of our essential immaturity and childishness.

Third World divorce will more often than not be due to sterility or the wife's inability to produce sons or her inability or unwillingness to do the hard labor necessary on the family homestead.

Western preachments about the desirability of limiting family size fall on virtually deaf ears among the uneducated here; if woman can't be a mother of many sons, of what value is she to herself or to anyone else?

This also applies to the desirability of women's liberation; the uneducated Third World woman asks, liberation from what? Family? The thought of living alone in a society of strangers with no one to turn to in case of trouble is horrifying.

All of this explains why birth rates continue to be very high in the unindustrialized portions of the Third World.

The population of Mexico has grown from 50-plus million to 70-plus million in two decades, and Mexico City has become the most populous city in the world. Shantytowns encroach on the suburbs of Caracas, Rio de Janeiro and Sao Paulo. Tens of thousands live and die on the streets of Calcutta. The people-jams of Lagos are legendary.

Where ethnic groups of the First and Second Worlds coexist in the same country with Third World cultural groups a demographic revolution is in progress. The best example of this phenomenon is the Soviet Union. While Great Russians, Ukrainians and the like are content to have one or two children the Islamic peoples of that vast country are rearing huge families. Already Great Russians comprise less than 50 percent of the Soviet population, while the numbers of Uzbeks, Kazakhs, Turks and other Islamic peoples grow at a rapid pace.

As mentioned earlier the same is happening at a slower pace in our country as the black and Hispanic populations grow.

It's in this area that one of the greatest communication gaps between the First and Second Worlds on one hand and the Third World on the other exists. Our values here — including our concern about too rapid population growth — are incomprehensible and inhuman to them until they absorb Western-style education and acquire ambitions to achieve Western-style affluence. Their values, irresponsible and anti-individual as we see them, are the same to us.

Chapter 9

The International State System

Origins of the European state system. As described earlier, during the Middle Ages, before the Reformation broke the unity of the Christian Church in Western Europe, the Pope claimed religious authority over all of the secular rulers of Christendom, while the Emperor of the Holy Roman Empire claimed a similar secular authority. In theory the sovereignty of ruler over subjects wasn't unlimited; the prince was subject to the law of God and to the authority of God's vicar on earth, the Pope, and to the secular authority of the Emperor.

As the Middle Ages waned and the Renaissance approached, the political and economic power of the secular monarchs grew. By the thirteenth century the authority of the Emperor had shrunk until it existed only in portions of German-speaking and Italian-speaking Europe; by the mid-fourteenth century Imperial political power had vanished. It was to revive in the early sixteenth century under the Hapsburg Emperor Charles V, but its power was then based upon the political and economic might of the House of Hapsburg, not upon any inherent Imperial power.

The growing power of the kings of France and the Great Schism of the fifteenth century destroyed the independent moral authority of the Church. During the Schism two and sometimes three church leaders at a time claimed to be Pope. The unseemly scramble for political power among those who shouldn't have had such ambitions was hardly edifying. Though the reunited Church sought to reclaim its moral authority the Protestant Reformation damaged its position beyond repair. Monarchs claimed power to rule their subjects in their own way, free from any outside interference. The result was international anarchy.

Without a law higher than that of the nation-state, might made right in international relations. Monarchs might behave honestly and responsibly in international relationships; generally it was to their advantage to do so. But few hesitated to act dishonestly or dishonorably when there was something to be gained by it. In fact, Niccolo Macchiavelli recommended such a course in *The Prince;* the end justifies the means in the governance of states and in the conduct of relationships between states.

From the fifteenth century on, European scholars claimed that there existed a natural law of nations; if this could be applied by the leaders of the nations there would be more order in the world. The monarchs began to take heed. International law Western-style slowly took form. In due course it was to become the accepted model for all civilized nations.

The basic nature of this law can be better understood if one understands the environment in which it originated.

The monarchs of Western Europe were members of a small exclusive caste. Because of the principles that persons of royal blood may marry only persons of royal blood and that there may be only one royal family within the state, the average monarch's spouse was a foreigner. Daughters, grandchildren, nieces, nephews and cousins might sit near or upon the thrones of other states. Most thrones were bound together by ties of blood.

Though these distant relatives would send their armies against each other on little or no provocation, they rarely sought to destroy each other or each other's states. Reigning monarchs were entitled to hold on to their thrones, and could expect to be treated with respect by others.

Since each member of the charmed caste wanted to rule his subjects as he saw fit, it seemed logical to accord to the other members the same right. Since no monarch wanted to believe that another had more prestige or rights than he, it was reasonable to insist upon the equality of monarchs and of states.

Each royal family possessed a dynastic claim to its throne and claimed to be the legitimate ruler of its state. Thrones usually changed hands peaceably, son succeeding father. Occasionally, however, dynasties changed through the power of the sword. Thus, in late medieval England the throne changed hands violently five times: Henry of Bolingbroke deposed Richard II in 1399 to become Henry IV; Edward of York deposed Henry VI in 1457 to become Edward IV; Henry VI regained his throne in 1471 only to lose it again to Edward IV in 1472; Henry Tudor deposed Richard III in 1485 to become Henry VII. Though these changes were in a sense affronts to the principles of legitimacy, they were accepted within the club of royalty.

Republics didn't fit into the monarchical pattern; only those possessing great military or economic power (such as the Swiss cantons or the Republic of Venice) earned the respect of the crowned heads. The United Provinces of the Netherlands forced their way into international society as a republic by winning their 80-year war for independence from Spain in 1648; the United States of America did likewise 135 years later by winning its Revolutionary War against Great Britain.

Powerful monarchs sometimes sought to expand their domains by making and seeking to enforce claims to thrones occupied by their neighbors when a ruler died without close relatives. Occasionally such claims were successful, as when King Philip II of Spain added Portugal to his domains upon the death of King Sebastian in 1578. (The king of Spain was also king of

Portugal for the next 60 years, until the Braganza family of Portugal claimed the throne of their country and militarily expelled the Spaniards during the 1640s.)

More often such claims failed, as when that of England's King Edward III to the throne of France during the 1340s set off the Hundred Years' War; it took a century of bloodshed and bitterness for the French to defeat this claim. The claim of King Charles VIII of France to the throne of Naples caused the French to invade the Italian peninsula in 1498. This plunged all of Italy into 60 years of bloody warfare, resulting in the weakening of France and the acquisition of the Neapolitan throne by the Spanish Hapsburgs.

Those who sought to expand their power illegitimately sometimes lost everything. Bohemia (now the most prosperous part of Czechoslovakia) was an elective monarchy at the beginning of the seventeenth century; the representative estates of the realm chose the monarch. In 1618 they elected Ferdinand of Hapsburg (a Catholic) as their King. But the next year they rescinded this choice, electing instead the Protestant Duke Frederick V of the Palatinate (a portion of Germany south of Frankfurt-am-Main, of which Heidelberg was the capital). Frederick accepted the election and the throne, though the Austrian Hapsburgs claimed the deposition of Ferdinand was unlawful. In 1620 an Austrian army marched into Bohemia to restore Ferdinand, defeating Frederick's army and deposing him from the throne (thereby commencing the Thirty Years War). Austrians and Bavarians then invaded Ferdinand's Duchy of the Palatinate and deposed him from that throne too; the Hapsburgs awarded part of the Duchy to Duke Maximilian of Bavaria for his assistance. Frederick died throneless ten years later.

Europeans were given a glimpse of what the future held for monarchy when the English deposed and executed King Charles I in 1649. The economic and military power of Oliver Cromwell's republican regime foreclosed any effort by other nations to restore the monarchy; the English themselves ended their republican experiment after Cromwell's death and restored their monarchy in 1660.

The French Revolution shook the royal club to its roots. The execution of Louis XVI and his queen Marie Antoinette was but the beginning. The armies of the French Republic were a menace to all thrones west of Russia, destroying many. The replacement of the Republic by the Empire of Napoleon was no improvement as the "Corsican Ogre" uprooted more dynasties and created new kingdoms for his relatives. By the time Bonaparte's ambitions were finally laid to rest at Waterloo many of the changes wrought by the French Revolution had become irreversible. The European map, particularly in German-speaking areas, changed forever.

Though Bonaparte's new kingdoms were destroyed and some of the old dynasties returned to power the restoration was temporary. The Latin American nations claimed independence from Spain and Portugal; 20 brand-new republics joined the list of independent nations. New monarchies also came upon the scene during the nineteenth century—Brazil, Greece, Belgium, Romania, Bulgaria, Serbia, Montenegro. More old monarchies were extinguished as Germany and Italy became united countries.

Other international communities came into intimate contact with Europeans during the nineteenth century and were forced into the European international system against their will. The Sultan of Turkey had claimed supremacy over the world's Muslim states as Caliph; Europeans treated him as just another monarch. The Emperor of China claimed to be Emperor of all civilized people; Europeans treated the claim with contempt. Western military power forced both Turkey and China, along with their satellites, to play the game of international relations by Western rules.

The nature of the community of nations changed forever during the twentieth century. The most powerful of the monarchs were swept away as a result of World War I (the Emperors of Germany and Austria-Hungary, the Czar of Russia and the Sultan of Turkey) and another host of new monarchies and republics, successor states of the Ottoman and Austro-Hungarian empires, joined the international club.

The totalitarian dictatorships established during the inter–World War years shook the international community to its foundations until most of them were destroyed in World War II. Many of the remaining monarchies were supplanted by republics in the late 1940s. Then began decolonization.

As the colonial powers began to set their colonies free, yet another wave of new republics almost tripled the number of Earth's independent nations within a period of 40 years. Sixty-odd nations were members of the United Nations in 1950; the number has now expanded to 159.

The game of international relations is still played according to the gentlemanly rules of former centuries, but the nature of the players has changed.

The old caste of royalty has been swept from nearly all of its thrones. In most nations where its remnants still reign, they rule no more; political power has passed into the hands of commoners almost everywhere.

In the past royalty sat upon its thrones supposedly by the will of God. Today the commoner presidents and prime ministers sit in their mansions supposedly by the will of their people. In the past national policies changed with glacial slowness. Today they change with mercurial quickness as elections and coups d'etat sweep aside one set of rulers and replace them with another.

States and Governments

Recognition of states. A potential state must meet four criteria to qualify for recognition by other states. These are (1) territory, (2) population, (3) government, and (4) independence.

A national territory need not be large. The smallest nation-state on earth is Vatican City, with an area of less than a square mile. The European micro-states of Monaco, San Marino, Liechtenstein and Andorra each contain less territory than a small American county. Several island nations of the Caribbean and Pacific have little more land area than the District of Columbia.

The national population also need not be large. The Republics of Nauru and Tuvalu have less than 10 thousand inhabitants; the European micro-states and several island nations have less than 100 thousand.

A government may take any form, but it must have some control over the territory and people of the nation. It should be located on the territory and among the people it's supposed to govern.

This government should be able to conduct its foreign relations free of the dictation of other nations, and must have the intent and the capacity to carry out international obligations.

The decision whether or not to recognize the existence of a state is the decision of individual national governments. It's to a large extent a political rather than a legal decision.

For pragmatic reasons, an entity possessing the four requisites of statehood will usually be recognized. Private business may be done with its citizens and it makes sense to deal with it as is.

New states may come into existence in various ways. Sometimes an empire breaks up as a result of defeat in war and splinters into new nations.

That happened to Austria-Hungary in 1918. From the ashes of the defunct empire arose three new nations — Czechoslovakia, Hungary and Austria. A large chunk of it became part of another new nation — Yugoslavia. Another large chunk joined a restored nation — Poland.

Sometimes small nations consolidate themselves into a larger nation. That happened when the 13 states governed by the Articles of Confederation joined to form the United States, and when 30-odd kingdoms, duchies and the like joined to form the German Empire.

Sometimes a portion of a nation secedes and establishes itself as a new nation. Belgium came into existence this way, seceding from the Netherlands in 1830, and Norway seceded from Sweden in 1905. Bangladesh was born in the same way, making good its violent secession from Pakistan in 1971 with the assistance of the Indian Army.

Singapore seceded from Malaysia without war in 1965. Malaysia accepted the secession without argument because it reduced the size of its Chinese minority and made it easier for the Malay majority to retain power in what remained of the nation.

Portions of a multi-ethnic empire may break away, as Greece, Romania, Bulgaria, Serbia, Montenegro and Albania separated from the Ottoman Empire during the nineteenth and early twentieth centuries.

The effort to establish a new state via the secession route doesn't always succeed. A civil war may well result in the destruction of the secessionists. Often the nations of the world stand by to see if the secessionists win before recognizing them. Thus, during the American Civil War the Confederacy met the four tests of statehood in 1861, but no nation gave it diplomatic recognition because it seemed unlikely that the new state would survive the war, as it didn't.

In the confusion caused by the Russian Revolution of 1917, parts of the Russian Empire sought to secede and claim independence. Some portions (Poland, Finland, Latvia, Lithuania and Estonia) succeeded. Other portions (Ukraine, Georgia, Armenia, and parts of Russian Central Asia) failed.

All of these met the definition of states; all obtained recognition from at least a few other nations before the post-revolutionary dust settled. Military force, not diplomacy, ultimately determined the fate of all these secessions.

In the late 1960s the members of the Ibo tribe sought to secede from Nigeria and establish the new state of Biafra. Nigeria resisted and bitter civil war ensued. Though the Biafrans met the tests of nationhood for awhile — and a handful of nations accorded them diplomatic recognition — Nigerian military force crushed the new state.

The majority of the nations of Africa and Asia obtained independence by having it granted to them by their former colonial masters. These states had no difficulty obtaining recognition because the world felt that the ending of the colonial empires was long overdue.

In two cases, however, the abandonment of a colony by a colonial power didn't necessarily result in the establishment of a new nation. In 1976 Spain abandoned her colony of Rio de Oro (or the Spanish Sahara) on the African coast south of Morocco. Morocco proceeded to occupy two-thirds of the phosphate-rich area and Mauretania claimed the other third. Some of the native inhabitants of the area organized the Polisario guerrillas to resist the Moroccan and Mauretanian occupiers, proclaiming the existence of the Saharan Arab Democratic Republic. With Algerian assistance the Polisario have kept a bitter little war going ever since. In 1982 Mauretania threw in the towel and recognized the Polisario, but Morocco occupied the former Mauretanian zone. The Organization of African Unity has recognized the independence of the SADR, as have most of its members, but the war goes on. As of now the outcome is in doubt.

In 1974 Portugal abandoned its colony of Portuguese Timor, the eastern half of the island of that name. West Timor had been Dutch and became part of Indonesia when the Dutch pulled out of the East Indies. The easterners attempted to establish the Republic of East Timor, but Indonesia laid claim to the territory and sent in troops. Indonesia now controls most of the area, though bloody guerrilla warfare continues there. No nation recognizes a Republic of East Timor.

Sometimes the world will refuse to recognize a secession even though it isn't militarily challenged by the former rulers. That happened when Ian Smith caused Southern Rhodesia to secede from the British Empire and set itself up as the Republic of Rhodesia. Most of the world refused recognition on moral grounds, because the Smith government was a government of a small white minority over a huge black majority. Black dissidents fought a bloody guerrilla war against Smith's government for over ten years. Though the guerrillas never won military victory, the Rhodesian government finally yielded power to the black majority, causing the creation of the republic of Zimbabwe—which was immediately recognized by most of the world.

Occasionally new nations are created at the command of older nations, without much attention being paid to world opinion. After the armies of Germany and Austria drove the Russians out of Russian Poland during World War I, the victors created a Kingdom of Poland in 1916 (which most of the world ignored). When Germany signed the Armistice with the Western allies in November of 1918, Josef Pilsudski took control of the governmental machinery of the Kingdom and proclaimed it to be the Polish Republic, present-day Poland.

Japan detached Manchuria from China in 1931 and proclaimed it to be the new nation of Manchukuo. Similarly Germany created Slovakia from the ruins of Czechoslovakia in 1939, and Croatia from the ruins of Yugoslavia in 1941. The allies of Japan and Germany recognized these nations, but no one else did. They vanished with the governments that created them in 1945.

The Republic of South Africa has created several supposedly new nations within its borders for some of its black tribes—Transkei, Ciskei, Bophuta-tswana, and Venda. These have defined territory, population, government and political independence, but no world nation other than South Africa recognizes them. The reason for their creation was so obviously to reduce South Africa's black population and to make it easier for the whites of that country to rule the remaining blacks that they are regarded as sham nations.

The majority of the population of Cyprus is Greek, but a sizable Turkish minority exists. In 1974 the constitutional government of Cyprus was overthrown by a military coup, and the rebels proclaimed their intention of uniting the island to Greece. The Turkish minority violently objected, and Turkey sent troops to the island to protect them. Later the Turkish-occupied part of the island established its own government and announced its secession. The Turkish Federated State of Cyprus claimed to be waiting for the government of the rest of the island to accept it as a federal state. In 1983 its rulers lost patience and declared independence as the Republic of North Kibris. The UN has refused to recognize the new state. Only Turkey does so; the independence of the area is still preserved mainly by the Turkish army of occupation (or protection, depending on how one views the problem).

There are organizations which promote the interests of states that don't now exist. The one with the highest profile is the Palestine Liberation

Organization. In November of 1988 an assembly of Palestinian Arabs containing many PLO members assembled in Algiers and proclaimed itself to be the parliament of independent Palestine. It declared the independence of a Palestinian state and announced its willingness to recognize Israel's right to exist. Thirteen Islamic nations have now recognized the independence of this Palestinian state, though most of the world has adopted an attitude of watchful waiting. Israel's government refuses to recognize it because of hostile Palestinian rhetoric that Israel's existence should be terminated and an Arab Palestinian state should occupy the soil where Israel now is.

A shadowy group seeks the establishment of the state of Kurdistan. The Kurds are an Islamic people with a distinctive language and culture living in the area where the borders of Turkey, Syria, Iraq, Iran and the Soviet Union meet. Some of them want to establish their own state in this area, as they actually did for a short period after World War I.

The Ottoman Empire disintegrated after its defeat in that war; in the confusion the Turkish Kurds declared independence. Kurdistan was recognized as a nation under the terms of the Treaty of Sevres, imposed upon a prostrate Turkey by the Western Allies in 1920. However, the resurgent Turkish nationalists of Mustapha Kemal "Ataturk" snuffed out the Kurdish Republic within a year or two and reannexed it to Turkey despite the treaty provisions; Europe recognized the annexation when the Turks forced revision of their peace terms in the 1923 Treaty of Lausanne.

The Iraqi Kurds have fought bitter wars against their masters, two within the last five years. The Iraqis used chemical weapons against the rebels in their relentless campaign of suppression. In early 1991, after Operation Desert Storm ended, the remains of Iraq's army utterly crushed the most recent Kurdish rebellion.

Iranian Kurds have made their displeasure with Iran known more than once, though they supported Iran's war effort against Iraq to aid their Iraqi brethren.

The Turkish Kurds have never really accepted the extinction of Kurdistan; even now they engage in terrorist activities in Turkey. None of the nations with Kurdish minorities wish to grant them local self-government, mush less national independence. The rest of the world isn't interested enough to disturb the local status quo; the vision of Kurdistan won't be realized soon, if ever.

Efforts have been made by individuals to create new states so that they might escape the taxation and other economic regulation of existing states. Marshall J. Langer describes two such in his work, *How to Use Foreign Tax Havens*.

Sealand consisted of a structure erected by the British six miles out in the English Channel to serve as a gun platform in World War II. It had a territory of sorts, thought it was a manmade territory. It had a government of sorts; its would-be creators declared themselves to be the government. Its government claimed to have independence, though no one on earth not involved in the

Sealand venture agreed. But it had no population, because no one lived on the abandoned platform permanently. Sealand's nearest neighbor, Great Britain, wasn't about to recognize it as a state because its founders were Englishmen seeking to escape many provisions of English law they found unpleasant. The rest of the world's nations went along.

Minerva consists of some reefs in the Pacific Ocean 250 miles off the coast of the kingdom of Tonga. They are uninhabited, for the good reason that they're mostly under water at high tide. Nevertheless an effort was made to declare this unpleasant corner of the globe an independent state. In a sense Minerva had a real territory. It had the same sort of government and independence as Sealand — but, again like Sealand, it had no population. Unlike Sealand, it could never have population; who can live on a reef that's under water at high tide?

The King of Tonga objected to the creation of such a neighbor, and declared the Minerva reef annexed to his domains. It's unclear whether the rest of the world acceded to this, but the world most certainly doesn't recognize the existence of Minerva as a state.

There exists an organization that is recognized by some 40 nations as a sovereign state, though it hasn't controlled any territory since 1798: the Knights of Malta. They began their existence during the Crusades as the Knights Hospitaler, or the Knights of St. John. They possessed fortresses in Palestine until expelled by the Muslims in 1291. They then moved to the island of Rhodes until the Turks drove them out during the 1520s. They then occupied the island of Malta until Napoleon's troops drove them out in 1798. Since then they've been a state without a territory, and will continue to be so. Many of the states that recognize them are nations of strong Roman Catholic belief; the devotion of the Knights to the Catholic Church is not forgotten by traditionalists.

Dependencies and colonies. Many nations claim sovereignty over lands that aren't attached to their home territories — islands or portions of another continent — or perhaps just nearby enclaves surrounded by the territory of a neighbor.

More than half of the land area of the earth was controlled by far-off governments in 1900 although decolonization has almost eliminated this phenomenon. Several countries still maintain control over distant possessions, however.

Among such American possessions are Puerto Rico, the American Virgin Islands, Guam, American Samoa, the Northern Caroline Islands and some other Pacific islands.

Great Britain retains Hong Kong (which will revert to China in 1997), Gibraltar, the Falkland Islands, several islands in the West Indies, and other remote scraps of territory.

France still holds French Guiana on the coast of South America, the

Caribbean islands of Guadeloupe and Martinique, the islands of St. Pierre and Miquelon off the coast of Newfoundland, the southwest Pacific island of New Caledonia, Tahiti and the other islands of French Polynesia, and a few other possessions.

The Netherlands rules the Caribbean islands of Aruba, Curacao, Bonaire and a few others.

Spain possesses two enclaves on the coast of Morocco (Ceuta and Melilla), the Canary Islands in the Atlantic and the Balearic Islands in the Mediterranean.

Portugal still holds an enclave on the Chinese coast (Macao) plus the Madeira and Azores Islands in the Atlantic.

Denmark rules the great island of Greenland plus the Faroe Islands in the north Atlantic.

Norway governs an Arctic colony, Svalbard, consisting of the island of Spitzbergen plus eight smaller islets.

Australia and New Zealand each rule scattered Pacific islands.

Recognition of governments. Sometimes two or more groups claim to be the legitimate rulers of a nation. The world's other nations must then decide which group to recognize as the true government.

The general rule in the world community is that if a government effectively controls the territory and people of the nation it's entitled to recognition. If it exercises control but its tenure is uncertain, de facto recognition is conferred. Such recognition may be revoked later if conditions change. If its control is certain, with no challenges in sight, de jure recognition will be conferred. This is theoretically permanent and irrevocable, as long as the government holds power.

When there's civil war in a nation and the forces of both sides control a substantial amount of the national territory and substantial numbers of the nation's people, problems arise.

In Spain the army sought to overthrow the government of the Republic in 1936. The coup in part misfired — in some parts of the country the soldiers took control — in other parts the government subdued the rebels and retained control. Bitter civil war ensued that was to tear the country to pieces for two and a half years. Both sides claimed to be the legitimate government of Spain. Neither wanted to divide the country.

Were the Nationalist rebels entitled to recognition as the government in the parts of the country they controlled?

The English courts answered "yes." Though the Republic was the de jure government of Spain, the courts reasoned that the Nationalists were the de facto government in the parts of the country they controlled because they fully exercised governmental powers there and were thus entitled to recognition. Ultimately they won the war and extinguished the Republic, then obtaining recognition as the de jure government of all of Spain.

If there is constitutional continuity between one group of rulers and another, no question of denial of recognition will arise. George Bush succeeded Ronald Reagan as president of the United States through constitutional processes; the change of government was unchallengeably legitimate.

Adolf Hitler lawfully succeeded Kurt von Schleicher as chancellor of Germany through another constitutional process, appointment to the post by President Paul von Hindenburg. Though the world knew that Hitler intended to destroy the constitutional basis of the German Weimar Republic, no one could doubt the lawfulness of his assumption of power.

Even when there's no constitutional continuity between a government and its successor, the successor will normally be recognized.

Fidel Castro assumed power in Cuba through the might of the gun, overthrowing his predecessor Fulgencio Batista. After Batista resigned Cuba's presidency and fled the country, there was no force within Cuba prepared to deny Castro's power. His government was therefore almost universally recognized (but not by the United States).

The Ortega government of Nicaragua assumed power in much the same way; when Anastasio Somoza resigned the presidency of that country and fled the Sandinistas had all of the remaining guns.

The government of Corazon Aquino in the Philippines too came to power by force, but under different circumstances. Her predecessor Ferdinand Marcos sought to retain his office by rigging presidential elections in which Aquino was his opponent. Though Marcos proclaimed himself to be the winner, huge numbers of his people refused to accept his claim and he left the country to avoid civil war. Though Aquino didn't win the election she very likely represented the wishes of a majority of Filipinos when she took office.

Although Americans like to think that the only legitimate governments are those holding office by expression of the will of the people, such governments have been a minority on this planet. Changes of government in the majority of the world's nations have come to pass through military coups, backstage political maneuver and the like. Pragmatism demands that we accord recognition to the effective government of a nation, whether we like its ruler or not. This has been the usual American policy.

Occasionally, however, we allow political preference to dictate policy in deciding questions of recognition.

In 1910 Francisco Madero led a revolt in Mexico which toppled the dictatorship of Porfirio Diaz. In 1912 Madero was elected president of Mexico in a free election but two years later he was overthrown and murdered by General Victoriano Huerta, who assumed the presidency. Though Huerta was only one of several who had risen to the presidency of Mexico via this disreputable route, and though the U.S. had recognized all of his predecessors, President Woodrow Wilson refused to recognize Huerta because he didn't represent the will of the people.

Civil war wracked Mexico as a result of the Huerta coup. Eventually Venustiano Carranza emerged as leader of the power most likely to topple Huerta, and the Wilson administration did what it could to help him succeed. He won and was duly recognized by Washington.

The United States very much disapproved of the coup through which Lenin's Bolsheviki assumed power in Russia in 1917. During the Russian Civil War of 1918–21, we recognized none of the contenders as Russia's legitimate government. Even after Bolshevik control of Russia was assured by victory in the civil war, we still refused to acknowledge the winners. We had no effective diplomatic dealings with the Soviet Union until 1933, when we finally conferred recognition.

Politics similarly causes the United States to deny recognition to the Castro government of Cuba.

Some of the world's governments are either imposed on their people by outside powers, or are kept in place by foreign assistance. Noteworthy were the governments of the Soviet Union's European satellites, imposed by Soviet military and political power after World War II and (in the cases of Hungary and Czechoslovakia) kept in place by military force. (Now that the Soviet Union is no longer willing to use force to keep these regimes in power, they have fallen.)

Soviet and Cuban troops have also aided Marxist-Leninist governments in Angola, Mozambique and Ethiopia in their struggles against guerrilla enemies. However, the Cubans have left Angola and the Soviets have sharply reduced their aid to all three of these regimes. The governments of Angola and Mozambique seek to survive by backing off from Marxism-Leninism and seeking Western economic aid; the Ethiopian regime is presently getting the worst of it in war against various groups of rebels.

Though the U.S. recognized the governments imposed on the nations of eastern Europe by Soviet arms it refused and still refuses to recognize the government of Kampuchea because it was imposed on that country by the Vietnamese.

The United States also refuses to recognize the government of Angola. When the Portuguese abandoned that colony in 1975, three armed factions battled for supremacy. Victory went to the Marxist-Leninist Popular Movement for the Liberation of Angola (MPLA) which received massive Soviet and Cuban assistance. Though most of the world recognized the victors, the United States held back. Since 1975 the National Union for the Total Independence of Angola (UNITA), under the leadership of Jonas Savimbi, has conducted a vigorous guerrilla war against the MPLA. Though the U.S. doesn't officially recognize Savimbi as the ruler of the country, it has aided him in various ways. We recognize the existence of the nation of Angola, but no government at the moment.

The United States recognizes the government of Mozambique, though a similar situation prevails there. Only one organization fought the Portuguese colonial power in that country—the Marxist-Leninist Front for the Liberation of Mozambique (FRELIMO). It assumed power there in 1975 when the Portuguese pulled out and it was recognized by most nations. An opposition movement, the Mozambique National Resistance Organization (RENAMO), commenced guerrilla warfare against FRELIMO in 1976 and now controls much of the country. Though RENAMO is anti–Marxist-Leninist, it has no American support, primarily because its major outside ally and supplier has been the Republic of South Africa.

Military force short of formal war is often used to overthrow governments. The Soviet Union used military force to establish a new government in Afghanistan in 1979. The United States used military force to overthrow the Marxist-Leninist government of Grenada and the corrupt government of General Manuel Noriega in Panama. United States–supported rebels overthrew the governments of Mohammed Mossadegh in Iran and Jacobo Arbenz Guzman in Guatemala during the 1950s, but efforts to accomplish the same thing in Cuba failed at the Bay of Pigs in 1961. French troops put an end to the reign of Emperor Jean-Bedel Bokassa in the Central African Empire, causing that country to once more become the Central African Republic.

Lesser powers sometimes do this sort of thing. The Kampuchean government of Pol Pot was overthrown by the Vietnamese troops who established the present government of that country. The tyranny of Idi Amin of Uganda was ended by Tanzanian military force. Libyan forces fight alongside Arab rebels against the Congoid-dominated central government of Chad, while French planes and pilots aid the government's fight against the rebels.

The most recent example of such conduct by a relatively small power is the Iraqi deposition of the government of the Emir of Kuwait in August of 1990. This was reversed by the allied victory in the Gulf War of early 1991.

Partitioned countries. Since World War II the territories of four historically recognized lands have been divided between sometimes competing governments. These divisions have caused war and diplomatic, legal and economic difficulty. The four are Korea, Germany, Vietnam and China.

Korea, which had been an independent nation for centuries, became a colony of Japan in 1910. The Allies promised to restore its independence after Japan's defeat in World War II. Americans accepted the surrender of Japanese troops in the nation south of the 38th Parallel, while Soviet troops accepted the surrender north of that line. Though the major powers had agreed to collaborate in creating a government for a unified Korea, this didn't happen. In the United States zone the Republic of Korea (South Korea) came into being, while in the Soviet zone the Democratic People's Republic of Korea (North Korea) arose.

When the North tried to unite the country by force in 1950, the Korean

War was fought. Americans too sought to unite the country by force later in 1950 after the Inchon landing and the destruction of the North Korean Army, so the Chinese entered the war. As a result of Chinese intervention the war ended in stalemate, both reunion efforts failed, and the two Koreas continue to exist. The U.S. continues to refuse to recognize the Democratic People's Republic as a state, while the Soviets refuse to accept the Republic of Korea, though both Koreas possess all of the requisites of statehood. (The USSR and most of the Communist world sent teams to the Seoul Olympic Games in 1988, despite their non-recognition of the government of the Republic of Korea. Only North Korea, Cuba and five other small nations boycotted the Games. As of July 1990, the two Koreas were talking of opening their mutual frontier, which has been sealed since the armistice of 1953.)

The victors over Nazi Germany agreed to reconstruct their enemy after the end of World War II, dividing the prostrate nation into four occupation zones, one each for the United States, Great Britain, France and the Soviet Union. Due to the Cold War of the late 1940s, collaboration between the former allies on this task virtually ceased. As it became clear that the Soviet Union wouldn't permit the union of its zone with a non–Communist Germany while the Western Allies wouldn't permit the creation of a Communist Germany, each side worked toward forming its own country. The result was the birth of two nations where before had been one — the German Federal Republic (West Germany) and the German Democratic Republic (East Germany). The Soviet Union recognized the Federal Republic during the 1950s, while the United States denied the legitimacy of the Democratic Republic and refused to recognize it. Only the detente of the 1970s led to the American policy change that recognized East Germany and the permanence of the division of Germany. Later the two Germanies reluctantly recognized each other; now, with the demise of the Communist government of the East, the partition ended with German reunification. Monetary and economic union occurred on July 1, 1990; political union followed.

After the Viet Minh broke the will of France to resist the establishment of an independent Vietnam, it was agreed in Geneva in 1955 that the Viet Minh would control that part of the nation above the 18th Parallel, while a non–Communist government in Saigon would control that part to the south. It was also agreed that free national elections would be held within two years to unite the country.

The elections were never held because the southern nationalists and their American backers doubted that the Viet Minh would permit free elections in the north. Thus the Republic of Vietnam arose in the south and the People's Republic of Vietnam in the north. The north tried to subvert and overthrow the government of the south from the beginning. In order to keep this from happening the U.S. intervened in the struggle. After the Americans abandoned this effort in 1973 it was fairly easy for the forces of the north to complete the conquest of the south. The Republic of Vietnam vanished—the People's Republic now comprises the whole country. The United States recognizes the existence of Vietnam as a nation, but doesn't recognize the Hanoi regime as its government.

China was partitioned because of an inconclusive civil war, the war of 1945–49. After the victorious Communist armies had driven the Nationalists from the mainland, Chiang Kai Shek established his government upon the last Chinese soil under Nationalist control—the island of Taiwan. From that time forward, two governments claimed to be the legitimate rulers of China: the Communist regime in Peking and the Nationalist regime in Taipei, Taiwan.

Since the U.S. had supported the Nationalists in the war and the Communists militarily opposed our forces in Korea, we continued to recognize the Taipei government as the true government of China, though the Communist rulers in Peking had effective control over more than 90 percent of the Chinese people.

This state of affairs continued until American policy toward Communist China changed during the Nixon years. Ultimately, under President Carter, we extended recognition to Peking and withdrew it from Taipei.

A curious situation now exists with respect to the international status of Taiwan. The island clearly meets all of the requisites of nationhood—yet no one recognizes it as a nation.

This is because its government doesn't consider itself to be the government of Taiwan. Rather, it claims to be the government of China. To the United States and the rest of the world, it's clearly not the government of China because the Peking regime rules China. So long as the Taipei government maintains this facade, it can't be recognized upon its own terms. (Of course, the world recognizes Taiwan as a political entity—international trade does much to fertilize its booming economy.)

Annexation of states. Recent history is filled with examples of extinctions of formerly sovereign states through the addition of their territory to that of other states. Annexations may be voluntary but most are involuntary.

The United States absorbed two sovereign nations in the course of its territorial expansion—Texas in 1845 and Hawaii in 1898. Both annexations were accomplished by treaties voluntarily entered into by the governments involved.

In late 1990 the German Federal Republic (West Germany) annexed the German Democratic Republic (East Germany) through the process of the east applying for admission to the west as additional states and the west accepting the applications. This was desired by both governments and a large majority of both populations.

Such voluntary annexation is uncommon. In 1772 Russia, Prussia and Austria forced Poland to cede to them half of its territory. In 1792 Prussia and Russia forced it to cede much of what remained. In 1794 the Polish people revolted against the government that ruled the rump of the country in an effort to preserve national independence. Russian troops extinguished the revolt and dispersed the revolutionary army. Russia, Prussia and Austria then divided the rest of the country among them. Poland vanished from the map until its restoration after World War I.

During the wars of the French Revolution and Napoleon, France annexed at various times Belgium, the Netherlands, all of the German-speaking territory bordering the North Sea as far north as Hamburg, much German territory on the left bank of the Rhine and all of French-speaking Switzerland, destroying several independent political units (such as the Republics of Geneva and Hamburg) in the process. (These annexations were reversed by the Congress of Vienna in 1814–15.)

In 1866 occurred the Austro-Prussian War. Allied with Austria were the German states of Hannover, Hesse-Cassel, Hesse-Nassau, and the Free City of Frankfurt-am-Main. The Austrian army was defeated in six weeks, and the war ended with Prussian troops in occupation of the territories of these Austrian allies. The government of the Prussian Chancellor von Bismarck declared these states annexed to Prussia; their governments were summarily deposed and their independence extinguished, never to be restored.

In 1898 began the Boer War between Great Britain and the south African republics of Transvaal and the Orange Free State. After a long bloody struggle the British won and extinguished the independence of these nations. They were incorporated into the Union of South Africa, a self-governing British colony which became independent as the Republic of South Africa. The two former nations are now provinces of the Republic.

Japan obtained a free hand in the ancient kingdom of Korea by defeating China in the Sino-Japanese War of 1894–95 and Russia in the Russo-Japanese War of 1904–05. In 1910 Japan deposed the Korean royal government and declared the peninsula annexed to itself. The consequences of this action have been explained earlier in this chapter.

Yugoslavia came into being at the end of World War I. The principality of Montenegro was incorporated into it without its government or people being consulted and its royal dynasty was deposed. In a sense the kingdom of Serbia was also incorporated into Yugoslavia, but the king of Serbia became the king of Yugoslavia, greatly multiplying his dominions.

The German government of Adolf Hitler extinguished two nations prior to the beginning of World War II. Austria was incorporated into and made an integral part of Germany in 1938; its independence was restored after Hitler's defeat in 1945.

Czechoslovakia was wiped off the map in 1939. Its provinces of Bohemia and Moravia were turned into the Protectorate of Bohemia-Moravia, a sort of German colony, while the province of Slovakia was recognized by Hitler as an independent country. Czechoslovakia too was restored in 1945; Slovakia vanished from the map as an independent country, though it continues to exist as a state of the Czechoslovak federation.

Hitler and Stalin collaborated to destroy Poland in September 1939. The Soviet Union annexed the eastern half of the country. Germany annexed a large part of the western half and ruled the rest as another colony. Poland too regained independence in 1945 but the Soviet Union retained most of the Polish territory annexed in 1939; how the new Poland acquired her present frontiers has been discussed in Chapter 1.

The Soviet Union terminated the independence of Lithuania, Latvia and Estonia by incorporating them into itself in 1940 through military occupation; the three lands became republics of the USSR. They still are; today their peoples seek to reverse the events of 1940 and regain national independence.

The major post–World War II annexation has been the extinction of the Republic of Vietnam by the military power of the People's Democratic Republic of Vietnam in 1975.

When we think of involuntary annexations, we think of small countries brutally overwhelmed by mighty imperialistic enemies. This isn't always the case.

In British India, the colonial government allowed many princes of pre-colonial times to continue to reign over their domains. When the British yielded control over the subcontinent to the governments of India and Pakistan they yielded only those territories over which they had ruled directly. It was left to the new republics to deal with the monarchies.

Most of these agreed to join India or Pakistan at once, but the major holdout was the largest. The Nizam of Hyderabad wanted to maintain the independence of his state, but the Indian government in New Delhi refused to consider it. Since Hyderabad was entirely surrounded by India, it was at the mercy of its huge neighbor. Indian troops marched in, and declared the Nizam deposed and his territory annexed.

Fate of the defeated in war. Several examples have been described of situations in which a wartime victor has annexed the territory of the vanquished. This, however, is not the usual fate of losers of wars.

As stated earlier, before the French Revolution the defeated usually kept their thrones and at least some of their territory. The Napoleonic Wars changed that state of affairs; Napoleon deposed dynasties, merged their territories into new kingdoms for his relatives and annexed the territories of other dynasties to France. His enemies avenged themselves by deposing his government and those of his relatives, but they left the territory of France almost intact.

The United States defeated the armed forces of Mexico in the Mexican War and occupied Mexico City, but didn't directly change the Mexican government (though the Mexicans themselves deposed President Santa Anna, leader of their losing effort). We settled for annexing large tracts of Mexican territory and paying compensation for it.

Prussia thoroughly defeated Austria in the war of 1866 and annexed the territories of some small Austrian allies as described above, but left Austria's government and territory intact.

Germany made no effort to change the government of France after the Franco-Prussian War, though it did annex the provinces of Alsace and Lorraine (and thus planted one of the seeds of World War I).

Germany would probably have annexed Belgium had it won World War I, but it seemed to have no intention of destroying the independence or the governments of its major opponents. Germany would have left the Czar on the Russian throne and the government of the Third Republic in place in France; it would simply have collected huge territorial and financial spoils from the losers (as it actually obtained from Russia in the Treaty of Brest-Litovsk and from Romania in the Treaty of Bucharest, both signed in the spring of 1918).

The victorious Allies on the other hand destroyed the Austro-Hungarian state, and would have done the same to Turkey had nationalist resistance of the Turkish people not been so formidable. Germany and Bulgaria suffered less drastic fates, simply losing some tracts of territory.

The Germans did not totally annex the territory of any conquered land in World War II. To be sure they annexed part of Poland and turned the remainder of their share of that land into a colony, but no other land met so draconic a fate. In Norway, the Netherlands and Greece puppet native governments were installed. Belgium was put under German military rule. Yugoslavia was partitioned and the monarch deposed, Croatia was spun off as an independent country, while the rest fell under either Italian military rule or the rule of a pro–German Serb puppet regime in Belgrade.

In Denmark the Germans left the democratic government in place, even allowing a free election to happen there in 1943. When the Danish government became uncooperative later in the war, however, the Germans deposed it and created a puppet successor.

France was a unique case. When it admitted defeat in June of 1940 the government headed by Premier Marshal Henri-Philippe Petain signed an armistice with the victors. A month later what remained of the Parliament declared the French Third Republic at an end. Petain put a new authoritarian constitution into effect and ruled France as a dictator. Germany recognized the Marshal's regime as the legitimate government of France and allowed it to exercise civil authority in the country and over French colonies, though much of France came under German military occupation. Great Britain and the United States recognized Petain's government and maintained diplomatic relations with it until the Germans occupied all of France in November of 1942. After that Petain's French government had the same international status as the other German puppet regimes. None of these governments survived the end of German occupation of their territories.

The Allies demanded unconditional surrender of Germany; therefore the Nazi regime fought to the bitter end.

Adolf Hitler appointed Grand Admiral Karl Doenitz as his successor as German Chancellor before the Fuhrer committed suicide on April 30, 1945. Doenitz was Chancellor of the Third Reich for a bit more than a week; it was his government that unconditionally surrendered on May 8, 1945.

His regime continued a shadowy existence at Flensburg, a remote city on the Danish border, for a few more weeks. Then British military police arrested Chancellor and Cabinet and declared the government ended.

From that time forward there was no German government in Germany. German bureaucrats enforced law under the direction of the Allied military governments of the occupation zones. Gradually German local governments were created and allowed to assume power. Still later state governments appeared. But it wasn't until 1949 that German governments—the German Federal Republic in the west and the German Democratic Republic in the east—were allowed to resume the trappings of national sovereignty.

In the Far East the Japanese established puppet regimes in most areas they occupied. Manchuria became the state of Manchukuo, in theory ruled by Henry Pu-Yi (the last Emperor of China, who was deposed as a very young child by the revolt of 1912) but in practice by Japanese military and civilian "advisors." A Chinese regime in Nanking exercised civil authority in Japanese-occupied China. The pre-occupation Thai government continued to rule Thailand, while puppet native governments replaced colonial regimes in Indonesia and Burma.

The American-supported government of the Philippines fled with General MacArthur in 1942; the Japanese created a new regime to replace it.

Though Japanese troops occupied French Indo-China in 1940, they allowed the French to continue governing until the spring of 1945. At that point they deposed the colonial regime and created a native government in its stead.

In the Philippines the puppet Japanese regime's power was destroyed by General MacArthur's liberating troops. The state of Manchukuo and the Japanese-supported government in China ended with the war. In Indonesia, Indo-China and Burma participants in the Japanese-sponsored regimes joined the nationalist resistance to the return of British, French and Dutch colonialists; some participated in the governments that took power after these lands achieved independence.

In Japan the constitutional civilian government unconditionally surrendered to the Allies in September of 1945. General MacArthur left it in place, governing the country through it. Thus, organized Japanese government never ceased to exist, even at the height of the American occupation.

As stated earlier, had the Allied forces won the Korean War the government of Kim Il Sung and the Korean Democratic Republic itself would have ceased to exist. Had the Chinese and North Koreans won the Syngman Rhee government and the Republic of Korea would have ceased to exist. The government of the Democratic Republic of Vietnam (North Vietnam) was in no danger during the Vietnam War; the issue was the continued existence of the Republic of Vietnam (South Vietnam).

In the other major international wars since 1945 there have been no total victors. Israel has won all four wars against its Arab neighbors, but the neighbors and their governments have survived defeat. (Had Israel lost even one of these wars, however, both the government and the nation might have ceased to exist.)

One of the objectives of both sides in the Iran-Iraq war was the overthrow of the opposing government, but since the fighting ended in a draw neither side achieved that goal. The allied objective in the Gulf War was the liberation of Kuwait, not the overthrow of Saddam Hussein's government. The objective was attained.

Post-war restorations. In the last two centuries there have been three world wars between gigantic coalitions—the wars of the French Revolution and Napoleon which ended in 1815 and the two World Wars of our century.

The Congress of Vienna redrew the European map after the wars of Napoleon. Though the loser, France, remained territorially intact, many small monarchies and republics destroyed by the French were not restored but added to the domains of victorious great powers. As already mentioned, those who made peace after World War I left Germany and Bulgaria substantially intact but destroyed the empires of Austria-Hungary and Turkey, thereby creating a host of new nations. Germany itself was for a time destroyed after World War II, but Japan was left substantially intact.

The peacemakers with Japan intended to restore the status quo in southeast Asia. Thus British rule was restored in Hong Kong, Malaysia and Burma, the French reoccupied Indo-China and Dutch rule was restored in Indonesia. But Indonesian nationalists of the puppet government established by the Japanese launched a bitter guerrilla war against the returning Dutch, who were forced to concede Indonesian independence in 1949. In Indo-China, particularly in Vietnam, nationalists launched an even more bitter war against the returning French (the beginning of the 30-year struggle for a unified independent Vietnam that didn't end until 1975). The British conceded independence to Burma without a struggle but fought a long successful war against guerrillas in Malaysia.

Great wars inevitably result in earthshaking changes, especially with respect to small states caught up in the struggle. The events of 1989 and 1990 indicate that the era of great power struggles may be at an end. If so, small states now have more power to determine their own destinies.

Chapter 10

Governmental Systems

Beginnings. In the spring of 1989 Americans celebrated the bicentennial of the inauguration of George Washington as first president of the United States. Thus the government created by the Constitution of 1787 has completed two unbroken centuries of existence. The fundamental law of the United States has become one of the oldest on earth.

The drafters of the Constitution knew that they were sailing uncharted waters when they began their work. The victory won over Great Britain in the Revolutionary War was unprecedented in world history. Unless some form of unity could be devised to hold the victorious 13 states together, the fruits of the great accomplishment could spoil.

What was needed was government powerful enough to impose national unity and defend national independence, but weak enough never to become a menace to the freedoms of the governed. Undesirable examples of government were visible everywhere and none provided a pattern worth copying.

Ancient government. The founding fathers of the United States knew their history and were well aware of the strengths and weaknesses of the forms of government invented by the states of Western culture.

Monarchy had of course been the prevailing form of government from ancient times until the eighteenth century. The only exceptions were the republican governments of ancient times and of the Middle Ages.

The philosopher Aristotle, writing in the fourth century B.C., divided governments into three sorts:

(1) Government by one person.

(2) Government by a small group of people.

(3) Government by all citizens of the state.

He claimed that no one of these forms was intrinsically superior to the others; the quality of government depended upon the nature of the persons doing the governing.

One-person government is potentially the best, said Aristotle and his mentor Plato. When one person rules the state for the benefit of the governed decisions are made quickly and the state profits thereby. The good person can work his will without danger of obstruction by selfish interests.

193

When the single ruler is concerned only with his own interests and those of his supporters the governed suffer. Aristotle called this sort of government tyranny and the ruler a tyrant. Ancient history provided many unsavory examples of this unpleasantness, illustrating emphatically that when there are no limits to the tyrant's power his villainy can wreak almost unbounded injustice.

One-person government is by its very nature unstable. No human being is immortal; the term of one person's government will end at his death. Such government may well suffer from succession problems; only in the most stable monarchies will power pass smoothly from the deceased ruler to a designated heir. Only in such lands will the cry be heard, "Le roi est mort; vive le roi!" (The King is dead; long live the King!) Otherwise, political intrigue or even civil war may rend the land until the identity of the new ruler is determined.

When a small group rules the state for the benefit of its citizens the state prospers. This condition Aristotle called aristocracy.

When the small group rules for the benefit of itself the citizenry suffer, though perhaps not as much as under tyranny. This Aristotle called oligarchy.

Aristocracy can be the most stable, durable government, as long as the aristocrats present a united front to the governed. It can also be the most beneficial for the state over the long term. Government by a group will not be terminated by the death of one of the rulers; the group never dies. By admitting new members as the old die or resign it perpetuates itself in power. As long as it doesn't lose its consensus as to how to govern, offend the governed so that they organize against it, or suffer total defeat in war it can survive indefinitely.

Government by all citizens is essentially government by majority vote. This is good when the majority rule for the benefit of all citizens (Aristotle terms this polity); it's bad when the majority rules only for itself (Aristotle's democracy). Ancient philosophers branded this the most unstable of governmental forms because majorities change, causing policies to change.

To Aristotle, average citizens aren't too likely to concern themselves with the good of the state; they have enough problems keeping their own lives in order. The ideal state should be an agricultural one, the majority of whose citizens are self-sustaining farmers. Such persons are by nature independent and self-reliant; they're not likely to fall under the influence of wealthy or corrupt patrons.

Rule by citizens in an urban state isn't likely to last long, Aristotle continued. Urban life isn't conducive to personal independence; the city dweller is very likely to fall under the influence of employers, moneylenders and demagogues. A handful of influential people may well manipulate popular votes for their own purposes.

Moreover, most of the citizenry of any state aren't very affluent. It's human nature for the poor to envy the rich. It's also human nature for demagogues to tell the poor that they should use their voting power to expropriate the rich and in essence "whittle them down to size." When this attempt is made, the rich minority are apt to organize themselves to protect their property and economic power. The result might be civil dissension, civil war, or the overthrow of the government.

In short, government by the citizenry lasts only as long as the majority doesn't overreach itself and attempt to oppress minorities—especially affluent minorities.

Human nature being what it is, ancient philosophers felt that a mixed government—one with elements of all three forms—would be the best. There should be one person as head of state with the authority to take quick action when necessary. There should be a small group involved in running the state to provide experience, continuity, and long-term planning. The citizenry should be able to participate so that they too have a stake in their state's governance.

One-person government was universal in the large states of ancient times; only small city-states could afford the luxury of experimenting with other arrangements. Instability was the rule in the city-states of ancient Greece, most of which began as monarchies. Eventually the monarch became too tyrannical for the upper classes of the state; they overthrew him and established an aristocratic republic. The new rulers presided over a growth in economic well-being; the citizenry became affluent enough to take an interest in how the state was governed. Eventually the aristocrats became selfish oppressors in the minds of the citizens, who overthrew the oligarchy and established popular rule. For awhile there was harmony as the citizenry ruled for the benefit of everyone. Then the demagogues obtained control and unleashed the class struggle between rich and poor; either the rich overthrew the popular government and established an oligarchy or a tyrant overthrew it in the name of order and stability and again set up one-person rule.

Athens went through this cycle; it's worth mentioning because its democratic phase is so well documented. At that time only free adult males had the rights of citizens; all had the right to attend the assemblies that conducted public business and the right to hold public office. Athenian citizens were divided into ten tribes and much of the government was based upon this tribal organization.

Though the assembled voters were the sovereign power of the state, they all obviously couldn't be in session every day to conduct public business. Every year a Council of 500 members, 50 per tribe, was chosen by lot to serve as a sort of supervisory committee of the people. This was divided into subcommittees of 50 members each, each subcommittee being composed of members of only one of the ten tribes. Every day one of these subcommittees was in session·

to serve as the government for that day. They alternated in office, each serving every tenth day. Each day a subcommittee was in office it elected a chairman who in essence was chief of state for that day.

Also chosen by lot for one-year terms were 6,000 jurors (600 per tribe) to serve in the high court of the state. Major trials were held before gigantic juries of 200 or more members; these rendered decisions by majority vote. (The philosopher Socrates was condemned to death by such a jury.)

Financial and military offices were filled by annual election, with unlimited eligibility for re-election. Ten generals were chosen to command the armed forces of the state, originally one per tribe, but later at large. These shared theoretically equal authority, but the assembly and the council could assign commands and thus prefer some generals over others.

All citizens were subject to military service; thus in wartime they could assess the talents of their elected generals first-hand and remove the incompetent from office.

In order to keep demagoguery under control the institution of ostracism was created. Once a year a special citizen assembly could be called. If at least 6,000 citizens attended (which was unusually high attendance at popular assemblies) each attendee would vote for one person to be banished from Athens for ten years. The unfortunate one who obtained the most votes was so banished. But he didn't lose his citizenship or property; when the ten years expired he could return and resume his life where it had left off.

During the time that Athenian democracy blossomed (the middle of the fifth century B.C.), Pericles was the most popular, respected leader of the state. He was repeatedly elected a general, formulating wise strategies in both war and peace. So long as he influenced state policy Athens prospered; after his death lesser men dominated the state. They devised the faulty strategies that assured Athenian defeat by Sparta in the Peloponnesian War, resulting in the destruction of Athenian power and the end of the democracy.

Victorious Sparta imposed an aristocratic restoration (the new aristocracy being composed of Athenians who'd favored Spartan victory). Later citizen rule was again restored, but by now Athens had become a relatively minor power among the city-states.

Nowhere in ancient Greece did citizen rule endure for more than a few decades. Aristocracies were the most stable government form, but all eventually fell to the superior military power of the Macedonian monarchy.

The Roman Republic was a mixed government that survived for more than four centuries and conquered the entire Mediterranean basin. Its monarchical element was the two consuls, its chief executives, elected for one-year terms by the Comitia Centuriata, the assembly of citizens organized into centuries on the basis of ownership of property. The consuls exercised military command known as imperium, and possessed considerable powers in peacetime (as long as they could agree upon how to exercise them). Other elected executive and judicial officers shared in the day-to-day duties of running the government (the Praetors who acted as judges, the Aediles who supervised public works and the Quaestors who handled financial matters). There were also Censors, elected for five-year terms, who supervised public lands and kept records of who had the rights of citizenship and who were entitled to seats in the Senate.

Its aristocracy was the Senate, composed of ex-office-holders who sat for life. The Senate provided long-term planning and wise advice.

Its democratic elements were the two assemblies of citizens—the afore-mentioned Comitia Centuriata which elected the consuls and praetors and the Comitia Tributa (the Assembly of Tribes) which elected other public officers and possessed legislative power.

The Roman people were organized into 35 tribes, four of which consisted of residents of the city, 31 of which represented citizens living outside the city. The four urban tribes had more members per tribe than the 31 rural tribes.

The Comitia Tributa was organized on a tribal basis. Each cast one vote, the majority of voters within the tribe determining how the vote would be cast. Since a voter had to come to Rome and attend the assembly in order to vote, large numbers of urban tribe members generally attended; the attendance of rural tribe members was smaller. Yet the rural voters cast 31 tribal votes to four for the urban tribes.

The Comitia Centuriata was organized into 193 centuries, each of which cast one vote and a majority of the voters of the century determined how its vote was cast. Makeup of centuries was determined by tribal membership and property ownership. There were five classes of property owners; the first and richest class was allotted 70 centuries. The other classes were allotted 122 centuries while the propertyless comprised the 193rd century. Ninety-seven centuries comprised a majority; if the rich voted together (as they did more often than not) they needed the support of only 27 of the other centuries to carry an election.

There was also a Concilium Plebis—Assembly of Plebeians (the poorer citizens) which had the right to elect the ten Tribunes. Any one Tribune had the right to veto an act of the Assembly of Tribes. This too voted by tribes, and could enact items of legislation (called plebiscita, hence our word plebiscite). The Tribunes had authority to veto plebiscita as well as acts of the Comitia Tributa.

Neither assembly was fully democratic, the rich dominating the Comitia Centuriata and the non-residents of Rome the other two assemblies. But there was enough diffusion of power within the state to insure (for better than three centuries) that no one individual could dominate the state, and enough political consensus that this cumbersome, complex government could establish a gigantic empire.

In a time of emergency a dictator was appointed, who could exercise absolute power for a period of six months. When his term ended, however, he was accountable to the people for what he'd done during his term. If he had abused his power, he could suffer severe punishment—even death.

Eventually the state outgrew its constitution. Political consensus vanished and power-seekers used extra-constitutional procedures and military force to pursue their objectives. The Republic evolved into the quasi-monarchical Principate of Caesar Augustus which evolved further into the Oriental monarchy of Diocletian and Constantine.

Medieval government. Monarchy was the Western condition during the Dark and early Middle Ages. The primitive tribal states of the Germanic successors of the Roman Empire became feudal monarchies which the Holy Roman Emperors sought to weld into a new universal empire.

The monarch's theoretical power derived from his position as chief feudal lord over all landowners within his domain, and his lawful right to claim military service from his vassals. As the economic revival of the West began, government became more complex and the royal need for money increased. Monarchs began to call assemblies of their subjects in order to request financial assistance. The subjects responded by requesting privileges from the monarchs. From Spain to Scandinavia rulers were soon sharing governmental power with their subjects in exchange for money.

These assemblies were organized by estates. In some places (such as France) there were three—the nobility, the clergy, and the third (representing everyone other than nobility and clergy). In others (such as Sweden) there were four—the nobility, the clergy, the town dwellers, and the peasantry. In still others the division was magnates (great nobility), lesser nobility, clergy and townsmen.

For several centuries the possibility existed that all European monarchies might evolve into constitutional realms. In most states this didn't happen.

The development of gunpowder weapons allowed kings to possess armies that gave them a monopoly on military power within the state. The economic development of Europe during the sixteenth and seventeenth centuries created huge pools of wealth from which the state could derive revenue by taxation. With modern armies it was possible for an enterprising king to compel his subjects to grant him the power to levy taxation by decree. Once he acquired such power he no longer needed to consult his subjects under normal conditions.

From Spain through France to central Europe the powers of the medieval estates had melted away by 1700. Only in England, Sweden, Poland and a few states in Germany did they retain authority.

In Poland the medieval estates eventually destroyed the power of the king and the country. In England they obtained the power to govern and reduced the king to a figurehead. In Sweden and the German states they retained at least a share of governing power. In Sweden they were able to reduce the monarch to a figurehead for much of the eighteenth century and govern alone, but in 1772 King Gustavus III destroyed their power and ruled as an absolute monarch. In Mecklenburg the nobles obtained control over the estates and ran the Duchy until 1918. In Wuerttemberg the estates developed into a Parliament bearing a resemblance to England's; Wuerttemberg was one of the most liberal states in Germany right up until 1918.

In Italy a regime of city-states reminiscent of ancient Greece arose, particularly in the area north of Rome and south of the Alps. Here all of the governmental forms described by Aristotle once more flourished. Milan knew aristocracy, tyranny imposed by the Visconti, a short period of democracy, the tyranny of the Sforza, and finally Spanish conquest. Florence knew aristocracy, two short periods of democracy, the benign Medici dictatorship maintained by a clever political machine, and in the end Medici monarchy imposed by outside military force. Only Venice and Genoa, ruled by aristocracies, survived as independent entities until the era of the French Revolution.

City-states also existed in Germany. Some were Free Cities of the Holy Roman Empire (such as Frankfurt-am-Main and Nuremberg), governed by closed aristocracies. Others were bishoprics of the Roman Catholic Church (such as Cologne, Trier and Mainz) in which the Bishop exercised secular as well as episcopal power. Still others were members of the Hanseatic League (such as Hamburg, Bremen and Lubeck), a confederation of trading states dating from the Middle Ages, ruled by merchant aristocracies. Hamburg, Bremen and Lubeck survived the Napoleonic Wars as independent city-states and became the only republics within the German Empire. Hamburg and Bremen today retain a portion of their ancient independence as states of the German Federal Republic.

By 1787 more or less absolute monarchy prevailed almost everywhere on the European continent, except in Switzerland, parts of Germany, the Netherlands and Poland. We'll now examine a few of the existing governments of that period.

Eighteenth-century English government. Though the Declaration of Independence denounces in ringing terms the tyranny of King George III of Great Britain, continental Europeans looked upon the English government as one of the most enlightened on earth.

The English Parliament had begun whittling away at the powers of the king during the Middle Ages. It abolished the monarchy after its victory in the civil wars of the 1640s and the restored monarchy of the 1660s trod warily in its dealings with the parliamentarians. When James II sought to enhance royal power during the late 1680s he was overthrown in the Glorious Revolution; the settlement that brought William III and Mary to the throne made it clear that, from then on, the monarch might reign but Parliament would rule.

The institutions of Cabinet and prime minister began to develop in the middle of the eighteenth century. By the 1770s English governmental institutions were beginning to resemble those of present-day Great Britain.

The power to govern the nation lay in the hands of Parliament. Then, as now, there were two houses: the Lords and the Commons. The House of Lords, successor of two of the estates of early medieval England, was the stronghold of the titled nobility; most of its members held their seats by hereditary right. A small minority was composed of the Bishops of the Church of England, survivors of the early estate of the clergy.

The House of Commons as its name suggests theoretically represented the common people. It was the successor of the other two early medieval estates, the townsmen and the country people. Its members were elected, buy by only a small percentage of the population.

A fifth of the members of the Commons represented the counties of England, most of which elected two members. The right to vote was limited to 40-shilling freeholders—those who owned land or property with an annual rental value of at least 40 shillings a year. Only a small proportion of people in rural England met this property qualification.

The rest of the members of the Commons represented the boroughs of the realm, cities incorporated by royal charter. Most boroughs elected two members and could determine their own voting qualifications.

Some boroughs existed under charters granted during the early Middle Ages. In fact, no new boroughs had been created since 1648. Once a borough came into existence its charter was never revoked, though it might have lost all of its population. There existed some "rotten boroughs" like Old Sarum, which elected two members of the Commons though no one lived within its boundaries. The owner of the land upon which the town had once stood appointed its members.

At the other extreme, there were sizable towns like Manchester which hadn't been granted royal charters and thus had no right to elect members of the Commons.

A wide variety of electoral franchises existed in populated boroughs, many of which allowed all freemen to vote. A freeman was a person who'd been granted town citizenship; only granted, freeman status could be inherited. One could be a freeman without living in the borough.

Many others used the scot-and-lot franchise, under which any man affluent enough to be liable for paying poor tax had the right to vote.

Next most numerous were the burgage boroughs. Burgages were pieces of property, each of which conferred one vote upon their owners. For each burgage owned, a person possessed one vote. If you owned one more than half of the borough's burgages, you could appoint the members of the Commons from that borough.

Then there were a fair number of corporation boroughs. Here the borough council elected the members of the Commons. Since borough councils were closed — the council itself filled vacancies caused by death or resignation — a handful of people controlled these Commons seats permanently.

A few boroughs had the "potwalloper" franchise. Every man who had lived in the borough for six months, had a family, and boiled a pot on his own hearth had the right to vote. These boroughs had the largest electorate.

And finally, a small number of boroughs used a freeholder franchise similar to that used to qualify county voters.

There was no rule of "one man, one vote." You could vote in as many boroughs as you could qualify to vote in. There were a few persons who could vote in ten or more boroughs through ownership of property or possession of multiple borough citizenships.

Voting was oral; when you voted you announced in public which candidates you supported. Landlords and employers didn't hesitate to instruct tenants and employees how to vote. Disobeying the instructions of the mighty on such matters could be costly. Beer, wine and hard liquor flowed liberally on election days and bribery was an accepted way of vote-getting in large boroughs.

A few hundred powerful men elected the majority of the members of the Commons. In all less than 5 percent of the adult males of Great Britain could vote.

The powers of the two houses were equal. No bill could become law without the assent of both.

George III was the head of the English state. Though he lacked power to make law, no act of Parliament could become effective without his assent. His power to withhold assent amounted to an absolute veto which could not be overridden.

The king appointed the prime minister, who was then as now the political head of state. There was no requirement that he have the confidence of Parliament but he could not secure passage of legislation without that confidence. Thus the prime minister who had no majority support there would soon resign or be put out of office by the king.

King George had the right to dissolve Parliament whenever he saw fit and call for new elections to the Commons. This authority might be exercised at the request of the prime minister, or by the monarch himself.

The king also had the power to influence votes in the House of Lords by exercising his right to create peers. He could conjure up a majority in the Lords by ennobling enough proponents of a point of view to create one. The last time this had been done was in 1713, but the memory of it was fresh enough that a monarch or prime minister could sway votes in the Lords by threatening to use this power.

George III made little use of these powers. He acquired and kept political influence in a more direct, subtle and effective way though bribery, appointments to high civil and military offices and ennoblement of selected loyal supporters. By the use of such methods he was able to assure that his prime ministers controlled Parliament, and that the government would operate according to his will.

The judiciary limited itself to trying and deciding cases. Though king and Parliament were theoretically subject to the common law, the judges asserted no political or legal control over them.

England's government of legislative supremacy was dominated by a landed and moneyed aristocracy. The rampant bribery and corruption disgusted our forefathers who were determined to avoid building English weaknesses into the new American government.

The above-described arrangements continued to exist until 1832, when the House of Commons was reformed. The rotten boroughs were abolished, as were some others with a handful of voters. The number of county seats was increased, and some counties were divided into separate constituencies. Several formerly unrepresented towns and cities obtained the right to elect members of the Commons. A uniform voting franchise (based on ownership of property of the value of ten pounds or more) was established for the boroughs.

Thus the door was opened resulting in the democratization of Great Britain and the creation of the present governmental system.

Strong monarchy—Prussia. In 1650 the Duchy of Brandenburg was one of the insignificant states of present-day Germany that was trying to rebuild itself from the devastation caused by the Thirty Years War. By 1789 it had been transformed into the Kingdom of Prussia, the most powerful nation of its size in Europe.

The dukes of Brandenburg had had to share government authority with provincial representative bodies created during the Middle Ages and with the councils of the towns. In the late seventeenth century the monarchs had destroyed the powers of these bodies, created a strong central bureaucracy, and begun the process of creating one of Europe's most powerful armies.

In the early eighteenth century the dukes assumed the title King of Prussia. By 1740 the little kingdom had become one of the most disciplined and prosperous in Europe. Its military machine under the command of King Frederick II (the Great) took on Russians, Austrians and French during the Seven Years War (1756–63) and emerged battered but victorious.

All power theoretically lay in the hands of the king. It was exercised by an educated competent bureaucracy operating under a system of almost military discipline. Frederick looked upon himself as the first servant of the state and expected his bureaucrats to have a similar attitude. This created strong, relatively efficient government maximizing state power on the international scene and creating relative economic prosperity in a poor area of Europe.

The price was, however, that the governed had no input into the determination of policy and that the state in the final analysis was only as strong as the personality of the king.

This governmental system continued to exist until the Prussian armies were utterly destroyed by Napoleon in 1806. Reformers strengthened the military system and the bureaucracy, reconstructing the army and allowing Prussia to play a significant role in the final defeat of Napoleon.

The Congress of Vienna allowed the annexation of much new territory to the Prussian domains, making it the great power of north Germany. Ultimately it became the kernel around which the German Empire coalesced in 1871.

Weak monarchy—France. Though France was the greatest power of Western Europe and in fact one of the mightiest powers of the world, its government had become one of the weakest and most inefficient in Europe.

Though King Louis XIV could exclaim, "L'etat, c'est moi!" (I am the State!) he was proclaiming a wish rather than an actuality. The French kings had in a sense shared power with a medieval representative assembly (the Estates-General), but they had never found it necessary to gain the assembly's consent to taxation. As the French economy grew and flourished, the kings were able to raise the taxes they needed through royal decree without consulting the Estates. As of 1787, the last meeting of these Estates had occurred over a century and a half previously (in 1614). The king indeed wielded absolute power in theory, but in practice his authority was limited.

First, the nobility and the clergy were by tradition exempt from taxation. Though the state was in financial difficulty and taxes upon the Third Estate (the non-noble, non-clergy part of the population) were high, the government feared to violate longstanding custom and subject the substantial assets of nobility and church to taxation.

Second, the powers of the monarch were not uniform throughout the kingdom. France had grown from a small piece of territory surrounding Paris (the Ile de France) to a kingdom the size of the present French Republic through an endless series of annexations. Some of the annexations had been due to conquest, others due to inheritance and diplomatic negotiations. Some of the treaties of annexation had reserved special privileges to the citizens and estates of the annexed provinces. Out of respect for law and custom, the monarchs allowed the special privileges to continue to exist. (An example: In Brittany the monarch couldn't levy taxes by decree; he was required to obtain the consent of the provincial estates to his taxation of the Bretons.)

Third, there existed powerful provincial courts, the Parlements whose judges held their positions through inheritance. The strongest of these was the Parlement of Paris, whose judges claimed that no royal decree was effective unless enrolled on the law books by them. They claimed the right to refuse to enroll decrees of which they disapproved, thus claiming a veto over royal legislation. King Louis XV decided to rid himself of these troublemakers by abolishing the Parlements, but this act caused so much political fallout that his successor Louis XVI restored them with their full powers.

Had the French monarchs possessed the will to assert their authority against these vested interests they could have immeasurably strengthened French government. But they lacked this essential willpower and thus shared authority with others, thereby weakening the power of central government.

By 1787 the French state was threatened with insolvency because of a progressively mounting government deficit. A strong monarch could have solved the problem in the following ways, among others:

(1) By declaring church and nobility subject to taxation and beginning to tax them, or

(2) Printing paper money to cover the deficit, or

(3) Declaring bankruptcy and repudiating all or part of the national debt.

King Louis XVI lacked the will to do any of these things. Instead he resurrected the Estates-General in 1789 and passed the buck to its members, unleashing the earthquake of the French Revolution.

The revolutionaries swept away the ancient barriers to the efficient exercise of governmental power in France. They abolished the old provinces and their special privileges; they abolished the Parlements and replaced them with judges chosen by the central government; they abolished the special privileges of nobility and clergy. They made possible the harnessing of French manpower and the French economy to the cause of defending the Revolution, allowing the Republic to take on all of Europe in a war that would last over 20 years and change human civilization forever.

Europe's largest republic—The Netherlands. The Dutch Republic was one of Europe's financial powers. For 80 years it had fought a bitter war against Spain to attain independence. By the time it succeeded, in 1648, it was well on the way to building one of Europe's great colonial empires.

The Netherlands was a union of seven provinces, dominated by the two richest—Holland and Zealand. Holland in turn was dominated by Amsterdam, its largest and richest city.

In effect the republic was an aristocratic union of towns and cities, ruled by closed city councils. Whenever a council member died or resigned the remaining councillors, called regents, chose his successor.

These councils elected the town's delegation to the provincial Estates, which in turn chose the provincial delegates to the Estates-General of the Republic, the governing body of the union.

The Estates-General appointed the captain-general and admiral-general of the Union, the commanders of the Army and Navy, the treasurer-general, ambassadors, and some minor officials. It ruled possessions of the Republic that weren't part of any province and controlled the Republic's foreign affairs and finance. Its delegates voted by province and all decisions had to be unanimous. Such decisions were binding upon the provinces.

The provincial estates had the power to choose an executive officer—the Stadhouder. This person acted as chief of state and often served as commander-in-chief of the provincial armed forces in wartime. The office wasn't always filled.

The same person could be—and often was—chosen Stadhouder of more than one province. Inevitably he was the head of the House of Orange and a descendant of William of Orange, the Dutch leader during the darkest days of the war of liberation from Spain. As Stadhouder of all the important provinces, he could act as a chief of state for the entire Republic.

For a time during the seventeenth century there was no Stadhouder in any province and the Grand Pensionary of Holland unofficially acted as chief of state. For half of the eighteenth century there was again no Stadhouder anywhere and the Republic functioned without any individual head of state.

However, in 1746 French armies threatened invasion; the Estates-General chose William IV of Orange as captain-general and admiral-general and made the offices hereditary in the Orange family. All of the provinces appointed William IV as hereditary Stadhouder at the same time.

In 1787 Stadhouder William V dominated the Republic by virtue of constitutional power and the prevailing political arrangements. The ruling Regents of the towns of the Republic had agreed to fill all vacancies on town councils with nominees chosen by William. William also chose the delegates of the towns to the provincial estates, and the delegates of the provinces to the Estates-General. Thus all of the officeholders of the Republic were appointees of the Stadhouder, allowing him to make the government in his image.

William's political machine, as we might call it, retained power until the French conquest of the Republic in 1795. The old form of government was never restored; when the Netherlands regained its freedom after Napoleon's downfall it became a monarchy under the House of Orange.

Aristocratic republic—Venice. Near the head of Italy's Adriatic Sea the proud Republic of Venice had flourished for a thousand years. Originally all of its citizens had participated in its governance through the right to elect the Grand Council, the major legislative body of the state. But they lost this power in the latter part of the thirteenth century; the Grand Council was "closed" and its membership restricted to those in families registered in the "Libro de Oro"—the Golden Book of the Republic.

The 1,000 to 2,000 aristocrats who comprised this Council governed the state for another five centuries. The Venetian constitution created a remarkable meshing clockwork of councils to rule the Republic: A Senate elected annually by the Grand Council to closely supervise the other organs, a Council of Ten to keep watch over subversives and maintain the security of the state, the six Savii Grandi who served as the cabinet of the Republic, the six members of the Signoria who advised the Doge (the chief of state), who was elected for life by an electoral college, and stood at the top of the governmental pyramid. The Doge served as ceremonial head of state, capable of influencing government policy if possessed of a strong personality.

The Grand Council also elected numerous other officials, such as colonial governors, military commanders, captains of warships, and so forth. There were enough elective offices within the Venetian Republic for all members of the Grand Council to gain experience in the art of governing.

No enemy had ever captured the city of lagoons; no violent coup had ever radically changed the constitution of the state. As of 1787 the constitution had operated smoothly without significant amendment for five centuries.

At one time the Republic had possessed an extensive empire in the eastern Mediterranean, but had lost it all to the Turks. It lived on, a medieval anachronism in a world immeasurably changed, surviving because of the wisdom of its rulers. Its life had but 11 years to run; Napoleon Bonaparte, that revolutionary destroyer of the past, would end the independence of the proud Republic in 1798. Bonaparte then ceded it to Austria; it remained an Austrian possession unti 1859, when it became part of Piedmont (which was soon to become Italy).

An ancient confederation—Switzerland. The Switzerland of 1787 was a confederation of 13 cantons. Its central authority was the Tagsatzung—an assembly of ambassadors from the sovereign cantons whose decisions bound the cantons only if they chose to be bound.

Each canton was a republic. The mountain cantons such as Uri, Schwyz and Glarus were governed by their adult male citizens while the larger lowland cantons such as Zurich, Bern, Basel and Lucerne were governed by small numbers of aristocrats. In Zurich and Basel the guilds of craftsmen and merchants controlled; in Bern a handful of patrician families devoted to government ruled.

Parts of present-day Switzerland weren't included in the territory of the thirteen cantons. Geneva was an independent aristocratic republic with only a loose attachment to the Confederation. Neuchatel was a monarchy ruled by the king of Prussia but not associated with the Prussian kingdom or the Swiss Confederation. St. Gall, Graubunden and upper Valais were independent associates of the Confederation, while most of the rest of present-day Swiss territory, including French-speaking Vaud and Italian-speaking Ticino, was ruled by one or more of the 13 cantons as virtual colonies. In 1787 this five-century-old association of proud states had but 11 years to live. Revolutionary France destroyed it during the same year that Napoleon destroyed Venice.

The Confederation was restored after 1815 in its old form, except for the addition of nine new cantons (Geneva, Neuchatel, the associated states and the liberated colonial areas). In 1848 the old Confederation was abolished and the present Constitution adopted, turning Switzerland into a modern federal state.

Anarchic commonwealth—Poland. Farther east the once-proud Polish Commonwealth lived out the last years of its history. During the fourteenth and fifteenth centuries the Jagellonian dynasty had made Poland one of the strongest nations of Europe. The extinction of the dynasty in the late sixteenth century opened the way to the decay of the state.

The Jagellonians had shared power with a representative assembly, the Sejm. Originally composed of representatives of most of the Polish people, the Sejm had fallen under the control of the nobility; by 1600 only nobles sat in it. These changed the constitution and made the monarchy elective. Over time the powers of the king dwindled to almost nothing; the nobility ruled Poland for its own benefit.

Paradoxically, this meant more popular participation in government than was found anywhere on earth except in the democratic Swiss cantons. Some eight percent of the Polish population was noble and they elected the Sejmiks, the governing assemblies of the provinces. The Sejmiks elected the members of the Sejm which governed the country.

The entire nobility elected the king. Thousands of them would assemble in response to the proclamation of a royal election; though each noble theoretically cast one vote in these assemblies the election was most often decided when the Magnates — the great landowners among the nobility — chose their candidate.

The members of the Polish nobility took pride in the "golden freedom" that prevailed in their country, freedom from government and from the demands of other nobles. In the mid-seventeenth century the adoption of the Liberum Veto anchored an extreme version of this notion within the government. From this time on the Sejm could enact no proposal into law if even one of its members voted against it. Government could not force any noble to do that which he didn't wish to do.

This provided the ultimate freedom for the individual noble, but it also brewed the poison that killed the Commonwealth. Russians, Prussians and Austrians bribed members of the Sejm to oppose measures to strengthen Poland's defenses. Thus the land became unable to protect itself against its rapacious neighbors. Already half of the territory of the Republic had been torn away and annexed by its trio of greedy neighbors in 1772. The proud nobles would lose the rest of their country and their golden freedom when the Russians, Prussians and Austrians wiped Poland off the map in 1795.

The Poles welcomed the armies of Napoleon as liberators; he restored a shadow independent Poland in the form of the Grand Duchy of Warsaw. The Grand Duchy, however, perished in the winter of 1812–13 as did most of the French soldiers then retreating from Russia.

After Napoleon's downfall most of Poland became part of Russia. The Germans and Austrians ejected Russia from Poland through victory in the east in World War I but the German defeat in the west during that war caused it to lose its Polish conquest. Thus was Poland restored to life in 1918 as a new centralized Republic.

Summary. The complex forms of government of the days prior to the

French Revolution have vanished in the storm of change transforming the world during the last two centuries. A study of them reveals clearly just how much the modern state has gained in power. The next two chapters will explore the structure and functioning of today's governments.

Chapter 11
National Governments

The American Revolution loosed upon the western world the idea of popular participation in government; the French Revolution amplified it. In the name of the sovereign people the French began a process of simplifying and strengthening government throughout Western culture.

Many of the small states of Germany and Italy were swept away, some during the wars of the Revolution and others when the Congress of Vienna redrew the boundaries of Europe. Conservative aristocracies ruled in the lands liberated from Napoleonic occupation and in France itself.

The liberated Latin Americans established republican governments with constitutions based on the American model (with the exception of the Brazilians, who retained monarchy until 1889). The efforts to create constitutional governments in that part of the world failed, however. Power flowed from the barrel of a gun in most of Latin America's republics from the time of liberation until the middle of the twentieth century.

Popular revolts on occasion shook Europe from 1820 on. In 1823 a French army suppressed popular revolt in Spain. In 1830 Belgium seceded from the Netherlands and rebels overthrew the Bourbon monarchy of France (replacing it with the Orleanist monarchy).

In 1848 all Europe was threatened with revolution. France overthrew the Orleanists and established the democratic Second Republic, Hungary and north Italy sought freedom from Austria and a popular assembly of delegates from all of Germany met in Frankfurt-am-Main to write a constitution for a German Empire. For a short moment it seemed that popular governments would emerge over all of that continent.

It wasn't to be; Prussian and Austrian military force crushed the rebels almost everywhere. The King of Prussia refused the German imperial crown and the dream of German unity temporarily died. Only in France did the handiwork of the revolutionaries survive, but it too was swept away when Napoleon III established the Second Empire in 1851.

The days of the aristocratic system were numbered, however; in many lands monarchs now granted constitutions to their subjects and popularly elected parliaments began to appear.

209

In 1871 Germany and Italy emerged as united nations (though by military force rather than by the exercise of popular will) while France ended a half-century of governmental instability with the creation of the Third Republic. By 1900 all adult males had voting rights in France, the United States, Germany and some smaller countries. By 1914 elected parliaments existed almost everywhere within the lands of Western civilization — even in Austria-Hungary and Russia.

Most of the world's remaining aristocracies perished in World War I. What remained were would-be democracies and dictatorships. During the 1920s and 1930s many fragile democratic experiments succumbed to dictatorships. The list includes Italy, Poland, Bulgaria, Yugoslavia, Austria, Portugal, Greece, Spain and Germany. Though World War II smashed the Fascist-type dictatorships of Germany and Italy, the Soviet occupation of Eastern Europe created new, seemingly permanent Communist autocracies. In the beginning most of the new nations created by decolonization also fell victim to dictatorships of one sort or another.

Democracy appeared to be locked into a long struggle with dictatorship for most of the years since the end of World War I. It began to gain ground during the 1970s with the fall of the Spanish, Portuguese and Greek dictatorships in Europe and gained more ground as one Latin American country after another embraced it. But only with the coming of the revolutionary events in Western Europe in 1989 has the future of democracy begun to glow. The powerful governments that exist almost everywhere may finally be harnessed to the popular will over the entire world.

Federal and Unitary Nations

The United States of America was the first federal government to appear upon the earth. Our constitution created a national government with a sphere of supreme authority, and state governments with their spheres of subordinate authority. The power of the federal government to infringe on the authority of the states was limited, while the states had no authority to encroach on the power of the federal government.

Though a few other federations have since been created most of the world's nations are unitary. All power belongs to the central government; whatever local governments exist are created by the central government, and exercise such power as it sees fit to delegate to them. These powers, and the very local government units themselves, may be altered or terminated by the central authority.

Among the federal nations of the world are the following:
(1) The United States of America
(2) Canada

(3) Mexico
(4) Brazil
(5) Argentina
(6) Switzerland
(7) Germany
(8) Austria
(9) Yugoslavia
(10) Czechoslovakia
(11) The Soviet Union
(12) Nigeria
(13) India
(14) Malaysia
(15) Australia
(16) The United Arab Emirates
(17) Venezuela

Some federations are among the world's largest nations, such as the U.S., Canada, the Soviet Union, and Brazil, and some are among the smallest, such as Switzerland and Austria. Some (the U.S., Canada, Australia, Switzerland, the United Arab Emirates and Malaysia) were formed when smaller political units were federated into a larger unit. Others (India, Nigeria, Yugoslavia, Czechoslovakia and the Soviet Union) are multi-lingual and multi-cultural states in which the larger national minorities have been given their own states and some measure of local self-government. India and Nigeria have recently created new states to meet the demands of racial and or linguistic minorities complaining of lack of self-government. Still others (Austria and to an extent Germany) preserve as states the provinces or sovereign states of defunct empires. Malaysia and the United Arab Emirates are federations of monarchies, a combination of ancient sultanates into somewhat artificial unions. Mexico is an artificially created federation, an effort to decentralize the unitary Spanish colonial government of that country. Brazil's federalism seemed necessary to provide efficient government for so gigantic a country while Argentina's federalism stemmed from the military victory of federalists over centralists in civil war.

There are wide variations among federal states as to the division of power between the central government and the smaller units. The general trend is for the federal government to steadily expand its power at the expense of the states until almost all governmental authority is federal. Some Americans complain that this process has gone too far, but American states have more power than do the states of most federations.

In the United States, most civil and criminal law is state law rather than federal. In Canada the criminal law is mostly federal while much civil law is provincial. In Switzerland, Germany and Austria nearly all civil and criminal law is federal.

In the United States state powers of taxation are almost unlimited and the states collect their own taxes. In Canada the provinces determine their rates of income tax but the federal government collects it for them (with the exception of Quebec). German state taxation power is narrowly limited by the federal authority, and much state revenue is granted by the federal treasury. In Switzerland on the other hand federal taxation is relatively light while many cantons levy heavy taxes and even local governments possess wide taxing authority.

In the United States, Mexico and Argentina federal courts enforce federal law while state courts enforce state law. In Germany, Switzerland and Canada the only federal courts are those at the apex of the judicial hierarchy; all others are state, provincial or cantonal courts enforcing both local and federal law.

In most federations the states or provinces or local governments control the police forces. In Mexico the highway police are federal, as they are in most of Canada (the Royal Canadian Mounted Police doing the job almost everywhere).

In federations with undemocratic political systems as we understand them (yesterday's Soviet Union, Czechoslovakia and Mexico), federalism has little practical meaning. Under authoritarian or totalitarian government, the power of the rulers is almost unlimited; the rulers of the states of the federation follow orders from the nation's capital without question.

In many federations (India, Mexico, Argentina and Brazil, for instance) the federal government has the authority to remove a state government from office if it isn't preserving order within the state. When those in charge of state government are in opposition to the government in the nation's capital, federal politicians may be tempted to use this power to remove the opposition state government from office. This isn't uncommon.

In the U.S., federal bureaucrats enforce federal law while state bureaucrats enforce state law. In Switzerland, Germany and Austria federal bureaucracies are relatively small, because state governments have the responsibility for enforcing most federal law.

In Canada the growth of federal power, and indeed the continued existence of a united nation, has been called into question by the Quebec problem. The demands of the French-speaking Quebecois for more cultural, economic and political autonomy have strained the bonds of Canadian unity. Also the western and Atlantic provinces resent the political and economic domination of the country by the central provinces of Ontario and Quebec; the particularism of the small provinces too strain the national consensus.

Though Yugoslavia has an undemocratic political system as we understand it, the demands of its disparate nationalities for local autonomy and self-government have resulted in progressive decentralization. The same process has begun in the Soviet Union and Czechoslovakia.

Several states are quasi-federal in nature, allowing special privileges to some or all local-government areas.

Belgium is constitutionally a unitary monarchy; the central government in Brussels exercises all power that it chooses not to delegate to the provinces. Because of the ethnic strife between Flemish-speaking Flemings and French-speaking Walloons a constitutional amendment divided the country into three linguistic areas — the Flemish-speaking north, the French-speaking south and the bilingual Brussels area. Flemish is the official language of the north, French the official language of the south, and both are official in Brussels and its suburbs. Each area has some autonomy with respect to language; otherwise the nation is still unitary.

An element of quasi-federalism exists also in the United Kingdom. Scotland was an independent nation until it and England united to create the United Kingdom in 1707. The Act of Union which united England and Scotland provided that Scotland would retain its own legal and judicial systems, as it does to this day. However, Queen Elizabeth II is as much Queen of Scotland as she is Queen of England, and the Parliament of the United Kingdom may legislate for Scotland as well as for England.

In Spain special local home-rule powers have been granted to Catalonia and the Basque country in order to permit these non–Spanish-speaking areas to better preserve their unique cultures. Italy allows similar privileges to the French-speaking Val d'Aosta and the largely German-speaking Alto Adige.

In Tanzania the island of Zanzibar possesses special privileges of self-government. It was an independent nation before its involuntary merger with Tanganyika in 1964. Self-government permits its Arab Muslim population some linguistic and cultural autonomy in a nation whose population is overwhelmingly Congoid and non–Muslim.

Constitutional Separation of Powers

National governments are either monarchies or republics. Monarchy is government by a hereditary (or occasionally elected) person who holds office for life and holds the title of emperor, king, prince, sultan, emir, duke, or whatever. A republic is ruled by a person or persons supposedly chosen by the governed to rule for a limited time period. Monarchy has been the prevailing form of government throughout most of human history but the French Revolution changed the trend. Today most national governments are republics.

Monarchies are either constitutional (in which the monarch has little or no governmental power) or absolute (in which the monarch rules as well as reigns). The United Kingdom is the prime example of a constitutional monarchy. Queen Elizabeth II is the head of state, but her function is almost totally ceremonial. She exercises virtually no governmental power.

Examples of other constitutional monarchies are Belgium, the Netherlands, Denmark, Norway, Sweden, Thailand and Japan.

Perhaps the most powerful monarch in today's world is the king of Saudi
Arabia, whose authority is theoretically unlimited. Other examples of powerful monarchs are the King of Morocco, the King of Jordan, the Sultan of
Oman, and the emirs of Bahrein, Qatar and the states of the United Arab
Emirates. The Emir of Kuwait was another powerful monarch until the Iraqi
army deposed him. (He was restored to his throne by the Gulf War victors and
is under great pressure to relinquish some of his power.) The only western
monarch who is more than a figurehead is the king of Spain.

Other monarchies are Swaziland and Lesotho in Africa, and Tonga and
Western Samoa in the Pacific.

When a monarchy is constitutional, the political ruler is usually called the
prime minister, who heads a parliamentary government.

Presidential government. The ruler of a republic is almost inevitably
called the president. This person is the ceremonial head of state, and may
also be the political ruler. Whether or not he or she exercises actual power
depends upon whether the nation's government is presidential or parliamentary.

The United States has a presidential government. There exists a separation of power between executive, legislative, and judicial branches. The Congress makes law and the president enforces it. The president can't dissolve the
Congress; the Congress can't remove the president from office (except by the
cumbersome process of impeachment). The president has little legislative
power; he may enact administrative regulations to supplement acts of Congress, he may legislate when authorized to do so by Congress, he may issue executive orders to accomplish his housekeeping duties and he may veto acts of
Congress (subject to overriding). The president alone cannot enact a legislative
program into law; without the cooperation of a majority of Congress he can't
get his political program enacted at all.

The majority of the world's republics have presidential forms of government. Most of the republics of the western hemisphere, Asia and Africa are
presidential rather than parliamentary.

Most of the world's presidents exercise more power than ours. Many have
the power to make law by decree when the national legislature isn't in session.
Some have the power to impose a state of siege in a time of national emergency, giving them authority to suspend civil liberties. Some may oust state
governments from office, as described above. In addition, the political systems
of many republics give the president such immense personal power as the head
of the ruling party that no countervailing power in the state can oppose his
will.

In a few republics with presidential governments legislative power exceeds
presidential power; Costa Rica is an excellent example. Many of the world's

federations, including the U.S., Mexico, Venezuela, Brazil, Argentina and Nigeria, have presidential governments.

Parliamentary government. In nations with parliamentary government, there's a fusion of executive and legislative power. In Israel the President is almost a figurehead, with little political power. The true head of state is the prime minister, who is the leader of the majority coalition of the Knesset, the Israeli legislature. The prime minister is an elected member of the Knesset. He and his cabinet sit in this body during its sessions and have the same voting rights as other members. The prime minister is appointed to office by the president and holds office only as long as he has the confidence of a majority of the Knesset. The legislative body may remove him from office at any time by voting a lack of confidence. However, the prime minister may respond to such a threat by dissolving the Knesset and calling for new legislative elections.

Thus, the power of the legislature to remove the executive from office is balanced by the power of the executive to force the legislature to run for re-election.

The United Kingdom is the prime example of a monarchy with parliamentary government. The political head of state is the prime minister, who is appointed by the monarch. He's an elected member of the House of Commons, as are the members of his cabinet, and he may be removed from office by the Commons at any time. With the consent of the monarch the prime minister may dissolve the Commons and call for new elections.

France has a hybrid presidential-parliamentary form of government. The president exercises numerous powers as head of state, but appoints a prime minister who exercises many of the functions of a prime minister in a parliamentary system. The prime minister may be removed from office by a majority of the National Assembly. He may dissolve the Assembly, and may legislate by decree when the parliament isn't in session. When parties of the president's political persuasion control the parliament, he has great power. But when opposition parties control parliament, he is obligated to appoint a member of his opposition as prime minister, who then exercises the most power.

Germany and Austria are examples of federal republics with parliamentary government.

Switzerland and Yugoslavia have neither presidential nor parliamentary governments. In both countries a multi-member executive governs. There is no premier; the president is the head of the executive board and serves as ceremonial head of state. No one person is the political head of state. For a spell during the middle of the twentieth century Uruguay too had such an executive but it was replaced by a single president.

The executive of the Republic of San Marino resembles that of the Roman Republic. Two capitani regenti (captains-regent) share authority in that postage stamp-sized land.

As mentioned before, monarchs acquire their thrones by hereditary right.

In Malaysia, sultans of the federal states elect a presiding monarch from among themselves, the Yang Di Pertuan Agong, who serves as head of state for the federation for a period of five years. Only a reigning state monarch is eligible for this honor. In the United Arab Emirates the seven ruling Emirs choose one of their number as president and another as vice president of the federation.

Presidents of nations with presidential forms of government are generally elected by direct popular vote. The major exception is the president of the United States, who is chosen by presidential electors chosen by popular vote.

Presidents of republics with parliamentary governments are often chosen by the national legislatures; the presidents of Israel, India, Turkey and Italy are examples. The president of Germany is chosen by an electoral college of federal and state legislators. The presidents of Austria, Portugal, Ireland and Iceland are chosen by direct popular vote though they exercise little power.

The Swiss Bundesrat — the seven-member executive council — is elected by the two houses of Parliament sitting in joint session. Parliament also elects the president and vice president from among members of the Bundesrat; by custom the posts are rotated between members in order of seniority.

The Yugoslav executive council consists of eight members, one each from the six constituent republics and two autonomous provinces. The presidency is rotated among the members, each republic and province getting the office once every eight years.

The captains-regent of San Marino are elected by the Grand and General Council, the Parliament of the republic.

Presidential terms of office vary in length. The captains-regent of San Marino serve only six months, the presidents of Switzerland and Yugoslavia for a year. The American four-year presidential term (limit of two terms) is one of the shortest for presidents who actually rule, the French seven-year term being one of the longest. Mexico limits its president to one six-year term; such limitations upon re-election are very common.

Prime ministers are constitutionally appointed by the head of state, but in practice they are generally chosen through more or less complex political dealings within and between the political parties.

Legislatures. Some nations have bicameral (two-house) legislatures; others have unicameral (one-house) legislative bodies. The lawmaking bodies of virtually all federal nations are bicameral, the majority constituted like the United States Congress. The members of our lower house, the House of Representatives, are apportioned among the states according to population. Our upper house, the Senate, consists of two Senators per state, regardless of population.

The legislatures of Mexico, Switzerland and Argentina are organized on the same principle. The lower house is apportioned according to population, two members of the upper house per state, canton or province. Brazil allows each state three senators, while each of Australia's six states elects twelve. The other federal nations grant their states unequal representation in the upper house, basing the apportionment primarily upon population.

Most unitary nations of Europe have bicameral legislatures, except those of the Scandinavian lands, Greece, Portugal, Luxembourg and Malta. Central American lawmaking bodies are unicameral, while those of South America are virtually all bicameral. African legislatures generally consist of one house as do those of Asia (India being a noteworthy exception).

In addition to those nations already mentioned, the following have unicameral legislatures: Israel, Turkey, Singapore, Thailand, Taiwan and New Zealand. All legislative power rests with this one body in these countries.

The lower house of a bicameral legislature is always elected by the voters. The huge majority of upper houses are similarly elected; a minority of nations use other selection methods.

Most Belgian senators are elected by the voters although a minority are chosen by the provincial legislatures and by the Senate itself.

In the Netherlands and Austria the members of the upper house are elected by provincial legislatures.

In Switzerland the cantons choose the method of electing their delegates to the upper house. The great majority have chosen popular vote as the election mechanism. A few very small cantons choose their delegates at the Landesgemeinde—the assembly of all voters at the cantonal capital. A few others allow the cantonal legislature to do the choosing.

The members of the German upper house (the Bundesrat) are appointed by the governments of the states and hold office at the will of these governments.

French senators are chosen by electoral colleges consisting mainly of councillors of local government bodies.

Some Irish senators are elected by designated professional groups but others are appointed by the prime minister.

Canadian senators are appointed to their positions for life by the governor-general upon nomination by the prime minister.

The members of the British House of Lords hold their seats by hereditary right.

The terms of office of legislators differ from country to country. Usually the members of the upper house serve longer terms than those of the lower house.

The two-year term of American representatives is one of the shortest in the world. By comparison, Australian representatives and Mexican deputies serve for three years, members of the Swiss Nationalrat, German Bundestag and Japanese House of Representatives serve for four years, and members of the British and Canadian House of Commons and French National Assembly serve for five.

American, Australian and Mexican senators serve for six years, as do Japanese Councillors. French senators enjoy one of the longest terms — nine years. In Switzerland terms of members of the Standerat (the upper house) are determined by the cantons. Most Standerat members serve four-year terms as do members of the lower house.

In the United States, one-third of the Senate is elected every two years. In Japan one-half of the House of Councillors is elected every three years. In Mexico, however, all senators are elected together every six years.

In nations with parliamentary forms of government the lower house of the legislature may be dissolved before its term expires (a noteworthy exception being Norway). But in countries featuring presidential forms of government this isn't authorized and the legislatures must serve out their terms.

In nations with bicameral legislatures and parliamentary government it may or may not be possible to dissolve the upper house. In some (such as Australia and Italy) it's possible and often done but not in others such as France and Japan.

In most nations the powers of the two houses of the legislature are equal; a bill may not become law without the consent of both houses. In a minority of nations, while the upper house may delay the effectiveness of legislation passed by the lower, it has no veto power. Examples here are Germany, Great Britain and Canada.

In bicameral nations with parliamentary governments, only the lower house may remove the prime minister from office by a vote of no confidence. This is true even when the legislative powers of the two houses are equal; the French and Australian Senates have no power to remove the prime minister.

Direct legislation. A few democracies allow their citizens some direct participation in legislating. In Switzerland this happens at all levels of government. Two hundred thousand voters may propose an amendment to the federal constitution, which must be submitted to the nation's voters for approval. The Parliament may debate the proposal, and it may submit a counterproposal to the voters, but the "sovereign," as the Swiss call the people, must vote the original proposal up or down.

The Parliament too may propose constitutional amendments, but these also must be approved by the voters.

One hundred thousand voters may demand that an ordinary act of the Swiss Parliament be submitted to a referendum, in which case the voters may veto the act of their elected representatives.

The voters may not initiate ordinary legislation at the federal level, though the majority of cantonal constitutions allow this. At the local level too, full initiative and referendum rights may exist.

In a few very thinly populated Swiss cantons, the voters assemble in the vast public square of the cantonal capital for the Landesgemeinde. Here public problems are debated by the assembled voters, public officials are elected, legislation enacted. It is the direct democracy of Athens clad in twentieth-century garb.

In some cantons similar assemblies of the voters of communes — the Swiss local government units — are held.

In the United States the initiative and referendum don't exist at the federal level but at the state level with respect to state constitutional amendments; these are usually proposed by the legislature and decided by the voters.

Some state constitutions allow initiative proposal of constitutional amendments, referenda on ordinary legislation and the initiation of ordinary legislation.

As limited as initiative and referendum rights are in our country, Americans have more such rights than any other people on earth except the Swiss. Italy and a few other nations permit referenda on ordinary legislation.

Judicial power. No judiciary on earth exercises more power than the American federal judiciary. Only the Supreme Court of the United States may radically change its nation's politics and culture by changing its constitutional interpretation. Our Supreme Court may frustrate the will of the political branches of government by declaring legislative acts unconstitutional, something few other national high courts may do.

The highest court of Australia has such power, but since the Australian Constitution has no Bill of Rights the possibility of a parliamentary act being unconstitutional is far less than in the U.S.

The highest court of Canada also has this power; since the Canadian constitution has a Bill of Rights the power is theoretically great. However, the Canadian federal parliament and the provincial legislatures have authority to declare a legislative act valid even if the courts declare that it violates the Bill of Rights. Thus, Canadian legislatures can override court decisions declaring legislation unconstitutional under such circumstances.

In the United Kingdom the judges may only interpret the law and they may not declare acts of Parliament null and void. This is true in most other lands.

In a few countries special courts have been created to consider the constitutionality of legislative acts. Such courts exist, for instance, in the German Federal Republic, Spain, France, Austria and Italy. In the latter three countries this power is rarely used; in Germany the Constitutional Court is a power to be reckoned with. The Spanish Constitutional Court is so new that its powers haven't yet been tested.

Judges acquire office in many ways. Among the methods in use are:

(1) Election by the voters.
(2) Election by a legislative body.

(3) Unfettered appointment by the political head of state.

(4) Nomination by a non-political commission and appointment by the political head of state.

(5) Appointment by a non-political official.

(6) Passing a civil service examination.

Most state court judges in the United States are elected by the voters, as are trial court judges in most of Switzerland, everywhere in the Soviet Union, and in some other Marxist-Leninist countries.

Appellate court judges are elected by legislatures in Switzerland, the Soviet Union, many nations of Latin America, and in a scattering of lands elsewhere.

The president of the United States has the power to appoint federal judges, subject to Senate confirmation. Many other presidents, monarchs and prime ministers have such power.

A few American states such as California and Missouri use the fourth method listed above.

Great Britain uses the fifth method. The appointing official is the lord chancellor, roughly the equivalent of the chief justice of the U.S. Supreme Court.

The sixth method is used in most non–Communist lands of Europe and in a few non–European countries.

Elected judges serve terms of years, and under normal political circumstances are re-elected if they wish to be. Appointed judges usually serve for life or good behavior, as do civil servant judges.

Constitutional amendments. The required procedure for amending constitutions varies widely. The procedure in federal nations may be more complex than that in unitary nations. Among the most cumbersome is that of the United States, the most widely used being proposal by a two-thirds vote of both houses of Congress and ratification by the legislatures of three-fourths of the states.

The Canadian system is even more difficult — proposal by majority vote of both houses of Parliament and ratification by all provincial legislatures. Thus, any one province may veto a constitutional amendment.

In Germany all that's required is a two-thirds vote of both houses of Parliament. Since the upper house is composed of representatives of state governments, the system fairly well protects state interests.

In Australia and Switzerland, an amendment supported by majority vote in both houses of Parliament must be submitted to popular vote. A majority of the total popular vote and a majority of the vote in a majority of states or cantons are required for the amendment to be adopted. (Also, as mentioned earlier, Swiss constitutional amendments may be proposed by initiative petition.)

Some unitary nations (such as Sweden, Norway and Italy) allow Parliament alone to enact amendments. Others (such as Denmark and Japan) require popular referenda on amendments proposed by Parliament. The French Constitution requires proposal by Parliament and approval by referendum, but President Charles de Gaulle on occasion proposed amendments by himself and submitted them to popular vote without consulting Parliament.

Since Great Britain has no written constitution, constitutional arrangements may be altered by simple Act of Parliament.

Political Systems

We Americans preach to the world that governments should govern according to the will of the governed, that political power should be derived from the people.

In half of the world's nations it doesn't work that way. Mao Tse-Tung stated the truth for many nations when he made his famous statement that political power flows from the barrel of a gun. Out of the 160-plus nations on the face of the earth, perhaps 80 allow something resembling free elections. Most of the others have dictatorial governments.

Totalitarian dictatorships. Totalitarian government seeks to dominate all facets of the lives of the nation's people, so that the governing person or party may hold power forever. We loosely classified yesterday's many Marxist-Leninist regimes as totalitarian, along with the Hitler government of Germany and the Mussolini government of Italy. In actuality, both Mussolini and Hitler exercised less than absolute control over their nations; Mussolini was never powerful enough to end the Italian monarchy (King Victor Emmanuel played a role in his overthrow in 1943), while Hitler didn't totally control the German armed forces or national economy until near the end of the Second World War. The power of Marxist-Leninist regimes has on occasion been virtually total (as in the Soviet Union under Stalin), but the nature of these varies. In most of yesterday's Marxist-Leninist lands the dictatorship was that of the ruling party organization, not the dictatorship of one individual.

Nikita Khrushchev and his successors in the Soviet Union survived Stalin's terroristic regime. They had no desire to return to the absolute one-person power that prevailed while the dictator lived. They preached the virtues of collective leadership of party and nation, denouncing Stalin's "cult of personality" and condemning the domination of social and political institutions by one person. The first among equals in the system was the secretary-general of the Communist Party of the Soviet Union, but the Party Central Committee reserved the right to remove him from office as it did Khrushchev in 1964.

Before the advent of Mikhail Gorbachev the constitutional branches of government were powerless facades. The Supreme Soviet (the federal parliament of the Soviet Union, chosen in elections with but one candidate on the ballot) routinely passed party legislative proposals without debate, without amendment, and without a single dissenting vote. The chief executive (a premier before the adoption of the constitution of 1977, a president afterward) exercised very little power unless he happened also to be (as he usually was) the secretary-general of the Communist Party.

Gorbachev began a revolutionary process that has already diminished the totalitarian nature of the Soviet Union. In the last Soviet federal election two or more candidates were allowed to compete for legislative seats. Though anti–Communists weren't allowed to run, many shades of opinion were represented by the candidates and the incumbent party leadership was subjected to harsh criticism during the campaign. Moreover, many anti-establishment Communists and non-party independents were elected.

In the present Supreme Soviet legislative proposals are genuinely debated and amended on the floor. Votes are rarely unanimous and occasionally the government concedes points to the legislators in order to avoid defeat on an issue.

In 1990 many republics of the country held elections to their parliaments and municipal councils; in some of them (notably Lithuania, Latvia, Estonia, Moldavia and the Ukraine) opposition political parties have participated and won substantial representation. In others (the Russian Republic, for instance) dissident Communists are now well represented and have even taken control of the city governments of Moscow and Leningrad.

The power of Mikhail Gorbachev still stems in part from his post as secretary-general; however, the Constitution of the Soviet Union has been amended to create a powerful presidency and Gorbachev now fills that office. Gorbachev has talked of resigning his party chairmanship in order to govern the nation solely as constitutional president—but the Congress of the Communist Party of the Soviet Union held in July 1990 reelected him to the General Secretaryship. He decided to retain the office.

The constitutional provision declaring that the Communist Party has the sole right to rule the state has been removed by amendment. New parties, some legal and some illegal, are springing up to participate in political debate.

The very future of the USSR as a federal state has been called into question. Lithuania's newly elected Parliament issued a unilateral declaration of independence, which was later modified. The parliaments of Latvia and Estonia have also declared in favor of national independence, as has that of Georgia.

The Parliament of the Russian Republic (Russia, the largest republic of the USSR, which occupies much of the land area of the Soviet Union and contains half the population) has resolved that from now on its acts will take precedence within its boundaries over acts of the federal Supreme Soviet. The parliaments of other republics have enacted similar resolutions.

Boris Yeltsin, recently elected president of the Russian Republic, has proposed that the Union of Soviet Socialist Republics (USSR) be replaced by the Union of Sovereign Soviet States (USSS), a confederation in which most of the governmental power will be possessed by the republics rather than by the federal government. President Gorbachev hasn't condemned the proposal.

Not only is the political structure of the USSR changing but its very federal constitutional basis is in some doubt. What the future holds for the Soviet Union remains to be seen.

Collective leadership prevailed within the parties of most other European Communist countries until the upheavals of 1989 began; most of these countries are no longer strictly Marxist-Leninist or totalitarian. The process started in Poland, the first country to allow non–Communists to contest a semi-free national parliamentary election. Though the Communists and their sympathizers reserved to themselves enough parliamentary seats to be assured a majority, candidates supported by the trade union Solidarity won almost all of the contested seats. Enough elected Communist sympathizers defected to the opposition to give it a parliamentary majority and permit installation of a non–Communist government.

The Hungarian Communist Party meanwhile voluntarily dismantled much of its system and changed its name. In a free election in the spring of 1990 Hungarian voters repudiated it, voting into power a coalition dominated by moderate conservatives.

The East German Communists held free elections in March of 1990 won by the conservative Allianz fuer Deutschland (Alliance for Germany). East Germany's economy was merged into that of the West. Political unification followed.

Massive popular demonstrations in Prague persuaded the Czechoslovak Communists to install a non–Communist President (Vaclav Havel), to permit organization of opposition parties and to schedule free elections for the summer of 1990. These were won by non–Communist supporters of Havel, ending Communist rule in Czechoslovakia.

In Bulgaria long-time Communist Party chairman Todor Zhivkov has stepped down; the party has changed its name to Socialist, allowed opposition, and held elections in June of 1990. The Socialists obtained 56 percent of the popular vote so the politicians of the old order remain in power.

In Yugoslavia the states of Croatia and Slovenia authorized formation of opposition parties and held free elections. Non-Communists were voted into power. The state of Bosnia-Herzegovina allowed similar elections in November of 1990; there too non–Communists assumed power. In Serbia, the largest Yugoslav state, the Communists retain control, as they do in the remaining states and in the federal government.

Albania is the only European Communist state in which a party collective leadership retains power, winning a semi-free election early in 1991.

The "personality cult" still prevails in two Marxist-Leninist lands: North Korea and Cuba. It also prevailed in Romania until December of 1989. There the family of Party Chairman Nicolae Ceausescu dominated the party and government, perpetuating the most repressive European Communist regime. Massive popular demonstrations plus the defection of much of the army triggered the most violent overthrow of a Communist government yet; the hated dictator and his wife were dispatched by a military firing squad. The present Romanian government consists mainly of anti–Ceausescu Communists; in the elections of May 1990 the National Salvation Front (the political grouping dominated by these Communists) won 66 percent of the popular vote against ill-organized opposition in a seemingly free election to retain authority.

Kim Il Sung has dominated the government of North Korea since the founding of the state in the late 1940s and with no organized opposition, is preparing to pass power to his son. Fidel Castro has similarly dominated the government of Cuba since the revolution of 1959. Though the Soviet-backed economy is a shambles Fidel's charisma enables him to retain power.

Collective leadership of the Communist Party high command prevails in China and Vietnam. The events of June 1989 (in Peking's Tien-An-Men Square) show that the Chinese Communist Party isn't about to share political power with dissidents. In Vietnam non–Communists possess no power; the organization which defeated so many mighty enemies in the 10,000-day war to unify the country isn't about to yield any of the fruits of victory to outsiders.

In Nicaragua Daniel Ortega leads the Sandinista movement, but doesn't dominate it. He permitted a free election there in early 1990 and lost to Violetta Chamorro. The Nicaraguan Army and civil service are still dominated by Sandinistas, who maintain power bases within the country.

Whether the Marxist-Leninist lands of Ethiopia, Angola, Mozambique and South Yemen were ever totalitarian is debatable. As mentioned earlier, the governments of Angola and Mozambique have turned Westward for economic assistance. Non-Communist rebels against the Marxist regime in Ethiopia are growing stronger; without massive Soviet help this government may fall.

South Yemen no longer exists as an independent nation, having consolidated with North Yemen to become the Republic of Yemen on May 22, 1990. The new government is decidedly un–Marxist; whether or not it will be democratic will be determined by future events.

Traditional dictatorships. Non-totalitarian dictatorial regimes have traditionally been labelled authoritarian. Such governments don't try to control all aspects of their peoples' lives. Rather they seek to preserve the social and economic status quo, letting the governed alone to live as they please, so long as they don't engage in political activity hostile to the rulers. Such governments have shorter lives than totalitarian regimes. They may end because of the death of the dictator, as the Franco regime ended in Spain. They may be overthrown by outside military action, as happened to Idi Amin's regime in Uganda. They may be upset by domestic military coup as happened to the Caetano government in Portugal. Or they may simply resign their powers as did the Greek colonels in the late 1970s and the Argentine generals in the early 1980s.

They may be replaced by democratic regimes, as in Spain and Portugal. Or they may be replaced by Marxist-Leninist totalitarianism as in Cuba and Nicaragua. Or another authoritarian regime may take power, as in Uganda.

Such regimes aren't as common as they were 30 years ago. Political forces favoring social change have gained strength all over the world. Today's dictator is obligated to engage in social organization to build a power base; without it any tenure of office may be short.

Military regimes. Dictatorial governments are often put in power by military muscle; the rulers so installed are often soldiers. The leadership may be just one person, or it may be by committee (or junta). Juntas are most common in Latin America.

Recent examples of one-person military rulers in South America have been General Pinochet in Chile, General Stroessner in Paraguay and General Noriega in Panama. Noteworthy examples from the middle of the century were Rafael Leonidas Trujillo in the Dominican Republic, Fulgencio Batista in Cuba and the Somoza family in Nicaragua. Juntas on the other hand have recently held power in Argentina, Uruguay and Brazil.

Latin American military rulers are generally authoritarian preservers of the status quo. They are almost inevitably generals who assume power to prevent leftists from causing social change, are likely to imprison opponents without bringing formal charges against them and to use torture. The duration of these regimes is usually relatively short (less than ten years); soldiers, untrained in political science and economics, find it difficult to deal with the economic and social problems of a nation. The 16-year rule of Pinochet in Chile and the 20-year rule of the Brazilian junta have been exceptional.

A different sort of junta ruled Peru during the late 1960s and early 1970s. Here a group of military reformers sought to change Peruvian society by expropriating foreign-owned industries and by bettering the lot of peasants and urban workers. They brought about a moderate amount of social change before they were ousted by a more conservative junta.

A greater variety of military governments exists in Africa. The junta has appeared only in Ghana, Nigeria and Malagasy. In Ghana their tenures have been short, while in Nigeria one faction of the military managed to hold power for 13 years. In Malagasy military rule seems to be permanent.

In some nations of French-speaking Africa individual generals or colonels may establish long-lived regimes, as did Mobutu Sese Seko in Zaire (1965), Gnassinghe Eyadema in Togo (1967), and Mathieu Kerekou in Benin (1972). Siad Barre established a similar regime in Somalia in 1969. All of the above-mentioned dictators except Siad Barre still hold power.

In English-speaking Uganda General Idi Amin held power solely through the exercise of brute force. General Jean-Bedel Bokassa established a similar regime in the French-speaking Central African Empire (now the Central African Republic).

A more unusual type of African military regime is that found in yesterday's Liberia, and today's Burkina Faso and Ghana. Master Sergeant Samuel Doe masterminded a coup that overthrew the conservative constitutional government of Liberia in 1980; as dictator he sought to open the doors of political and economic opportunity to the poorer elements of Liberian society. Flight Lieutenant Jerry Rawlings has sought to accomplish the same thing since taking power in Ghana. These low-ranking military people have tried to break the power of their countries' established oligarchies but they haven't been in power long enough to cause permanent change.

Captain Thomas Shankara made many changes in Burkina Faso from the time he took power in 1983 until he was overthrown in 1987. He too sought to make a true revolution in his country.

The Doe regime in Liberia has come to its end. Charles Taylor's National Patriotic Forces of Liberia have launched civil war against Doe's supporters and recently seemed to be in the last stages of winning it. However, Taylor's forces have split; a third faction under the leadership of Prince Johnson occupies much of Monrovia, the national capital. Doe was captured by Johnson's forces and killed. What sort of government will emerge from the chaos is an open question.

Asian military regimes tend to be dominated by one person and to last for a long term; examples are the government of General Mohammed Zia ul-Haq in Pakistan (ended by his death in an air crash), that of General Suharto in Indonesia (who has been the major power there since 1965), and General Ne Win in Burma (who ran the state from 1962 until a coup ended his regime in 1988).

Personalist civilian dictatorships. In the nineteenth and early twentieth centuries many dictatorships were managed by one civilian who maintained control over the state through power of personality and control of the necessary guns by loyalists. Nations such as Paraguay and Haiti have been ruled by such persons throughout most of their history.

More recently, civilian Milton Obote has twice ruled Uganda, once before Idi Amin's bloodbath and once afterward. Both of his reigns were violent, his second even more than his first. When Spain granted its colony of Spanish Guinea independence in 1968 Francisco Macias Nguema established a bloody-fisted personalist dictatorship that lasted a decade. Only isolated, poor lands whose populations have little political consciousness are now subject to such regimes.

Modern dictatorships. Barry Rubin points out in his work *Modern Dictatorships* that many of the world's non–Marxist-Leninist dictatorial governments hold power with the consent of a good portion of the national population. Some of these rulers are military, others are civilian. What they have in common is an organized power base within the society that maintains their rule, often allowing them to pass power to a successor when they die.

Examples of early populist dictators were Juan Perón in Argentina, Achmed Sukarno in Indonesia, Kwame Nkrumah in Ghana, and Gamal Abdel Nasser in Egypt. Nkrumah's regime fell because he couldn't control his military and his power base vanished. Perón lost power for the same reason, but his movement lived on (giving him a second shot at governing Argentina 15 years after his overthrow); the country's current President Menen was elected to office as the candidate of the Perónist Justicialist Party. Sukarno ruled for 16 years before military deposition, while the political organization established by Nasser still governs Egypt.

Examples of the newer generation of populist dictators who seem to hold permanent power with the consent of the governed include Muammar Khaddafi in Libya, Hafiz al-Assad in Syria and Saddam Hussein in Iraq. (Saddam Hussein's grip upon power in Iraq seems unshaken by his defeat in the Gulf War.)

The present Iranian system seems to be an authoritarian populist dictatorship by the Ayatollah Khomeini's successors. Ali Khamenei succeeded Khomeini as religious head of state, but the most visible exerciser of political power is now President Hashemi Rafsanjani. No one person has near absolute power, but no opponents of the regime are allowed anywhere near the corridors of authority.

No party systems. Nations may also be classified according to how many effective political parties they allow to exist. There are a few where no parties exist—Saudi Arabia and other nations on the Arabian peninsula and a few lands in sub-Saharan Africa. Some of these are nations that have been so isolated from the modern world that their peoples have not developed significant political consciousness. Here the elite rule because no one else has the knowledge or inclination to get involved. Others are nations ruled by dictators—military or civilian—who have abolished all political parties in order to wipe out organized opposition.

A variation on the no-party theme exists in certain areas of the United States, where some or all public officials are chosen in non-partisan elections. The legislatures of Nebraska and Minnesota, city and county officials in California, and city officials in many other parts of the U.S. are elected that way, as are mayors of many Canadian cities. Candidates for non-partisan offices do not run as nominees of political parties. In theory, parties do not participate in such elections. Election campaigns are contests between individuals and the governments elected are therefore governments of individuals (though political parties on occasion get unofficially involved).

One-party systems. Probably the majority of nations allow only one party to exist. In many African nations those who rule have organized a political party to perpetuate their power. Periodic elections happen in which only one candidate's name appears on the ballot and the victor amasses 99.7 percent of the votes or thereabouts.

In a few one-party states (Tanzania and Zambia are examples) contested elections happen, but all candidates must be members of the ruling party.

In the southern United States another sort of one-party system existed between roughly 1880 and 1950. The Democratic Party so dominated the politics of these states that often the Republicans didn't bother to run candidates for state offices. They would run presidential electors in presidential election years, but the Democrats would win 2 to 1 in states like Virginia and North Carolina while racking up over 90 percent of the vote in Mississippi and South Carolina. All of these states nominated party candidates for office in direct primaries; the Democratic primary was the equivalent of a general election.

In other nations, more than one party exists, more than one candidate's name appears on the ballot for each office, the opposition fields candidates, but the official party always wins the election. In many of these the winds of change are blowing, however and the hold of the dominant party is weakening.

In Singapore the People's Action Party (PAP) has held power since 1959. Though elections are held every four years and the seven or so opposition parties contest every election, the PAP normally polls 75 percent or more of the popular vote and wins every seat in Parliament. Defenders of the system say this is because the PAP provides excellent government and the voters are happy with its performance; opponents say that PAP uses fraud and manipulation to retain power. The Singapore situation is unique; the island republic's population is ethnically diverse. Seventy-six percent of the people are Chinese while the 24 percent minority consists of Malays and Indians. Most political parties are ethnic; PAP is essentially a Chinese party (though it nominates non–Chinese as parliamentary candidates and allows non–Chinese to hold cabinet posts). Fragmentation of the Chinese vote between two or more parties might endanger Chinese political control of the Republic, which many Chinese don't want to risk.

In Mexico, before 1988, several opposition parties were allowed to campaign against the ruling PRI (Party of Revolutionary Institutions) at election time, but the ruling oligarchy didn't permit them to win any meaningful political power. Minority parties were guaranteed some representation in the national Chamber of Deputies, but that was all.

In the elections of July 1988 the PRI presidential candidate Carlos Salinas de Gortari announced his intention to have an honest election. As President-to-be his command carried clout within the PRI organization. The opposition took advantage of the new ground rules to make a serious bid for victory. Due to the facts that there were two major opposition candidates and that in some states the PRI machine continued to vote tombstones and stuff ballot boxes Salinas and the ruling party won. PRI claimed only 50.36 percent of the presidential vote for Salinas; he probably had less than an absolute majority.

Salinas's major opponent, leftist Cuauhtemoc Cardenas, at one stage in the count claimed victory and probably did better than the 31 percent of the vote the government claimed he'd won.

For the first time opposition parties won state-wide elections; four non–PRI candidates won election to the federal Senate.

The ruling party suffered a close call and the Mexican political climate may have been permanently changed in 1988. In state elections in 1989, the PRI candidate for governor of Baja, California, was defeated; for the first time ever the PRI permitted an opposition party to win an election for state governor.

In the Republic of South Africa opposition parties made futile noises against the ruling Nationalist Party, but the white voters of the Republic (there are no others) paid no heed for many years. There most voters agreed that the black majority of the nation's population must not attain political power. The Nationalists were the party of white supremacy par excellence, and vocally defended the country against the verbal and economic assault of most of the rest of the world. Despite Nationalist intransigence on racial matters, growing black militance and foreign pressure against the Republic to relax apartheid seemed to demonstrate to those who would observe reality that strict racial segregation was no longer a viable policy.

Recently, under the leadership of President Pieter Botha and his successor President Frederick de Klerk, the Nationalists moved to the left and relaxed many of the discriminatory laws and regulations offensive to blacks. This caused the bitter-end proponents of apartheid to secede from the Nationalists and form the Conservative Party. At the same time leftist opponents of the Nationalists composed their differences and formed the Democratic Party.

During the election campaign of 1989 it appeared for a spell that the Nationalists might lose the parliamentary majority that they've held since 1948. However, Nationalists argued during the campaign that to throw them out would be to open Pandora's box and bring unpredictable change to the land. Enough South African voters found this unthinkable that, though the Nationalists suffered losses in popular votes and parliamentary seats they retained their majority. The country is less a one-party land than it's been for many years. The end of Nationalist rule, and indeed of white minority rule, may be in sight.

Several democratic nations have political systems in which numerous parties compete for power, elections are free, votes are honestly counted, but one party seemingly governs forever even though it seldom, or never, polls a majority of the popular vote.

In Japan, the Liberal Democratic Party has governed the country for over

30 years. Sometimes it holds a majority in the Japanese House of Representatives, sometimes it doesn't. Always it's by far the largest party in the nation, and never can the opposition parties unite to throw it out of office. The farmers and industry support it; it has access to far greater financial support than do any of its opponents. As mentioned earlier, the Liberal Democratic Party lost control of the House of Councillors for the first time ever in 1989, and its domination of the House of Representatives appeared to be in danger (though it retained an absolute majority in the lower house in the election of February 18, 1990, and will thus continue to govern alone).

In Italy, the Christian Democratic Party has dominated all governments since the 1940s. Almost never has the Democristiana (DC) held a majority in the Italian Chamber of Deputies but it has always been the largest party. Its power is seemingly perpetual because its primary competitor is the PCI, the Communist Party of Italy. The non–Communists of Italy will not allow the Communists to share power in that country, but if they're to be kept out of power the DC must support the government to insure it a parliamentary majority. Thus the prime minister is almost always DC; if he isn't the majority of cabinet members at least are DC. In recent elections Italy's Socialists and environmentalists have gained support at the expense of the Communists. The weaker the Communists become, the more possible it will be for a coalition of parties to rule Italy without the participation of the Christian Democrats. In addition, the Communists now proclaim devotion to democracy; once they convince enough opposition leaders of their sincerity they may well be allowed to participate in government at the national level. (They already govern several major Italian cities in coalition with Socialists, and in general provide competent, honest government.)

In India the Congress Party has enjoyed almost permanent power in the world's largest democracy. Many parties compete against the Congress Party for power but before 1989 it was defeated only once, as a reaction to Indira Gandhi's half-hearted effort to establish a dictatorship in the mid–1970s. It was replaced by the Janata, a multi-party coalition whose members had nothing in common except dislike of the Congress. Janata quickly fell apart; its government was so chaotic and incompetent that the Congress Party triumphantly returned to power at the next election and remained there until late 1989. In the latest Indian election the Congress lost its majority in the Lok Sabha (the House of the People, the lower house of Parliament) but remained the largest party. However, an opposition coalition has mustered a parliamentary majority and has at least temporarily ejected the Congress Party from power.

Two-party systems. Most English-speaking nations and a few non–English-speaking democracies have two-party systems. The purest of these is found in the United States.

Because of the peculiar nature of our federal system it's almost impossible for third parties to challenge Democrats and Republicans. Due to the electoral college system, a presidential election is actually 51 separate state-wide elections to choose electors from the 50 states plus the District of Columbia. Ballots are prepared at the state level; political parties are defined by state law. Third parties must qualify for a spot on state ballots under state law, and 51 different sets of requirements must be met to get on those ballots.

Add to that the facts that our laws providing for public financing of presidential campaigns make it difficult for third-party candidates to qualify for assistance, and that the direct primary system allows people of any ideology to call themselves Democrats or Republicans, and it's clear that the system makes the founding and growth of third parties almost impossible. Why should the aspiring politician go the difficult third-party route when there are so many advantages to being a Democrat or a Republican?

In Brazil during the 1970s a two-party system was mandated by law. The generals who ran the nation created the parties and commanded that they compete in semi-free elections. They saw to it that their preferred party ARENA — Alliance for National Renovation — always controlled the Congress and most state and local governments. They allowed the tame opposition, the MDB — Brazilian Democratic Movement — to control the state of Guanabara (of which Rio de Janeiro is the capital) and a few city governments, but no more. The system ended when the generals decided to allow multiple parties to exist once more in the late 1970s. Brazil's political system has since evolved into a relatively open multi-party one.

In other nations with two major political parties, major third, fourth and even fifth parties exist. However, only the two largest parties have an opportunity to govern.

In Canada, only the Liberals and the Conservatives have a chance to be the largest party in the House of Commons and to govern, though the New Democratic Party wins a fair number of seats in every parliament and now controls the Ontario provincial legislature. The Social Credit Party competes in provincial elections and has won a few in the West, but is at present an insignificant force in federal politics. The Parti Quebecois has governed Quebec and is presently the main opposition party in the provincial legislature there, but it doesn't contest federal elections.

In the United Kingdom, the prime minister will be either a Conservative or a Laborite, although the Liberal-Social democratic Alliance received about 20 percent of the vote in recent elections to the House of Commons. Since 1987 the Alliance has disintegrated into its component parts (the Liberal Democrats and the Social Democrats), neither now being strong enough to threaten the two major parties. In 1989 the Greens polled 15 percent of the vote in electing British members of the Parliament of the European Community and became the third-strongest party of the realm. Whether they will retain such strength in the next House of Commons election (to be held at the latest in 1992) is anyone's guess.

In West Germany, the Christian Democrats and the Social Democrats polled at least 80 percent of the vote between them in every election; though it was rare for either to get over half of the vote, one or the other has always governed the German Federal Republic. No other party has polled even 10 percent of the vote in many years.

In Austria the Social Democrats and the Austrian People's Party obtain 85 percent to 90 percent of the votes between them; occasionally the Social Democrats win over 50 percent alone. In Colombia the major parties are the Liberals and Conservatives; the elected presidents of the country have always been one or the other, and there's no real possibility of a third party breaking into the charmed circle (though a third-party candidate finished second in the presidential election of 1990). In Uruguay Blancos and Colorados compete; until recently no third party has been strong enough to challenge.

Multi-party systems. In most democratic nations, many political parties exist and for the most part there is no majority party.

One variation on this scheme of things is that which exists in Norway and Sweden. In these two countries political warfare is a competition between a very powerful socialist party and less-powerful anti-socialist parties. The Norwegian Labor Party and the Swedish Social Democratic Party always poll over 40 percent of the votes in national elections; they're always the largest party in their respective parliaments. When they and their leftwing allies control over half of the seats in their parliaments, they govern. When their opponents control over half of the seats, the opponents govern in a multi-party coalition. The government is either socialist or non–socialist.

The Israeli situation is similar. Two large party groupings win 80 percent or more of the parliamentary seats—the Labor Party and the conservative Likud bloc. Recently the balance between Labor and Likud has been so delicate that neither can rule alone; they must both hold office together or one must form a coalition government with two or three minor parties.

In the Netherlands, Belgium and Denmark there are so many parties that none can hope to win over half of the seats in parliament for itself. Who governs is determined by complicated negotiations between the party leaders. Thus some Belgians call their country a particratie (a nation governed by the political parties) rather than a democratie (one governed by the people).

In Switzerland at least a dozen parties compete for votes at each election, but a four-party coalition has run the nation for the last 30-odd years and seems prepared to hold office forever. The Social Democratic Party, the Radical Party, the Christian Democratic Party and the Swiss People's Party garner between them at least 75 percent of the vote at every election. No other party ever comes close to breaking into the Big Four.

Nature of political parties. The nature of political parties varies tremendously from nation to nation, and even within nations. Some represent belief in a political or social ideology with adherents over all the earth, such as the

Communist parties found almost everywhere. (However, all Communists are not alike. In fact, three separate Communist parties compete for votes in India.)

The Social Democratic and Labor parties found in so many democratic countries are also very similar; almost all such believe in democratic Marxist Socialism and find their support primarily among working people and members of labor unions.

Most Christian Democratic parties began as organizations of Roman Catholic political activists. Some have developed broader political appeal, attracting Protestant and non-religious voters.

Some parties represent the traditional establishment of a nation. Their members think of themselves as the natural rulers of the country and seek to preserve what they perceive to be the national character. Such are the British Conservative Party, the Japanese Liberal Democratic Party, the Swiss Radical Party, and perhaps the Indian Congress Party.

Still other parties represent broad coalitions of diverse interest groups which value winning elections and gaining power over preserving ideological purity. Such are the American Democrats and Republicans and the Canadian and Colombian Liberals and Conservatives. The lack of strong ideological differences between such parties leads to their characterization as Tweedledum and Tweedledee, and causes ideological opponents such as George Wallace in the 1968 American presidential election to charge that "there's not a dime's worth of difference between them."

Most democratic nations have small one-issue parties devoted to a single burning cause. The Welsh Nationalists exist only in Wales, and want local self-government for that corner of Great Britain. Scottish Nationalists want the same privilege for Scotland. The Israeli Religious Party wants the Israeli Government to enact the religious obligations of orthodox Jews into law. The Swiss National Republicans want severe restrictions upon the immigration of foreign workers into Switzerland.

Some nations have political parties constructed to advance the political fortunes of one person — their leader. Most noteworthy was the Perónista Party of Argentina, the political vehicle of Juan Domingo Perón. (After Perón's death it changed its name to the Justicialist Party and still governs the country.) Other examples were the APRA Party of Peru, the creature of the radical reformer Raul Haya de la Torre; and the French Union for the New Republic (UNR), the vehicle of Charles de Gaulle. Such parties have appeared even in the United States — most noteworthy being the Progressive Party of 1912 (the creature of Theodore Roosevelt) and the American Independent Party of 1968 (the creature of George Wallace).

Two of the most successful totalitarian parties became personalist before assuming power — the Fascists of Italy (the tool of Benito Mussolini) and the National Socialist German Workers' Party of Germany (the tool of Adolf Hitler).

In general, one-party government is strongest but least democratic. Two-party systems provide strength in democratic systems, at the cost sometimes of underrepresenting schools of thought that don't fit into the major parties. Multi-party government tends to be weakest, because it depends on horsetrading between the leaders of the various parties and because one small party can destroy a coalition of stronger parties if it wishes by simply pulling out and supporting the opposition.

Majoritarian and consensual democracy. In some democratic nations virtually all major political parties are involved in the government and virtually the same people govern forever, regardless of election returns. In others parties representing only a bare majority of the voters or legislative representatives govern, while a numerous minority opposes the government. Here the personnel of government may change when the outs eject the ins from power (if they ever do).

The first type of democracy is consensual — the best national example being Switzerland. The second type is majoritarian — the best example being Great Britain.

Swiss government at the federal level and in virtually all cantons and communes in German-speaking Switzerland is conducted by the four-party coalition mentioned earlier in the chapter. Hardly ever is one of the four great parties excluded, or a fifth party allowed into the circle.

In French-speaking Switzerland other parties may participate in the governing coalition (Liberals in a few cantons, Communists in Geneva), but the rules are the same; the major groups are never excluded and the coalition participants almost never change.

Government is, then, by consensus of all major political groups; only small minority parties are "outs"; the huge majority of votes and parliamentary seats are won by the blanket coalition of "ins," who seem to remain in power forever.

In Great Britain one-party government has been the rule since 1945. The leader of the largest party in the House of Commons is chosen to be prime minister; this person selects a cabinet of ministers drawn entirely from his party. Members of Parliament from this party constitute the Government party — the ins. All members of Parliament from other parties constitute the Opposition — the outs. Usually the Government holds a majority of seats in the House, occasionally holding only a plurality. Everyone knows that its power is temporary; never since 1945 has one party held power for 15 years running.

Almost always the Opposition holds at least 40 percent of the seats in the House. Government and Opposition both know that soon the political wheel will turn, the ins will be thrown out and the outs will come back to power.

Two-party democracies almost always are majoritarian. The major exception is Austria. From 1945 into the mid–1960s the Austrian Peoples' Party and the Social Democrats ruled the country in a consensus "Grand Coalition" representing the votes of over 90 percent of the Austrian people. Then the consensus broke down and the Social Democratic Party ruled, either alone or in coalition with small parties. Now, however, the consensus has returned and the Social Democrats lead a restored coalition.

In essence Italy and Japan are majoritarian, in that those who govern almost never enjoy the confidence of a two-thirds majority in Parliament. However, the outs have no opportunity to oust the ins from power—a small majority rules forever, while a large minority is permanently held at bay.

The multi-party regimes of Norway and Sweden—socialists and antisocialists alternating in office—are rather majoritarian. The broad multi-party coalition regimes of the Netherlands and Denmark are more consensual. The United States occupies a middle ground; when the presidency and Congress are controlled by the same party we in a sense have majoritarian government—where control is divided we have consensual government. Since our Congress has become permanently Democratic, our two alternatives are Democratic majoritarian government when a Democrat sits in the White House and two-party consensual government when a Republican sits there. With the election of George Bush to the presidency in November of 1988 the Republicans won their fifth presidential election of the last six and their seventh of the last ten, while the Democrats won their nineteenth straight majority in the House of Representatives in 1990. The United States may be on the road to a permanently Republican president ruling with a permanently Democratic congress.

Democracy and authoritarianism. In many nations of Latin America and in a few nations elsewhere, democratic government has alternated with military authoritarianism. Uruguay for long enjoyed the reputation of being the most democratic nation of Latin America; Colorados and Blancos battled for electoral control of the nation for a century in free elections. Its Colorado rulers established the most comprehensive welfare state in the Western Hemisphere and its people enjoyed a North American–style standard of living. Then inflation ran amuck, living standards plummeted, and the leftist Tupamaro urban guerrillas destroyed the peace of the land. The military expelled the civilian leadership and temporarily ended democracy. Only recently have the generals stepped aside and restored civilian rule.

Chile lived under multi-party presidential-style democracy for over 30 years, its political system permitting the Marxist Salvador Allende to win the presidency with 36 percent of the popular vote in 1970. Popular discontent with his rule combined with the American CIA led to his overthrow in 1973; the leader of the coup, General Augusto Pinochet, ruled the land for 16 years. In October of 1988 Chileans voted in a free election on the question of whether General Pinochet should hold office for eight more years. Over 55 percent of the Chilean voters said "no." The General therefore called a free presidential and congressional election for December 14, 1989; the winner was Christian

Democrat Patricio Aylwyn, a moderate leftist opponent of both Allende-style leftism and the Pinochet dictatorship. In early 1990 Pinochet's rule ended. The short-term prognosis for the restored Chilean democracy is good.

Though violent governmental change is almost unknown in Brazil, that country too has switched governmental forms on occasion. For better than half a century after independence it was the Western Hemisphere's only monarchy. A bloodless coup created the Old Republic in 1889; the effective rulers of the country were a close-knit group of oligarchs who manipulated a limited number of voters to keep themselves in power. In the 1930s Getulio Vargas established his Estado Novo (New State), a mild authoritarian dictatorship modelled to a degree upon Mussolini's Fascist Italy. When the democracies triumphed in World War II Vargas stepped aside and permitted the creation of a democratic government; from 1945 until 1964 Brazil was a rather typical multi-party democracy (except that illiterates, a large percentage of the population, weren't permitted to vote). Then a military coup brought the generals to power and the two-party controlled democracy described earlier came into existence. In the early 1980s the generals began converting this system into another true democracy, this time allowing even illiterates the right to vote. In November and December of 1989 the first presidential election since 1960 was held. On December 17 the voters chose the moderate conservative Fernando Collor de Mello as president, narrowly rejecting Socialist Luis Inacto da Silva. Congressional elections were held in October of 1990; hopefully the new democratic government will function more effectively than the old one of 1945–64 did.

Argentina has vacillated from one government form to another, in recent years with confusing rapidity. Conservative oligarchs were in charge in 1900. In 1912 they expanded the right to vote and yielded power to the middle class; for almost two decades democracy reigned.

In 1928 the aged Ypolito Yrigoyen was elected president of Argentina; his government was so corrupt and inept that the military overthrew it with popular blessing in 1930. The army now took power behind the scenes until 1945.

Juan Domingo Perón established his demagogic semi-dictatorship with military backing, but lost his uniformed support as he became more radical; the armed forces ousted him in 1955.

Arturo Frondizi was elected president in 1958, but deposed by the military in 1962. Arturo Illia was elected president in 1963, but was deposed by the military in 1966. Seven years of military rule followed, after which Juan Perón won the presidency again in 1973, his wife Isabel being elected his vice president. Juan died in office and was succeeded by Isabel. The military removed her in 1976 and instituted a hard-line dictatorship which lasted until 1983. In that year democracy was restored and Raul Alfonsin was elected president, serving out his six-year term. In the latest presidential election the outs

(Perónist Carlos Menen's Justicialist Party) defeated the ins (Alfonsin's Radical Party) and the government changed hands without violence. This bodes well for democracy's continuation for a spell in Argentina.

Nigeria began its independent existence as a parliamentary democracy in 1961. This was overthrown by the military in 1966, which ran the government for over a decade. In the late 1970s the generals stepped aside to allow civilian rule under presidential democracy. Five years of civilian corruption were all that the generals could take; once again the country is under military control.

The norm in Bolivia and Pakistan is authoritarianism, with short intervals of democracy. The secession of Bangladesh in 1971 destroyed the credibility of the Pakistani authoritarians and permitted the semi-democratic regime of Zulfikar Ali Bhutto to come to power. Only a few years later the military lost patience with him and overthrew him, establishing the authoritarian rule of General Mohammed Zia ul-Haq. The recent death of General Zia in a plane crash destabilized his system; in November 1988 his successor permitted a free parliamentary election which was won by political forces led by Benazir Bhutto, daughter of Zulfikar Ali Bhutto. She was the Pakistani prime minister, the first female head of state to rule an Islamic country, until August of 1990. She was dismissed from office by President Ghulem Izhek Khan, who at the same time dissolved Parliament and called for new elections. The president, under pressure from the military, did all he could to undermine Bhutto's strength with the voters. Her party was defeated soundly at the polls.

Turkey too has switched systems with regularity. The authoritarian system of Mustapha Kemal Ataturk and his successors yielded to two-party democracy after World War II. Rampant political corruption caused the military to assume power in the late 1950s. In the 1960s the soldiers moved aside and multi-party democracy came into being. Weak government and escalating domestic violence ensued, so once more the military stepped in to restore order. Recently the soldiers have once more relinquished power, and multi-party democracy again reigns.

Party discipline. Another consideration to be taken into account is that of party discipline. Are legislators elected to vote their conscience on legislation, or must they vote as the party leaders dictate?

In the United States, party discipline in legislative bodies is almost non-existent. Legislators don't vote as the party leadership tells them but as they wish. Since the direct primary allows a person to receive a party nomination for a legislative seat without the support of a party organization, and since most legislative candidates conduct their campaigns for office independent of the party organization, elected legislators feel that they owe little to the party. After all, they got themselves elected; the party didn't elect them. This contributes to the difficulty a president or governor faces in getting a legislative program enacted. What duty does a Democratic Congress person owe a Democratic president, or a Republican state senator a Republican governor?

The direct primary to choose party nominees for public office is almost exclusively an American device. In nearly all other countries, party nominees for public office are chosen by the party organization. The legislator must keep the party happy in order to be assured of renomination at election time and independent candidates stand little chance of election in all democracies.

Without direct primaries, party organizations can exert great influence on legislators. But the greatest enemy of legislators' independence is the notion that they're elected as party delegates, not as individuals. As the character in *HMS Pinafore* stated it, "I always voted at my party's call, and never thought of thinking for myself at all." The role of the legislator in most democratic nations is exactly that — vote always at your party's call, and never think of thinking for yourself at all — that is, if you want to keep on being a legislator.

In Great Britain and most other democratic lands, party discipline is very strong; party whips get out the vote on important legislative proposals and make sure that party members vote the right way. In Switzerland on the other hand legislators are more likely to vote their consciences, because the fate of the governing coalition never rides on legislative parliamentary votes.

Until recently Italian members of parliament voted by secret ballot on pending legislation. Party discipline was relatively weak because the leadership couldn't determine who voted against it. It was to improve discipline that the secret ballot was abolished for most parliamentary votes in Italy in 1988.

The good of party discipline is that a majority can enact its program into law without difficulty. Without party discipline majorities shift about like the desert sands, the behavior of the legislature becoming almost unpredictable.

Conclusion. There are as many variations of democratic government as there are democracies. No two democratic governments are alike. Though the number of such governments has increased dramatically recently, there is still no democracy in half of the nations on Earth. In these the rulers still hold power by force, open or concealed. There power still flows from the barrel of a gun.

Chapter 12
Nomination and Election Systems

The right to vote. We Americans take it for granted that, if a country is to call itself democratic, all adult men and women should possess the right to vote. Such a broad electoral franchise is a creation of the twentieth century.

The original Constitution of the United States just allowed popular election of members of the House of Representatives; only those people could vote for congressmen who could vote for members of the lower house of their state legislature. (Senators were to be elected by state legislatures, the president by electors chosen as state legislatures directed.) In the beginning almost all states limited the franchise to male property owners. As a result, up to half of all adult males (and in some states more) could not vote.

By the time of Andrew Jackson (circa 1830) these property qualifications had been for the most part abolished; the United States was a land of universal manhood suffrage for free white males. (By now in most states presidential electors were chosen by direct popular vote, thus voters now chose both congressmen and the president.) The abolition of slavery and the fourteenth and fifteenth amendments in theory extended the franchise to ex-slaves (though they were prevented by various subterfuges from using it for a century). The Seventeenth Amendment provided for popular election of United States senators beginning in 1914. The Nineteenth Amendment extended the vote to women, who voted for the first time in the election of 1920. The Twenty-Sixth Amendment extended it to 18-year-olds.

France permitted universal manhood suffrage under the constitution of the First Republic (circa 1792), but quickly abolished it. It was restored under the Second Republic (1848) and again abolished, but it came to stay with the Third Republic of 1871. French women didn't obtain the vote until after World War II.

While Great Britain broadened its franchise in 1832, and again in 1867, it didn't attain true universal manhood suffrage until the twentieth century. English women, most of them, obtained the vote after World War I.

Universal manhood suffrage came to Germany with the Second Reich in 1871. All male Germans could vote for members of the largely powerless

239

Imperial Reichstag, the lower house of the federal Parliament. German women got the right to vote with the establishment of the Weimar Republic in 1919.

The last major European state to accord women the right to vote was Switzerland—only in 1971 was its constitution amended to allow this. The principality of Liechtenstein didn't climb aboard the bandwagon until 1984.

Virtually all nations that allow any type of voting now permit universal male and female suffrage. Whether this right to vote is meaningful depends upon the political and constitutional system of the nation in question.

Nomination of candidates. An essential part of any election system is the procedure for selecting the names of the candidates who will compete for office. In most lands this process is anything but democratic.

The traditional method for choosing candidates almost everywhere is that of nomination by party organizations. Only party insiders participate in this process.

In nations where citizens vote for the party rather than the candidate the nominee doesn't necessarily need glamor or competence; party loyalty is much more important. What has the candidate done for the party lately? How likely is he to vote as directed on pending legislation if elected? How many party bigwigs back the candidate?

In the United States candidates for Congress or the state legislature will live in the district they seek to represent. In virtually all other democracies this isn't true; thus in Great Britain a person living in London might be nominated by his party for a Parliamentary seat in the highlands of Scotland or the coal-mining country of South Wales. Virtually all countries that elect legislators from single-member districts do the same thing. For example, a candidate from Marseilles may run for a French National Assembly seat in Paris. Those the party leadership want elected they nominate for districts where the party is strong; up-and-coming candidates with voter appeal may be nominated for districts where the contest will be close (here charisma may make a difference). And marginal candidates may be nominated for districts where the party is almost sure to lose.

In nations electing legislators from multi-member districts by proportional representation, major parties may well elect at least one candidate per district (and perhaps many more). The party organizations here not only determine which candidates will run in which district, they also determine the order in which the names of the district's candidates are printed on the ballot.

The name leading a major party list will certainly be elected. The farther down the ballot a candidate's name is placed the less are his or her chances for election. The reasons for this will be explained later in the chapter.

To sum up: In most nations the voters who elect legislators have no input into the nomination process. Not only that, the candidates are very likely not to be residents of the district in which they seek election.

The American system of candidate nomination is atypical; never have we entrusted the nomination process solely to party organizations. In the early days of the Republic we did indeed entrust nomination of legislative candidates to the party. Candidates for executive offices were nominated by the legislative caucus—presidential candidates by the party Representataives and Senators, gubernatorial candidates by the party's members of the state legislature.

During the time of Andrew Jackson (the late 1820s and the 1830s) the caucus was replaced by the convention. Those who supported the party in the voting precincts would assemble in precinct caucuses to choose members of the county convention, which would nominate candidates for county offices and choose delegates to the state convention. The state convention would nominate candidates for state office and choose delegates to the national convention.

The convention was democratic in the sense that all party voters could theoretically participate in the system. It proved to be not so democratic because most voters didn't choose to participate so the machinery fell into the hands of the party activists and their organizations. Almost always the organization could control the convention and nominate its own but occasionally, insurgents could assemble a powerful organization of their own and seize control of the convention and the party.

In order to break the control of the party organization over nominations the direct primary made its appearance around the turn of the century. Where it is used candidates are nominated by the party's voters in a preliminary election, conducted like a general election.

This quickly became the method of nominating party candidates for state and local government office in the majority of American states. By 1950 the direct primary was virtually universally used to choose candidates below state level, but New York, Connecticut, Indiana and a few other states retained it for choosing candidates for state-wide offices. Today it has disappeared as a nomination device, except at the national level. The only important nominations still made by conventions are those for president and vice president.

Even here, the voters make the party choice in state primary elections. Most national convention delegates are elected in primaries; the party nominee almost invariably locks up the nomination through primary victories long before the national convention assembles. The last Democratic nominee who did not clinch his nomination by winning primaries was Hubert Humphrey in 1968; the last such Republican nominee was Thomas E. Dewey in 1948.

Vice-presidential nominations are not subject to any voter input. By tradition a party's vice-presidential nominee is chosen by the presidential nominee who announces his choice to the convention for ratification. The last Democratic vice-presidential nominee to be chosen by the convention delegates and not by the presidential nominee was Estes Kefauver in 1956; the last Republican to be so chosen was Calvin Coolidge in 1920.

Those who wish to place their names on a party's primary ballot do so by filing petitions signed by a required number of registered voters with a designated authority. The organization may indorse primary candidates and work to assure their nomination, although this effort doesn't always succeed.

The convention system virtually assured that only Democrats had a voice in nominating Democratic candidates and only Republicans had a voice in nominating Republicans. In 1952, however, Democrats participated in Republican precinct caucuses by the thousands in states such as Texas and Georgia to choose convention delegates favorable to Dwight D. Eisenhower. Delegates so chosen helped "Ike" win the GOP nomination; these ex–Democrats also helped Eisenhower carry several southern states in the general election.

Most states conduct "closed" primaries. Voters register as Democrats, Republicans or independents. Only registered Democrats may vote in the Democratic primary and registered Republicans in the Republican primary. Independents generally may not vote in primaries, though some states let them choose on the day of the primary.

A minority of states conduct "open" primaries, in which the voter is free to choose which primary to participate in. In these states (of which Wisconsin is the most noteworthy example) voters may participate in the primary with the most interesting contests, regardless of normal party affiliation.

Washington and Alaska conduct "blanket" primaries in which the voter is given a ballot containing the names of all of the parties' candidates for all offices. Here the voter may vote for a Democrat for governor, a Republican for United States senator, a Democrat for state attorney-general and so forth. The best Democratic vote-getter among the party's candidates for Governor receives the Democratic gubernatorial nomination; the best Republican vote-getter among the GOP candidates gets the GOP nomination. This is true even if the top two Democrats get more votes than the top Republican—the Democrat who ran second has been defeated.

Louisiana also has a blanket primary, but in that state all candidates compete against each other in the primary. Any candidate getting 50 percent plus one of the total vote is elected; for that office there will be no general election. If no one obtains an absolute majority the top two vote-getters face each other in the general election, even if both belong to the same party. Many Louisiana contests are decided in the primary, so the general election ballot is likely to be very short.

For many years California allowed candidates to cross-file in primaries. That is, a Democrat could run in both the Democratic and Republican primaries, as could a Republican. Despite the fact that California primaries have always been closed, Republicans could vote for Democrats in the primary if they were on the Republican ballot and vice versa. Occasionally a candidate would win both major-party nominations on primary day and clinch the election. The state abolished this system in 1959.

New York retains a modified version of this system. Candidates may run in the primary of a party other than their own if they obtain permission from the other party's governing committee to do so. Such permission may be hard to come by. However, New York has a unique party system. Four parties have virtually permanent places on the ballot (Democratic, Republican, Liberal and Conservative), though only Democrats and Republicans generally win elections. Liberal Democrats are likely to seek both Democratic and Liberal nominations, while conservative Republicans seek both Republican and Conservative nods. Sometimes a liberal Democrat loses the Democratic nomination while winning the Liberal contest. He may choose to contest the general election as a Liberal. Often this will split the Democratic vote and allow the Republican to win. Conservative Republicans sometimes use the same tactic when they lose the GOP nod but win the Conservative.

Minor party and independent candidates are nominated by petition as are candidates for office in areas where non-partisan elections are mandated.

Conventions choose nominees in a few areas outside the United States. Canadian parties choose their candidates for the House of Commons in district conventions, their provincial leaders in provincial conventions and their national leaders in national conventions. In Mexico the opposition parties choose presidential candidates in national conventions. (In the ruling PRI, however, the outgoing president in essence nominates his successor.) In a few Latin American countries (such as Colombia and Argentina) direct "closed" primaries exist.

Introduction to electoral systems. The system for determining the winners of elections can have great influence over who runs the nation.

Legislators may be elected from single-member districts, where each district elects one legislator, or from multi-member districts, where each district elects more than one legislator.

In single-member districts there can be no minority representation, because only one legislator is elected from that district. Where such districts exist, there are four possible election systems.

In nations where the president is elected by direct popular vote, again there can be but one winner. Here too there are four possible election systems.

First-past-the-post. The system used by most English-speaking nations is first-past-the-post. The candidate with the most votes wins, whether he has an absolute majority (50 percent plus one of the votes) or not. Thus, in a three-candidate race the following can happen: A gets 40 percent of the vote; B gets 36 percent; C gets 24 percent. A wins because he gets the most votes, though 60 percent of the voters vote for someone else.

Several countries elect their president by first-past-the-post, including Colombia, Mexico and Venezuela; it was also the system used in Brazil between 1945 and 1964. American state governors are also elected this way.

In American gubernatorial elections the victor almost inevitably obtains more than 50 percent of the vote because there are almost inevitably only two major candidates, thanks to the rigid American two-party system.

In countries with multi-party systems which elect presidents using first-past-the-post, there may be three or four major candidates; the winner may obtain far less than an absolute majority. In the Venezuelan presidential election of 1968 the results were:

Rafael Caldera	1,075,375
Gonzalo Barrios	1,044,081
Miguel Burelli Rivas	825,233
Luis Prieto Figueroa	716,820

Caldera obtained only about 29 percent of the vote. Though over 70 percent of Venezuelans who voted for president in 1968 did not vote for him, he still won the election.

Most nations which elect their presidents by popular vote do not use first-past-the-post in order to avoid outcomes like the above. Instead they use the run-off system which will be described later.

First-past-the-post usually magnifies the victory of the largest party in a general legislative election where all seats (or a large number) are up for grabs. In the most recent British elections the Conservative Party has won over 55 percent of the seats in the House of Commons with little more than 40 percent (44.9 percent in 1979, 43.5 percent in 1983, 42.3 percent in 1987) of the popular vote.

In the Canadian election of 1984 the Progressive Conservatives won 75 percent of the seats with only 50 percent of the popular vote.

In the Indian election of 1985 the Congress Party won nearly 80 percent of the seats with a bit less than half of the popular vote.

In recent elections in Singapore, the People's Action Party has won all of the parliamentary seats with 75 percent or so of the vote. (Singapore politicians were shocked when a candidate of the Workers' Party defeated the PAP in an election to fill a vacant parliamentary seat in 1981, becoming the first member of the Opposition to sit in Parliament in almost two decades. A greater shock happened in 1984, when PAP received only 65 percent of the votes and the Opposition elected two members of Parliament out of 65. In 1988 PAP's share of the popular vote fell to 64 percent but the Opposition lost one of its two parliamentary seats.)

This system magnifies the power of parties with concentrated voter support in a few areas and dilutes the power of parties with scattered support. In the British election of 1983 the Conservatives received 43.5 percent of the popular vote, Labor received 28.3 percent, while the Liberal-Social Democratic Alliance received 26 percent. The Conservatives won 397 seats, Labor 209 and the Alliance 23. Conservative voters are numerous in all parts of England except in inner cities; in English inner cities, Scotland and Wales Conservative candidates often run third or worse. Labor voters are found in huge numbers in Britain's large cities and in Scotland and Wales, but are rare in rural England. Alliance voters are widely scattered across the countryside, having no areas of concentration. In rural and suburban areas of England Conservative candidates won with handsome pluralities but were often buried under massive landslides in England's inner cities and in industrial areas of Scotland and Wales. Where the Conservatives were weak Labor won overwhelming majorities of popular votes. In the big cities the Alliance often ran second to Labor; in rural areas of England it often ran second to Conservatives, but under first-past-the-post rules second is no better than ninety-sixth. Labor's concentrated voters won it much representation for its 28-plus percent of the popular vote; the Alliance's scattered voters won it virtually none for its 26 percent.

It's also possible for the party with the most popular votes to lose an election under first-past-the-post. In the South African election of 1948 the governing United Party and its coalition partner the Labor Party polled 52 percent of the popular vote while the Nationalist-Afrikaaner opposition polled 42 percent (6 percent going to small parties). However, the Nationalist-Afrikaaner opposition won 79 parliamentary seats to 73 for United-Labor and took control of the government, setting in motion its policy of apartheid—mandated segregation of the country's racial groups. Though the legislative apportionment system didn't deliberately overrepresent rural areas and underrepresent the cities the United Party won most of the urban seats by large majorities while the Nationalists won more numerous rural seats by generally smaller majorities. Thus the majority of South Africans voted against the racial segregation policies of the victorious Nationalists at the time the Nationalist government began putting them into effect. In 1953 the popular vote between the two party alliances split virtually 50–50 (with United Party-Labor holding a slight lead), but the Nationalist-Afrikaaner group gained several seats from its opponents. Only in 1957 did the Nationalist-Afrikaaner group obtain a popular vote majority (55 percent), producing a two-thirds majority in Parliament.

In 1951 the British Labor Party obtained 13,948,883 popular votes to 13,718,199 for the Conservatives, but the Conservatives won 321 parliamentary seats to Labor's 295, ousting Labor from power. In February of 1974 the reverse occurred as the Conservatives received 11,872,180 votes to Labor's 11,645,616 but Labor won 301 seats to 297 for the Conservatives, ousting the Conservatives from power. .

Gerrymandering. In the United States gerrymandering is a commonly used device for maximizing one party's representation in the legislature as against another's. Legislative district boundaries are drawn so as to cram as many minority party voters as possible into as few districts as possible; thus the minority wins a few seats by huge majorities while the majority wins many seats by narrow majorities. Thus in some recent California elections Democrats have won majorities in the state legislature and the state's delegation to the House of Representatives though Republican candidates have won a majority of popular votes. In Indiana the reverse has happened. Though Democrats have won popular majorities Republicans have elected legislative majorities. Gerrymandering is an accepted part of the American political game as the legislative majority at reapportionment time does all it can to make its majority permanent. In most other nations the drawing of election district boundaries is deliberately made non-political.

Before the United States Supreme Court declared the practice unconstitutional during the 1960s another type of gerrymander was common in the United States; legislative districts of widely differing population would be created. The majority party would create many districts of small population where its voters were numerous and a few districts of gigantic population where the opposition's voters prevailed. Sometimes this sort of thing was mandated by state constitutional provisions regarding apportionment of representation in the state legislature.

Before the apportionment revolution of the 1960s, the Ohio Constitution provided that each of the state's 88 counties was entitled to elect one member of the Ohio House of Representatives and that there would be 136 total members of the chamber. After each county was assured its one representative only 48 more seats were available for distribution among counties of large population. The result was that Vinton County with a population of 10,000 elected one representative, while Cuyahoga County with over a million residents elected only 17 representatives. In a sense a Vinton County vote was worth more than seven times a Cuyahoga County vote. Rural counties thus controlled the Ohio House, and since most Ohio counties voted Republican in those days the Chamber was, as some wags stated, constitutionally Republican. Now that rural votes and urban votes are equal in Ohio legislative elections, the Ohio House is usually controlled by the Democrats.

The California Senate has 40 members while the state has 58 counties. Before the apportionment revolution no county could elect more than one senator; the counties with the smallest populations were grouped into two- or three-county districts. Los Angeles County with a population of six million plus elected one senator as did San Luis Obispo County with a population of less than 200 thousand and mountain multi-county districts with less than 100 thousand residents.

A series of decisions by the United States Supreme Court ruled these representation systems unconstitutional; when legislators are elected from single-member districts the populations of the districts must be as nearly equal as possible.

The Supreme Court has also declared racially inspired gerrymandering unconstitutional. Before the 1960s state legislatures would sometimes draw district boundaries in such a way as to insure that no racial minority would have a majority in any district, thus denying it legislative representation. Now boundaries must be drawn in such a way as to give the minorities a fair chance to win representation proportionate to their share of the voting population.

An interesting sort of gerrymander exists in the Australian state of Queensland. There the National Party, the party of Australia's farmers and the third largest party in the country, dominated the state government by creating urban single-member districts of large population and rural single-member districts of small population. Nationals would win the rural vote and Laborites the urban vote, but the Nationals would get the most representation. (In 1989 Labor won control of the state legislature despite this gerrymander and may now redistrict the state to abolish it.)

The second ballot. This system was used in elections to the lower house of the French Parliament for most of the twentieth century. It was abolished for the National Assembly elections of 1986, but was restored just two years later. The second ballot was also used for the election of the president of the Weimar Republic of Germany. It's still used in the election of judges, upper house members and cantonal and local executive bodies in Switzerland. If no candidate receives over half of the votes in an election, a second election is held a week or two weeks or a month later. In Switzerland everyone who was on the ballot in the first election may remain on in the second; no one is eliminated. However, new candidates may enter the race and old ones may drop out as the parties trade horses to maximize their chances in the second go-round. The person who gets the most votes on the second ballot is elected, whether the most is an absolute majority or not.

The president of the Weimar Republic of Germany was elected under the same rules. The possibilities are illustrated by what happened in the German presidential election of 1925. Karl Jarres, the candidate of the Nationalist Party and the Peoples' Party, led the first ballot with 10,787,870 votes. Social Democrat Otto Braun came in second with 7,836,676, third was Center Party candidate Wilhelm Marx, with 3,988,659 and fourth was Communist candidate Ernst Thaellmann with 1,885,778. Three other candidates split the few remaining votes.

The Social Democrats knew Braun couldn't overtake Jarres on the second ballot, so they caused Braun to withdraw and threw their support to Marx. The Nationalists and Peoples' Party now feared that Jarres couldn't beat Marx, since Marx now had Social Democratic support — so these two parties plus supporters of all other candidates except Thaellmann gave their support to Field Marshal Paul von Hindenburg, a new candidate, on the second ballot. Thus the two leading candidates dropped out of the race after the first ballot.

The result of the second ballot was Hindenburg 14,655,766, Marx 13,751,615, and Thaellmann 1,931,151. Thus Hindenburg, who hadn't been a candidate on the first ballot, won the election while Marx jumped from a poor third-place on the first ballot to near victory on the second.

Chapter 12

Under the current French election law no new candidates may enter the race between the first and second ballot. Those candidates who don't receive at least 12.5 percent of the vote on the first ballot are eliminated, and survivors are of course permitted to drop out. Dealmaking between ballots is still possible, but the possibilities are limited since new candidates can't enter. More often than not the second ballot is a two-person race between the best votegetter on the left and the best votegetter on the right.

This system effectively damaged the ability of the Communists to elect National Assembly members in the early days of the Fifth Republic. In the 1960s particularly, when a Communist finished first or second in a district where there was no majority, all of the other parties would throw their support to the non–Communist who finished first or second. The second ballot would pit the Communists against the non–Communists who would almost always win.

Communists became more respectable to their left-wing cousins from the late 1960s on as socialists and other liberals began to support them against rightist opponents on the second ballot. Hence the above-mentioned left-right confrontations in today's elections.

Run-off. In some American city elections, in a few American state party primary elections and in French, Austrian, Polish, Portuguese, Brazilian, Chilean, Peruvian, and Argentine presidential elections the run-off is used. If there are more than two candidates, and if no one gets 50 percent plus one votes, a second election is held between the top two vote-getters. In the run-off someone's bound to be elected with over half of the votes.

Under this system, people are voting for someone on the first ballot, the person they really want to see elected. In the run-off supporters of the losers on the first ballot are most likely voting against someone, the one of the pair of survivors they least want to see elected.

The system works to the disadvantage of candidates perceived as extremist who have less than majority support and against candidates of minority ethnic groups. In the past liberal candidates in Texas Democratic primaries have suffered from this perception. The 1972 Texas primary for the nomination for U. S. Senator was a contest between liberal Ralph Yarborough, moderate Barefoot Sanders, and some minor conservative candidates. The result of the first primary was:

Ralph Yarborough	1,033,606
Barefoot Sanders	787,504
Hugh Wilson	125,460
Tom Cartlidge	66,240
Alfonso Veloz	53,936

Yarborough led Sanders by over 220,000 votes but the combined opposition obtained 1,037,142 votes; the liberal missed out on victory by a mere 3600 votes out of a total of more than 2,000,000 cast.

In the run-off the losers supported Sanders, and the voter turnout dropped by over 100,000. The result:

Sanders	1,008,499
Yarborough	928,132

Yarborough lost over 100,000 votes in the run-off, while Sanders gained over 200,000 to win the nomination. (He lost the general election to Republican John Tower, however.)

The 1924 Louisiana Democratic gubernatorial primary illustrates how run-offs work against candidates of ethnic minority groups. The three candidates in the race were Hewitt Bouanchaud, a French-speaking Roman Catholic; and English-speaking Protestants Henry Fuqua and Huey Long. The result of the first primary was:

Bouanchaud	84,162
Fuqua	81,582
Long	73,985

Long was thus eliminated. (He made a second run for the governorship in 1928 and won, beginning the period of Long domination of Louisiana politics.)

Long was neutral in the run-off campaign, but the outcome of it was almost foreordained. The result:

Fuqua	125,880
Bouanchaud	92,006

Though voter turnout in the run-off declined slightly, both contenders gained votes. Clearly, most Long supporters voted for Fuqua in the run-off as he gained over 44,000 votes; Bouanchaud managed a gain of only 7,900. The English-speaking Protestants ganged up on the French-speaking Catholic to defeat him.

Preferential voting. In Australia, preferential voting is used in parliamentary elections to the federal House of Representatives and to most state legislatures. Under this system voters don't just put an "X" before the name of the candidate they want to see elected. They write a "1" before the name of their favorite candidate, a "2" before their second choice, and so on.

When the votes are counted the "1s" are counted first. If any candidate gets 50 percent plus one of the "1s" he wins. If no one gets this majority, the candidate with the fewest "1s" is eliminated and his ballots are counted for the "2s" marked on them. If anyone now has a majority, he wins; if not, the new low person is eliminated and his "2s" (or "3s," as the case might be) are counted. Eventually someone will obtain the magic 50 percent plus one of the votes and be elected.

This method of voting preserves the Australian three-party political system, consisting of Laborites, Liberals and Nationals. Labor is the party of the urban working class, the Liberals represent the urban middle class and the Nationals represent the country folks. The Nationals are the permanent third party and can never hope to govern by themselves at the federal level, but the single transferable vote allows their voters to back their party without helping Labor gain power. Most National voters will cast their "2" for a Liberal rather than a Laborite. The Liberal voter will usually give his "2" to a National rather than to a Laborite. Thus Liberals and Nationals routinely gang up on the local Laborites, making it difficult to impossible for Laborites to win seats without absolute majority support. However, in recent years the Labor Party has shed its radical image and more Liberal and National voters are willing to cast their "2s" for Labor. These have helped Labor retain power in Canberra since 1982.

In addition, two new Australian political parties have come on the scene—the Democrats and the Greens. These tend to draw "1s" from all three major parties. In the election of March 1990 Labor drew only 39.5 percent of the "1s" cast by the voters; the Liberal-National coalition drew less and the Democrats and Greens between them drew over 20 percent. Because of "2s" cast by Democrats and Greens, Labor managed to retain a small majority in the House of Representatives and remained in office.

The Irish use this system to elect their President.

The block vote. In multi-member districts, three basic systems are used to determine the winners. Simplest is the block vote in which the voter has as many votes as there are positions to be filled. He generally votes a straight party ticket. Since there is usually no run-off or second ballot the candidates who get the most votes win. Thus the party with the most supporters in the district wins all of the legislative representation. This system was used in the election of members of the British House of Commons from the beginning until multi-member districts were abolished around the turn of the century. Before the 1970s it was commonly used in American large cities to elect state legislators and in most American cities to elect city councils. It's now unconstitutional in this country in legislative elections because it dilutes minority voting power.

For instance, the 17 members of the Ohio House of Representatives from Cuyahoga County under the old legislative apportionment were elected county-wide by block vote. Since the Democrats were (and still are) the permanent majority in the county the 17 state representatives were always Democrats. Today the county delegation to Columbus is elected from single-member districts and it includes a few Republicans.

City council members were elected at large by block vote in many municipalities all over America before the 1960s. In Nacogdoches, Texas, the five-member City Commission was so elected by non-partisan ballot—three members one year, two the next. Over 30 percent of the city's population is black, and there were black candidates running for the council at each election, but none ever won. Today four commissioners are elected from single-member districts and one is elected at large. One of the districts has a black majority and elects a black commissioner.

The block vote is still used in the election of presidential electors in the United States, however. The candidate winning a plurality of the popular vote of a state wins all of that state's electoral votes. Outside this country it's used to elect city councils in other English-speaking lands and in France.

Limited vote. The next simplest voting system in multimember districts is the limited vote. Members of the Japanese House of Representatives are elected from districts choosing three to five representatives. The voter may vote for one candidate only. Thus, the chances of one party winning all seats from the district are slim; if a minority party concentrates its votes in the right way it's sure to win some representation.

Japanese parties nominate only the number of candidates for a district they think have a chance to win. The Communists choose only one, knowing that they must concentrate their votes on this candidate to stand a chance of victory. In a five-member district the Liberal Democrats may run three candidates, figuring that's all the representation they can elect. It's fatal to run too many candidates; if the party vote is spread too thinly, weaker parties concentrating their votes on fewer candidates will win seats their strength really doesn't entitle them to win.

The districts from which Japanese representatives are elected are somewhat gerrymandered resulting in overrepresentation of rural residents. Since the Liberal Democrats are stronger in the country than in the city, the apportionment helps them to keep control of the House.

The Spanish Senate is chosen by a less limited system. Each province of the country elects four Senators, but each voter has but three votes. Thus the largest party of the province elects three Senators while the second-largest elects one.

A similar system has been used to elect city councils in the United States. In Cincinnati the city council at one time consisted of nine members elected by the voters at large. Each voter was allowed to cast only six votes, however. The result was that the majority party would elect six council members and the minority party three.

In Argentina a compromise between limited vote and proportional representation was until recently used to elect members of the national Chamber of Deputies. Under the Saenz-Pena law, enacted in 1912, voters in each province voted a straight party ticket in these elections. The party receiving the most votes got two-thirds of the province's deputies. The party finishing second got the other third and parties finishing third or worse got no representation. This system has now been replaced by proportional representation.

A similar system was used to elect members of the Spanish Chamber of Deputies between 1931 and 1936.

Soviet elections. Before the Soviet election system was reformed by President Gorbachev, Soviet legislators were "elected" from single-member districts. There was only one nominee on the ballot; the voter could vote for him by depositing the ballot unmarked in the ballot box. One could vote against the nominee by crossing out his name but there was no way to vote for any other candidate. If over 50 percent of the voters didn't cross out the name of the nominee he was elected, and if over 50 percent did cross out his name he was defeated and a new election would be required. Virtually always over 98 percent of the voters approved the official nominee.

Now that Gorbachev has introduced multi-candidate elections the ground rules have changed. Some legislators come from multi-member districts, others from single-member districts. Either way, they are elected under the run-off system. Any candidate receiving 50 percent plus one of the vote is elected on the first go-round. If seats are left unfilled, candidates amounting to twice the number of seats remaining to be filled face each other in the run-off.

Poland used a similar system in 1989; the other East European ex-satellites use or will use proportional representation or a combination of single-member districts and proportional representation in their legislative elections.

Proportional representation—party list systems. The most complex election system is proportional representation. Under that system, if a party gets 30 percent of the popular vote in a district it should get that much of the legislative representation from that district. The idea is to give parties the percentage of representation in the legislature that they receive of the popular vote.

This system is less than a century old. It was devised to avoid the under-representation of small parties that resulted when the first-past-the-post, second ballot, or run-off systems were used.

There are many schemes for determining how the representation is to be divided. The most accurate system was that used to elect the German Reichstag under the Weimar Constitution, in effect in Germany from 1919 to 1933. A party was entitled to one representative for each 60,000 votes polled in the national election. The number of representatives in the Reichstag therefore varied according to how many people voted in each election, but the representation was an absolutely accurate mirror of the popular vote. Czechoslovakia used a similar system between 1919 and 1938.

The d'Hondt highest average system is used in the Netherlands, Belgium, Austria, Spain and many non–European nations. It is biased to an extent in favor of large parties and against small ones. Assume a district entitled to elect eleven legislators. The district party vote is as follows:

Labor	Liberal	Farmer	Radical	Center	Green	Anarchist
99,000	69,000	65,000	38,000	32,000	21,000	11,000

The first step is to divide each of the vote totals of the parties by one, two, three, four and five. This produces the following table:

Labor	Liberal	Farmer	Radical	Center	Green	Anarchist
99,000	69,000	65,000	38,000	32,000	21,000	11,000
49,500	34,500	32,500	19,000	16,000	10,500	5,500
33,000	23,000	21,667	12,667	10,667	7,000	3,667
24,750	17,250	16,250	9,500	8,000	5,250	2,750
19,800	13,800	13,000	7,600	6,400	4,200	2,200

The next step is to list the 11 largest numbers in the above table and the party column from whence they came:

99,000	Labor
69,000	Liberal
65,000	Farmer
49,500	Labor
38,000	Radical
34,500	Liberal
33,000	Labor
32,500	Farmer
32,000	Center
24,750	Labor
23,000	Liberal

These indicate the winners of the 11 seats—four Laborites, three Liberals, two Farmers, one Radical and one Centrist.

The Saint Lague system is a variant on d'Hondt that is less biased against small parties. It's used primarily in Scandinavia. Assume the same vote distribution in our 11-person district. The same type of table used above is created, but the divisors are 1.4, 3, 5, 7 and 9. That produces the following table:

Labor	Liberal	Farmer	Radical	Center	Green	Anarchist
70,714	49,286	46,429	27,143	22,857	15,000	7,857
33,000	23,000	21,667	12,667	10,667	7,000	3,667
19,800	13,800	13,000	7,600	6,400	4,200	2,200
14,143	9,857	9,286	5,429	4,571	3,000	1,571
11,000	7,667	7,222	4,222	3,556	2,333	1,222

The top 11 numbers from this table and the party column from which they come are:

70,417	Labor
49,286	Liberal
46,429	Farmer
33,000	Labor
27,143	Radical
23,000	Liberal
22,857	Center
21,667	Farmer
19,800	Labor

15,000	Green
13,800	Liberal

Thus, the Laborites win three seats, the Liberals win three seats, the Farmers win two seats, while the Radicals, Centrists and Greens win one seat each.

The Hagenbach-Bischoff largest remainder system is used in Switzerland, Israel and a few other countries. It is biased to an extent in favor of small parties. It would operate in our hypothetical 11-member district this way:

The first operation is to add together all of the votes cast and divide by one more than the number of legislators to be chosen (12, in our case). This is the district electoral quota — each party is entitled to one seat per quota. The figures:

TOTAL VOTE	335,000
QUOTA	27,917

The Laborites have three quotas, the Liberals and Farmers two each, while Radicals and Centrists have one apiece. Nine seats are accounted for.

To determine the tenth and eleventh, we compare the remainders after the quotas are subtracted from each party's total vote:

21,000	Green
15,250	Labor
13,167	Liberal
11,000	Anarchist
10,083	Radical
9,167	Farmer
4,083	Center

The Greens have the highest remainder and Labor the second-highest; these two parties take the remaining two seats. Thus Labor wins four seats all told, Liberals and Farmers take two each, while the Radicals, Centrists and Greens obtain one each.

The Dutch and Israeli national systems provide the most proportional results today. In Israel there's but one election district — the entire nation. The Knesset has 120 members. Any party receiving one percent of the popular vote obtains representation in the Knesset its percentage entitles it to; thus if a party gets 30 percent of the popular vote it will end up with 30 percent of the seats in the Knesset.

In the Netherlands too the nation is one gigantic district. Any party obtaining 1/150 of the national vote is entitled to representation in the 150-seat Second Chamber.

The fewer the districts and the more legislators they elect, the more legislative representation will mirror the popular vote. And the more the districts and the fewer representatives they elect, the more the system will discriminate in favor of large parties, even under the largest remainder system.

In most countries using districts, the districts are of relatively equal size, electing relatively the same numbers of legislators.

In Switzerland on the other hand each canton is a district, electing the numbers of members of the Nationalrat (the lower house of the legislature) that its population is entitled to. The canton of Zurich elects over 30 members and the Inner Rhodes of Appenzell elects just one. A minor party in Zurich could elect a legislator with five percent of the cantonal vote; only the majority can win in the Inner Rhodes of Appenzell. The four parties of the governing coalition sweep the board in the small and middle-sized Swiss cantons while only in the heavily populated cantons electing large numbers of legislators do the opposition parties obtain representation.

The election system of the German Federal Republic is unique, in that it's in effect a proportional system designed to discriminate against small parties. Half of the members of the Bundestag (the lower house of the Parliament) are elected from single-member districts on a first-past-the-post basis. The other half are elected from the states and nationally by proportional representation.

German citizens cast two votes in a parliamentary election — one for the district representative and one for a party. The party votes determine how the proportional representation seats will be divided.

No party gets any seats unless it gets five percent or more of the national party vote or it wins three district seats. The seats are distributed in such a way that the total representation accorded to the large parties mirrors their respective shares of the popular vote.

For many years only three parties obtained representation — the Social Democrats, the Christian Democrats and the Free Democrats. The government was, and still is, a coalition between the Free Democrats and whatever major party they choose as a partner.

The situation became more complex when a fourth party, the Greens, climbed above the five percent threshold and won representation in the Bundestag. The Greens are an anti-pollution, anti-nuclear weapons party. An alliance between them and the Christian Democrats is out of the question. It's now possible that a Red-Green (Social Democratic-Green) coalition could come to power.

Due to the collapse of most of the Communist governments of Eastern Europe a merger of East and West Germany occurred. Germany-wide elections to a single parliament took place December 1990. West German rules prevailed, except any party obtaining five percent of the vote in either East or West Germany was entitled to representation. The West German Greens polled only 3.9 percent and were eliminated from Parliament, but East German Greens and Democratic Socialists (Communists) won representation.

Systems similar to that of West Germany were used in Hungary and other eastern European countries in their 1990 elections.

The system under which the Mexican Chamber of Deputies has been elected resembles West Germany's. Approximately three-quarters of the deputies were elected from single-member districts under the first-past-the-post system. One-quarter were elected nation-wide by proportional representation.

These were all reserved for opposition parties, and were divided in proportion to the parties' popular vote. Until the most recent election the ruling PRI routinely swept almost all of the single-member districts; if it lost a half-dozen out of the 300-plus of these it was unusual. However, in July of 1988 the opposition carried 51 of the single-member districts.

These district deputies plus the deputies elected by proportional representation gave the opposition over 45 percent of the seats in the Chamber. The PRI's comfortable majority in the Chamber shrank almost to the vanishing point.

The PRI has changed the system to try to restore its majority. In the congressional elections of 1991 the party winning the most popular votes in the nation (as long as it gets at least 33 ⅓ percent) will be guaranteed 51 percent of the seats in the Chamber. The PRI obviously counts upon being the largest party.

This system resembles the Acerbo law under which the Italian Chamber of Deputies was elected in 1924. That law (enacted at the command of Benito Mussolini who had become prime minister in 1922) provided that the party receiving the most popular votes would obtain two-thirds of all the seats in the Chamber. Mussolini and his henchmen duly saw to it that his Fascists emerged as the largest party. Before the next election (held in 1929) Mussolini abolished all parties but the Fascist; the Acerbo law no longer served any useful purpose and was repealed.

A similar law governed the Italian Chamber of Deputies election of 1953. If any party or alliance of parties obtained 50 percent plus one of the popular vote it would get two-thirds of the seats in the Chamber. The idea was to allow the Christian Democrats and their allies to obtain a huge majority in the Parliament, weakening the power of the Communists to obstruct them. The voters resented this power grab; the Christian Democrats and their allies fell one percentage point shy of the sought-after absolute majority and representation was determined by ordinary proportional representation principles. The law was repealed by the newly elected Parliament.

In some systems a person votes for individual legislative candidates and the votes are counted for both the candidate and his or her party. Almost always the voter is limited to choosing among candidates of the party of his choice, however. The party count determines how many party candidates will be elected and the candidate count determines which candidates are elected. Thus the voter determines not only how the seats will be divided among the parties but also which party candidates are elected.

Brazil used a variant of this system before 1964. Each state elected its members of the Chamber of Deputies this way: The names of all candidates for the Chamber were printed on the ballot. The voter picked one candidate.

That one vote was counted for both the candidate and his or her party. The votes of all candidates of a party were added together to determine the party vote in the state. The party's percentage of the state-wide vote determined the number of deputies to which it was entitled. If, say, a party was entitled to four seats from the state, its four candidates with the most votes were declared elected.

Switzerland is unusual in that voters have the right of Panachage; in cantons electing more than one member of the Nationalrat citizens may vote for candidates from different parties. In a canton that elects seven members of the Nationalrat, the voter has seven votes. He may choose to vote a straight party ticket, in which case he casts his votes for the seven candidates of the party of his choice (it would never nominate more than seven). He may cast up to two votes for individual candidates—so he could cast two votes each for his three favorite party candidates and one vote for his fourth favorite. Or he may split up his votes among candidates from different parties, giving each two votes or one as he prefers.

Straight-ticket ballots would count as seven votes for the party in this canton. Ballots where a person voted for individual candidates are counted for the candidates; all votes for candidates of a party are added to the straight ticket votes to determine party totals. The seats are divided among the parties ratably according to these totals, the candidates with the most votes being elected. The straight-ticket votes help the candidates listed at the top of the ballot. These people have an advantage in Swiss elections, but they can be defeated by citizens who vote for people as well as parties.

The Grand Duchy of Luxembourg also grants its voters the right of Panachage.

Other systems (as in Israel) allow votes only for the party, not for individual candidates. The party lists the candidates in order on the ballot and the voter must accept the list as arranged. If the party ends up electing ten members of the Knesset, the first ten names on the party list are elected.

Party organizations enjoy much more power under Israeli-type systems than they do under the Swiss type, but their power is immense under both. After all, they nominate the legislative candidates.

Proportional representation—the Hare system. The Hare system is an adaptation of the Australian single transferable vote to elections of legislators from multi-member districts. The Australian Senate is elected in this way, as is the lower house of the Irish parliament, the unicameral parliament of Malta, and the legislature of the Australian state of Tasmania. At one time it was used in city council elections in New York City and some other American cities, but it has almost totally passed out of use in this country.

In the Hare system, the voter is presented a ballot with the names of all of the legislative candidates from his district on it. He marks a "1" beside his favorite candidate, a "2" by his second choice, and so on. If there are 40 names on the ballot he may keep writing numbers until he reaches 40.

All of the "1s" are counted first. The total number of votes cast is then divided by the number of legislators to be elected plus one. This magic number is the electoral quota; any candidate meeting or exceeding it is elected. Any candidates having surplus votes, who received more than the quota, have the "2s" counted on their surplus ballots—these votes being transferred to the lucky surviving candidates. If these put any others "over the top," more surpluses are created and transferred.

After all surpluses are disposed of the low remaining candidate is declared eliminated and the "2s" (or "3s" or "4s" or whatever) are counted, the ballots being transferred to the highest-ranked candidate still in the race. The process of eliminating low candidates and dividing their votes among survivors continues until the quota of legislators is elected.

As long as voters choose a straight-party ticket—not placing numbers before any candidate not of their party until they've numbered all of the candidates from their party—the system elects legislators in proportion to the strength of the parties. The candidate's party is usually printed on the ballot so the party-line voter's job is easy.

Since each Australian state elects 12 Senators, 6 at each election, there are at least 15 names on the ballot, maybe even 20 or 25. When the Senate has been dissolved so that all 12 Senatorial seats are up for grabs these numbers will double. Irish and Maltese ballots are shorter.

The old system for electing the New York City Council was a unique marriage of the Hare system with the system of electing the Reichstag of the German Weimar Republic. The quota for electing a Council candidate was 75,000. The number of council members a city borough would elect depended on how many votes were cast there. The count would continue until there were less than 75,000 ballots which hadn't contributed to the election of a candidate within the borough. The size of the Council would vary from election to election, but the party representation within it accurately reflected the popular vote.

A Hare system ballot is difficult for the voter to mark—how do you choose whom to mark number 25 and whom number 26? The vote count may take days because of the numerous transfers of ballots from one candidate to another.

But the system has two advantages: it produces proportional results and allows party voters to determine their legislative representatives, not the party organizations.

In Ireland a type of gerrymandering sometimes influences the outcome of parliamentary elections. The Dail Eirann, the lower house of Parliament, is elected from small districts. Some of these elect three members, some four, and some five. It takes about 25 percent of the vote to elect one legislator from a three-member district, 20 percent in four-member districts, and 17 percent in five-member districts. Large districts are good for small parties while small districts are detrimental. Conversely, small districts are good for large parties and small districts are not. (For instance, if a party can poll 51 percent of the vote in a three-member district it will elect two-thirds of the district's legislators—two of three. If it does the same in a four-member district it gets only half of the representation—two of four.) When party control of the Dail changes, district boundaries are often redrawn and sizes of districts reshuffled to help the winners retain power at the next election.

Even the Hare system occasionally allows the party finishing second in popular votes a legislative majority. In the 1981 Maltese election, the Labor Party got 49.1 percent of the vote and 34 seats in Parliament. The Nationalist Party got 50.9 percent of the vote, but only 31 parliamentary seats.

Frequency of elections. There are more elections in Switzerland than anywhere else on earth. Three or four times a year the Swiss are called to the polls to vote in referenda. Most federal, cantonal and local officials serve four-year terms. Since these offices aren't filled at the same time, at least three elections of public officials take place each four years.

American elections are also very frequent. With us state and federal officers are elected at the same time. Since members of the House of Representatives and many state legislators serve two-year terms, and since candidates for such offices are nominated in primary elections, and since several states hold run-off primaries when no candidate gets an absolute majority in a first primary there may be three state-wide elections in every even-numbered year—the first primary, the run-off primary and the general election. Municipal officers are usually not elected at the same time as state and federal officers; separate elections are held to fill these posts.

American election ballots are among the longest in the world. On presidential election day voters may have to choose their favorite candidates for president of the United States, United States senator, United States representative, state governor, state attorney-general, other state executive posts, state senator, state representative, county sheriff, county commissioner any many other state and local offices. To keep straight who's running for what and who is the best candidate for what is difficult, to say the least.

Blanket ballots used to make things worse. In some large American cities, a primary election ballot was sometimes the size of a large tablecloth in the days before voting machines.

Before the reapportionment revolution of the 1960s Cuyahoga County, Ohio, elected its 17 members of the Ohio House of Representatives at large.

Since the Democratic nomination for these posts was the equivalent of election, many hopefuls vied for these spots in the Democratic primary. There were often more than 100 candidates for these 17 nominations. Virtually no voter could know the qualifications of so many candidates; the primary was in essence a gigantic lottery in which candidates with simple names or names identifying them with large ethnic voting blocs stood the best chances of victory.

Such huge ballots are typically American. In nations with popularly elected presidents, the president isn't normally elected at the same time as the national legislature. In other federal nations, state or provincial elections are seldom held at the same time as federal elections. Local elections are held at still other times. There are no primary elections, only general elections. Thus only one election is necessary per office (unless the run-off or second ballot is used). Ballots are short because there are few offices to be filled per election. Voters may theoretically therefore make more intelligent choices.

American election campaigns are notoriously long. It takes us over a year to elect a president. By contrast, campaigns for the British House of Commons are limited by law to three weeks. Campaigns in most other democracies are concluded in three months or less. More time and money are expended in electioneering here than in other lands.

Voter behavior in democracies. Rates of voter participation in elections vary immensely from nation to nation. A few countries, such as Australia, insure turnouts of over 90 percent by making voting compulsory and subjecting non-voters to fines. Participation in elections is voluntary in most nations, however.

Fifty percent and less of American and Swiss voters go to the polls on election day, while in many continental European nations turnouts of over 80 percent aren't uncommon. It's paradoxical that in the two nations whose political and constitutional systems are most attuned to the will of the individual voter the most potential voters refuse to participate in the system. (Swiss voters aren't always so blase about elections, though. In the federal referendum of November 1989 the voters were asked to approve a constitutional amendment which would have, if adopted, abolished the Swiss Army. The pre-election campaigns of the proponents and opponents attracted great public interest; 70 percent of all eligible voters went to the polls, setting a modern record for voter turnout. Observers were shocked to learn that the amendment to abolish the army got 30 percent of the vote.)

Is this non-participation good or bad? It's argued on one hand that substantial non-voting makes for minority rule; those who need the most from the system are the ones who don't make use of it. American liberals argue this quite loudly, because black and Hispanic participation in American elections is lower than the average.

On the other hand it's argued that a vote cast in ignorance is worse than no vote cast at all. Believers in this notion point to the example of Weimar Germany in the early 1930s. In 1928 the turnout for the Reichstag election was low for Germany as 30,753,200 persons voted, of whom 3,264,800 voted Communist and 810,100 voted Nazi. The extreme anti-democratic vote was about 13 percent.

In 1930 34,960,900 persons voted. The Communist vote rose to 4,592,100, the Nazi vote to 6,409,600. Total turnout increased by over 4,000,000 votes and the extremist anti-democracy vote rose by almost 5,000,000. The National Socialist German Workers' Party (Nazi) came from nowhere to become second-largest in the nation as over one-third of the vote was cast for extremists.

In July 1932 the voter turnout jumped to 36,882,400; the Communists polled 5,355,300, and the Nazis 13,745,700. The total vote was up 2,000,000 and the anti-democratic vote rose by more than 8,000,000. The Nazis polled over 35 percent of the votes and became the largest party. Their vote combined with that of the Communists exceeded 50 percent. Over 6,000,000 new voters made their wishes known between 1928 and 1932. Logic indicates that most of them added to the Nazi and Communist totals.

A bit more than six months later Adolf Hitler became the political head of state and destroyed the democratic republic. Liberals rightfully point out, however, that what happened in Weimar Germany has apparently happened nowhere else.

Among those who vote, two tendencies are noteworthy. Many tend to vote for parties rather than for candidates, or to re-elect incumbent office-holders.

In nations like Israel, where the legislature is elected by party-list proportional representation and executive officers are chosen by legislatures, there's no voting for individuals at all. In nations like the United States where legislators are chosen from single-member districts and all executive officers are directly elected, all voting is for individuals. (Some states encourage party-line voting through use of the party-column ballot, with which one may vote a straight-party ticket by making only one mark on the ballot. Others discourage this by using the office-type ballot, where one must vote for one's favorite candidate for each office.)

So prevalent is the tendency of Americans to vote for the person rather than the party that Republican presidential candidates often win landslide victories while Democratic congressional candidates win the majority of contested legislative races. The ultimate example of this sort of voting is illustrated by the behavior of Arkansas in November of 1968. Voters there elected American Independent Party presidential electors, a Republican governor and a Democratic United States senator on the same day.

However, we Americans often combine voting for people at the top of the ballot while voting for the party lower down. In rural areas of many southern states, voters often cast their ballot for Republicans for president, governor,

United States senator, or congressperson. For minor state and county offices, however, they still vote straight Democratic.

In the Italian, Swiss and German city-states of the Middle Ages it was traditional to re-elect holders of public offices as long as they desired to serve. Only in times of catastrophe were incumbents denied re-election.

This tradition lives on in today's Switzerland The Parliament re-elects members of the Bundesrat who desire it without meaningful opposition. Since 1959 it's been the convention that the seven-member Bundesrat will contain two Radicals, two Christian Democrats, two Social Democrats and one member of the Swiss People's Party. At each election the legislative caucuses of each party nominate the required number of candidates, and those nominated are duly elected by huge majorities. When this doesn't happen the Swiss are astounded.

The last time it didn't happen is a matter of interest. The Social Democrats nominated for one of their Bundesrat seats the first female candidate for such a post ever—the leftist activist Liliane Uchtenhagen. The non–Social Democrat majority of Parliament couldn't stomach the thought of electing a radical woman to the Bundesrat, so it unofficially nominated another Social Democrat for the post, the moderate Otto Stich. Most of the Social Democrats voted for Uchtenhagen, but the majority voted for Stich, so he was duly elected. The majority obeyed the convention and elected a Social Democrat to the contested seat, but rejected the official party nominee.

The results infuriated both the Social Democrats and Swiss feminists. The Social Democrats threatened to drop out of the governing coalition, but soon changed their minds, deciding that participation in the government on the majority's terms was better than not participating at all.

At the next Bundesrat election Parliament appeased the wrath of the feminists. A Radical incumbent chose not to seek re-election, so the Radical caucus nominated for the seat a conservative woman acceptable to the non–Socialist majority. Elizabeth Kopp was almost unanimously elected. (Late in 1988 Mrs. Kopp was forced to resign her post as described in an earlier chapter.)

Members of cantonal and municipal executive councils are generally elected by popular vote rather than by legislative bodies. These more often than not have no opponents on the ballot when they seek re-election. The party leaders agree among themselves as to how the posts at stake will be divided, and they nominate only the number of candidates needed to fill the seats allotted by the inter-party agreement. The Stille Wahl (still election, or uncontested election) is common. The party leaders co-operate to make sure that no candidate has meaningful opposition. Sometimes minor parties nominate candidates for such posts just to create a contest but almost inevitably the major party candidate wins by a huge majority. The voters seemingly approve of the arrangements made by party leaders.

Never do the Swiss eject the "ins" from office in wholesale lots. Political change is evolutionary rather than revolutionary; meaningful election contests happen only when an incumbent has died in office or declined to seek re-election. When the voters of the canton of Bern denied re-election to some executive councillors guilty of corruption in office it made headlines all over the country, simply because the defeat of incumbents seeking re-election is so rare.

The American tradition throughout most of our history has been the opposite. We haven't hesitated to "throw the rascals out" when we've thought they deserved it. Though we deny re-election to our presidents only under unusual circumstances, we haven't accorded such respect to members of Congress or state governors in the past. Many have been the memorable landslides in which the "ins" were cast forth from legislatures or governors' mansions in huge numbers to be replaced by hordes of power-hungry "outs."

More recently, however, American behavior toward incumbents has become more Swiss than the Swiss. In November of 1990 96 percent of the incumbent members of the United States House of Representatives seeking re-election were victorious, continuing a trend which began in 1976. In the Swiss parliamentary elections of 1987 on the other hand, 14 out of 160 members of the lower house seeking re-election were defeated; thus the re-election rate was only a bit over 90 percent.

Many state legislatures too are becoming the permanent preserve of one or the other major party. The legislative landslide has become almost an historical curiosity in the United States.

In other nations with single-member legislative districts this hasn't happened. Since party organizations nominate candidates in these countries, and since members of the legislature usually need not be residents of the district they represent a close rapport between legislator and constituents doesn't exist as in the U.S.

The memorable landslide still happens out there, as when Canadian Conservatives massacred Liberal members of Parliament by the dozen in that country's 1984 election, or when Laborite members of the British House of Commons bit the dust in large numbers in 1979 and 1983.

In most English-speaking countries, the winner of a national election wins big; the swing of small numbers of voters from one party to another tips the balance in many legislative districts. Changes in popular vote percentage are magnified manifold in single-district victories.

In countries using proportional representation the landslide is rare to nonexistent. Since the percentage of legislative representation of a party is directly tied to the percentage of popular vote, only earth-shaking changes in voter allegiance produce earth-shaking changes in the composition of legislatures. Most of the "ins," of whatever party, remain "in" forever. The status quo in countries like the Netherlands, Belgium, Denmark and Italy seems eternal.

In Sweden, Norway, Austria and the former German Federal Republic the balance between the left and right is so close that a shift of two or three percentage points in popular vote can alter the balance of power. The competition resembles that between the two parties of an English-speaking country.

One hears more and more often that it really doesn't matter whether the democratic voter casts a ballot or not. Votes may come and votes may go, but the system goes on forever. Up to a point this is true, but on the other hand it's the participation of the voters that has kept the system as it is in democracies. The more voters who refuse their electoral privilege, the more power falls into the hands of those who keep on voting.

Particratie—how prevalent? It has already been mentioned that some Belgians feel that they are governed by the political parties rather than by themselves. Voters in other democratic nations feel the same way.

In early May of 1990 Israel was gripped by a severe political crisis. The Likud-Labor grand coalition had broken down as one bloc or the other tried to assemble a Knesset majority. The 120-member parliament was divided into two 60-member blocs; there was no majority and therefore no effective government.

Because of the electoral system described above several small parties held the balance of power between the two big party groups. They bargained shamelessly for advantage in the ongoing negotiations to form a viable coalition.

At last two parliamentarians deserted the Labor bloc for Likud, which formed a government with a 62–58 majority. So far (late May 1991) the majority is holding.

Public opinion polls show that the two big blocs are so evenly balanced in appeal to the voters that an election might not resolve the virtual deadlock. Some national leaders therefore are proposing revision of the electoral system.

So simple a remedy as raising the popular vote threshold to five percent in order to gain parliamentary representation would help. It would deprive a few very small parties of representation and eliminate some of the selfish bargainers in the recent negotiations. The minuscule parties naturally oppose this; no one is likely to vote for his own execution.

Another idea is to eliminate or modify the rigid party list system and the one national constituency; elect members from small districts and allow citizens to vote for candidates as well as for parties. Incumbent legislators, many of them, don't like this notion. Under the present system they need neither charisma nor political vision to hold their seats. They just need enough pull within the party to be listed high on the candidate list. The thought of appealing to voters as individuals and subjecting oneself to their choice is terrifying.

The major blocs regard any alteration of the system with suspicion. Changes in the status quo could bring about unpredictable results. Now that the immediate crisis is resolved the subject of reform has lost its urgency.

Similar problems exist in other democracies, particularly those with multi-party political systems. Where no majority party exists an artificial majority must be constructed from two or more parties which will naturally involve inter-party bargaining, something German-speaking purists have derided as "Kuhhandel" — cattle-trading.

Where consensual democracy exists virtually all parties are involved in governing and election results don't seem meaningful; no matter how the votes are distributed the same people continue to govern.

Where majoritarian government exists voters may "throw the rascals out" by electing the opposition party to power. Once in office, however, the majority in a nation like Great Britain proceeds to govern as it will. With the support of a disciplined party majority it can work its will (within limits) during the term for which it was elected, regardless of popular passions. Those who voted to install the new majority may get more (or less) than they anticipated.

Where popularly controlled parties exist (as in the United States) the voters choose among candidates rather than parties and something resembling anarchy holds forth in the national capital. In our country the president and his appointees manage foreign policy while domestic policy depends upon the mood of Congress. With representatives and senators voting their conscience on all proposed legislation majorities shift about like sand dunes on the floor of the desert. Almost everything seems to get done on an "ad hoc" basis without much advanced planning. A handful of party leaders don't dominate the system as happens in other democracies — but all too often, nobody dominates.

There seems to be no such thing as an ideal democratic political system. No wonder, since it has been said that even though democracy is a horrible governmental system it's far superior to any of the possible alternatives.

Chapter 13
Nationality and Human Rights

Nationality. Nearly all people, things and organizations possess nationality in that they are thought of as "belonging" to a nation. Individuals may acquire nationality by birth or by naturalization. How is a matter of national law.

Nationality confers a package of rights and duties upon a person. Among the rights are the following: (1) the right to come "home" whenever the national desires, (2) the right to assistance from his country's diplomats when he has difficulties abroad, and (3) unlimited rights to vote, hold public office, and otherwise enjoy the benefits of membership in the national community. Among the duties are: (1) The duty to pay taxes, perhaps even if the national lives abroad and earns income abroad, and (2) the duty to perform military service when such duty is imposed.

Rights of aliens. Theoretically every nation has absolute authority to keep aliens off its soil. No one has an absolute right in international law to visit a country of which he isn't a national.

Few, if any, nations refuse entry to all aliens, but many won't allow certain aliens to visit certain places. For example, no nation gives aliens (or even its own citizens) unrestricted access to military installations.

Saudi Arabia won't allow non–Muslims to visit the city of Mecca. The Soviet Union and China won't permit aliens to visit many localities within those nations. Burma excludes most foreigners altogether, as does North Korea.

Many Western European nations allow other western Europeans to cross their frontiers without passports, a national identity card being sufficient identification. For many non–Europeans, such as Americans, a passport is required.

During much of the twentieth century the United States has been more inhospitable. Not only do we require passports of most of our foreign visitors, we also require a visa (official U.S. government permission to visit). Among Western European nations, only France presently requires visas of visiting Americans. Communist nations generally require visas of all foreign guests as well as transit visas of people crossing their states to reach another state. Thus

266

a person traveling from Japan to Western Europe via the Trans-Siberian Railroad would need a Soviet transit visa permitting him or her to cross the Soviet Union on the journey.

Many nations restrict the rights of their own nationals to travel abroad. Citizens of the Soviet Union need special permission to travel outside their country, and such permission is difficult to come by. Americans may travel to Canada and Mexico without passports, but need them to visit more distant places. Also, American passports aren't valid for travel to Cuba, North Korea, Vietnam and Kampuchea. He who goes to one of these lands without special government permission commits a criminal offense.

It's much easier to visit another nation than it is to establish permanent residence there. The U.S. limits the number of persons admitted per year for permanent residence, giving preference to close relatives of American citizens and those who have job skills in demand.

Most other nations also impose such restrictions. During the 1950s and 1960s Australia had a very generous immigration policy because it wanted to increase its population. However, the global recession of the 1970s created unemployment problems even in "the land down under" and the government changed its policy, severely restricting immigration.

Citizens of member nations of the European Community have the right to establish residence in other member nations of the Community. Great Britain is generous in allowing citizens of nations of the British Commonwealth to immigrate. France is similarly generous to citizens of former French colonies.

Aliens have two basic rights in their host countries, the right to personal security and to basic justice. No country can guarantee an alien freedom from the attention of criminals, but it can guarantee the same quality of police protection accorded its own citizens. It should not allow or encourage its own citizens to harm its guests.

Formerly, the powerful nations of the world used gunboat diplomacy to assure good treatment of their citizens abroad. It was only 80 years ago that President Theodore Roosevelt told the government of Morocco after bandits had kidnapped an American citizen there, "Perdicaris (the American citizen) alive or Raisuli (the bandit leader) dead!" In due course Perdicaris appeared, very much alive.

It's also worth remembering, however, that in 1891 rioting against Italians in New Orleans nearly caused war between the United States and Italy, which claimed New Orleans authorities hadn't supplied Italian citizens with minimum personal security.

The requirement that aliens be granted basic justice isn't necessarily a requirement that they be granted due process of law American-style. It's simply that the courts of a nation must treat aliens as they treat their own citizens.

Thus the Saudi Arab in the United States is indeed entitled to due process of American law. And the American in Saudi Arabia would be entitled to no more than due process of law Saudi style, which could include amputation of the right hand for theft.

The argument is made that all national governments owe to all persons within their borders respect for basic human rights. In the best of all possible worlds this would be accepted without argument. However, many of the world's governments don't grant such rights to their own citizens. If a state treats its own inhumanely, can it be expected to treat aliens any better?

Virtually all nations give only to citizens the right to vote, hold public office or practice learned professions—particularly law.

The right to live in another nation does not necessarily include the right to work there. No alien present in the United States has the right to work here unless his or her visa permits it.

In our age of high unemployment this state of affairs is almost universal. Work permits for aliens are hard to come by everywhere.

It wasn't always so. Twenty years ago there was a labor shortage in most western European nations. Many countries rolled out the red carpet to encourage foreigners to come and accept the many jobs that were available. Alien Gastarbeiter—guest laborers—became an appreciable part of the populations of Switzerland, the German Federal Republic, and other nations.

Then came the recession of the mid–1970s. The number of jobs began to shrink, lay-offs became necessary, and difficult questions arose. Could an employer legitimately lay off aliens while retaining citizens with less seniority? Would laid-off aliens be entitled to the same welfare-state benefits as unemployed citizens?

It was generally accepted that the Gastarbeiter couldn't be discriminated against in lay-off decisions just because they were aliens, and that they were entitled to the same welfare-state benefits as citizens because they'd paid the same social security taxes as citizens. Besides, as mentioned earlier, they had taken over certain unpleasant ways of making a living (such as collecting garbage) that citizens were happy to abandon to them.

Asylum. Most nations will take in residents of other nations for humanitarian reasons despite their laws restricting immigration. This is the granting of asylum. Because of poor economic conditions, overpopulation and the like some countries are very reluctant to do this but other nations have long traditions of being hospitable to the world's oppressed.

Refugees from war and revolution in Vietnam, Kampuchea and Laos have flooded the Orient for almost two decades. Some nations are hospitable to them, others are not.

Japan is one of the reluctant. It is a crowded island nation and its population is one of the most homogeneous on earth, so this is somewhat understandable. "Japan for the Japanese" is in many ways the national policy.

Hong Kong, one of the most crowded pieces of real estate on earth, is very reluctant to grant asylum. Though it took in many Chinese refugees from Communism during the 1950s and 1960s, its government now asserts that the lifeboat is full; there's room for no more. Malaysia too isn't known for rolling out the welcome mat; it isn't anxious to increase the number of non–Malays on its soil. Thailand allows refugees from Indochina to establish refugee camps along its frontiers but prefers not to allow them to settle in its interior. That many of these unfortunates try to reach Europe, North America and Australia is explained in part by the unwillingness of most nations of east and south Asia to accept them.

The nations of the Sahel — the southern fringe of the Sahara Desert — have experienced horrible demographic problems because of the desert's inexorable expansion. Land that once supported agricultural and herding communities has been swallowed up by the desert in Mauretania, Mali, Niger, Chad and Burkina Faso. People whose homes have literally dried up have moved south seeking moister lands and the opportunity to re-establish themselves. There's no place for them in their native countries, so they've tried to cross national frontiers into more hospitable (climatically) countries such as Nigeria, Benin, Ghana and the Central African Republic. These nations, only marginally richer than their dessicated northern neighbors and themselves beset by economic and demographic problems, don't need more people. Thus the refugees are turned away and forced to remain in their own countries.

Malawi and Zimbabwe harbor numerous refugees from the brutal civil war in Mozambique; people fleeing a similar condition in Angola have found refuge in Zaire and Zambia.

Some poor nations have strained meager resources to accept large numbers of refugees. Thus India accepted thousands of Bihari and Bengali refugees from Bangladesh during the fighting of 1971, while Pakistan and Iran have accepted thousands of Afghans since the Soviet occupation of 1979. An influx of Palestinian Arab refugees into Jordan after the Israeli victory in the Six-Day War and occupation of the West Bank of the Jordan destabilized the politics of that country, inducing King Hussein's government to expel them in 1970. They moved to Lebanon and have contributed to the destabilization of yet another country.

The German Federal Republic has had to deal with large numbers of displaced persons ever since the end of World War II. Some of the non–German inmates of Hitler's concentration camps remained there after the war for lack of another place to go. German expellees from the areas of Germany awarded to Poland after the war crowded in during the late 1940s, as did the German speakers expelled from Sudetenland by the Czechs. Hungarians fleeing the repression of the revolt of 1956 flooded in. Gastarbeiter from Turkey and other lands have chosen to remain in the Republic despite the depression of the 1970s. More Turks have come in during the 1980s as refugees from the political and economic instability in their native country.

Switzerland, though hospitable to individual refugees, has followed a policy of refusing to grant asylum to large numbers of people because of limited living space. On this principle, it turned away Jewish refugees during World War II. Because of pressure from human rights activists in the last few years, Switzerland has recently relaxed its asylum policy. Chilean refugees from General Pinochet's dictatorship, Zaireans fleeing poverty and political repression in their country, Tamils fleeing the civil war in Sri Lanka, Kampucheans fleeing Pol Pot's massacres, Tibetans running from Chinese repression of their ancient culture and Poles hostile to General Jaruzelski's government in their homeland have found refuge there. Swiss opponents of this policy speak darkly of the "Ueberfremdung" (overforeignization) of the land, but to date the Swiss government shows no sign of relaxing its liberal asylum policies.

United States policy in this area has been inconsistent. We were reluctant to admit Jewish refugees before and during World War II, though we admitted large numbers of displaced Europeans afterward. Because of ideological hostility to the Soviet Union we've accepted refugees from Communism without much question, though we're reluctant to accept them from countries ruled by non–Communist dictators. Those who escape from Cuba in small boats find welcome as political refugees, while those who escape from Haiti in small boats may well be sent home because they're merely economic refugees for which we have no space. Cuban refugees have turned Miami, Florida, into an Hispanic city, while the Asian population of California has grown by leaps and bounds due to settlement of Vietnamese and Kampuchean refugees there. We're reluctant to accept the tens of thousands of Hispanic economic and political refugees flocking across our virtually unguarded Mexican border, but since they're here and many of them do economically useful work we've amended our immigration laws to allow them to stay. Americans too are beginning to grumble about the "overforeignization" of our country.

In the best of all worlds all nations would accept refugees in the name of common humanity, but on our overcrowded planet with its almost universal political and economic problems there's no space for the dispossessed. Most nations are tempted to react to the problem as the Swiss did during World War II—"Go away. The boat's too crowded already!"

Rights of citizens. The notion that citizens of a country should have rights in international law is of recent origin. The traditional point of view has been that a government should be free to treat its citizens as it pleases, otherwise it would not be sovereign within its own territory.

The most atrocious treatment government may mete out to a group of its own citizens is to subject them to genocide—to attempt to exterminate them. The horrible example that's called to mind is the effort of the Nazis to exterminate European Jewry. This, unfortunately, isn't the only example.

Before World War I there were a sizable number of Armenians living in Turkey. When Turkey became involved in the war it suspected the loyalty of its Armenian subjects, because their brand of Christianity was akin to the Eastern Orthodoxy of the Russian enemy and thus anathema to Turkish Muslims.

The Turks attempted to exterminate this potentially disloyal minority, and nearly succeeded. It's said that anywhere between 600 thousand and one million Armenians were killed in 1915.

In 1930 Josef Stalin decided that private ownership of land in the Soviet Union should end. Lenin had rewarded the Russian peasantry for supporting the Bolsheviks in the Russian Civil War by allowing them to acquire the land expropriated from the great noble estates at the time of the Revolution, but Stalin felt that this private land ownership was contrary to Marxist ideology.

Many peasants resisted collectivization — especially the kulaks, those who had made themselves prosperous. In order to break the opposition of these, Stalin deliberately created a famine in the Ukraine and some other areas of Russia. Many kulaks starved to death; others were deported to Siberian labor camps and worked to death. Hundreds of thousands of Russians and Ukrainians died.

Before the European colonists came to Rwanda and Burundi in central Africa, a small number of Tutsi lorded it over a much larger number of Hutu. The Tutsi retained their dominion under the Germans and later under the Belgians. When Belgium granted these lands their independence in 1962, the Hutu gained control of Rwanda and slaughtered Tutsi by the tens of thousands. In Burundi, controlled by the Tutsi, there was deceptive calm for ten years. Then the ruling Tutsi, fearing an imminent Hutu uprising that would subject them to the fate of their Rwandan brothers, made a pre-emptive strike, killing between 100,000 and 200,000 Hutu. Though the slaughter was soon stopped, Tutsi and Hutu in these two lands still hate each other. Either may once again try to commit genocide against the other at any time.

When the Khmer Rouge of Kampuchea won their civil war against the government of Lon Nol in 1975 and took control of the country, their leadership decided to drastically change the basis of the national economy. To the Khmer Rouge cities were hotbeds of degeneracy and parasitism, and educated people were worse than useless. In order to turn their country into a land of simple virtuous peasants, the Khmer Rouge executed the educated by the thousands and forced city-dwellers into the countryside to fend for themselves. The name of the game became "Root, hog, or die." If they couldn't support themselves on the uncleared land allotted to them, they didn't deserve to live. This ruthless policy caused the deaths of hundreds of thousands. At least a fifth of all Kampucheans perished.

The Indonesians have resorted to genocidal massacre in their efforts to suppress the guerrillas of East Timor. Over 100 thousand of the original 800 thousand East Timoreans have perished in the nasty little war. Guerrillas still harass the invaders and the Indonesians continue their brutal repression.

Spain granted independence to its African colony of Spanish Guinea in 1968 resulting in the birth of the new Republic of Equatorial Guinea. Francisco Macias Nguema became president and quickly obtained dictatorial power for himself. During a decade-long reign of terror he either massacred or expelled over 100 thousand of the 300 thousand-plus citizens of his country. He was overthrown and executed in 1979 but the country still hasn't recovered from the effects of Nguema's brutality.

Paraguayans are accused of attempting to exterminate the Ache Indians of the interior of their country; they stand in the way of economic development.

Similar charges are levied against Brazil with respect to the various Indian tribes of the Amazon Valley. Here, apparently, genocide isn't a matter of government policy. It's simply that, as development of Amazonia proceeds and more and more of the rain forest is destroyed, the habitat of the Indian tribes is also destroyed. For the long haul, only those Indians able to adapt to Brazilian culture will make it.

Massacres of less than genocidal scope have happened in numerous lands since World War II. Nigerians of various ethnic groups killed thousands of Ibos just before the Biafran secession. Idi Amin caused the deaths of thousands of Ugandan citizens. Hindus and Muslims died in the tens of thousands in communal rioting set off by the partition of British India. Bengali Muslims died by the tens of thousands when Pakistani troops sought to prevent the secession of Bangladesh. The surviving Bengalis took vengeance against Muslim Biharis who fought with the Pakistanis against independence for Bangladesh— thousands of Biharis were killed. Tamils and Sinhalese have killed hundreds of each other in Sri Lanka. Hindus and Sikhs have done likewise in India since the Indian Army stormed the Golden Temple of Amritsar. When Indonesia suppressed its Communist Party in 1965 over a half million actual and suspected party members were killed.

In today's Bangladesh over 100 million people are crammed into an area much smaller than that of Japan. In the thinly settled Chittagong Hill Tracts primitive people who speak languages unrelated to the Bengali spoken by the crowded lowlanders and who are not Muslim occupy precious land. The land-hungry Bengalis do what they can to force these people out of their ancestral homes. But the culture of the hill people doesn't fit them to participate in the affairs of Bangladesh.

"We need your land, but we don't need you!" is the message the Bengalis send these tribesmen. "Go away, or die!" Some flee to India, some to Burma, and more die in their homeland. In Uganda massacre and disorder didn't stop with the overthrow of Idi Amin in 1979. Milton Obote became President in 1981 and loosed a reign of terror against his opponents until he was overthrown in 1985. Only recently has President Yoweri Musaveni been able to restore order and personal security in that unhappy land.

In Sudan and Ethiopia drought, famine and civil war have brewed a devilish combination that has caused the deaths of between two and four million people. In Sudan there is ethnic and cultural incompatibility between the majority Muslim Arabic speakers of the north and the minority black Christians and animists of the south. The two groups fought a brutal civil war in the late 1960s and early 1970s which resulted in the grant of local self-government to the southerners. Recent attempts by the central government to impose Islamic law upon the entire nation have rekindled the war. The fact that the drought has hit hardest the southern areas where the war rages has compounded the resulting famine.

Multi-ethnic Ethiopia threatens to come apart at the seams as various minority ethnic groups seek to overthrow the domination of the mostly Amhara ruling group and its Marxist leader Colonel Mengistu Haile Mariam (who is not an Amhara but rather an Oromo). The most successful of the rebels at the moment are the Muslim Eritreans, inhabitants of the major province along the Red Sea coast. The partly Christian, partly Muslim Tigreans, inhabiting the province just south of Eritrea, have also won victories recently. The seat of the fighting in this bitter conflict is another area hit very hard by the present African drought. Tens of thousands starved in this area before the civil war heated up; it's estimated that the total casualties caused by war and famine may exceed two million.

Though the most powerful man in Ethiopia is Oromo (Colonel Mengistu), many of the Oromo people are unhappy with the present state of affairs in their country. In their provinces too low-level guerrilla warfare against the central government simmers.

The inhabitants of Ogaden, Ethiopia's southeastern province, are Somalis. Many of these yearn to detach their province from the rule of the Amharas and incorporate it into neighboring Somalia. During the 1970s troops from Somalia invaded Ogaden to help the native Somalis and drove the Ethiopians out. When the Soviets reorganized and re-equipped Colonel Mengistu's army it and its Cuban allies returned with a vengeance, reconquering the province in 1978 and driving 650 thousand refugees over the frontier into Somalia. Ever since, low-level guerrilla warfare against Mengistu's forces has gone on in Ogaden.

Violence and instability have now spilled over into Somalia itself. President Siad Barre of that country operates another of Africa's oppressive dictatorships. Some northern malcontents, armed with weapons left over from the fighting in Ogaden, have risen against his government, encouraged by the Ethiopians. Heavy fighting has occurred in the north of Somalia causing tens of thousands of refugees to flee to Ethiopia.

There seems to be no end to the destruction of human life and property in this unhappy corner of the world.

In many lands racial and ethnic discrimination exist. The Republic of

South Africa is held up as the most egregious example of this sort of thing, but it isn't the only guilty nation.

In Vietnam the Vietnamese majority discriminates against minority Montagnards and other ethnic groups. Laotians discriminate against Meo tribesmen. In Iran the Farsi majority discriminates against Baluchi, Kurdish and Azerbaijani minorities, while in Pakistan Punjabis discriminate against Sindhis, Pathans and Baluchis.

In the Yugoslav republic of Serbia, the Albanians of Kosovo and the Hungarians of Vojvodina complain of Serb discrimination against them, while the Hungarians of Transylvania, a portion of Romania, lodge similar complaints against Romanians.

Though the Soviet Union has boasted that there's no discrimination against non–Russians on its soil, it's simply untrue. The master race of the Soviet Union has been the Great Russian — the majority ethnic group of the Russian Federated Soviet Socialist Republic, the largest republic of the USSR, which has some 48 percent of the total population of the country.

To be sure the Soviet government allows each major ethnic group its own Republic and minor groups autonomous areas within the Republics. These ethnic groups may receive primary education in their languages, and publications in these languages are encouraged. And each Republic is governed in its own language. Yet, Russian has been the language of the federal government and of the federal and party bureaucracies. It is the language of command in the Red Army. No non–Russian has been able to rise to a position of importance without command of the Russian language.

Either the secretary-general or the assistant secretary-general of the Communist Party in each Republic of the Soviet Union has for many years been a Great Russian. Nearly all members of the Politburo and the Central Committee of the Communist Party of the Soviet Union are Great Russians. Ukrainians and Byelorussians have been allowed to play minor roles in these organizations but rarely have other nationalities looked in.

There have been occasional exceptions. Josef Stalin's true name was Josef Vissarionovich Djugashvili; he was a Georgian. Edward Schevarnadze, recently Foreign Minister of the USSR, is also a Georgian. Anastas Mikoyan, an Armenian, held various second-rank positions of power during his lifetime.

But never has a person from one of the Muslim republics held high federal office. Great Russians have dominated the state and the party and some of them mean to continue to do so. After all, it was their nationality which created Holy Russia and the Soviet Union in the first place.

Mikhail Gorbachev's new order may well change this state of affairs if allowed to run its course. If the prime position of the Communist Party within the state is terminated it won't much matter who controls it. If the USSR truly evolves into the USSS, a confederation of semi-independent republics, the Great Russians will control only the Russian Republic.

However, Great Russians still control the federal bureaucracy, the armed forces and the central police forces (the KGB secret police and the MVD interior police). The old regime won't truly end until these organizations are shorn of much of their power. Will this happen under the new order? Time will tell.

In some of the republics of the USSR where secession sentiment is strong, Russians now complain of reverse discrimination. Moldavia has declared Moldavian to be the one official language of the Republic; the large Russian-speaking minority bitterly complains. Lithuania, Latvia, Estonia, Azerbaijan and Uzbekistan have enacted similar legislation making their respective local languages official; Russian minorities complain there too. Native dislike of Russian settlers is strong in non–Russian republics, particularly in the Muslim lands of central Asia. The potential for growth of reverse discrimination is great.

We Americans too are still accused of discrimination. Though we have ended legally mandated racial segregation and have accorded equal political rights to all of our citizens perceived inequality still exists.

Though many blacks have served as mayors of American cities and have held seats in the House of Representatives for many years only one has served in the United States Senate during the twentieth century—Edward Brooke of Massachusetts. Not until 1989 was a black elected state governor, L. Douglas Wilder in Virginia.

New Mexico and Arizona have elected Hispanic governors in the 1970s and 1980s, as did Florida in 1986. Hawaii's two United States senators are of Japanese ancestry, as was one of California's a few years ago (Dr. S. I. Hayakawa).

Though some Americans aren't ready to elect a black or Hispanic president at this moment, the role played by our minorities in politics grows progressively larger. We may not ever totally eliminate discrimination from our society, but we have made giant strides in that direction.

As a general rule the multi-ethnic nations with the fewest ethnic problems are those where each group lives in its own defined area.

Though Switzerland has its four official languages, its three major ethnic groups don't live intermingled with each other. Most cantons have only one official language and the huge majority of its people speak that language. Thus Zurich is overwhelmingly German-speaking, Geneva overwhelmingly French-speaking and Ticino overwhelmingly Italian-speaking. In Zurich the schools instruct pupils in German, Geneva instructs pupils in French and Ticino instructs them in Italian. There's no talk of bilingual education—if a Zurich family with children moves to Geneva the children must learn French because there are no German-language public schools in Geneva. If a family with minor children moves from Geneva to Zurich it faces a similar problem because there are no French language public schools in Zurich.

In the canton of Ticino, as mentioned above, most residents are Italian speakers. In one of the canton's communes immigrants from the German-speaking north became the majority and voted to establish German-speaking public schools in the commune. The cantonal government objected; by cantonal law all instruction in Ticino public schools must be in Italian. In the ensuing litigation the Bundesgericht—the Supreme Court of Switzerland—held for the canton. Cantonal authorities have exclusive power to determine languages of instruction in their schools.

A few cantons (Bern, Fribourg, Valais) are bilingual (German and French); here communes may adopt their own official languages. There are few bilingual areas in these cantons, however, as linguistic frontiers are clearly discernible.

In trilingual (German, Romansch and Italian) Graubunden a different situation prevails. German speakers and Romansch speakers coexist side by side in most of the canton. Romansch communes often adjoin German communes; as people move from one commune to another the majority language within a commune may change. The locality may then, by referendum, change its official language.

Though over 70 percent of the Swiss speak German, the majority make no effort to lord it over the minorities. Though German-speaking Bern is the national capital, the nation's highest court sits in Lausanne, a major French-speaking city. By custom at least two members of the Bundesrat are French or Italian speakers. There is no one language of command in the armed forces; units of German speakers use German while units of French speakers use French and units of Ticinesi use Italian.

Though the German-speaking areas of the country are the most highly developed, many French-speaking areas enjoy a high standard of living. A French Swiss may hold a high-paying job working for a French-speaking employer without ever needing to take orders from a German speaker or to use German in the workplace. Ticino is less economically developed, but even here one may live well without using any language other than Italian.

Each of the three major language groups has no desire to join its linguistic fatherland. The Ticinesi have no wish to become Italians, living much better as Swiss. Similarly, Genevois have no wish to become French, or Zurchers to become German. They enjoy so much more freedom and prosperity as Swiss than do their linguistic brethren in Italy, France and Germany that they all share a common incentive to make the Swiss enterprise continue to be successful.

Hardly any Swiss complain of discrimination; each linguistic group is king on its home turf and this is accepted as right and proper.

The governments of India and Nigeria have attempted to establish the same sort of environment by guaranteeing to each fair-sized ethnic and linguistic group its own state.

Canada, however, is the major exception to the above rule. Its minority ethnic group (French speakers) are concentrated in the province of Quebec, where they are supreme. Yet the fabric of united Canada threatens to unravel as many Quebecois think secession. Why?

The major reason is that the Quebecois perceive themselves as a French-speaking island in an English-speaking sea, one that threatens to engulf their language and unique culture. To the west is Ontario, the richest of Canada's provinces. To the south is the massive United States. To the east are Canada's English-speaking Atlantic provinces. To the north is the empty forbidding Arctic.

While English Canada industrialized, Quebec lagged behind. While many students at English Canadian universities earned degrees in applied science, engineering and business the students of Quebec pursued the traditional disciplines of law, theology and medicine.

Canada's largest private-sector employers are managed by English-speaking Canadians; English is the language of business. Even in Montreal (Quebec's largest city) the largest companies are managed by English speakers and their business gets done in English. Those Canadians who would rise in the world must master English; those who do not have been (and, say Quebecois, still are) at a grave disadvantage.

Many Quebecois feel that they cannot attain economic equality with other Canadians without giving up their French culture. They deeply believe that they shouldn't be forced to do this.

The Canadian federal government has leaned over backward to soothe Quebecois sensibilities. The majority of Canadian prime ministers since 1950 have been Quebecois (as is the present incumbent, the Progressive Conservative leader Brian Mulroney). Mulroney's successor will almost certainly be Quebecois, as the Liberal Party leadership convention of July 1990 chose Jean Chretien, a French speaker from rural Quebec.

More federal money is spent in Quebec than is extracted from the province in federal taxes. By federal law no one may hold a job with the federal government or with a public corporation (such as Air Canada or the Canadian National Railway) who is not fluent in French, even if he or she is to work in Alberta or British Columbia where French speakers are rare.

Quebec has responded by making French the one official language of the province, requiring that all street signs and the like in the province be in French and that all public education within the province also be in French. Thus, nine of Canada's ten provinces are more or less bilingual by federal law, while Quebec strives to make itself unilingual.

It may well be that both Quebecois and English Canadians have lost the will to compromise upon the issues involved here. If so, Quebec will secede from Canada as Singapore seceded from Malaysia and, it is hoped, with a minimum of hard feelings and hatred.

One of the more subtle ironies of the Canadian situation is that the

Quebecois aren't particularly interested in the wellbeing of French speakers who live outside their province. New Brunswick, Nova Scotia and Ontario have sizable French-speaking minorities. Quebec would apparently allow the English-speaking majority in these provinces to deal with the French-speaking minorities as they will so that Quebec will have the same privilege with respect to its English-speaking minority.

Canada excepted, the nations with the most serious ethnic strife are those which can't give each group its own state and those which refuse to allow ethnic minorities any sort of self-determination.

Malaysia, though a federal nation, has problems with its Chinese and Tamil minorities because they are scattered throughout the country. Every state has a Malay majority, along with Chinese and Tamil minorities; nowhere are the minorities a majority.

Ethiopia's endemic civil war stems in part from the fact that the Amhara, a minority within the state, seek to dominate without much consideration for the cultures and aspirations of the non–Amhara.

For the same reason Burma has never known internal peace since independence. The Burmese majority refuses to grant any sort of self-determination to the non–Burmese minorities living along the fringes of the country. Many of these have conducted guerrilla warfare against the central government for decades.

Strife between Flemings and Walloons threatened to tear Belgium apart because, though the competing linguistic groups live in separate areas the nation is unitary; who rules in Brussels rules all Belgians. The establishment of defined linguistic areas within the country (as described earlier) may have defused the problem.

Our American minority problem is exacerbated because our minorities, like those in Malaysia, are scattered through our population. No state (unless one calls the District of Columbia a state) has a black majority nor an Hispanic majority. (Puerto Rico would be the exception should it become the fifty-first state.) Nowhere can our minorities call themselves a majority except in certain cities. But since the local self-government powers of cities are very limited, American minorities have no turf to call their own. This helps to explain their extreme sensitivity.

Chapter 14
Economic Systems

Many Americans believe that free-market principles are the natural basis of all economic systems, and that all systems operated in this way until the leftists of the late nineteenth and early twentieth centuries began to interfere. This is not true; governments have interfered with and attempted to dominate markets throughout most of recorded history. A political climate suitable for the free market has existed in limited parts of the world only for the last two centuries.

The first relatively prosperous Western economy was that of ancient Crete. We know that Cretan fleets sailed the eastern Mediterranean, selling and buying. Archaeological remains prove that the islanders possessed a rich leisured civilization, but we don't know how the economy functioned. Catastrophe ended Cretan power—whether it was the Santorini volcanic eruption of circa 1500 B.C. or foreign invasion we don't know.

Many centuries later the Greek city-states recreated prosperity based on a slavery-based classical economy. Cheap slave labor and active interstate trade produced the leisure class that governed Athens in its heyday. The quest for gold possessed many Athenians, as it does so many modern men and women. Money spoke as loudly as it does today.

In Sparta the legendary Lycurgus and his successors created the macho anti-materialist state that has fascinated a class of philosophers and politicians for two and a half millennia. All male Spartans were reared to be professional soldiers. Economic activity was for commoners, helots and slaves. Spartan money was made of iron, to insure that it had no value outside the city. The ascetic Spartan militarists preserved the independence of their city for over half a millennium, destroyed the power of the materialistic Athenians in the Peloponnesian War, and dominated all of Greece for a few decades of the fourth century B.C.

Roman conquest of the Mediterranean basin expanded the classical economy and increased its prosperity. Large-scale production of food increased and immense riches were created. At the beginning of the Christian era unheard-of economic well-being existed throughout the free trade area of the Empire.

By modern standards the economic base was incredibly weak. Since much of the labor force consisted of slaves, and since thousands of prisoners of war (the major source of slaves) had fallen into Roman hands during the wars that rounded out the Empire, labor was very cheap. There was no incentive to improve the primitive technology of the time. (Though the Greeks of Alexandria discovered the principles upon which the steam engine operated, steam-driven devices were never anything more than toys.)

Capital was limited. An adverse balance of international trade began to drain away such hard money as there was; Roman imports of Chinese silk and Indian spices were paid for in gold because Rome produced nothing its Chinese and Indian suppliers were willing to buy.

The Western European economy entered a period of continual regression at the beginning of the third century A.D. Government instability, inflation, high taxation and a growing shortage of slave labor interfered with production and long-distance trade. At the beginning of the fourth century the Emperor Diocletian sought to stem the decline through rigid price controls but the effort failed. Black markets sprang up all over the Empire and the government wasn't powerful enough to suppress them. After Diocletian's controls were abandoned the degeneration accelerated. Money became worthless, replaced by bartering. Income declined to the point that it was insufficient to pay the heavy taxes which had started to erode capital.

Those who still possessed liquid wealth began to leave the empire; in response government forbade the affluent to change residences or occupations. Agricultural laborers were forbidden to leave their place of employment and sons were required to take up the occupations of their fathers.

The boundaries of the empire shrank; the legions abandoned England, Germanic tribes flooded into what's now France, and in 410 the armies of Alaric the Goth sacked Rome itself. In 476 the Gothic king deposed the last West Roman emperor. West of the lands of the eastern Emperor the old political and economic system was dead.

High taxes and the restrictions on personal liberty were also dead. In that sense the Germanic conquerors brought liberation. But long-distance trade dried up because of insecurity and lack of goods to trade; production slowed because of lack of capital, hastening the steep descent to the poverty of the Dark Ages.

For 500 years west Europeans lived in a subsistence economy, but the seeds of eventual recovery had been planted. In Benedictine monasteries the anchorites, isolated from the world, began producing large quantities of food, clothing, tools and the like through disciplined division of labor and time. The rise of the feudal system introduced manorial agriculture, raising food production. In the slowly growing towns handicrafts began to prosper. By the eleventh century Italian cities were growing prosperous through reviving production and commerce. Long-distance trade routes began to multiply.

The insecurity of political and economic life meant that cooperation had to be the cornerstone of economic activity. Travel was exceedingly dangerous as highwaymen infested the forests bordering on the trade routes. Robber barons ventured forth from their castles to plunder passing mercantile caravans. Mercenary nobles enriched themselves by collecting tolls at bridges and ferries. No caravan was minimally safe unless escorted by a large number of soldiers; many merchants had to collaborate to finance the hire of such protection.

In the towns producers of handicrafts organized themselves into guilds in order to control production, prices and admission of new master craftsmen to practice.

Developments of the later Middle Ages spurred economic progress. The invention of double-entry bookkeeping made possible the development of modern accounting. The slow rise of the nation-state made long-distance trade safer through the suppression of highwaymen and robber barons. States took over the privileges of laying tolls upon caravans, reducing the number of places where tolls were levied.

Most important was the introduction of banking and commercial paper. Without these two devices trade could only be conducted on a cash or barter basis. Banks made it unnecessary to carry around large sums of cash; the merchant could deposit his precious metal with a banker and take back a warehouse receipt or receipts for it. Later he could pay for a purchase by transferring his deposit receipt.

Banks also expanded the amount of available cash. When a merchant deposited 1,000 gold ducats with a banker, the banker might lend out 10,000 ducats against the deposit in the form of warehouse receipts which were of course redeemable in gold coins. So long as the world accepted a banker's receipt for 1,000 gold ducats as the equivalent of the actual cash, few of the banker's receipts would be presented for redemption and the banker could issue many more receipts than he had gold ducats. Thus the money supply was multiplied. (If for some reason the trading community lost confidence in a banker disaster ensued. If more receipts were presented for redemption than the coins held by the banker in cash reserve the bank failed and its receipts became worthless. Thus a sizable portion of society developed a distrust of banks and bankers which continues to the present day.)

The first factories began producing textiles as the banking economy grew. More and more persons became rich through buying, selling and lending.

An intellectual opposition to economic activity for the sake of creating wealth existed almost from the beginning of the economic revolution, both inside and outside the Roman Catholic Church.

To church people, buying and selling encouraged the merchant to commit some of the seven deadly sins. The desire to show off one's opulence was unjustifiable pride. The unhappiness one may well feel upon seeing the success of a competitor was very likely sinful envy. The feeling that no matter how rich you are you can and must get richer was avarice. To become upset with too-successful competitors was anger. The desire to use one's wealth to buy and consume vast quantities of the best food and wine was gluttony. To use such wealth to attract members of the opposite sex was lust. The only one of the seven deadly sins no successful businessperson would commit was sloth — laziness.

The church condemned as usury the lending of money at interest. The selling of goods for the highest price the market will tolerate was unfair — the seller should sell for the just price — that price which guaranteed a fair return on his effort and no more.

Outside the Church the opposition condemned inequality of property ownership; some went farther and condemned the private ownership of property. The Waldensians of the Middle Ages would have abolished property altogether, as would the Taborite sect of the Hussites.

Wat Tyler led a rebellion of the English peasantry against their social betters in 1381, the rebels demanding a better economic deal and chanting,

> "When Adam delved and Eve span,
> Who was then the gentleman?"

The gentlemen in question — the feudal nobility — would have none of this radicalism and most efficiently suppressed Tyler's revolt.

A radical sect of Anabaptists under Jan van Leiden gained control of the German city of Munster in 1534 and established an essentially communist state; all property and even women were declared to be common possessions of the male believers. An army of Catholics and Protestants, united in their detestation of these people, stormed the city in 1535 and slaughtered its defenders.

Ultimately most of the Catholic Church made its peace with the new order, while non-Church opposition was either suppressed or driven underground.

After the Reformation the revolution obtained the support of the followers of John Calvin. To the original Calvinists individuals are saved or damned at birth; nothing could change that predestination. One of the best pieces of evidence that one belongs to the elect is success in one's life work. Therefore, if one works very hard and succeeds, this is almost certain proof of forthcoming salvation.

Since it was most praiseworthy to devote one's life to the pursuit and accumulation of wealth, residents of Calvinist states went at it with gusto.

As the nation-state increased in size and strength its appetite for revenue grew and its powers of taxation increased. Rulers soon realized that the ease of extracting taxes from their subjects depended on the health of the state's economy; therefore the wise sovereign did whatever he could to improve the realm's economic base.

The more hard cash reposed within the realm, the more healthy the state's economy, allowing the philosophy of mercantilism to take root. According to mercantilists the nation-state is in a sense a profit-making organism; its external trade must be regulated in a way that minimizes the outflow of cash. The main cause of such an outflow is an adverse balance of trade, so exports must exceed imports. Domestic industries must be developed wherever possible to reduce dependence upon imports, and production of goods that may be profitably exported should be stimulated.

Though competition is to be expected in the tough scramble for external markets, it is inefficient and wasteful within the domestic economy. Therefore monopoly in the production and distribution of goods is to be encouraged.

When colonies are acquired their production and trade are to be regulated for the benefit of the mother country; thus their exports must be made to the mother country only and their imports must come from nowhere else. (British mercantilist restrictions of this sort on the trade of the American colonies was one of the causes of the American Revolution.)

The beginning of the Industrial Revolution caused some to question the benefits of mercantilism, but it wasn't until the publication of Adam Smith's *The Wealth of Nations* in 1776 that a strong case was made for the abolition of mercantilism and the establishment of the free market economy.

The immense growth of world trade caused by the European expansion into Asia and the conquest of America caused a great increase in the European money supply and of international banking. The huge quantities of Aztec and Inca gold brought home by the Spaniards triggered inflation in Iberia; the supplies of silver produced by the mines of Mexico increased it. As the Spaniards spent the precious metal abroad to finance their wars in Italy and the Low Countries the inflation spread and the European cost of living skyrocketed. The precious metal ended up doing little to increase the prosperity of Spain as most of it came into the possession of north European bankers.

During the 80-year war for independence fought by the Dutch against Spain, Amsterdam became the financial center of Europe. Dutch merchants and bankers didn't hesitate to improve their profits by selling war materials to the Spanish enemy for cash. The Dutch Republic continued to be the financial center of the West until it was overtaken by London in the eighteenth century.

In the seventeenth century foreign trading companies of an as yet unheard-of size developed. The Dutch East India Company pioneered Dutch expansion into Ceylon and Indonesia, the British East India Company began the expansion into India and the British West India Company invested in the sugar islands of the Caribbean. These firms issued stock to shareholders leading to large-scale (for the time) trading in securities.

About 1720 two remarkable speculative booms and busts stirred up hostility to corporations that hasn't yet died in some parts of the West. In France John Law founded the Louisiana Company to develop the immense land area later to be sold by Napoleon to the United States in 1803. Speculators drove the price of the company's stock sky-high, anticipating the profits to be earned by the venture, and immense sums flowed to Paris to participate in the mad boom. Very little of the company's capital was actually invested in Louisiana; when the public realized that there would be few if any profits the speculative bubble burst and many investors lost everything.

At about the same time, in London, a similar speculative boom erupted in South Seas Company stock. As in Paris, the boom was followed by a tremendous bust, many English speculators being wiped out. As a result French, English and other persons caught up in the madness resolved that no good could come of trading in the stock of corporations. The law positively discouraged the organization of such.

The beginnings of the Industrial Revolution caused unprecedented growth of the English economy. That plus the founding and growth of the Bank of England and other banks made possible the generation of huge quantities of capital in Great Britain. It was the ability of the government to tap these resources as much as anything else which made possible the English victories over the French in the eighteenth-century wars. The English credit system enabled the nation to finance immense deficits; the absence of a similar credit system in France caused the deficit-plagued government of Louis XVI to summon the Estates-General in 1789, setting off the French Revolution.

The greatest triumph of the English credit system was yet to come. The French financed the 23-year series of wars of the French Revolution in large part with wealth seized from their continental enemies; Napoleon in particular thought that Great Britain's economy couldn't stand the strain of a long war but he was wrong. The islanders emerged after Waterloo with a record public debt, but they emerged victors.

The English economy was now the strongest in the world, a mixture of free enterprise and mercantilism. With the triumph of the proponents of Free Trade around 1840 and the repeal of protective tariffs on agricultural products Great Britain embraced the free market.

Meanwhile the new United States, grateful to have escaped the stifling incubus of English mercantilism, unconsciously adopted the principles of Adam Smith in almost all ways. Hostility toward government regulation and control of the economy was the norm, but government action to aid the economy was equally the rule. Tariffs were raised to protect the nascent industry of the country from foreign competition, and government subsidization promoted the growth of desired new industries. Behind the tariff wall the American industrial machine grew, unhindered by high taxation or other governmental interference and helped by a massive, prosperous domestic market.

Though the United States dollar became and remained a "hard" currency (because such paper money as was issued by the federal government was redeemable in precious metals) much of the economic growth along the frontier was financed by the "softest" of money, state bank notes. All frontier banks made loans in this medium. Though in theory these notes were redeemable in the federal government's coin or currency, the issuing banks had nowhere near enough cash reserves to redeem outstanding notes at par. When banks ran out of cash reserves they failed and such failures caused minor disasters. Yet the majority of these frontier banks survived and their notes continued to be accepted as good money.

As a result of the Civil War the state bank notes disappeared; the federal government levied a tax on them that drove them from the marketplace. From that time on only national banks could issue bank notes, so the amount of money in circulation on the frontier declined.

In the United States more than elsewhere the corporation came to be accepted as the major form of business organization. Small- and medium-sized firms were numerous before the Civil War and the growth of gigantic industries afterward (such as railroads, oil, steel and coal) promoted the growth of massive organizations. So great were the capital requirements in some industries that these huge sums could not be raised by selling stock or bonds to the public; the age of finance capital dawned. The perception grew that investment bankers were taking control of the economy.

This era of government subsidization without regulation was in many ways the heyday of the American free market. Goods and services of immense variety and low cost in money were available to all, but not without other costs. Many skilled handicrafts died out, their practitioners unable to compete against factories. More and more Americans earned their livings as employees of industrialists; it was in this era that our ancestors were subjected to the full discipline of time managed to the second.

Our economy began to experience speculative booms and busts; from the beginning the busts sent shock waves through the political system. The Panic of 1837 cost President Martin van Buren re-election in 1840. The Panic of 1857 aided the rise of the Republican Party and indirectly contributed to the election of Abraham Lincoln in 1860. The Panic of 1873 contributed to the end of post–Civil War Reconstruction in the South by causing economic concerns to overshadow public interest in the future of the ex-slaves of the South and caused for the first time anti–free market and pro-regulation sentiment.

This was exacerbated by post-war monetary developments. During the Civil War the federal government (as well as the Confederate government) issued millions of dollars worth of greenbacks—fiat paper money not redeemable in precious metals—to help finance the war effort. These were in part responsible for the inflation of the war era; advocates of hard money strove to get them withdrawn from circulation after the war ended while advocates of inflation wanted more issued.

Neither side won here; the Civil War greenbacks remained in circulation but no more were printed. A period of sometimes stable and sometimes falling prices set in as a shortage of cash plagued farmers and other residents of newly settled lands. As the value of money rose debtors were unmercifully squeezed. Westerners demanded an increase in the money supply along with regulation of the activities of big business. These feelings were expressed through the media of the Greenback Party of the late 1870s and the People's (or Populist) Party of the 1880s and 1890s. William Jennings Bryan expressed this sentiment when he shouted an imprecation against advocates of hard money in a famous speech to the Democratic National Convention in 1896, "You shall not crucify mankind upon a cross of gold!"

The demanded inflation never came to pass, but the era of business regulation dawned. The Supreme Court placed its stamp of approval on state regulation of business in the 1876 case of Munn v. Illinois; Congress entered the regulation arena by enacting the Interstate Commerce Act of 1887 and the Sherman Act of 1890.

In 1893 the greatest depression yet shook the nation and populist ideology seized control of the Democratic Party three years later when Bryan won its presidential nomination and the pro-regulationists took (and kept) control. The end of the unrestricted free market was at hand.

Theodore Roosevelt contributed to it through vigorous enforcement of the Sherman Act. Woodrow Wilson contributed much more through the Federal Reserve Act, the new federal income tax, the Federal Trade Commission Act, the Clayton Act, and later the unprecedented economic mobilization that followed America's entry into World War I.

Public utilities were subjected to stringent regulation as natural monopolies, and Workman's Compensation programs rendered employers liable to employees injured on the job, even when the employer wasn't negligent.

European economies moved in other directions before World War I. Great Britain imposed income taxes long before the United States did. In the first decade of the twentieth century it enacted legislation encouraging the formation of labor unions and exempting them from liability for most of their members' wrongdoings. The foundations of the British welfare state were laid by the Liberal Party government that took office in 1906.

Industrialization was encouraged by Prince Bismarck after the creation of the united German Empire in 1871. Government offered much assistance to industrialists who in return cooperated with the state. Cooperation was preferred to competition within Germany's domestic economy; cartelization was endemic.

In order to discourage the growth of the German Social Democratic Party, Bismarck created the German welfare state during the 1870s and 1880s; it was the first nation to create systems of unemployment compensation, workers' compensation and government medicine. This pattern was to be copied by other nations later.

In Russia the Czar's government sought to guide industrialization through subsidies and construction of state-owned industries. At approximately the turn of the century the private sector of the Russian ecconomy began to grow but it lagged behind other European nations economically.

The currencies of most major Western nations were redeemable in gold, upon which foreign exchange rates were based. Inflation was rare; never had the environment of international trade been more stable or more inviting.

Nineteenth-century opposition to the free market. The French Revolution was for the most part a middle-class revolution. It wasn't opposed to private property or the acquisition of wealth—rather, it was an effort to destroy aristocratic barriers to the pursuit of wealth and social position by non-aristocrats. The only revolutionary event that could have threatened private property was the conspiracy of Gaius Gracchus Babeuf and his confederates to overthrow the French Directory and establish a socialist state. Babeuf's plot was discovered by the authorities before it could be activated and he met his end on the guillotine, becoming a martyr to the cause of Marxism-Leninism.

During the first half of the nineteenth century various utopian socialists preached that it would be to the advantage of humanity to abolish private property; only in that way could equality and happiness be achieved. They preached to peoples' consciences, without much success. Private parties sought to establish small socialist utopias in Europe and the new world, but all failed.

In the middle of the nineteenth century Karl Marx presented his theory of scientific socialism. He didn't urge the establishment of socialism through appeal to the human conscience, but argued instead that socialism is the wave of the future and will come to pass whether we like it or not. Capitalism had overthrown feudalism as the prevailing economic order and the bourgeoisie (middle class) had replaced the landed aristocracy as the dominant class in society. It's inevitable that the proletariat (the working class) will overthrow the bourgeoisie and establish its dictatorship. Private ownership of the means of production will end and socialism (from each according to his ability, to each according to his work) will be the form of economic organization. The dictatorship of the proletariat will continue until all traces of capitalist mentality are removed from human minds and all people will be willing to exert maximum effort on the job for the benefit of society. At this point communism will be established (from each according to his ability, to each according to his need). The state will wither away and all people will live in prosperous egalitarian happiness.

Marx exhorted European proletarians to pursue this dream in his Communist Manifesto of 1848; its closing words still thrill true believers: "Workers of the world, unite! You have nothing to lose but your chains!"

The only proletarians who made serious efforts to establish socialism by force were the workers of Paris. In 1848 they rose against the Second Republic and were violently suppressed by the army. In 1871 they took advantage of the confusion caused by France's defeat in the Franco-Prussian War to establish the Paris Commune, as the kernel of a socialist France, but this effort too was drowned in blood by the army.

Nevertheless, the Marxist dream has galvanized the minds of many for a century and a half. Some Marxists have sought to help history through the democratic process; these are the world's Social Democrats. Other more impatient believers have sought to speed the process through the use of force and violence despite the French experience; these are the Communists.

Communist anarchists preached the abolition of capitalism through the abolition of government and private property. Unwilling to wait for the state to wither away, they'd destroy it at the beginning of their revolution.

Anarcho-syndicalists too preached the abolition of the state and of private property, but they would turn over the management of the units of production to those who worked in them.

Before World War I, only the Social Democrats had a strong power base. The German Social Democrats became the largest party in the Reichstag in 1912, the British Labor Party was the fourth-largest party in the House of Commons and the French Socialist Party was a power to be reckoned with in France.

Marxist believers in violence gained control of the Social Democratic Party of Russia in the first decade of the twentieth century.

Anarchists and anarcho-syndicalists developed strength in Italy, Spain, Mexico and other Latin countries, but not enough to put their notions into practice.

World War I. Some pre–World War I writers worried that the European alliance systems could trigger a world war of unprecedented length and ferocity. Others argued that a lengthy world war was impossible because national economies weren't strong enough to finance such a struggle. Europeans marched off to battle in August of 1914 expecting to be home for Christmas; no one foresaw what was to come.

By the beginning of 1915 all of the belligerent armies were suffering from shortages of weapons and munitions. All of the national economies involved were harnessed to support the war, imposing unprecedented regulation.

All of these nations mobilized their credit resources to the hilt. Germany borrowed capital to finance the war effort from its own people, while Great Britain and France borrowed from their own and from the United States as well.

Even the U.S. began regulating its economy after entering the war in 1917; very high income tax rates were imposed upon the upper and middle classes, the railroads were subjected to management by the federal government, and many other restrictions and regulations came into being.

In the end no nation left the war due to a lack of financial resources; first Russia and later Germany and its allies simply suffered military defeat and moral collapse.

Communists gained power in Russia in 1917. For the first time dedicated Marxists would have the chance to restructure a formerly capitalist society.

Between the wars. Though the American Republican administrations of the 1920s are depicted as foes of business regulation, the record doesn't quite bear out this accusation. The Federal Reserve Board subjected the nation's banking and monetary system to control throughout this period, promoting through easy-money policies the borrowing that fueled stock-market speculation. The new broadcasting industry was held to stringent regulation, while for the first time the government began regulating labor-management relations with the Railway Labor Act.

The Great Depression ended a decade of conservative government and opened the door to a period of economic revolution. Banking, agriculture, securities markets, airlines and other industries were subjected to strict regulation. The organization of labor unions was encouraged. Unemployment compensation and the Social Security system were created. A minimum wage law was enacted. The dollar was devalued and gold demonetized as the age of American fiat money dawned. Extremely high rates of income tax were imposed. The employee's portion of the Social Security tax was withheld from his or her pay packet; for the first time Uncle Sam made tax collectors of the nation's employers. The American economy had become a mixture of free enterprise and government regulation.

The British economy stagnated during the inter-war period. Conservatives dominated the government most of the time. Unemployment was high, even before the depression; it grew much worse after 1929. Only the coming of World War II brought recovery.

Though Germany suffered economic dislocation and hyperinflation after the war, German big business grew even bigger during this period. It eliminated many domestic rivals and all of its debts during the hyperinflation of 1923. At the same time the German federal, state and local governments paid off their debts in worthless money while the middle classes lost everything.

The Great Depression hit all Germans hard; unemployment rose to levels higher than elsewhere in Europe. Many business owners and managers supported Hitler and the Nazis; to appease them Hitler suppressed the Nazi left wing (which favored an economic revolution) and left private property in place. In return for large profits and destruction of labor union power business accepted stringent controls during the dictatorship.

Germany was the only nation to end the Depression within its borders before 1939. A combination of massive public works financed by government, massive rearmament and military conscription did the job.

In Italy Marxists threatened to take control following World War I, so Benito Mussolini was handed political power in 1922 to prevent this. He created a "Corporative State" economy based vaguely upon syndicalist premises but controlled by the state; for the most part private ownership of property wasn't disturbed.

In 1931 a revolt overthrew the Spanish monarchy and a republic dominated by the political left was created. In 1936 a coalition of Socialists and Communists won control of the national parliament, which conservatives saw as a threat to private property. The Army rebelled and civil war resulted. In some areas of the country governed by the Republic anarchists took control and sought to abolish both private property and government; in other parts Communists sought to establish proletarian dictatorship. All were eventually suppressed by the army and property rights were preserved.

In France the Radical-Socialist-Communist Popular Front under the Socialist Leon Blum took power in 1936, the first truly leftist French administration. It nationalized part of the economy and strengthened the rights of labor unions and working people. Some conservative French people voiced their disgust by growling, "Better Hitler than Blum!"

In all of Scandinavia and in other parts of western Europe Socialist governments took power at various times between the wars; the welfare states of the Netherlands, Belgium and Scandinavia took form at this time.

Lenin and the Bolsheviks sought to abolish the free market within the Soviet Union and to create an almost total command economy. Lenin expropriated almost the entire Russian economy in 1918 without compensation, but when production fell to nothing in the early 1920s he instituted the New Economic Policy which restored the free market at lower levels of the economy, stimulating production and reviving the nation.

To Stalin the NEP was contrary to Marxist ideology; he abolished it and created the command economy which prevailed in the USSR until the advent of Mikhail Gorbachev. The employment of one person by another was forbidden. Virtually the entire economy was placed under the control of central planners in Moscow. They determined what would be produced, how much would be produced, who would produce it and to whom it would be delivered.

Every production unit would be assigned a production quota that it was expected to meet or exceed. In general, the quantity produced was of the highest concern and quality was secondary.

The financial resources of productive enterprises were furnished by the state. Managers were expected to manage finances efficiently, but weren't necessarily expected to operate at a profit. Prices were set by the planners, to encourage or discourage consumption.

Thus came into being the command economy that produced the huge quantities of weaponry that equipped the Red Army, the largest in Europe during the late 1930s.

The stable international monetary environment had vanished with the firing of the guns of August 1914. The German hyperinflation of 1923 was the worst of the interwar period, but massive inflation also shook Austria, Poland, Czechoslovakia and Russia. Italy and France too saw their price levels rise by several hundred percent.

With the coming of the Great Depression international trade began to dry up as all nations erected massive tariff walls to keep out imports and reserve their domestic economies to their own producers. The international business environment hadn't much improved by 1939.

World War II. It was preparation for war that ended the Great Depression throughout the Western world. No country truly mobilized its economy at the beginning—even Germany reserved much productive capacity for civilian goods since Hitler expected a short war.

After the fall of France Winston Churchill caused total mobilization of the British economy; he saw that the road to victory would be long and rocky. Stalin, his country still neutral, also ordered a nearly total mobilization to prepare for possible German attack. The United States geared up for rearmament and the supplying of Great Britain.

Only after Hitler failed to knock the Soviet Union out after his 1941 invasion did he order full mobilization of the German economy; it was the U.S., Great Britain and the Soviet Union versus Germany the rest of the way.

The German economy worked wonders in allowing Hitler to continue the struggle for another three years, producing prodigious quantities of weaponry as late as 1944. In the end, however, it suffered almost total destruction along with Hitler, his party, his army and his country.

In the United States too the economy was subjected to unprecedented regulation. Government allocated raw materials to industry, reserving much of the existing supply to war production. Food, shoes, rubber products, gasoline and other consumer goods were rationed. Rigid price and wage controls were imposed. The income tax was raised and for the first time most Americans became income tax payers. Withholding of income tax from the wages of employees was begun.

The Soviet Union emerged with the largest army in the world, the United States emerged with by far the largest economy in the world, while Great Britain emerged well-armed but financially and economically exhausted.

Post-war Western economies. World War II in Europe ended with the Red Army in occupation of everything between the Elbe River and the Soviet frontier. Communist governments and Soviet-style economies were imposed upon Poland, Romania, Bulgaria, Hungary, Czechoslovakia and the Soviet occupation zone of Germany. The Cold War had begun.

The productive capacity of the U.S. helped to make possible the economic reconstruction of Western Europe, including ex-enemy West Germany. For a period American business dominated the world economy and the American dollar the international money markets as the Bretton Woods agreement made the dollar the world's major reserve currency. Free trade became the watchword of the West; unhampered trade between nations was essential for quick recovery from the shock of war.

The Cold War and world-wide demand for American products kept the American economy in high gear until the mid–1950s. Then came a slowdown and an increase in unemployment. European and Japanese competition reduced American advantages in world markets. American foreign aid and military spending sent increasingly large quantities of money outside the country (as did direct foreign investment by American business); some people began to claim that the greenback was overvalued.

Though the wartime regulations were repealed in the late 1940s and no new regulations were devised during the 1950s, the trend went in another direction during the 1960s. The civil rights movement caused the enactment of strict anti-discrimination legislation. The Occupational Safety and Health Act mandated workplace safety. The various environmental protection statutes imposed strict anti-pollution controls. Consumer protection legislation imposed strong safety standards upon manufacturers of products used by the public.

The Vietnam War stimulated some parts of our economy once again, but progressively higher inflation caused continuing erosion of the value of the dollar at home and abroad. In 1971 the greenback was dethroned as world reserve currency when the Bretton Woods system collapsed. The era of floating currency exchange rates began. The dollar fell to new lows on world money markets as American imports increased and the foreign trade deficit mounted. The Swiss franc and German deutschmark replaced the dethroned dollar as kings of world finance.

For awhile the Arab oil embargo and high petroleum prices of the mid–1970s threatened to turn the United States into a total debtor nation; the succeeding oil glut delayed the inevitable for a few years. High American interest rates caused foreign funds to flow into the United States in the late 1970s and early 1980s. Despite the mounting foreign trade deficit the dollar soared in value abroad.

The tax cuts of the Reagan years were supposed to stimulate investment in the American economy and generate increased tax revenue through business expansion. Since the cuts were targeted toward individuals and the "reforms" actually discouraged business investment, consumption by Americans increased while investment in capital assets decreased. Moreover, there was no cut in government spending to match the tax cuts as annual federal deficits rose to record levels. The American national debt soared from one trillion dollars to nearly three trillion dollars during the decade of the 1980s. The dollar again fell to new lows abroad.

Most of these annual deficits were financed by foreigners through their purchase of government debt securities or by direct investment in the U.S. economy. At last the inevitable happened — the United States was transformed from the world's leading creditor nation into the world's leading debtor.

Though the deregulation movement of the 1970s and 1980s reduced government control of the airline industry and a few others, the United States is far from possessing an absolute free market economy. American tax law still discourages business investment in capital goods. Increasing protectionist sentiment demands the closing of the American economy to foreign imports and foreign investment. Sentiment for re-regulation of airlines grows. Uncle Sam's annual deficits don't shrink; government spending continues at its usual high level. The United States no longer has things its own way in any market. Here and abroad, the European Community and the Japanese provide formidable competition.

In Great Britain the Labor Party assumed power for the first time in 1945 as revolutionary changes took place. The nation to a large extent disarmed as railways, coal mines, the steel industry and many other portions of the economy were nationalized. A system of socialized medicine was instituted. By the time Labor left office in 1951 Great Britain possessed one of the world's comprehensive welfare states.

The British economy was looked upon as "the sick man" of Europe during the 1950s, 1960s and 1970s as inflation soared and productivity dragged. Then Margaret Thatcher assumed power in 1979 and turned things around to an extent. She began to dismantle some of Britain's public sector, selling off government enterprises and turning them into private enterprises. Thus Great Britain has joined the United States in having a privately owned telephone system. Privatized British firms (government-owned enterprises sold off to the public) include British Telecom, British Airways, British Petroleum and Rolls-Royce.

At the same time productivity has risen and British products have become more competitive on world markets. The British patient for the moment has recovered from his economic illness.

West Germany had to start from scratch to rebuild its economy. New modern plants replaced the older structures flattened by wartime bombing and shelling. Some large German firms were nationalized after the war ended although most remained under private ownership. German discipline and cleverness wrought an economic miracle; by 1960 the West German economy had become one of the strongest in Western Europe.

Today much of it remains privately owned. German tax policy encourages investment and growth in the private sector. However, employees are entitled to participate in management and taxes upon industry help to finance a more massive welfare state than that created by Bismarck.

With the birth of the European Community in 1958, the process of integrating the economies of Western Europe into one gigantic market began.

Most of this task will be completed by 1992; the economy of a newly reunited Germany will lead the Community into the twenty-first century.

Some of the French economy was nationalized after the war, particularly those firms whose managements collaborated with the Germans during their occupation of the country (such as the automaker Renault). During the Fourth Republic (1945–1958) economic weakness plagued the country but between 1958 and 1982 there was relative prosperity. Under the presidency of the Socialist Francois Miterrand (1982 to the present) there were further nationalizations, but since 1986 there have been a reversal of policy and increasing government adherence to free market principles.

Post-war Italian governments undid Mussolini's Corporative State; though Italy's public sector is relatively strong, free market ideology has a large following.

The Soviet command economy has created and maintained the largest armed forces in the world since the end of World War II. It put Sputnik into orbit in 1957 and landed a robot on Venus. But it has been unable to feed the Soviet people or to provide them a decent standard of living. It's ideal for the creation of large military forces for a totalitarian dictatorship but until recently the Soviet people had nothing to say about the allocation of national resources. It can also provide something resembling full employment; when a production unit isn't required to operate at a profit it can employ and pay excess labor. That is of no consequence to the managers when the state picks up the tab for operating deficits. It can also provide cheap housing (of low quality and quantity, each individual Russian having fewer square meters of personal living space than most other Europeans). It can provide cheap food, when such is available.

Though in theory thorough planning was supposed to create the ultra-rational economy, entirely under the control of human reason, it didn't work out in practice. The Soviet economy is too complex to be effectively controlled by a group of bureaucrats in Moscow.

Gorbachev has apparently realized that human reason operating alone cannot create and operate an acceptable civilian economy. His program of perestroika seeks to inject free market elements into the Soviet economy though how far he intends to carry this remains to be seen. Soviet bureaucracy opposes the change; their managers aren't mentally equipped to manage under free market conditions.

Poland and Hungary never developed true Soviet-type economies. Land remained under private ownership in Poland while Hungary allowed very small private businesses to exist. These two liberated nations intend to purge virtually all command elements from their economic systems, creating Western European–style free market economies. They are embarking upon a noble and difficult experiment.

How are the state enterprises of these lands to be turned over to private ownership? Who will the owners be? Must they pay the state for the property they're acquiring? If so, where will they obtain the money?

Where will these enterprises acquire managers who know how to operate under free market conditions? What will happen to all those who lose their jobs when excess employees are terminated? How long will it take for the new free market to begin to encourage production and get goods on the shelves of retail stores?

The former East Germany is embarking on a similar enterprise, but there the transformation will go much easier. With German reunification the eastern German economy is being integrated into that of western Germany. Western German private industry and government will provide the capital and expertise to make the transition less painful than in Poland, Hungary and elsewhere. Even so, sudden economic difficulty plagued East Germany after the July 1, 1990, economic union. Unemployment is growing as inefficient enterprises lay off excess labor, while new enterprises aren't yet in operation to hire it.

Czechoslovakia, whose economy much resembled that of the Soviets, is just now embarking on the conversion to the free market. How far and how fast the new government will travel down this road are yet open to question.

In Yugoslavia "market socialism" has prevailed for many years. Small private enterprise may compete with the state and many larger enterprises are in a sense quasi-private because they are managed by their workers. A group of ordinary people desiring to found such an enterprise may obtain capital and assets from the state. Functioning as a cooperative, the workers hire management to run their undertaking, and management serves as long as the workers desire to keep it in office. The decisions of what to produce and where to sell the production are worker decisions.

Since price controls have diminished in Yugoslavia, most prices are determined by the law of supply and demand. The enterprise is expected to operate at a profit and if it becomes insolvent it's liquidated.

Profits belong to the workers to dispose of as they see fit. This money may be reinvested in the enterprise, or paid out to the workers as a form of dividend.

The Communist hold on Yugoslavia's government has yet been greatly shaken; the revolutionary reforms in other lands of Eastern Europe have caused political and economic fallout here. There may well be an enlargement of the Yugoslav private sector.

The Chinese economy. In China economic ambition has always coexisted with socialistic notions. Chinese have always been encouraged to work hard, but the intellectual mandarin always had a higher status than the rich merchant. Anyone who became rich through economic activity always ran the risk of having both enterprise and wealth confiscated by the government.

Twice in Chinese history idealistic reformers sought to eliminate most private property from the national scheme of things. The first such person was

Wang Mang, who temporarily deposed the Han dynasty and ruled as Emperor from A.D. 8 to A.D. 23. He declared that all the land within China was the property of the nation, distributing some of the expropriated property to the landless. He also expropriated enterprises that manufactured liquor and refined iron and salt. He put the government into the business of lending money to the needy, and sought to have the state buy up and store surplus produce in time of plenty to resell to the public when it was scarce. Wang Mang's reforms offended too many powerful interests. He came to a violent end and his new order was quickly terminated.

In the year 1069 the Emperor Sung Shen-Tsung appointed Wang An-Shih as his chief minister. Wang immediately began a reform program that bore some resemblances to that of Wang Mang a millennium earlier. Again the government lent money to needy farmers at low rates of interest and bought surplus produce in times of plenty to resell in times of scarcity. All ablebodied rural men were compelled to join a national militia which was given both police and military duties. The government gave money to farmers with which to buy horses; the horses belonged to the government, but farmers could use them for agricultural purposes in peacetime. In war the state would claim the horses for use as cavalry mounts.

All of this required the expenditure of much money and taxes rose to unheard-of levels, leading to popular protest against some of these policies. When famine struck in 1074 the cry was raised that Wang had lost the Mandate of Heaven and that the Emperor should dismiss him. To still the outcry Shen Tsung demanded Wang's resignation. These experiments were terminated forthwith.

A devotion to egalitarianism has always been an important part of Chinese culture. One component was the notion that all people were entitled to try their hand at the examination for entrance to the mandarinate. Another is the notion that family members have the duty to support each other, and that no family member should live better than another just because he happens to have more earning power. Another is the notion that all rural people should have access to land, and their holdings should be substantially equal. (This last principle was breached far more often than it was observed; it provided a platform for many a Chinese rebel intent on raising a military force.)

Chinese reformers were always most interested in promoting the well-being of agriculture. Other economic activity took place subject to either governmental indifference or hostility. Much of this economic activity took place far away from the seat of central authority, in the southeastern seaports of the country.

Here Chinese overseas trading began; here merchant families became rich and remained that way, faw away from the Emperor's tax collectors. From here the Chinese emigrants wandered south and east to the Philippines, Indonesia,

Malaysia and Burma (and eventually to Hawaii and the west coast of the United States). Their hard work in manufacturing, selling and buying has always paid better for the long term on foreign soil than in their native land.

Socialist ideas were still very much alive in twentieth-century China; thus Mao Tse Tung's Communists preached a doctrine that wasn't at all outlandish to Chinese peasants. His socialist state was very much within the scope of Chinese tradition.

In Mao's China, employment of one person by another was forbidden. In post–Mao China, this prohibition has relaxed — in the interest of promotion of economic growth more and more small businesses are coming into existence. In large cities like Shanghai, private corporations with hundreds of employees now exist.

Economic liberalization has slowed since the events in T'ien An Men Square in July of 1989, though the rulers are leaving in place the reforms enacted before that time.

Japan's economy. Like China, Japan's economy was primarily agricultural before modernization. The farmer and the soldier enjoyed much higher status than the merchant in old Japan.

Under the Tokugawa merchants came into their own. Though their social status didn't much increase the peace and prosperity of the land encouraged domestic trade and thus enriched clever buyers and sellers.

As a result of the forced modernization during the last century Japan has developed a unique form of free market. Government encouraged and participated in the industrialization of Japan; the state actually constructed factories during the 1880s and 1890s with public funds and then sold them to individual and corporate buyers. For more than a century government, banking and industry have collaborated in the building of a strong national economy. Before World War II a small clique of industrialists, bankers, bureaucrats and military officers controlled the economy and the nation. It was only through keeping the Japanese people on very short rations that they were able to manage the conquest of much of China and all of southeast Asia.

The Japanese economy was completely mobilized for war before the attack on Pearl Harbor, but it was unable to produce the amount of weaponry turned out by the Germans. It was systematically starved of oil and raw materials by the American submarine blockade and later totally wrecked by bombing.

Like the Germans, the Japanese rebuilt from scratch with American aid and constructed new ultra-modern production facilities. Government, banking and industry renewed their traditional cooperation, laying the groundwork for creation of the world's second biggest economy.

Japan has one of the largest per-capita incomes of the world, but the Japanese standard of living is considerably lower than that of the United States. Japanese save more of their income than do most other peoples. Moreover, the Japanese cost of living is one of the highest in the world.

It's said that the market value of the land in the Tokyo metropolitan area is so high that the U.S. government couldn't afford to buy it all. The price of houses is so high that Japanese banks are offering home buyers 100-year mortgages; with prices at today's high levels ordinary Japanese couldn't afford to buy homes otherwise. For their money they get few square meters of living space. These crowded conditions Americans and West Europeans would find most uncomfortable.

Food prices are tremendously high. Most Japanese consume Japanese rice, though rice from the United States and Thailand is much cheaper. The government discourages import of foreign rice so that Japanese rice farmers may retain their markets and continue to farm. Japanese beef is much more expensive than the imported American product, but imports of foreign beef are also discouraged.

Consumer products are marketed mainly in small "Mom and Pop" retail stores; Japanese law positively discourages the growth of large retail outlets. It's government policy to protect these small retail businesses so that their owners can continue to earn their livings as they're accustomed. The network of wholesalers and distributors supplying these small outlets helps to keep prices of such goods very high as middlemen are of course entitled to their profit.

Japanese work longer hours and have less holiday and vacation time than do Westerners. As workers they are less individualistic and work as much for their employer and their country as they do for themselves.

Government, banks, industrial corporations, and employees collaborate to insure the prosperity of "Japan, Inc." in today's world. It's difficult for Westerners to compete against such dedication.

Other far eastern economies. South Korea, Taiwan, Hong Kong and Singapore are experiencing immense economic growth. Hong Kong possesses perhaps the purest free market economy on earth; taxes are very low and government regulation is minimal. The other three lands possess more activist governments.

Wage levels are lower in these lands than they are in Japan and employees work longer hours. However, there are more individualism and competitive spirit there than in Japan, thus firms from these countries are able to cut into Japanese market shares around the world. Until their wage levels approach the Japanese, they will have a competitive advantage over their Oriental big brother in markets where size doesn't confer advantages.

Malaysia, Thailand, Indonesia and the Philippines lag behind the above-mentioned, but their economies are relatively prosperous. Burma stagnates in the genteel poverty generated by its Socialist rulers, while Vietnam refuses to abandon Marxist orthodoxy and breathe life into its economy.

Islamic economies. In the world of Islam a variety of economies exists.

First, there are the oil-based economies of the Middle East—Saudi Arabia, Qatar, the United Arab Emirates, Bahrein, Kuwait, Iraq, Iran and

Libya. The former quintet are conservativve lands of the Arabian peninsula where governments seek to maintain the traditional style of relationships between rulers and ruled while using oil revenues to selectively modernize their domains. (Iraqi destruction of Kuwaiti oil wells will deprive Kuwait of substantial oil revenues for several years.) Iraq, Iran and Libya have relatively large, somewhat educated populations and use much of their oil revenues to maintain well-equipped armies and air forces. Iran and Iraq financed years of very costly modern warfare from oil sales; Libya too maintains huge armed forces while fomenting terrorism around the world. "Arab socialism" prevails in Iraq and Libya, modernity with a slight Islamic leavening in Bahrein, and Islamic fundamentalism in the others (though the meaning of the term varies from country to country; Saudi fundamentalism is as different from the Iranian brand as night is from day).

Second, there are the quasi–Western economies of modernized nations such as Egypt, Turkey, and Tunisia. There is no commitment to the pure free market in any of these lands; in all of them rulers have used socialist rhetoric during the last 40 years. All three of these lands are relatively prosperous and devoted to free market principles.

Third come the lesser-developed lands such as Morocco, Jordan and Pakistan. Lack of oil and slower modernization keep these lands poorer than the rich, but much richer than the very poor.

Algeria has been the most socialist of the oil lands; its private sector is relatively small.

Syria is the mightiest non-oil power of the Middle East. Its economy is under the stringent control of the government which maintains one of the most powerful of Islamic armies.

Lebanon, partially Islamic, had the most free economy in the Middle East before civil war tore the country apart. Its economy barely functions today.

Albania languishes under Marxism-Leninism, the poorest of European countries. That part of Afghanistan controlled by the government in Kabul does likewise; in areas controlled by the rebels a Third World economy prevails.

Several Islamic lands are among the poorest of the Third World. Included here are Bangladesh, Sudan, Mali, Niger, Mauretania, Djibouti, Somalia, Yemen, and Oman.

In the world of Islam, traditional economic notions hinder the westernization of some national economies but could fuel the growth of a unique economic order.

The Islamic holy scriptures forbid the practice of Riba, which is usually, though loosely, translated as usury. Riba isn't only lending money at too high a rate of interest, however—any lending of money at interest is theoretically forbidden.

To literally abide by this injunction would make Western-style banking in Islamic lands impossible, because Western banking is based upon paying and collecting interest. However, in several Muslim lands Islamic banks have been created which try to do business without paying or collecting interest.

It's done by making depositors co-owners of the bank, while the bank becomes a co-owner of the business of its borrower. The return earned by the depositor on his deposit is a share of the profit (if any) earned by the bank. The return earned by the bank on its loans is a share (if any) of the profit earned by the borrower's enterprise.

These banks finance consumer purchases by buying what the consumer desires from a supplier for cash and then reselling it to their customer at a higher price. The bank retains title to the merchandise until the customer pays off his debt in full; if he does not the bank retains the payments he made and repossesses what was sold.

The Islamic scriptures also forbid the practice of Gharar loosely defined as gambling. Again, the true meaning of the term is broader than that; no Muslim should enter into a contract the performance of which could be influenced by the unexpected or the unforeseen. Thus, all sales should be cash sales in which goods and price change hands simultaneously.

Contracts to be performed in the future are Gharar, because the thing to be sold might be damaged or destroyed, one of the parties could die, or whatever. Any purchase of an item with intent to sell it in the future for a higher price is Gharar, because this is speculation, a form of gambling. Insuring against a risk is Gharar, because the insured wagers with the insurance company that the peril insured against will happen.

Certain transactions are Haram—forbidden by spiritual law. Included here are the purchase and sale of hogs or the products of hogs, of alcoholic beverages, or of musical instruments or other forbidden items.

In nations such as Saudi Arabia where Islamic fundamentalism is enshrined in the national law, the economy operates without Riba, Gharar or Haram transactions. The forbidding of such lends a unique flavor to these economies.

Believers in Islam say that the faith holds the potential for creating the most just and prosperous economies the world has known. Islamic concern for the poor and helpless mitigates the capitalist drive to concentrate only on the acquisition of wealth, while Islamic belief that the producer is entitled to the fruits of his or her enterprise without government interference encourages private initiative. The problem is that no Islamic nation until now has had both the capital and the management expertise to create a really modern economy.

Non-Islamic Afro-Asian economies. In the Third World economic philosophy varies greatly from nation to nation. Immense poverty reigns almost everywhere. In India and Sri Lanka a mixture of the free market and socialism prevails. In nations like the Republic of the Congo, the People's Republic of

Benin, Ethiopia, Angola, Mozambique, the Cape Verde Islands and Guinea quasi–Marxism-Leninism stifles economic development. In Tanzania and Zambia non–Marxian Socialists rigidly control the nation's economy, while the Ivory Coast has become one of the most prosperous nations of sub–Saharan Africa by encouraging foreign investment in its economy.

There are as many economic climates in the Third World as there are nations; because of the political instability in so much of the region the economic climate can change as rapidly as the unpredictable tropical weather.

Latin-American economies. Some of the most prosperous Third World nations are found in the Western Hemisphere, as are some of the poorest. Mexico, Venezuela, Brazil, Argentina, Uruguay and Chile are relatively prosperous. (Though Mexico, Brazil and Argentina have huge foreign debts and are plagued by inflation, free market spirit is strongest in Brazil and Venezuela and weakest in Argentina and Mexico.)

Among the very poor nations of the world are Haiti, Guatemala, Honduras, Guyana, Suriname, Paraguay and Bolivia. Guyana and Suriname proclaim themselves to be socialist. The others survive with pockets of more or less free market prosperity in their cities and primitive subsistence in the countryside.

In between are nations such as Costa Rica, Trinidad and Tobago, the Dominican Republic, Jamaica, Colombia, Ecuador, Panama, El Salvador and Peru. Trinidad and Tobago claims to be socialist, the others do not. Nowhere does anything like an unrestricted free market prevail.

Summary. For the moment the free market American-style seems to have won its struggle against the Marxist command economy. However, its struggle against the Japanese cooperative economy may have just begun.

Is it better to develop our unique Western strengths in this competition to come, or should we strive to be more Japanese than the Japanese? Considering the great differences between the two cultures, the best answer would seem to be to emphasize our own economic virtues. Whether or not we'll manage to do it is another question.

For now the huge majority of Third World governments do not promote free market economics. Since the cultures of these poverty-stricken lands don't emphasize the work ethic as the north European and Chinese cultures do, this is not surprising. Yet the only viable, quick route to increased prosperity seems to be that followed by South Korea, Taiwan, Hong Kong and Singapore: Set free the ingenuity and acquisitive instincts of the people; encourage them to do the work which will create economic development and prosperity.

Chapter 15
The Future

The revolutionary events of 1989 and 1990 have conjured up new visions of freedom, peace and prosperity for the world. The superpower competition may become less strenuous and the split between the First World and the Second may be healed. The Pope's vision of a Europe united culturally and spiritually from the Atlantic to the Urals is many steps closer to fulfillment.

Partial disarmament may release more economic resources for the struggle to better the lot of mankind. The dismantling of the Marxist-Leninist command economies and the freeing-up of the genius of millions of ordinary human beings to do their economic thing may well greatly increase the prosperity of our planet.

Yet we must not let our relief at the apparent demise of Marxism-Leninism lead us to believe that Utopia lies just around the corner. The Iraqi occupation of Kuwait and the hi-tech war it conjured up indicate too well that peace on earth with goodwill toward all men and women lies far down the pike. Let's speculate as to what the twenty-first century might bring.

Present Trends

Racial mingling. Mobility is causing an unprecedented mingling of human bloodlines. The homogeneity of human populations diminishes everywhere on earth, particularly in the industrialized lands of Western culture. There are more Hispanics and Asians in the United States, more Arabic-speaking and black persons in France, more Turks in Germany, more foreign workers of all kinds in Sweden, more Asians in Australia, more south Asians and Orientals in the Arabian peninsula, than ever before.

The trend will continue. There is no evidence that the low Western birthrate will rise in the near future; with us children are and will continue to be economic (and in the minds of some of us personal) liabilities. The median age of Western populations slowly rises and the number of working people supporting each pensioner inexorably declines. Today's labor surpluses in the West

302

may become tomorrow's labor shortages and tomorrow's Westerners may welcome vigorous Third World immigrants to help do the necessary work and to pay the taxes needed to support the ever more numerous retirees.

On the other hand birthrates in Third World lands as yet unsaturated by Western culture remain high, industrial development remains limited, unemployment is astronomic. These lands can be, and some are, massive exporters of labor. The future supply of large numbers of ambitious young people will be found in the Third World. The future demand for human brains and brawn will center in the First. Hence the mingling of the races can only accelerate.

Cultural futures. Western culture continues to dominate the planet and to threaten other cultures with modification or extinction. There are no indications that this trend will reverse itself. Wherever radio, television and motion picture theaters are found (except where stringent government censorship exists) people are deluged with the sights and sounds of our culture. The mighty seductive power of Western gadgetry and individualism is difficult to resist.

For the most part we Westerners remain the masters of technology, controlling the pace of the planet's material advancement. With the progress being made in certain areas of biology we may even acquire the capacity to control the future evolution of the human race through genetic engineering.

The coming acceleration of racial intermingling described above will hasten the triumph of Western culture; already Third World Gastarbeiter don't feel at home in their native lands when they return from Germany or Great Britain or the United States. After knowing the individual freedom of the West they spiritually smother in the confines of their traditional culture. Western individualism is a heady brew. Once sipped, it changes the imbiber forever.

The only challengers to the West on today's horizon are the Japanese. If they are able to retain their cooperative approach to economic activity they'll at least hold their own in the cultural and economic competition of the twenty-first century. But the enticing power of Western do-your-thingism isn't lost upon some younger Japanese, particularly those who go abroad as children and live for a spell in a Western country; it may well be that even in Japan individualism will triumph. If it does, however, we can bet that it will be modified to suit Japanese conditions.

Language. As Western culture and technology bind the peoples of the world ever closer together, most of the world's languages will become outmoded and will disappear.

This has already happened to many Amerindian and Australian aboriginal languages, and even to European languages such as the Cornish once spoken in Cornwall (extreme southwest England) and the Manx once spoken on the Isle of Man.

If there is ever to be a lingua franca of the world spoken by all educated persons English is the leading candidate. It's already the language of the world's air traffic controllers, and the leading business language. Its grammatical simplicity makes it easy to learn although if we could somehow reform its spelling we'd make it much easier.

However, the languages spoken by hundreds of thousands of people are not going to disappear. All over the world linguistic minorities of any size exert great efforts to preserve their ancient speech. There is linguistic diversity in most of the nations of the world; as racial homogeneity of a nation becomes diluted linguistic homogeneity suffers the same fate. (For some purposes Spanish is already an official language in the United States. Public notices on many subjects appear in both English and Spanish in California, Texas and other states with large Hispanic populations.)

Never will all or even most of the world's educated people speak English with the fluency of a person reared in an English-speaking family. The number of people who speak English will rise spectacularly during the twenty-first century, but that will not excuse Americans and other English speakers from studying other languages. The basic fact won't change, that we can't truly understand a person of another culture unless we speak his or her language fluently.

Religion. To an extent the influence of Christianity has expanded as that of Western culture has, but the culture has far more influence than the religion. The most successful Christian missionaries these days are fundamentalist Protestants and Roman Catholics. The number of Christians in countries of non–Western culture grows as their number in Western lands shrinks.

The basic dilemma facing today's Western Christians is: shall we try through political and social action to restore Christian principles to the culture (and risk a backlash from anti-clericals), or do we leave the culture as is and seek to adapt to it (abandoning some traditional notions in the process)? To my knowledge the United States is the only country in which Christians have attempted the first approach on a large scale although their success has been minimal. The fundamentalists have reached only the already converted. Concerted political evangelism only turns off the uncommitted and turns on vocal opposition (especially when such evangelism is accompanied by personal and financial corruption on the part of some ministers).

Mainstream Protestant denominations have for the most part done the second, accepting abortion on demand, easy divorce, abolition of prayer in public schools and the like. The Roman Catholic Church is split on the issue; the Vatican hierarchy resists the second approach while modernists favor it. The majority of practicing Catholics in the U.S. and northern Europe would probably support the modernists.

Since the Western mood is materialistic, anti-moralistic and individualistic, the first approach seems doomed to failure. The second guarantees denominational survival, perhaps, but little more. In the absence of a moral revival among Westerners—which doesn't seem to be in the cards at the moment—Christian influence seems bound to diminish in our culture.

The religion which is least threatened by Western cultural developments is Islam. Islamic missionaries enjoy success everywhere on earth and rarely do Muslims convert to another faith.

As stated earlier, Islam in theory governs every aspect of the Muslim's life; it's a total belief system. The maxim, "Render unto Caesar that which is Caesar's and unto God that which is God's" has no place in it. Islam offers a theology that everyone can grasp—"There is no God but God, Mohammed is his prophet." It offers a complete blueprint for the ideal society and the ideal personal life and eternity in Paradise to the dedicated true believer. In short, it offers total certainty and security.

The popularity of Islamic fundamentalism stirs conflicting emotions in conservative Western breasts. On the one hand it's good that there are forces that successfully oppose the crass materialism of our popular culture, but on the other hand the social objectives of Islamic fundamentalism are far removed from those of fundamentalist Christians. Prohibition of alcoholic beverages and gambling may be good things, but how about segregation of women or amputation of the thief's right hand?

Fundamentalist Protestants may joyfully devote their lives to the cause of the Faith as they understand it but most other Christians will not. The fact that large numbers of Muslims will do as our Protestants do in the cause of a religious belief of which we have little understanding and for which we have no sympathy we find almost incomprehensible.

Hinduism will adapt to the twenty-first century as it has to all others; its great diversity will continue to protect it through thick and thin. Buddhism will do likewise. Both Eastern religions may in fact expand their influence in the Western world. Through them Western spiritual rebels may obey the command of Timothy Leary: turn on, tune in, drop out—abandoning a materialistic culture they find stifling to embrace a more human (to them) system of belief.

Family, marriage, gender, children. What will transpire with the family and marriage in the world will depend to an extent upon the road Western culture follows in these areas. Some Westerners despise both as obstacles to the realization of human individuality: how can I truly be myself when others dominate a portion of my life? Yet several axioms of human existence argue for the continuation of both institutions. These are:

(1) Human procreation is necessary in order to continue the species. We can't forego our own reproduction.

(2) The Western child requires at least 16 years of nurture before becoming self-sufficient.

(3) Human beings are gregarious creatures. Though we can't stand prolonged intimacy with our kind we can't stand much loneliness either.

(4) We can't always be totally self-sufficient. There are times (such as when we're ill) when we must be dependent upon someone else.

Some of us forget that the purpose of male-female association is, biologically speaking, reproduction. The individualist wants the pleasure of the association without the consequences (pregnancy, motherhood, sexually transmitted diseases). The pill has virtually eliminated the possibility of pregnancy for its users; abortion on demand eliminates undesired motherhood; penicillin and other wonder drugs have reduced the virulence of most STDs. Before the advent of the AIDS virus it appeared that any human being, male or female, could choose to live a life of unlimited libertinism without fear of unpleasant physical consequences. It's no wonder that the culture change made possible by these developments has been termed the Sexual Revolution. For the first time in human history harmless promiscuity seemed to be open to all.

The reality of AIDS has shattered the dream, postulating terrifying physical penalties for the indulgent; the great revolution has in a sense been cut short. It's no wonder that some people hysterically demand that society embark upon a crash program to find a vaccine and cure; the glorious revolution must not be strangled in its cradle. (The fact that the sexually continent and those married couples who don't indulge in extra-marital affairs are least likely to get AIDS is to these people irrelevant. AIDS research and treatment hold out hope to the supporters of the revolution—a true cure may yet be found.)

We also forget that the biological purpose for the existence of female creatures is motherhood. Most are programmed with an almost irresistible desire for it. The average woman feels that her life will be wasted if she doesn't become a mother. The logic of this biological programming is most apparent in this age; if adult human beings followed the dictates of pure reason today many would not reproduce. Child rearing is so confining and so expensive in a time like ours! Hence our present low birthrate. If women's biological programming wasn't so powerful it would be much lower.

We can't escape Schopenhauer's Porcupine Dilemma in this life. We're covered with sharp psychic quills and the closer we cuddle to another person, the more likely it is that we'll prick him and he'll prick us and the relationship will become occasionally painful. In order to get rid of the pain we want to shed the partner. Yet because of our gregariousness we've got to find someone to cuddle up to, preferably someone of the opposite sex. Serial polygamy—semi-permanent marriage with the right to change partners on occasion—is one solution. Free love—changing partners as one changes shirts or blouses—is another. So long as this can be managed without reproduction there are no major problems. Once children are born, though, it becomes a different game. You can't cast off a child as you can an adult partner who bores or irritates you. Who takes the responsibility for rearing the kids? Who pays the bills?

It's now theoretically possible for reproduction and childrearing to be separated from everyday human life. Test-tube babies (embryos created through the fertilization of human eggs outside a human body) are a reality. At present such an embryo can live for only a few days if not implanted in a human womb. Science seeks to extend the potential in vitro life of such embryos; the inhuman baby hatcheries of Huxley's *Brave New World* have come several steps closer to reality.

We now know that parthenogenesis—the development of a human egg into a living embryo without fertilization by sperm—is possible. Should this become practicable on a large scale the male half of the race will become biologically useless.

Another dream that's on the way to becoming a reality is cloning—the production of a duplicate of a living creature from one of its cells. This has been done with plants and lower forms of animal life. So far no warm-blooded creature has been duplicated in this way, but it's certainly not impossible.

Thus, continuation of the existence of the human species outside the reproductive system nature devised looms upon the horizon, but until these potential biological techniques come into common use we'll still have to conceive and rear our own young.

Today commitment to careers stands in the way of commitment to rearing children. Many parents farm out child-care chores to others: babysitters, grandparents, day-care centers, schools and the like. Children and parents can become strangers to each other. As more mothers enter the workforce this practice will increase.

If there's no real commitment between partners, why should they care for each other in sickness, especially if the sickness is chronic or permanent?

Some say—let the state or private nursing homes care for the sick and disabled. Life's too short to impose such responsibilities upon other people. As a result, dependent people are cared for by overworked, underpaid bureaucratic-minded employees who treat their charges at best as ciphers and at worst as demanding nuisances. (In this age where can we find large numbers of truly loving people who will devote their lives to caring for dependent strangers for pay?)

Thus, it seems that we can't do without either family or marriage unless we want to utterly dehumanize our collective existence.

We Westerners will do our best to marry the concept of women's liberation to those of marriage and family. It's already apparent that the only way a woman can attain complete independence is by foregoing motherhood—which more and more Western women do (some at the cost of eternal yearning for the children that never were). The demands of biology won't permit the great majority of women to do so, so they try to combine career and motherhood. We haven't found any ideal way for women to accomplish this; perhaps we can do better in the twenty-first century.

Whatever we do on that front, the cause of women's liberation will continue to prosper as the influence of Western culture penetrates to the remote corners of the planet. Modern education on the one hand and the notion that the only fitting role for women is motherhood and submission to men on the other are not compatible.

The spread of urbanization and compulsory education also insures that children become economic liabilities rather than economic assets; this makes declining birthrates a certainty as economic development progresses. Thus there will be less mothering done in many areas during the twenty-first century.

States and government forms. There has been an amazing proliferation of independent states during the twentieth century. The odds favor a continuance of the trend, though a reversal isn't out of the question.

There are several more potential nations out there waiting to be born. Sentiment exists in some European dependencies for independence, particularly on the French Pacific island of New Caledonia. Other possibilities are the British West Indian islands of Anguilla and Montserrat, the Netherlands Antilles and French Polynesia.

It's quite possible that Lithuania, Latvia and Estonia will be allowed to secede from the Soviet Union and regain the independence they lost in 1940. Less likely, but not impossible, would be the secession of the Soviet republics of Georgia, Armenia and Azerbaijan. One could even imagine the USSR coming apart at the seams as Austria-Hungary did in 1918, with the Ukraine, Byelorussia and the Islamic republics of Central Asia becoming independent states.

As the ties holding Yugoslavia together become more and more strained, it too may well splinter into its component parts. There may be independent republics of Slovenia, Croatia and Serbia some day soon.

Israeli occupation of the West Bank of the Jordan can probably not endure forever. The time for the birth of an independent Palestinian state draws nearer.

Once again Scots agitate for some sort of separation from England; one day the Act of Union of 1707 may be repealed and the St. Andrew's Cross flag might again fly over an independent Scotland.

The desire for independence hasn't died in many Quebec hearts; the failure of the Meech Lake Accords in Canada has caused agitation for "Quebec Libre" to rise again.

If and when the status of Puerto Rico as a United States commonwealth ends, it's possible that it could be spun off as an independent republic.

On the other hand the European Community may well evolve into a United States of Europe, its 12 members becoming states in a federal union. If the west Europeans take such a plunge, other regional federations (such as a union of the Central American republics) might take place.

Democracy marches forward all over the world as many peoples demand the power to rule themselves. Is this democratization permanent, or a mere passing phase? It's too early to tell. If Mikhail Gorbachev doesn't reverse his Glasnost policy (or he isn't overthrown by vindictive Communist hardliners); if Latin American armies remain in their barracks; if Corazon Aquino doesn't become a coup victim; and if Islamic fundamentalists don't take power in any Arabic-speaking country the prognostication for expansion of democracy remains favorable. It would also help if the leadership of China returns to a policy of liberalization.

The power of many African dictators remains unchallenged, though Samuel Doe of Liberia and Siad Barre of Somalia are gone and Colonel Mengistu is on the ropes in Ethiopia. Iraq's Saddam Hussein belonged upon that list until he ordered the Iraqi army into Kuwait; it's possible that this move will precipitate his downfall but he may also emerge from the crisis stronger than ever.

The gun retains its political power over much of the world.

Human rights. The end of Communist dictatorship in Eastern Europe is a great step forward in the battle for human rights. However, the struggle is far from won.

Genocide may again raise its ugly head. Tutsi and Hutu may have another go at each other in Rwanda or Burundi. The Bengalis of Bangladesh still covet land in the Chittagong Hill Tracts. The clearing of the Amazon rain forests still threatens the future existence of Brazilian Indians.

Mass death still runs rampant in Ethiopia and Sudan with no end in sight in either unhappy country. Discrimination of one kind or another exists in more places than one can count. Human beings don't seem ready to treat each other as members of one family.

Economic systems. Through the collapse of the command economies of eastern Europe the free market has seemingly won its battle against Marxism-Leninism. The winning ideology is not the pure ideology of Adam Smith, but Smith combined with a sizable shot of democratic socialism. Aside from places like Hong Kong, the purest sort of free market is found in today's United States, but even here the admixture of government intervention is great.

Though Ronald Reagan spoke of restoring the pristine free market in this country he wasn't very successful. During the 1980s Americans voted conservative for president and liberal for Congress. We wanted the benefits of the free market (low regulation and low taxes) but we also wanted to keep the benefits of the welfare state (Social Security, Medicare, government-insured student loans and Small Business Administration business loans). In America only the Libertarian Party believes in a totally free economy; its presidential candidate, Ron Paul, polled 432,179 votes in 1988 (about one half of one percent of the total popular vote, finishing in third place).

A restoration of the free market of the 1920s seems out of the question; what is more likely is an expansion of government regulation (re-regulation of airlines, public health insurance, mandatory maternity leave for employees, strengthened anti-discrimination legislation and higher taxes).

In Western Europe the relatively free market combined with a comprehensive welfare state seems likely to continue. European socialists have lost their taste for nationalizations and the management of large public sectors within their economies.

Eastern Europeans want to keep most of the Communist welfare state in place after they've eliminated their command economies. Free medical care, guaranteed employment and low-cost housing are after all valuable benefits, even when medical care is of low quality, pay is low and housing is crowded.

Objections to the free market are still heard, even in the U.S. and Western Europe. People all over the world question the ethics of businessmen. The ideological objections to economic activity raised by the medieval church still seem to have validity; seeking to maximize profit equals avarice in the minds of many Christians.

The very nature of a free market guarantees conflict with religious ethical systems. In business as in life, survival is the first law of nature. Insolvency — inability to pay debts as they mature — is death for a business and the only way to avoid insolvency is to earn a profit.

The prevailing wisdom of the market says that if you build a better mousetrap the world will beat a path to your door and you will prosper. But what you do well today a competitor may do better tomorrow. In a competitive market you never have it made; you don't dare rest upon your laurels.

The best way to assure a profit is to produce and sell a product that market participants will buy — but what if your competitors sell equally good products and your profits begin to fall? How do you stop the decline? Do you:

Design a better product through use of your own resources?

Spy on your competitors in any way you can to learn why their products are better?

Copy your competitor's product, at the risk of infringing upon his patent rights?

Promote your product through half-true advertising that exaggerates its virtues?

Reduce the quality of the product and the coverage of its warranty to cut production and repair costs?

Lay off some of your employees to cut labor costs, though you know they'll have problems finding other jobs?

Some businesspeople facing such a problem will act in accordance with the ethical systems they use in their personal lives, doing nothing that's even slightly dishonest, nothing that would cause harm to others. But others will do what they feel they must in order to preserve their investment, furnishing ammunition to the anti-free marketers.

Some compare the competitiveness of business in a free market economy to war, claiming that one can and should apply the ethics of war to business conflict. Those who follow this line of thinking hold that one must let nothing stand in the way of victory—morality, human beings, competitors or whatever.

Others hold that business is like a poker game; you never tell the truth about your situation except where it will benefit you. Bluffing and outright lying are acceptable and the only rule of combat is that the survivor with the best hand wins. Thus, the free market comes across as callous and heartless.

The fact that free-market economies boom and bust disturbs opponents of the system. To be sure, in boom times there are plenty of jobs and everyone lives well. But the boom time is the time of the speculator, the gambler who wagers borrowed money on potential rises in the price of land, stock or commodities. "Why should someone who produces nothing get rich through gambling?" ask many non-speculators. "There's something wrong with a system that makes this possible!" they thunder.

In bust times there are few jobs and little money. Many an ex-employee suffers because of the ill-fortune of the ex-employer. Ordinary creditors and shareholders of failed businesses lose 100 percent of their claims against and investments in the failed business while the bankers who hold mortgages on solid firm assets collect almost 100 percent of theirs, the critics grumble.

In boom times, "them that has, gets," they continue. The rich get richer while everyone else progresses just a little or breaks even. "Them that has keeps in bust times; it's the little guy who gets wiped out, who never gets anything out of the rotten system!" critics bellow.

There is some validity to these oversimplified complaints, of course. Some business people aren't particularly honest or ethical, but the same can be said of lawyers, doctors, ministers, athletes, politicians, husbands, wives, children, professors, students, or any other class of human beings one can mention. The failing is a human failing, not just one of business people or of the free market.

It's true that speculators get rich in boom times, and that the rich get richer. The complainers forget that the general standard of living within a free market economy rises during these times; it truly isn't only the big guy who benefits. On the other hand, the rich may well benefit more than anyone else.

It's also true that the little guy hurts more in bust times. But critics forget that there's no such thing as absolute security in this world; nobody, but nobody, has it permanently made. No economy guarantees absolute security, that no one will suffer, or that everyone who participates in it will be treated equally.

The rule that "Them that has, gets" applies just as much in the command economy as it does in the free market. In the free market, those who have and get are the rich; in the command economy they are the members of the Nomenklatura—the party bigwigs.

It's theoretically possible that the command economy could create a society of economic equality. The economy of Mao's China perhaps came closest to attaining that objective; even the members of the Nomenklatura had to perform manual labor every year so that they'd remember how the other half makes a living, and the pay differentials between supervisor and supervised were small. However, the equality that emerged was the equality of relative poverty. Mao's successors had to eliminate equality to attain economic growth and they succeeded.

The conclusion must be this: The free market is an imperfect economic system, because in some ways it encourages rather disreputable behavior by some participants, and it guarantees security to no one. Horrible as its critics say it is, no one has devised a system that works better. In fact, the performance of the alternatives has been much worse.

The World Ecological Crisis

The greatest threat faced by the triumphant free market will be the planet's ecological crisis. The components of the crisis are in a sense legion— rapidly growing world population, food shortages, expansion of deserts, loss of topsoil to wind and water erosion, the greenhouse effect (gradually warming climate), acid rain, smog, proliferating solid waste, water pollution, extinction of endangered wildlife species—the list goes on and on.

Some say that there is no crisis and, even if there is, we can adapt to it without changing our style of life (by eating synthetic foods, learning to adapt to more crowded living quarters, living and working in hermetically sealed buildings to keep out the smog—and as to the endangered animal species, who needs them anyway?). Believers in this point of view possess political clout though the facts aren't on their side.

Some aspects of the crisis are not caused by human economic activity; the growth in world population, for instance, is a product of the success of Western culture in lowering the human death rate. Desert expansion, loss of fertile topsoil to erosion and the like are caused by human agricultural activity, much of which is conducted by farmers and herders living in subsistence economies.

The United States was one of the first nations to become concerned about these problems; in response it has enacted probably the most stringent environmental protection legislation of any country on earth. Yet the problems are still as severe here as anywhere else, due in large part to our massive industrial production.

Air pollution. Industrial processes that emit smoke and vapor into the air are in part responsible for air pollution. The exhaust emissions of motor vehicles and aircraft are also contributing factors, as are gases emitted into the atmosphere from aerosol cans. Among the unpleasant results of air pollution are:

(1) Smog in the world's large cities, from Mexico City to Tokyo to Paris to Los Angeles.

(2) The killing of forests, to an extent in the United States, to a greater extent in Europe.

(3) The falling of acid rain, the killer of forests and sterilizer of lakes.

(4) The slow destruction of architectural masterpieces by corrosive atmospheric gases produced by smog (The Parthenon in Athens and Notre Dame in Paris among others).

(5) Damage to the ozone layer of the earth's atmosphere, allowing more of the sun's ultra-violet radiation to reach earth's surface, which will cause an increase in skin cancer and other evils.

(6) Accumulation of carbon dioxide in the earth's atmosphere, which may produce a "greenhouse effect" appreciably raising the earth's surface temperature and changing the climate of many areas (and also reducing the size of the earth's ice caps, raising the levels of the oceans and permanently flooding low-lying areas).

Air pollution by industry has been reduced in some developed countries by law and regulation; reduction of pollutant emissions by automobiles is proving an almost intractable problem.

Water pollution. Industrial producers create water pollution by dumping liquid wastes into the nearest stream. Other contributors are municipalities which discharge sewage into waterways, farmers (through overuse of chemical fertilizers and insecticides carried into streams by rainwater and irrigation water), feed lot owners (through dumping of animal wastes) and oil companies (through various sorts of oil spills).

Among the results are:

(1) Pollution of human and animal drinking water.

(2) Eutrophication of streams and lakes, depriving their living creatures of oxygen and thus killing them.

(3) Causing aquatic animals used by us for food (fish, shrimp, oysters and the like) to absorb toxins into their tissues, making them unfit for human consumption.

(4) Destruction of shoreline environments.

Deliberate industrial and municipal pollution of streams has been reduced by law and regulation in developed countries, but it still occurs. Accidents are now the worst culprits in this area.

Noise pollution. The amount of noise produced by modern society is literally nerve-wracking and sometimes deafening. Those who live or work near a busy city street are assailed by the racket of automobiles, motorcycles, emergency vehicle sirens, giant trucks and the like. The screech of jet aircraft engines plagues those who live or work near airports. A variety of noisy machinery thunders and hammers and screeches away on construction sites and inside factories. Even in offices the buzzing of telephones and the chatter of computer printers can be annoying. Silence becomes more and more golden.

Noise produces stress which produces nervous disorders and other physical complaints. Excessive noise can damage one's hearing. A less noisy world would be a more relaxed, healthy world.

Toxic wastes. Toxic waste disposal has become a great problem. Some industries produce large quantities of such wastes. When it was impractical to dump such into flowing streams, the cheapest solution to the disposal problem was to put the stuff into metal drums or the like and bury it, applying the hoary maxim, "Out of sight, out of mind."

The difficulty is that the buried waste doesn't remain out of sight. Steel drums and other such containers don't have eternal life. They rust or burst and their contents escape, poisoning subsoil and ground water. Result: people and animals too close to the polluted soil and water develop cancer and horrific forms of chemical poisoning (as did residents of the Love Canal area in New York State). The poisoned area must be closed off; steps must be taken to cleanse the soil and remove the wastes, a terribly expensive process.

One solution is the construction of waste disposal areas where the poisons are stored and treated in an effective manner. The establishment of these is almost inevitably bitterly resisted by residents of the area. No one wants an assemblage of potentially deadly toxins for a neighbor.

Toxins on the job. The use of toxic substances in industrial production is another problem. Fifty years ago no one knew that asbestos fibers can cause lung cancer when inhaled; asbestos was a common insulation material. The world is just now learning of its error as large numbers of former asbestos workers become cancer patients. Lead is another producer of occupational disease. How many other unsuspected carcinogens and other sorts of toxins may be in use in our workplaces?

Nuclear pollution. The use of nuclear power plants and nuclear weapons systems creates two pollution dangers: escape of radiation from a plant facility and of misdisposal of nuclear waste. Examples of the former are the Chernobyl disaster in the Soviet Union and the Three Mile Island affair in the United States. The nuclear waste problem stems from the presence of spent fuel rods and other forms of waste in power plants. These will emit very highly dangerous levels of radiation for tens of thousands of years. Where can such materials be stored so that they'll remain undisturbed for so long a time period? When one considers the basic instability of the earth's crust one suspects that the true answer is NOWHERE.

A nuclear accident can poison wide areas and massive numbers of people. The consequences—poisoned land, birth of deformed children, a rising incidence of cancer—could endure for decades if not centuries.

Nuclear problems are caused by governments in most of the world, not by private industry; most nations do not permit private industry to operate nuclear facilities. The U.S. is the major exception. Most nuclear power plants here are owned and operated by private power companies under the supervision of the Nuclear Regulatory Commission. The private firms are primarily responsible for accidents, though they're insured by the federal government.

Solid non-toxic waste. Solid non-toxic waste is another problem. Western society — particularly the American variant — has become the throw-away society. The packing and packaging materials, diapers, food scraps, worn-out artifacts and wrecked motor vehicles that we discard every day create tremendous problems. What do we do with all of this stuff?

We used to burn what was inflammable and bury the rest. This isn't as viable a solution as it used to be since the burning creates air pollution and we don't have the space for burying that we once had. Before the age of plastics much garbage was biodegradable; it would become part of the soil some time after burial. Plastics though are not bio-degradable, remaining where buried forever.

Though local government assumes the responsibility for disposing of the mountains of garbage generated by Americans every day, the free market is in part responsible for producing it. Many products are fancily presented for marketing purposes in attractive but excessive packaging. In the name of efficiency most beverages are marketed in throw-away containers because it's cheaper to use a container once than it is to collect and re-use those already existing. We produce scads of use-and-throw-away products: diapers, razors, pens and paper towels, to name a few. We've even talked of marketing paper throw-away clothing.

We're running out of landfill space near our big cities. What do we do with the garbage when such surplus land is gone? Recycling is an obvious answer, but as mentioned above in the context of beverage containers, throwing away is easier (and cheaper). There are consumer costs involved in encouragement of recycling (container deposits, for instance); there are labor costs in collecting materials to be recycled; there are freight costs to move them to recycling plants. Somehow we must overcome such economic disincentives.

Logging. Logging operations destroy ecosystems, causing the death of many wild creatures. They also expose the topsoil of logged-over areas, encouraging massive soil erosion. When care is taken not to disturb the plant cover of the soil, erosion damage is minimized; when the area is immediately replanted in trees, the forest will eventually regenerate.

When forest clearance is undertaken to claim new land for agriculture or ranching, horrendous environmental damage can ensue. Forest soils may not be fit for agriculture or grassland. When exposed to sun and rain they may lose their fertility and the landscape becomes desert. When huge areas are denuded of forest cover (as occurs in Brazil, Indonesia and central Africa) the very climate may be altered. The photosynthesis conducted by the leaves of forest plants removes carbon dioxide from the atmosphere, replacing it with oxygen and water vapor. Clearing the forest reduces the recycling of the carbon dioxide and retards the liberation of oxygen and water vapor. Thus the atmosphere becomes drier and more capable of retaining heat.

Agriculture. Irrigation of agricultural land in formerly desert areas (which is done by both small farmers and big agribusiness in places like California's Imperial Valley) can result in salinization of the soil, rendering it virtually unfit for agriculture for centuries to come. The irrigation water soaks the soil to a considerable depth, dissolving subsurface minerals. As the surface water evaporates the lower-lying water rises to the surface bringing the dissolved minerals along. As this evaporates the minerals remain behind and the salt content of the soil increases as its fertility decreases.

Plowing up grassland for the growing of grain (as has been done by small farmers and agribusiness in areas like eastern Colorado and western Texas) leaves the soil open to wind erosion; small-scale replays of the Dust Bowl of the 1930s have recently occurred in these areas. If the current tendency toward summer drought there continues, wind erosion will get worse.

Mining. Strip mining and placer mining can change the very contour of the mined land. Spoil banks can render the land unsightly and change drainage patterns. Moreover, fertile topsoil may be buried under heaps of infertile subsoil, destroying the fertility of the area. Loose subsoil is very likely to wash away in storms, polluting watercourses downstream.

Use of pesticides. Plants that provide food for us can be eaten by other animal species (such as corn borers and grasshoppers). Food stored by us may be eaten by other animals (mice and rats), or rendered inedible by molds and other fungi. Unwanted animals (moles and gophers), insects (ants, termites and cockroaches) and plants (thistles, crabgrass) continually invade our farms, gardens, yards and houses. We have devised a myriad of chemical weapons for use against the intruders—insecticides, herbicides, fungicides, rodenticides and others. Though this weaponry may control the enemy pest for the short term, its undesirable long-term side effects are two in number.

First, the poisons don't kill only the intended victims. Insecticides may kill valuable insect species (bumblebees, honeybees, ladybugs) along with grasshoppers and boll weevils. Furthermore they may accumulate in the tissues of animals which feed upon affected insects (fish, birds) and either kill them or interfere with their reproduction. Herbicides may be poisonous to animals (including people!) as well as to undesired plants. The residues of fungicides and rodenticides applied near stored human and animal food may render the saved foodstuff poisonous or carcinogenic to its intended consumer.

Second, insecticides select for their own failure. The life span of most insects is very short (sometimes less than a year); during a human generation 30 to 50 insect generations may be born and die. No insecticide will be fatal to all members of a species dosed with it and inevitably some individuals will prove immune to it. The susceptible ones die in their millions and reproduce no more but the immune ones survive in their hundreds and continue to reproduce. Each new generation contains more immune individuals. Eventually (within a few years) the species has regenerated itself, immune to the toxin that slaughtered most of it. We must return to the drawing board to produce a new insecticide to which the pest is not yet immune.

Extinction of animal species. Commercial activity may result in the extermination or threatened extermination of animal species. Whaling has placed several varieties of that aquatic mammal in danger. Large-scale fishing has decimated the populations of several species of fish. The fur industry has caused some fur-bearing animals to become endangered. Private poaching threatens the African elephant and rhinocerous among other creatures. Destruction of natural habitat through deforestation, urbanization and the like puts others in jeopardy. Indiscriminate use of pesticides in some areas threatens still others.

Costs of pollution control. Pollution abatement is not a direct cost of production in most polluting industries. Economically speaking, the best way to dispose of pollutants is the cheapest way — send the gas up the chimney, dump the liquid pollutants into the river, bury the toxic waste in the nearby fields, do the same with the nuclear wastes.

Pollution abatement equipment is expensive; installing it may require massive capital expenditures. For some firms the costs may be unbearable, for others meeting them may require increases in the price of the product. For still others it may be a concealed blessing as the pollutant might be used to produce a byproduct which can be profitably sold.

Some of the excessive packaging placed on small products sold in self-service retail stores is intended to discourage shoplifters; this is a reaction to a cultural problem. On the other hand excessive packaging for marketing purposes, throw-away beverage containers and throw-away products themselves are all examples of the market thinking "profit" to the exclusion of all else.

The costs of logging and mining rise when the loggers and miners must restore the land they tear up in the course of their operations. It's cheapest to walk off and let the mess be; the labor and material costs of restoration can be immense.

To conduct whaling and fishing operations in such a way as to not threaten the existence of the harvested species is difficult. To cut back on operations may cost people their jobs and their livelihood.

Yet, to totally exterminate the species in question will cost all participants in the industry their jobs and their livelihood, permanently.

The market itself doesn't compel firms to engage in pollution abatement or to otherwise show concern for the environment. The ecologically aware manager may feel that he's a fool to spend money on pollution abatement when the competitors do not—if he increases his expenditures by so doing he may put himself and the firm at a competitive disadvantage. He decreases the profitability of the firm—a cardinal sin.

The compulsion here must come either from law or from the conscience of industrial managers. Actually, of course, the compulsion is applied by Mother Nature herself. If we do not stop our assault upon the environment, we'll render our planet uninhabitable and the question of profit will become irrelevant.

Opponents of the free market argue that since profitability and environmental protection are incompatible we can't trust the free market to end pollution; we need a type of economy in which government may command the obedience of industry and thus pollution abatement.

In theory a command economy devoted to environmental protection could very effectively eliminate industrial pollution. The question is, what sort of standard of living might such an economy produce?

The Marxist-Leninist command economies did a worse job of controlling pollution than did the free market economies. To Communists the name of the game was increased production, not profitability. No expenditure of money and effort was to be made upon projects that did not directly increase production. Pollution abatement does not immediately increase production, therefore it was an objective of small or no consequence. Therefore the level of environmental pollution in eastern Germany, Czechoslovakia, Poland and the Soviet Union is higher than that in western Germany, France or Great Britain.

The free market now has a clear field within which to strive to advance the well-being of humanity. Humanity may not long survive with its present standard of living (or survive at all!) unless it devises mechanisms to deal with the environmental crisis (existing or yet to come). Perhaps it can devise a way to turn inventive minds loose on solving environmental problems for profit. If it does not, its enemies will assail it with a virulence unknown to the twentieth century.

It and all of the cultures of humanity must bear in mind the lesson Garrett Hardin wrote of in *The Tragedy of the Commons,* and consider the truth of several axioms of ecology (and life itself) discussed by Hardin and by Barry Commoner in various works.

The sad inevitable fate of the commons. A commons is a resource—a tract of land, the earth's oceans, the earth's atmosphere—which has no owner but is open to all who desire to use it.

Hardin explained the fate of the commons this way. Assume a tract of pasture open to use by all cattle owners in a neighborhood; it's owned by them in common. No one cattleman is responsible for maintaining the tract. How may each of the co-owners get maximum benefit from the pasture?

In the long run, maximum benefit would flow from a cooperation agreement between the co-owners limiting grazing on the tract to that which the land can bear without permanent damage. The agreement will be of no value, however, unless all co-owners agree to it and abide by it. In the absence of this consensus, each co-owner will think short-term and crowd as many of his animals as possible onto the pasture.

This will of course destroy the usefulness of the land in the long term, but since in the absence of consensus the destruction is bound to happen why not get maximum benefit from the land while possible?

To use restraint in exploiting a commons is a losing strategy when others who have access to it will not do likewise. Grab what you can while the grabbing's still good is the most logical game plan; why should the other guys get the lion's share of the benefits?

This way of thinking may well result in the extinction of certain species of whales, as mentioned above. The whaling nations of the world know full well that this industry on the scale practiced in the last half-century will result in such extinction and that only restraint will preserve the hunted species. Yet Japan and the Soviet Union have not shown restraint, encouraging whalers of other nations to behave likewise. This commons faces almost certain destruction.

Human thinking must outgrow simple short-term economic logic if the commons of the planet are to be preserved. Even this may not save us from ecological catastrophe unless we pay more attention to the following axioms.

We cannot do nothing; not to act is to act. Often we take no action against a problem in the hope that it will solve itself and go away. Sometimes the strategy succeeds but more often it fails. Inaction preserves the status quo. If we do nothing to promote change something or someone else will. When the change happens, then, we have no control over its nature or course.

We cannot reduce environmental pollution by doing nothing. To refuse to act against it is to allow it to continue and get worse.

We can't do just one thing, everything affects everything else. Everything we do as societies or as individuals has consequences—some of them unforeseen. Every bargain we make for ourselves is a package deal, and inside every package are good and evil. Consider an example.

Most human beings in developed countries would rather move about by private automobile than by public transportation. One is free to go when one wishes to where one wishes without concern for public transportation routes or schedules. The individualism of the user is catered to; sales of autos, gasoline, tires and the like boom; industries serving the auto and its drivers prosper and multitudes of jobs are created.

As a result large numbers of people are killed and injured each year in auto accidents. Much law enforcement manpower must be used to police streets and highways against drunk drivers and speeders. Smog fouls the air of our large cities causing human respiratory diseases and damage to irreplaceable architectural treasures and death to nearby forests. More and more land is paved over to provide freeways and parking lots.

Any human choice of conduct will have far-reaching side effects. No one can perfectly foresee all of the results of his or her actions and we are not programmed to think long-term. As the economist John Maynard Keynes said, in the long run we're all dead. That realization lies in the breasts of all of us; we feel that the problems of the remote future aren't ours.

If we think a bit more before we act, however, some unpleasant side effects of our actions may be prevented.

There's no such thing as a free lunch. Never do we get anything for nothing. Everything must be paid for, whether in money or in another form.

In the economic sphere most of us understand this very well. That's why Josef Stalin put a provision in the Soviet Constitution of 1936 stating that every Soviet citizen is obligated to do productive work, according to the principle "He who does not work, neither shall he eat." If we don't support ourselves, someone else must support us, or perhaps no one will.

In spheres other than the economic our comprehension of the principle is not so good. The price we pay for a benefit may not be reckoned in money at all.

We develop forms of fruits and vegetables that are resistant to damage while being shipped and resistant to spoilage as they sit on the grocer's shelf— then we find that they have little flavor. We grain-feed beef cattle in order to produce tender steaks—then we're concerned because of the high fat content of the steaks.

One of the costs of the existence of the automobile in large numbers is smog. A cost of the throw-away society is mountains of garbage. A cost of nuclear electric power is nuclear waste which will be dangerous to life for 100,000 years.

Every one of life's packages contains a mixture of good and evil. We pay to enjoy the good by learning to live with the evil.

If anything can go wrong, it probably will. Murphy's Law doesn't state an inevitability, but a strong probability. Our species does not possess crystal balls in 100 percent working order and since everything we do produces side effects, some are likely to be unanticipated and negative. Most human undertakings turn out to be more difficult than anticipated.

Everything has to go somewhere. Nothing can be utterly destroyed. Nothing can be truly thrown away. If we burn it it's transformed into gases and ash. If we smash it it's converted into rubble. If we dissolve it in a liquid it remains a component part of the liquid.

If we move it somewhere else to get it out of our hair it bugs its neighbors in the new location. If we dump it in the nearby river it goes downstream to aggravate whoever resides in that direction. If we bury it it will remain there forever if it isn't biodegradable; if it is biodegradable it will decompose and quite likely get into the local groundwater. If it's poisonous or radioactive it must be packaged in stout containers, but we have yet to devise such that are rust-proof, corrosion-proof, radiation proof, leak-proof and earthquake-proof. Containers, like people, do not have the gift of eternal life (though poisons and radioactive materials seem to). Moreover there's no guarantee that it will stay buried since the crust of Mother Earth isn't as stable as we wish. If we dump it into the sea the ocean currents will carry it to who knows where. Even if we fire it off into outer space (too expensive a disposal method to be viable) it might come back in the form of meteorites, and it would certainly pollute the atmosphere.

The human reaction to unpleasant garbage or the like is to put it somewhere where it doesn't bug us any more. Then we wash our hands and congratulate ourselves that the problem's solved—out of sight, out of mind. Just because it's out of sight does not mean it should be out of mind. It's still out there, somewhere.

We refuse to recognize evil until it arrives, if then. One of the most tragic characters in Homer's *Iliad* is the Trojan princess Cassandra, who could foresee the future. She knew the consequences of bringing the Greek horse inside the walls of Troy and warned her people of them, but they refused to listen and suffered disaster.

Of course, he who cries "Wolf!" when there is no wolf deserves contempt and forfeits his credibility. We tend to assume that prophesiers of disaster are all like the religious fanatics who claim that the world will end next week.

Yet we didn't believe that Hitler was exterminating the Jews of Europe until allied armies occupied the concentration camps in 1944 and 1945, after the deed was done. We didn't believe the horrible tales of Stalin's crimes until they were described in detail by Alexander Solzhenitsyn and others—after Stalin was dead. We didn't believe the warnings of Winston Churchill that Hitler was determined to begin a world war—until German troops shot their way into Poland.

We don't recognize our true Cassandras until it's too late.

Nature knows best. This is a principle with which most human beings viscerally disagree. Ever since our species began changing its environment to provide a better life we have engaged in an unending battle with the forces of Nature. It's an article of faith that people can master Nature; that people know what is best for themselves.

Yet there is no more wondrously complex mechanism on earth than a functioning ecosystem. Tens of thousands—perhaps millions—of species of creatures coexist side by side, each making its minute contribution to the continued life of the system. The survival of each species helps guarantee that of the system; the survival of the system helps guarantee that of each constituent species. The system is far more complicated than the most elaborate computer, but it can function flawlessly, almost automatically—sometimes for millennia. Its built-in checks and balances prevent any one species from permanently increasing in numbers and upsetting it.

Since all things in the universe are subject to the laws of thermodynamics even ecosystems don't live forever. The dinosaurs reigned for millions of years but suddenly became extinct. Changes in climate and other cosmic disasters can overwhelm any earthly system.

Human intelligence allows us to tinker with ecosystems as we strive to increase our lifespans, comfort and numbers. The scientific and technological revolutions of the last two centuries have permitted our kind to dominate the planet in a manner that was never before possible. In so doing we have ripped the fabric of countless long-established ecosystems and created the ecological crisis described in this chapter.

Nature doesn't concern itself with the well-being of individual members of a species—the individual is meaningful only as it contributes to the well-being of the species. And the species is meaningful only as it contributes to the survival of the ecosystem.

Humanity in general values survival of its own species above that of ecosystems—if a system discourages expansion of human numbers we seek to replace it with another more "humanity-friendly." Westerners in a sense value the human individual as highly as the species. If a system limits the life (physical and psychic) of individual human beings they seek to replace it with one more "man-and-woman-friendly." In so doing we seek to impose upon our planet an order of things designed by our intelligence, to replace the pre-existing order of things which has ruled life on earth quite well for geologic ages.

Are we better system designers than Mother Nature?

So often we blindly engage in head-on combat against natural forces. We know that when we build cities upon flood plains they're subject to flooding, but we build them there anyway though we must spend millions on flood control systems. We know that devastating wildfire sometimes sweeps the dry hills of southern California, but we build expensive housing developments there anyway. We know that felling large areas of tropical rainforest can adversely affect the climate of our planet, but we do it anyway. We know that plowing up grassland for agriculture encourages wind and water erosion of topsoil, but we do it anyway.

In our pride we believe that our intelligence is great enough to allow us to discover and understand all of the laws governing the universe. Furthermore we want to believe that we can repeal those we don't like through the exercise of human ingenuity.

The universe is a far more complex place than our ancestors of a century ago believed. It may indeed be possible for the human mind to discover and comprehend how it all works, but such an intellectual triumph is, as of now, far down the highway of time.

For the foreseeable future, we cannot emerge victorious from head-to-head combats with the forces of Nature. Instead we must learn to accept our limitations.

The ultimate human limitation. Garrett Hardin sums up the natural limitations upon humanity (and indeed upon everything in the universe) with these three depressing statements.

You can't win.

You are bound to lose.

You can't get out of the game.

If by winning we mean acquiring eternal health, youth and life we indeed can't win; there are no fountains of eternal youth. If by losing we mean dying, we are indeed bound to lose. The only playing field of the game is our universe, which is bound by the above-stated rules. There is no other universe available to us, and the only way to leave the game is to die.

The universe is like a spring-wound clock. Everything in it uses energy as it does its thing. Just as the clock ultimately stops when its spring runs down, the universe will ultimately stop when its cosmic spring does likewise. The ultimate fate of the universe is entropy—eternal stillness.

For individual human beings the equivalent of entropy is death; for the human species the equivalent is extinction. Can we change the ground rules of the universe to make possible our physical immortality? Can we insure that our species will physically survive forever?

Unless physicists have misstated the laws of thermodynamics it's impossible. All physical things are made to end; this ultimate outcome is inevitable.

Can we accept this cosmic limitation upon ourselves? Life being what it is, the human creature must be a congenital optimist. The Westerner says that things must and will be better during his lifetime. The Easterner says that though there's no hope for better things in this lifetime adherence to the laws of Karma insures that the soul will ultimately attain Nirvana. However and whenever, both agree that the triumph of the good guys is assured.

It's interesting to note, however, that the triumph the Easterner hopes for is spiritual rather than physical—Nirvana isn't of this world. Before the Western intellectual revolution our ancestors too held out no hope for triumph in the physical world—Martin Luther called it the Devil's Inn (Der Teufels Wirtschaft). As Thomas Nashe expressed it 300 years ago:

Heaven is our heritage, Earth but a player's stage.

Mount we unto the sky.

For us too in those days the triumph of the good would take place in Heaven, not on earth.

For modern Western peoples this world is the only one that counts. We mean to create the nearest thing to heaven on earth here that our species has yet seen. If we proceed cautiously, always aware of our intellectual limitations and working within their boundaries, it's barely possible that we might come close.

But if we behave with the arrogance of King Canute of old (who sought to command the tide not to rise) and with the blindness of King Priam and his people (who refused to listen to the warnings of Cassandra) our present economic and physical prosperity will end.

At best, a bureaucratically directed command economy may be resurrected that provides us with adequate food, clothing and shelter but not much else. Worse, severe ecological catastrophe may destroy the superstructure of the present economy and Western civilization may regress to where it stood in A.D. 500—at the beginning of a new Dark Age. Or—the worst cast—ecological disaster may render Planet Earth uninhabitable for our species. The physical human saga will end with a big bang or an almost unheard whimper, while the cockroaches take charge of what remains of our heritage.

Glossary

Absolute Majority fifty percent plus one (or more) of all votes cast in an election.

Alawi a small Shi'ite sect found mainly in northern Syria. Non–Alawi Muslims charge that members of this sect worship Ali as God and are thus not true Muslims, though most Alawi deny this. Alawites wield great political power in Syria because Hafiz al-Assad, president of the nation, is Alawi.

Albigensians a sect of Christian heretics who flourished in Italy and south France during the eleventh and twelfth centuries. They believed that the God of the Old Testament was the creator of this evil world and that the Roman Catholic Church served this evil God. They were virtually exterminated during the thirteenth century.

Altaic Languages a family of languages spoken from Asia Minor to northeast Asia. The major member of the family is Turkish.

Anarchism the notion that all government is evil and should be abolished.

Arians early Christian heretics who believed that the nature of Jesus Christ was essentially human. They were numerous in Western Europe from the fifth century to the seventh, but disappeared soon thereafter.

Assassins a fanatical Ismaili Muslim sect of the twelfth and thirteenth century whose members were expected to kill enemies of the true faith at the command of their leader. The Assassins became high on drugs before undertaking their assigned tasks, and thus performed fearlessly — the assassin often died alongside his victim. The sect was exterminated by a Mongol army during the thirteenth century.

Authoritarian Dictatorship a dictatorship in which the rulers allow the ruled to live as they please as long as they don't engage in political opposition to the regime.

Baltic Languages a small group of Indo-European languages spoken along the east shore of the Baltic Sea. Only two now exist, Lithuanian and Latvian.

Bantu Languages a group of languages spoken in Africa from Kenya and Tanzania south to the Republic of South Africa. Most noteworthy of the group is Swahili, the national language of Tanzania.

Blanket Primary a direct primary in which the voter is given a ballot containing the names of all candidates for public office of all parties and may vote for candidates of two or more parties as nominees. Thus, for instance, a registered Republican could vote in the Democratic primary for Governor, State senator, and sheriff while voting in the Republican primary for other offices.

Block Vote a voting system used in multi-member legislative districts in which the voter has as many votes as there are seats to be filled in the district. This usually assures that the candidates of one party sweep the election in the district.

Bodhisattva in Buddhism, a saint who achieves so much sanctity during his life that, after he has achieved Nirvana, he has the power to transfer surplus merit to others to help them reach the same goal.

325

Bolsheviks   the majority faction of the pre–World War I Russian Social Democratic Party. Under Lenin's leadership they seized power in Russia in October of 1917 and established Communist dictatorship in that country.

Bourgeoisie   the middle class. In Marxist theory it rules the state under capitalism and must be deprived of all political and economic power before a communist society can come to pass.

Brahmin   a member of India's priestly caste, the highest ranking of the four castes.

Bundesrat   the seven-person executive body of the Swiss federal government. Also the upper houses of today's German and Austrian federal parliaments.

Bundestag   the lower house of today's German federal parliament.

Burgage   in pre-1832 England, a parcel of land within a borough which conferred upon the owner one vote for members of the House of Commons. A voter was entitled to one vote per burgage owned; thus the owner of a majority of burgages within the borough could nominate the borough's members of the Commons.

Capitani Reggenti   Captains Regent, the two chief executive officers of the Republic of San Marino.

Celtic Languages   a group of Indo-European languages spoken along the western fringe of Europe. Only four now exist—Breton, Welsh, Irish Gaelic and Scots Gaelic.

Chamber of Deputies   the lower house of the Mexican congress, the Italian parliament, and numerous other national legislatures.

Chancellor   the political head of state in Germany and Austria.

Closed Primary   a direct primary in which only registered party members may participate (registered Democrats in the Democratic primary, registered Republicans in the Republican primary).

Comitia Centuriata   the Assembly of Centuries in which Roman citizens of the Republic annually elected the Consuls and other high public officials.

Comitia Tributa   the Assembly of Tribes in which Roman citizens enacted legislation and annually elected minor public officials.

Communism   an economic system based on common ownership of property operating on the principle "from each according to his ability, to each according to his need."

Communist Anarchism   the notion that both government and private property are evil. The optimal society is one where all property is owned in common and no government exists.

Concilium Plebis   the assembly of the plebeians (the lower class of Roman citizenry) which elected the tribunes and enacted certain types of legislation.

Consensual Democracy   the type of democracy in which all or virtually all parties have a hand in governing. Only small non-system parties are in opposition; this insignificant opposition is permanent.

Consuls   the two chief executive officers of the Roman Republic.

Corporation Boroughs   in pre-1832 England, boroughs in which the Corporation (the City Council) elected the borough's members of the House of Commons.

Cyrillic Alphabet   the alphabet in which Russian and several other Slavic languages are written.

Dail Eirann—the lower house of parliament in the Irish Republic.

De Facto Recognition   recognition of the existence of a national government by other states on the basis that, as of now, it has governing authority in a defined area though the continuance of that authority is uncertain.

De Jure Recognition   recognition of the permanent, legally sanctified existence of a national government by other states.

Devanagari   the alphabet used for writing Hindi and several other Indic languages.

Dharma   the moral obligations of the believing Hindu.

D'Hondt Proportional Representation   the most commonly used proportional representation system, which favors large parties over small parties.

Direct Primary   a device by which the voters choose party nominees for public office by casting ballots in a preliminary election.

Docetists   Christian heretics who flourished during the second and third centuries. They believed that Jesus only appeared to die on the cross, because no divine being would submit himself to such a degrading, painful death.

Doge   the head of state of the Republic of Venice, elected for life by an electoral college.

Donatists   Christian heretics who flourished in North Africa before the Arab conquest, believing that lapsed sinners can't be readmitted into the Church, and that sinful priests may not administer valid sacraments.

Dravidians   the dark-skinned inhabitants of southern India, thought to be descendants of those people of the subcontinent displaced by Aryan invaders 4,000 years ago. They speak languages of the Dravidian family, unrelated to the Indo-European tongues spoken farther north.

Druzes   a near–Muslim sect found in the area where the borders of Syria, Lebanon and Israel intersect. They claim that Hakim, an Egyptian sultan of the eleventh century A.D., was God. In the past they have shared in the exercise of political power in Lebanon.

Ebionites   a Jewish-Christian sect which observed Jewish law while worshiping Jesus as the Son of God. It existed from the first through the sixth century.

Endogamous Marriage   the condition under which a man must marry a woman from his own clan or tribe, perhaps even a first cousin.

Exogamous Marriage   the condition under which a man must marry a woman from another clan or tribe.

First Estate   in medieval European representative estates, the representatives of the clergy.

First-Past-the-Post   the election system used in most English-speaking countries in which the winner of an election is the candidate who polls the most votes, whether he or she obtains an absolute majority or not.

Forty-Shilling Freeholder   a person who owned or leased property with a rental value of at least 40 shillings per year. In pre-1832 England, such persons had the right to vote for county members of the House of Commons, and also for borough members in a few communities.

Freeman   in pre-1832 England, a citizen of a borough. In many boroughs, all freemen had the right to vote for members of the House of Commons.

Frelimo   the Front for the Liberation of Mozambique. This Marxist-Leninist guerrilla organization battled the Portuguese for the independence of Mozambique. When the Portuguese pulled out in 1974 they turned over government authority to Frelimo, which has ruled the country ever since.

Gastarbeiter   the foreign workers brought to Western European countries during the 1960s and early 1970s to counter the effects of the chronic labor shortages of those years. They have become a permanent part of the labor force of these countries.

Genocide   the extermination or attempted extermination of a religious, cultural or linguistic group.

Germanic Languages   the group of languages descended from the speech of the original Germanic migrants to Europe. The major members of the group are German and English.

Gerrymandering   the practice of drawing boundaries of single-member legislative districts in a way that maximizes the seatwinning potential of the majority party and minimizes that of minor parties.

Gharar   in Islamic law and custom, uncertainty. Contracts, the outcome of which may be influenced by unforeseen factors, are deemed Gharar and are almost always unenforceable.

Gregorian Calendar   the calendar devised by Pope Gregory XIII in the sixteenth century under which most of mankind now lives. Every fourth year is a leap year except in years ending in 00, with the exception of years divisible by 400.

Gnostics   a group of sects, Christian and non–Christian, that flourished during the second and third centuries. They believed that a person must find his way to God through personal gnosis (knowledge) of the Eternal, acquired by each in his own way. Only a small group of the elect are capable of accomplishing this.

Grand Council   the legislative assembly of the Venetian Republic. Its membership was limited to the adult male members of families listed in the Libro de Oro — the register of Venetian nobility.

Great Schism   the division within the Roman Catholic Church during the late fourteenth and early fifteenth centuries, during which two and sometimes three persons claimed to be Pope.

Greenhouse Effect   the gradual warming of the earth caused by the accumulation of carbon dioxide and similar gases in the atmosphere, making it more difficult for accumulated heat to be diffused into outer space.

Group Marriage   the marriage of several men to several women.

Guru Granth Sahib   the holy scripture of the Sikhs.

Hagenbach-Bischoff Proportional Representation   the "largest remainder" system of proportional representation, working to the advantage of smaller parties.

Hajj   the pilgrimage to Mecca, which must be performed by the believing Muslim at least once in his or her life.

Hajji   the Muslim who has made the pilgrimage to Mecca.

Hangul   the written form of the Korean language.

Haram   that which is forbidden by Islamic law.

Hare Proportional Representation   applies single transferable vote principles to multi-candidate elections. The voter marks a "1" before his one favorite candidate, a "2" before his second-favorite, and so forth. A candidate needs a quota of votes to win — in a five-candidate race one-sixth plus one, in an eight-candidate race one-ninth plus one, and so forth. Low candidates are eliminated and their votes transferred until the required number of candidates reach the quota.

Harijan   in India, a person who has no caste; an untouchable.

Hiragana   one of the native syllabaries used for writing Japanese, primarily handwriting.

House of Commons   the lower house of the parliaments of Great Britain, Canada and certain other English-speaking countries.

House of Councillors   the upper house of the Japanese parliament.

House of Lords   the upper house of the British Parliament, most of whose members hold their seats by hereditary right.

House of Representatives   the lower house of the United States Congress, the Australian and Japanese parliaments, and some other national legislatures.

Indic Languages   the Indo-European languages native to the Indian sub-continent, the major of which is Hindi.

Indo-European Languages   the family of languages spoken from the British Isles to India, including the Germanic, Romance, Slavic, Indic and other linguistic groups.

Initiative the process by which citizens may propose legislation and constitutional amendments in Switzerland and in some American states.

Ismailis a minor sect of Shi'a Islam, sometimes known as Seveners. They believe that Ismail was the seventh Imam, a belief denied by Twelvers. The spiritual leader of today's Ismaili is the Aga Khan.

Jains members of an Indian religion who believe that human souls may be reincarnated as insects and other sorts of animals; thus they don't believe in taking any kind of life except in dire emergencies.

Julian Calendar the calendar devised by Julius Caesar under which Western people lived until it was replaced by the Gregorian calendar. Every fourth year without exception was a leap year by this calendar.

Junta a committee of dictators (usually military officers) who run a nation under collective leadership.

Kamikaze in Japanese, literally, the Divine Wind—the typhoons that wrecked the fleets carrying Mongol invaders to Japan's shores during the late thirteenth century. Also the suicide fliers of 1944–45 who sought death by crashing their aircraft on the decks of American warships.

Kanji the Japanese term used for the Chinese characters of written Japanese.

Karma in Hinduism and Buddhism, the debits and credits earned by a soul during an incarnation.

Katakana one of the native syllabaries used for writing the Japanese language, primarily in signs and the like.

Khalsa the community of the world's Sikhs.

Kharijites the "third force" of Islamic believers who are neither Sunni nor Shi'a. Originally they were the Puritans of Islam who believed that the faith could not forgive relapsed sinners. They have modified their beliefs in recent times. Most of them, now known as Ibadis, are found in the sultanate of Oman.

Knesset the Israeli parliament.

Kshatriya a member of India's second (warrior) caste.

Landesgemeinde in some small Swiss cantons, the annual assembly of citizens on the public square of the cantonal capital to elect public officers and enact legislation.

Latin Alphabet the alphabet in which English and many other world languages are written.

Liberation Theology the notion adhered to by some radical Roman Catholic clergy (mainly Latin-American) that the major goal of the Roman Catholic Church should be the liberation of people from poverty and injustice in this world rather than the liberation of the soul in the next.

Libertarian Anarchism the notion that government is humanity's greatest curse and private property is its greatest blessing. No government should exist so that people are free to accumulate property and to use it as they see fit (without harming others).

Liberum Veto in the Polish Commonwealth of the late seventeenth and eighteenth centuries, the right of any one member of the Sejm to veto legislation or to dissolve the current session of the body.

Libertarianism the philosophy that seeks to create a government empowered only to preserve public order and national independence, on the principle that the best government is that which governs least.

Libro De Oro the Golden Book of the Venetian Republic, containing the names of all noble families whose male adult members were entitled to sit in the Grand Council.

Limited Vote a voting system used in multi-member legislative districts in which the voter has fewer votes than the number of legislators to be elected. This system makes it next to impossible for a majority party to win all of the seats, thus insuring some minority representation.

Lotus Sutra the holy scripture of Nichiren Shoshu Buddhism.

Mahayana Buddhism the Buddhism of China, Korea and Japan which is more worldly and less ascetic than the Theravada of south and southeast Asia. It is divided into many sects.

Mahdi in Shi'a Islam, the Hidden Imam who will return and bring liberation to the world's oppressed.

Majoritarian Democracy the form of democratic government in which the party or group of parties holding a small parliamentary majority rule the state, while a large minority stands in opposition, not participating in government.

Malayo-Polynesian Languages the family of languages spoken from Madagascar to Southeast Asia to the islands of the Pacific. The major members of this family are Indonesian, Tagalog and Malay.

Mandate of Heaven in Chinese culture, the right of those who control a government to rule. As long as the rulers provide peace and prosperity they hold the Mandate of Heaven and rebellion against them is wrongful. However, when disorder and famine stalk the land the rulers have lost the Mandate and it becomes virtuous to overthrow them, by violence if necessary.

Marcionites a sect of Christians of the second century who believed that the only legitimate Christian scriptures were the Gospel of Luke and certain epistles of Paul. They rejected the entire Old Testament as being solely Jewish scripture. They were declared to be heretics by the orthodox church.

Messiah in Judaism, the wise powerful person who will come to the world and liberate the Jewish community from its oppressor.

Moksha in Hinduism, the moral virtue created by the accumulation of good Karma.

Monogamous Marriage the marriage of one man to one woman.

Monophysites Christians who believe that the nature of Jesus Christ was divine, with no human admixture. They were declared to be heretics in the fifth century, but their belief dominates the Coptic Church of Egypt and the national church of Ethiopia.

MPLA the Popular Movement for the Liberation of Angola, the Marxist-Leninist group which won a bloody civil war for control of Angola after the Portuguese pulled out, and which still governs the country.

Nanosecond one billionth of a second.

Nationalrat the lower houses of the Swiss and Austrian federal parliaments.

Nichiren Shoshu Buddhism a Japanese form of Buddhism which preaches the necessity of group action to reform the world. It participates in Japanese politics and actively seeks converts throughout the world.

Nirvana in Hinduism and Buddhism, the goal of human existence. When the soul achieves Nirvana, it becomes one with the universe and is liberated from the wheel of Samsara—the endless cycle of reincarnation.

Nomenklatura the privileged class of bureaucrats and Communist Party bigwigs which governed Marxist-Leninist countries in the heyday of Communist dictatorship.

Open Primary a direct primary in which a person may vote in any party primary he or she chooses regardless of party affiliation or membership. (Thus, a registered Democrat may vote in either the Democratic or Republican parimary, but not both.)

Ostracism   an institution of classical Athens by which the assembly of citizens could choose a person to be expelled from Athenian territory for a period of ten years. It was a way of disposing of unpopular politicians wihtout killing them or confiscating their property.

Panachage   in Switzerland and Luxembourg, the right of a citizen to vote for legislative candidates of two or more parties on Election Day.

Parlements   the appellate courts of pre-revolutionary France, whose judges held their seats by purchase or by inheritance.

Parliamentary Government   government in which there is a fusion of legislative and executive power. The political head of state serves at the pleasure of, usually, the majority of the lower house of parliament and is a member of that house. The legislature may remove the political head of state from power through a vote of "no confidence," while the political head of state has, usually, the power to dissolve the legislature and call for new elections.

Parthenogenesis   the reproduction of a sexually reproducing species through unfertilized eggs.

Particratie   the state of affairs in which a supposedly democratic country is ruled by a few party leaders rather than by the people.

Party List Proportional Representation   a type of proportional representation in which a person votes for a list of legislative candidates nominated by a party with little or no choice of individual candidates.

Pinyin   the system used by the Communist Chinese for writing Mandarin in the Latin alphabet.

PLO   the Palestine Liberation Organization, consisting of Palestinian Arabs who strive to establish an independent, self-governing Palestinian state.

Plurality   the highest number of votes polled by a candidate or party in an election, which may or may not be an absolute majority.

Polisario   in the former Spanish Sahara, a group that engages in guerrilla warfare against Moroccan troops to drive them out of the country and establish the independence of the Saharan Arab Democratic Republic.

Polyandrous Marriage   the marriage of one woman to two or more men.

Polygamous Marriage   the marriage of one person of one sex to two or more persons of the opposite sex.

Polygynous Marriage   the marriage of one man to two or more women.

Potwalloper   a person who owned or leased a house with a hearth upon which he could boil a pot. In pre-1832 England, many boroughs conferred the right to vote for members of the House of Commons upon such persons who had been residents of the borough for six months.

Premier   the French term for the political head of state in parliamentary governments.

President   the head of state of most republics. In presidential government he or she is the political as well as ceremonial head of state; in parliamentary states the president serves only as ceremonial head of state.

Presidential Government   a type of government organization in which a strict separation of power between executive and legislature exists; the president may not dissolve the legislature and the legislature may not remove the president from office (except possibly by the complex process of impeachment).

Prime Minister   the English term for the political head of state in parliamentary governments.

Proletariat   the working class. In Marxist theory, it will wrest power from the bourgeoisie, establish the dictatorship of the proletariat and destroy capitalism and the power of the bourgeoisie. After that has been accomplished the state will wither away and communism will come to pass.

Pure Land Buddhism a Mahayana sect found throughout the Far East and in areas elsewhere that are influenced by Chinese culture. Believers achieve Nirvana by calling upon the Bodhisattva Amitabha to exert his power to liberate the soul from reincarnation in this world.

Qu'ran the holy scripture of Islam.

Referendum the process by which voters approve legislation and constitutional amendments in Switzerland, some American states and a few other nations.

Reichsrat the upper house of the parliaments of the German Empire and of the Weimar Republic. The lower house of the parliament of the Austrian half of the Austro-Hungarian Empire also went by this name.

Reichstag the lower house of the parliaments of the German Empire and the Weimar Republic.

Relative Majority a plurality of votes received in an election when there is no absolute majority.

Renamo the Mozambique National Resistance Organization, which seeks to overthrow the Frelimo government of Mozambique and take its place. It has engaged in guerrilla warfare against Frelimo for over a decade and controls much of the nation's countryside.

Riba in Islamic law, the charging of interest upon loans. This is forbidden; Islamic banking functions without the charging or collecting of interest.

Rinzai the sect of Zen Buddhsm in which masters seek to help postulants achieve Satori through mental harassment.

Romance Languages the group of languages descended from Latin, the language of the Roman Empire. Major members of the group are French, Spanish, Portuguese and Italian.

Rotten Borough in pre-1832 England, a borough which had been granted the right to elect members of the House of Commons during the Middle Ages and continued to possess that right though no one resided within its boundaries. The members of the Commons for such boroughs were nominated by the owner of the land upon which the borough town once stood.

Runoff an election system under which a candidate must receive an absolute majority (50 percent plus one) of all votes to be elected. If no one accomplishes this on a first vote, a second election is held between the top two vote-getters on the first ballot; the winner is assured more than half of the vote cast (barring a tie).

Saint-Lague Proportional Representation a system of proportional representation (used mainly in Scandinavia) which works more to the advantage of small parties than does D'Hondt.

Salah in Islam, the mandatory prayers which must be uttered by the believer five times a day.

Samsara in Hinduism and Buddhism, the wheel of seemingly endless reincarnation to which the human soul is bound until it accumulates enough merit to attain Nirvana.

Satori the process (a sort of psychic lightning bolt) by which the believer in Zen Buddhism attains enlightenment.

Satyagraha the non-violent resistance to perceived oppression popularized by Mahatma Gandhi and others in pre-independence India.

Sawm in Islam, the obligatory fast of the month of Ramadan, during which the believer must not eat during daylight hours.

Scientific Socialism   the socialist theory of Karl Marx which holds that the coming of a communist society is inevitable. Feudalism (rule by aristocrats) must yield to capitalism (rule by the middle class) which must yield to socialism (rule by the working class while capitalist mentality is eliminated from the population) which must yield to communism (the elimination of government and the state).

Scot and Lot Franchise   in pre-1832 England, a few boroughs used this franchise. It limited the right to vote for members of the House of Commons to those who paid the poor tax.

Second Ballot   an election system under which a candidate must receive at least 50 percent plus one of all votes cast to win on the first ballot. If this produces no winner a second ballot is held in which no candidates are eliminated (as in Switzerland) or candidates polling very small percentages of the vote are eliminated (as in France) and the candidate with the most votes wins.

Second Estate   in medieval European representative assemblies, the representatives of the nobility.

Sejm   the Diet of the Polish Commonwealth and the lower house Parliament in the present-day Republic.

Semitic Languages   the major linguistic family of the Middle East. The most widely spoken language of the family is Arabic.

Senate   the upper legislative body of the United States, Mexico, Brazil, Argentina, Australia, France, Italy, Belgium and other countries.

Shehada   the fundamental statement of Islam. "There is no God but God, and Mohammed is his prophet!"

Shema   the fundamental statement of Judaism. "Hear, O Israel! The Lord our God, the Lord is One!"

Shi'a   the major minority grouping of Muslims. They believe that the Imam is the most important leadership figure, and that Ali and his son Hussein were true leaders and suffered martyrdom in the cause of religious truth. There are several variants of Shi'a in the Islamic world.

Shogun   the effective ruler of Japan for almost a millennium, obtaining power either by inheritance or through military force. The Shogunate wasn't abolished until the Meiji Restoration of 1868, at which time the Emperor once more theoretically acquired the power to rule.

Single Transferable Vote   an election system in which the voter marks a "1" before the name of his favorite candidate, a "2" before his second favorite, and so on. The "1s" are counted first—any candidate receiving an absolute majority of those is elected. If there is no absolute majority the candidate with the fewest "1s" is eliminated; his votes are distributed among the remaining candidates according to the "2s" marked thereon. If any candidate now has an absolute majority, he's elected; if not, this process goes on until someone receives the necessary majority.

Sino-Tibetan Languages   the major linguistic family of the Far East. The most widely spoken member of the family is Mandarin Chinese.

Slavic Languages   the group of languages descended from the speech of the original Slavic settlers of eastern Europe. The major language of the group is Russian.

Socialism   an economic system organized on the basis of common ownership of property on the principle of "from each according to his ability, to each according to his work."

Soto   the form of Zen Buddhism in which the believer seeks satori through solitary meditation.

Stadhouder   the chief executive officer of a Dutch province during the time of the Dutch Republic. At times the head of the House of Orange served as Stadhouder of all seven provinces and thus of the entire Republic.

Standerat   the upper house of the Swiss federal parliament.

STD   sexually transmissible diseases, including AIDS, syphilis, gonorrhea, herpes and several more.

Sudra   in India, a member of the fourth (laborer) caste.

Sufis   the mystics of Islam, who believe that the individual may attain contact with God by his own efforts, without necessarily following required Islamic ritual.

Sunni   the majority group of believers in Islam, to whom the Caliph has been the most important leadership figure and to whom Hussein, son of Ali, was a rebel against legitimate authority.

Supreme Soviet   the present legislature of the Soviet Union.

Szlachta   the nobility of the pre-partition Polish Commonwealth which ruled Poland until it lost independence in 1795.

Tantric Buddhism   the Buddhism of Tibet and Mongolia, whose believers follow magic practices.

Tao Te Ching   the nearest thing to holy scripture possessed by the Taoist faith.

Theravada Buddhism   the ascetic, inward-looking Buddhism of Sri Lanka, Burma and Thailand.

Third Estate   in the pre-revolutionary French Estates-General, the representatives of all of society who were not clergy or nobility.

Twelver Shi'a   the most important of Shi'a groups. They believe that there have been 12 Imams and that the twelfth, Mohammed al Muntazar, went into occultation in the ninth century A.D. He still exists as the Hidden Imam and will return some day to liberate the true believers from oppression. The rulers of Iran are Twelver Shi'a, as are most Iranians.

Unita   the National Union for the Total Independence of Angola, an organization which has fought a bitter bloody war against MPLA for control of Angola. Led by Jonas Savimbi, it controls a large area of the country.

Uralic Languages   the family of languages spoken by isolated groups in eastern Europe and western Siberia. Most noteworthy family members are Finnish and Hungarian.

USSR   the Union of Soviet Socialist Republics. The Soviet Union.

USSS   the Union of Sovereign Socialist States, a loose confederation into which the present Soviet Union may evolve.

Utopian Socialism   the notion that private property will be eliminated by the action of the people when they realize that a socialist system is more just than the regime of private property. To the utopians socialism isn't necessarily inevitable—its coming depends upon people becoming enlightened enough to install it.

Vaisya   in India, a member of the third (merchant) caste.

Yang Di Pertuan Agong   the head of state of the federation of Malaysia. He must be a reigning monarch of one of Malaysia's constituent states, and is elected to the post for five years by the votes of his fellow monarchs.

Zaidis   a minor sect of Shi'a Islam which is also known as Fivers. They believe that the fifth Imam of the faith was Zaid, a notion denied by Twelvers and Seveners. The major leader in modern times was the Imam of Yemen until he lost his power in the North Yemeni coup of 1962. The majority of Zaidi are still found in Yemen.

Zakat   in Islam, the obligatory annual contribution of two and one-half percent of the believer's net worth to the cause of aiding the poor.

Zen Buddhism   a form of Mahayana Buddhism whose members seek enlightenment in this world through meditation.

Bibliography

Races of Humankind

Braudel, Fernand. *The Structures of Everyday Life.* New York: Harper and Row, 1981.
Castro, Americo. *The Spaniards.* Berkeley, California: University of California Press, 1971.
Coon, Carleton S. *The Living Races of Man.* New York: Alfred A. Knopf, 1965.
Crosby, Alfred W., Jr. *The Columbian Exchange.* Westport, Connecticut: Greenwood Press, 1972.
Crow, John A. *The Epic of Latin America,* 3d ed. Berkeley, California: University of California Press, 1980.
Curtin, Philip, Steven Feierman, Leonard Thompson and Jan Vansina. *African History.* London: Longman Group, Ltd., 1978.
Garn, Stanley M. *Human Races,* 2d ed. Springfield, Illinois: Thomas Publishing Company, 1971.
Prawdin, Michael. *The Mongol Empire,* 2 ed. New York: The Free Press, 1967.
Roberts, J.M. *The Pelican History of the World.* Harmondsworth, England: Penguin Books Ltd., 1980.
Toynbee, Arnold. *Mankind and Mother Earth.* New York and London: Oxford University Press, 1976.
Williams, Eric. *From Columbus to Castro.* New York: Vintage Books, 1984.

Western Culture

Anderson, Perry. *Lineages of the Absolute State.* London: Verso Editions, 1979.
_____. *Passages from Antiquity to Feudalism.* London: Verso Editions, 1981.
Brown, Lawrence R. *The Might of the West.* New York: Joseph J. Binns, 1963.
Ehrlich, Paul R., Loy Bilderbeck and Anne H. Ehrlich. *The Golden Door.* New York: Wideview Books, 1979.
Johnson, Paul. *Modern Times.* New York: Harper and Row, 1983.
Jouvenel, Bertrand De. *On Power.* Boston: Beacon Press, 1962.
Kennedy, Paul. *The Rise and Fall of the Great Powers.* New York: Vintage Books, 1989.
Lincoln, W. Bruce. *The Romanovs.* New York: Anchor Press Books, 1981.
McNeill, William H. *The Rise of the West.* Chicago: University of Chicago Press, 1963.
Nisbet, Robert. *History of the Idea of Progress.* New York: Basic Books, 1980.
Parret, Geoffrey. *A Country Made by War.* New York: Random House, 1989.
Vernadsky, George. *A History of Russia.* New Haven, Connecticut: Yale University Press, 1967.

Von Laue, Theodore H. *The World Revolution of Westernization.* Oxford, England: Oxford University Press, 1987.

Non-Western Cultures

Davidson, Basil. *The Lost Cities of Africa,* revised ed. Boston: Little, Brown & Co., 1970.
Davis, William Stearns. *A Short History of the Near East.* New York: Macmillan, 1922.
Hall, D.G.E. *A History of Southeast Asia,* 3d ed. London: Macmillan Press Ltd., 1968.
Kiernan, Thomas. *The Arabs.* London: Sphere Books, 1978.
Li, Dun J. *The Ageless Chinese,* 3d ed. New York: Charles Scribner's Sons, 1978.
Packard, Jerrold M. *Sons of Heaven.* New York: Collier Books, 1987.
Sastri, Nilakanta. *A History of South India,* 4th ed. Oxford, England: Oxford University Press, 1978.
Wittfogel, Karl A. *Oriental Despotism.* New York: Vintage Books, 1981.

Languages

Baugh, Albert C., and Thomas Cable. *A History of the English Language,* 3d ed. London: Routledge and Kegan Paul, 1978.
Bodmer, Frederick. *The Loom of Language.* London: Merlin Press, 1981.
Chan, Shau Wing. *Elementary Chinese.* Stanford, California: Stanford University Press, 1961.
Duff, Charles, and Paul Stamford. *German for Beginners.* New York: Barnes & Noble, Inc., 1960.
Girsdansky, Michael (revised and edited by Mario Pei). *The Adventure of Language.* Greenwich, Connecticut: Fawcett Publications, Inc., 1967.
Keller, R.E. *German Dialects.* Manchester, England: Manchester University Press, 1979.
Mitchell, T.F. *Colloquial Arabic.* New York: David McKay Co., Inc., 1976.
Nakanishi, Akira. *Writing Systems of the World.* Tokyo, Japan, and Rutland, Vermont: Charles E. Tuttle Company, 1980.
Sampson, Geoffrey. *Writing Systems.* London: Century Hutchinson, Ltd., 1985.
Simon, Paul. *The Tongue-Tied American.* New York: Continuum, 1988.
Vaccari, Oreste, and Mrs. Enko. *Complete Course of Japanese Conversational Grammar.* Tokyo, Japan: Vaccari's Language Institute, 1965.

Christianity

Arrington, Leonard J., and Davis Bitton. *The Mormon Experience.* New York: Vintage Books, 1980.
Bokenkotter, Thomas. *A Concise History of the Catholic Church* (revised ed.). New York: Image Books, 1990.
Estep, William R. *The Anabaptist Story,* revised ed. Grand Rapids, Michigan: William B. Eerdmans, 1975.
Frend, W.H.C. *The Rise of Christianity.* London: Darton, Longman and Todd, 1984.
Hughes, Philip. *A History of the Church* (3 volumes). London: Sheed and Ward, 1979.

Johnson, Paul. *A History of Christianity.* Harmondsworth, England: Penguin Books Ltd., 1978.

Kraus, C. Norman, ed. *Evangelism and Anabaptism.* Scottdale, Pennsylvania: Herald Press, 1979.

Lewy, Gunther. *Religion and Revolution.* New York: Oxford University Press, 1974.

Ling, Trevor. *A History of Religion East and West.* London: Macmillan Publishers Ltd., 1968.

Martin, Walter. *The Kingdom of the Cults,* revised ed. Minneapolis, Minnesota: Bethany House Publishers, 1985.

Mead, Frank S., and Samuel S. Hill. *Handbook of Denominations in the United States* (8th ed.). Nashville, Tennessee: Abingdon Press, 1985.

Ware, Timothy. *The Orthodox Church.* Harmondsworth, England: Penguin Books Ltd., 1983.

Non-Christian Religions

Causton, Richard. *Nichiren Shoshu Buddhism.* London: Rider & Co., Ltd., 1988.

Humphreys, Christmas. *Buddhism,* 3rd ed. Harmondsworth, England: Penguin Books Ltd., 1963.

Johnson, David L. *A Reasoned Look at Asian Religions.* Minneapolis, Minnesota: Bethany House Publishers, 1985.

Johnson, Paul. *A History of the Jews.* New York: Harper and Row, 1987.

Martin, Malachi. *The Encounter.* Garden City, New York: Dial Press, 1983.

Momen, Moojan. *An Introduction to Shi'i Islam.* New Haven, Connecticut: Yale University Press, 1985.

Mortimer, Edward. *Faith and Power.* New York: Vintage Books, 1982.

Peters, F.E. *The Children of Abraham.* Princeton, New Jersey: Princeton University Press, 1982.

Ross, Nancy Wilson. *Three Ways of Asian Wisdom.* New York: Clarion Books, 1968.

Sen, K.M. *Hinduism.* Harmondsworth, England: Penguin Books, 1968.

Smith, Huston. *The Religions of Man.* New York: Harper & Row, 1986.

Stutley, Margaret. *Hinduism.* Wellingborough, Northamptonshire, England: Aquarian Press, 1985.

Zaehner, R.C. *Hinduism.* Oxford, England: Oxford University Press, 1962.

Other Cultural Considerations

Adler, Nancy J. *International Dimensions of Organizational Behavior.* Boston: Kent Publishing Company, 1986.

Akbar, M.J. *India, the Siege Within.* Harmondsworth, England: Penguin Books Ltd., 1985.

Balasz, Etienne. *Chinese Civilization and Bureaucracy.* New Haven, Connecticut: Yale University Press, 1964.

Benedict, Ruth. *The Chrysanthemum and the Sword.* Boston: Houghton Mifflin, 1987.

Carson, Gerald. *Men, Beasts and Gods.* New York: Charles Scribner's Sons, 1974.

Eichhorn, Werner. *Chinese Civilization.* New York: Frederick A. Praeger, 1962.

Gibney, Frank. *Japan the Fragile Superpower.* New York: Meridian Books, 1975.

Godlovich, Stanley, Rosalind Godlovich and John Harris, eds. *Animals, Men and Morals.* New York: Grove Press, 1971.

Harris, Marvin. *Cannibals and Kings.* New York: Vintage Books, 1977.
————. *Cows, Pigs, War and Witches.* London: Fontana Books, 1977.
————. *The Sacred Cow and the Abominable Pig.* New York: Touchstone Books, 1985.
Landes, David S. *Revolution in Time.* Cambridge, Massachusetts: Harvard University Press, 1983.
Morris, Ivan. *The Nobility of Failure.* New York: Meridian Books, 1975.
Ramos, Samuel. *Profile of Man and Culture in Mexico.* Austin, Texas: University of Texas Press, 1962.
Reynolds, Reginald. *Cleanliness and Godliness.* New York: Harcourt Brace Jovanovich, 1974.
Rifkin, Jeremy. *Time Wars.* New York: Touchstone Books, 1987.
Shoumatoff, Alex. *The Mountain of Names.* New York: Touchstone Books, 1985.
Terpstra, Vern, and Kenneth David. *The Cultural Environment of International Business* (2d ed.). Cincinnati, Ohio: Southwestern Publishing, 1985.
Van Wolferen, Karel. *The Enigma of Japanese Power.* New York: Vintage Books, 1990.

Family, Marriage, Women

Auerbach, Nina. *Woman and the Demon.* Cambridge, Massachusetts: Harvard University Press, 1982.
Bohannon, Paul, and John Middleton, eds. *Kinship and Social Organization.* Garden City, New York: Natural History Press, 1968.
————, and ————, eds. *Marriage, Family and Residence.* Garden City, New York: Natural History Press, 1968.
Briffault, Robert. *The Mothers.* New York: Atheneum Books, 1977.
Daly, Mary. *Gyn/Ecology.* Boston: Beacon Press, 1978.
De Riencourt, Amaury. *Sex and Power in History.* New York: Delta Books, 1972.
De Rougemont, Denis. *Love Declared.* Boston: Beacon Press, 1963.
————. *Passion and Society.* London: Faber and Faber, 1966.
Derrett, J. Duncan M. *An Introduction to Legal Systems.* London: Sweet & Maxwell, 1968.
Eisler, Riane. *The Chalice and the Blade.* New York: Harper and Row, 1987.
French, Marilyn. *Beyond Power.* New York: Ballantine Books, 1985.
Greer, Germaine. *Sex and Destiny.* London: Pan Books Ltd., 1985.
Hewitt, Sylvia Ann. *A Lesser Life.* New York: Warner Books, 1987.
Mount, Ferdinand. *The Subversive Family.* London: Unwin Paperbacks, 1982.
Tillion, Germaine. *The Republic of Cousins.* London: Al Saqi Books, 1983.
Wilson, Anthony. *The Female Pest.* London: Anthony Wilson, 1985.

The International State System

Berman, Harold J. *Law and Revolution.* Cambridge, Massachusetts: Harvard University Press, 1983.
Brownlie, Ian. *Principles of Public International Law,* 3d ed. Oxford, England: Oxford University Press, 1978.
Janis, Mark W. *An Introduction to International Law.* Boston: Little, Brown & Co., 1988.
Langer, Marshall J. *How to Use Foreign Tax Havens.* New York: Practicing Law Institute, 1973.

Mitteis, Heinrich, translated by H.F. Orton. *The State in the Middle Ages.* Amsterdam: North Holland Publishing, 1975.

Shaw, Malcolm N. *International Law,* 2d ed. Cambridge, England: Grotius Publications, 1986.

Governmental Systems

Brock, Michael. *The Great Reform Act.* London: Hutchinson & Company, 1973.

Crawford, Michael. *The Roman Republic.* Cambridge, Massachusetts: Harvard University Press, 1978.

Freeman, Kathleen. *Greek City States.* New York: W.W. Norton & Co., 1950.

Hammond, N.G.L. *A History of Greece to 322 B.C.,* 2d ed. Oxford, England: Clarendon Press, 1967.

Meyers, A.R. *Parliaments and Estates in Europe to 1989.* London: Thames & Hudson, 1973.

Norwich, John Julius. *A History of Venice.* New York: Alfred A. Knopf, 1982.

Palmer, R.R. *The Age of the Democratic Revolution* (2 volumes). Princeton, New Jersey: Princeton University Press, 1959.

_____. *The World of the French Revolution.* New York: Harper Torchbooks, 1971.

Sealey, Raphael. *A History of the Greek City States 700–338 B.C.* Berkeley, California: University of California Press, 1976.

Taylor, Lily Ross. *Party Politics in the Days of Caesar.* Berkeley, California: Unviersity of California Press, 1964.

Zamoyski, Adam. *The Polish Way.* London: John Murray Ltd., 1987.

National Governments

Cammack, Paul, David Pool and William Tarnoff. *Third World Politics.* London: Macmillan Education Ltd., 1988.

Dahl, Robert, ed. *Political Opposition in Western Democracies.* New Haven, Connecticut: Yale University Press, 1966.

_____. *Regimes and Oppositions.* New Haven, Connecticut: Yale University Press, 1973.

Decalo, Samuel. *Coups and Army Rule in Africa.* New Haven, Connecticut: Yale University Press, 1976.

Finer, Samuel E. *The Man on Horseback,* 2d ed. Harmondsworth, England: Penguin Books, 1976.

Fishkin, James S. *A Critique of Political Theories.* Baltimore, Maryland: Johns Hopkins University Press, 1979.

Hammond, Thomas T., ed. *The Anatomy of Communist Takeovers.* New Haven, Connecticut: Yale University Press, 1975.

The Information Please Almanac. Boston: Houghton Mifflin Co., 1990.

Lijphart, Arend. *Democracies.* New Haven, Connecticut: Yale University Press, 1985.

McDonald, Forrest. *Novus Ordo Seclorum.* Lawrence, Kansas: University Press of Kansas, 1985.

Moore, Barrington, Jr. *Social Origins of Dictatorship and Democracy.* Boston: Beacon Press, 1966.

Rubin, Barry. *Modern Dictators.* New York: Meridian Books, 1987.

Spiro, Herbert J. *Government by Constitution.* New York: Random House, 1959.

Ungar, Sanford J. Africa. New York: Touchstone Books, 1986.
Wheare, K.C. *Federal Government,* 4th ed. New York: Oxford University Press, 1964.
————. *Legislatures.* Oxford, England: Oxford University Press, 1967.

Nomination and Election Systems

Bogdanor, Vernon. *The People and the Party System.* Cambridge, England: Cambridge University Press, 1981.
————, and David Butler, eds. *Democracy and Elections.* Cambridge, England: Cambridge University Press, 1983.
McDonald, Ronald H. *Party Systems and Elections in Latin America.* Chicago: Markham Publishing Company, 1971.
Rae, Douglas W. *The Political Consequences of Electoral Laws,* revised ed. New Haven, Connecticut: Yale University Press, 1971.
Roberts, Geoffrey K., and Jill Lovecy. *West European Politics Today,* revised ed. Manchester, England: Manchester University Press, 1988.
(See also current almanacs and the numerous works describing the governments and political systems of individual nations.)

Nationality and Human Rights

Brogan, Patrick. *The Fighting Never Stopped.* New York: Vintage Books, 1990.
Chalk, Frank, and Kurt Jonasson. *The History and Sociology of Genocide.* New Haven, Connecticut: Yale University Press, 1990.
Drzemczewski, Andrew. *European Human Rights Convention in Domestic Law.* Oxford, England: Clarendon Press, 1983.
Humana, Charles, compiler. *World Human Rights Guide.* London: Pan Books, 1986.
Nielsen, Niels C., Jr. *The Crisis of Human Rights.* Nashville, Tennessee: Thomas Nelson, Publisher, 1978.
Seager, Joni, and Ann Olson. *Women in the World.* London: Pan Books, 1986.

Economic Systems

Allen, Frederick Lewis. *The Lords of Creation.* New York: Quadrangle/New York Times Book Company, 1935.
Braudel, Fernand. *The Perspective of the World.* New York: Harper and Row, 1984.
————. *The Wheels of Commerce.* New York: Harper and Row, 1982.
Chandler, Alfred D., Jr. *The Visible Hand.* Cambridge, Massachusetts: Harvard University Press, 1977.
Henderson, W.O. *The Industrial Revolution in Europe.* Chicago: Quadrangle Books, 1961.
Kirkland, Edward C. *Industry Comes of Age.* Chicago: Quadrangle Books, 1961.
Lindblom, Charles E. *Politics and Markets.* New York: Basic Books, 1977.
Moskoff, William. *Comparative National Economic Policies.* Lexington, Massachusetts: D.C. Heath & Co., 1973.
Shelton, Judy. *The Coming Soviet Crash.* New York: Free Press, 1989.
Sobel, Robert. *The Age of Giant Corporations.* Westport, Connecticut: Greenwood Press, 1972.

Solo, Robert A. *The Political Authority and the Market System.* Cincinnati, Ohio: Southwestern Publishing, 1974.

Sowell, Thomas. *Marxism.* New York: William Morrow, 1985.

Vernon, Raymond, and Louis T. Wells, Jr. *Economic Environment of International Business,* 3d ed. Englewood Cliffs, New Jersey: Prentice-Hall, Inc., 1981.

The Future

Boyle, Stewart, and John Ardill. *The Greenhouse Effect.* London: Hodder and Stoughton, 1989.

Brown, Lester R. *The Twenty-Ninth Day.* New York: W.W. Norton, 1978.

Cherfas, Jeremy, and John Gribbin. *The Redundant Male.* London: Triad-Paladin Books, 1985.

Drucker, Peter. *The New Realities.* New York: Harper and Row, 1989.

Ehrenreich, Barbara. *Fear of Falling.* New York: Harper Collins, 1989.

Fisher, Helen E. *The Sex Contract.* London: Grenada Books, 1982.

Hardin, Garrett. *Nature and Man's Fate.* New York: Mentor Books, 1959.

_____. "The Tragedy of Commons." *Science.* December 13, 1968.

Johnson, Stanley. *The Green Revolution.* New York: Harper and Row, 1972.

King, Dr. John L. *How to Profit from the Next Great Depression.* New York: Signet Books, 1988.

Leiss, William. *The Domination of Nature.* Boston: Beacon Press, 1974.

Merchant, Carolyn. *The Death of Nature.* New York: Harper and Row, 1980.

Nisbet, Robert. *The Present Age.* New York: Harper and Row, 1988.

Oltmans, William L., ed. *Growth.* New York: Capricorn Books, 1974.

Schneider, Stephen H., with Lynne E. Mesirow. *The Genesis Strategy.* New York: Delta Books, 1976.

Tiger, Lionel. *Optimism.* New York: Touchstone Books, 1979.

Walworth, Ralph Franklin. *Subdue the Earth.* New York: Delta Books, 1977.

Index

A

Abbasid dynasty 41
Abortion 164, 165, 166, 171
Abrazo 134
Abu Bakr 101
Acerbo Law 256
Aden 43
Adowa, Battle of 56
Aediles (Roman) 196
Afghanistan 2, 28, 30, 37, 63, 107, 185, 299
Aga Khan 104
Agriculture, ecological harm done by 316
Ahriman 110, 151
Ahura Mazda 110, 151
AIDS 306
Aigun, Treaty of 51
Ainu 2
Air pollution 312, 313
Aisha, widow of Mohammed 101
Akihito 52
Alamut 104
Al-Andalus 9
Alaska 28, 66, 242
Alawi 104
Al-Azhar 122
Albania 63, 177, 223, 299
Alberta 277
Albigensians 82, 110
Aleutian Islands 66
Alexander, King of Macedonia 14, 39, 46
Alexander II, Czar of Russia 28
Alexandria 90
Alfonsin, Raul 236
Algeria 65, 159, 299
Ali, Fourth Islamic Caliph 100
Aliens, rights of 266–270
Allende, Salvador 235

Altaic languages 63
Amar Das, Guru 109
Ambika 107
American Civil War 33, 36, 178, 285
American Independent Party 233, 261
American Revolutionary War 31
American Samoa 181
American Virgin Islands 181
Amerindian languages 66
Amida Buddha 113
Amin, Idi 185, 225, 226, 272
Amish 83
Amitabha 113
Amritsar 109
Amsterdam 204, 283
Anabaptists 282
Anarchosyndicalism 288
Ancient Government 193–198
Andorra 177
Angad, Guru 109
Angkor Wat 46
Anglo-Iranian Oil Company 44
Angola 62, 184, 224, 269, 301
Anguilla and Montserrat 308
Animal species, extinction of 317
Anne, Queen of England 154
Annexation of states 187–189
Antioch 90
Apache Indians 58
Appenzell, Inner Rhodes of 255
APRA Party (Peru) 233
Aquino, Corazon 162, 183, 309
Arab Socialism 299
Arabic alphabet 70
Arabic language 2, 63
Arabic numerals 71
Araucanian Indians 57
Arbenz Guzman, Jacobo 185

ARENA (Alliance for National Renovation, Brazil) 231
Argentina 5, 61, 62, 162, 211, 212, 215, 225, 227, 234, 236, 237, 243, 248, 252, 301
Arians 81
Aristide, Jean-Bertrand 162
Aristocracy 194
Aristotle 193, 194
Arizona 13, 58, 156, 275
Arkansas 67, 58
Armageddon, Battle of 83
Armenia 64, 178, 308
Arthur, King of Britain 153
Aruba 182
Ashikaga Shogunate 53
Ashkenazic Jews (Ashkenazim) 95, 96
Asoka 46, 112
Assad, Hafiz al 133
Assassins, Order of 104
Assyria 39, 94
Assyrian Christians 93
Asylum 268–270
Athaliah, Queen of Israel 151
Athens 14, 195, 196, 219, 279, 313
Atlanta 36
Augustine 15, 91
Augustinian 22, 43
Aung San Suu Kyi 161
Australia 1, 2, 12, 13, 183, 211, 217, 218, 219, 247, 249, 250, 257, 267, 269, 302
Australian languages 66
Australoid race 1
Austria 61, 62, 68, 177, 179, 187, 188, 190, 210, 211, 215, 216, 217, 219, 232, 234, 248, 252, 264, 290
Austrian People's Party 232, 234
Austro-Hungarian Empire 29, 35, 36, 96, 176, 192, 210, 308
Austro-Prussian War 188
Ayatollah 103
Aylwyn, Patricio 236
Azerbaijan 275, 308
Azores Islands 182
Aztecs 18, 57

B

The Bab 105
Babeuf, Gaius Gracchus 287
Babylon 39, 45, 94
Baghdad 40, 43
Bahais 105

Baha'ullah 105
Bahrein 13, 214, 298, 299
Bai, Lakshmi 160
Baja California 229
Balearic Islands 182
Balfour Declaration 43
Bali 106
Baltic languages 61
Bangladesh 4, 64, 159, 237, 269, 272, 299, 309
Banking, development of 281
Bantu languages 65
Bar Kochba Revolt 94
Barbados 5
Barre, Siad 225, 275, 309
Basel 68, 118, 206
Basij militia 103
Basque language 59
Bastille Day 118
Batista, Fulgencio 183, 225
Bavaria 175
Bay of Pigs 37, 185
Belgium 59, 61, 176, 177, 188, 190, 209, 213, 214, 217, 232, 252, 263, 271, 278, 290
Belize 5, 57
Bell, Alexander Graham 34
Belshazzar, King of Babylon 39
Bemba (Zambian tribe) 130
Benedict XVI, Pope 87
Benedictines 16, 119, 280
Bengal 11
Benin 66, 225, 269, 301
Berber languages 65
Bering, Vitus 28
Berlin 34
Bern 68, 206, 276
Beverages 136, 137
Bhindranwale, Sant Jarnail Singh 109
Bhutto: Benazir 159, 237; Zulfikar Ali 237
Biafra 178, 272
Bismarck, Prince Otto von 188, 286, 293
Black Muslims 105, 106
Blanco Party (Uruguay) 232, 235
Blanket Primary 242
Block Vote 250, 251
Blum, Leon 290
Bodhisattva 113
Boer War 188
Bohemia 175
Bohemia-Moravia, Protectorate of 188
Bokassa, Jean Bedel 185, 226
Bolivia 5, 57, 162, 237, 301

Bolshevik Revolution 44
Bombay 111
Bonaire 182
Bonaparte, Napoleon 20, 28, 175, 189,
    203, 206, 284
Booth, John Wilkes 33
Bophutatswana 179
Borobudur 46
Bose, Subhas Chandra 47
Bosnia-Herzegovina 223
Botha, Pieter 229
Botswana 66
Boudicca (Boadicea) 152
Bourgeoisie 287
Boxer Rebellion 34
Boxing Day 118
Brazil 5, 61, 62, 176, 211, 212, 215, 217,
    225, 231, 236, 243, 248, 257, 272, 301
Bremen 199
Breslau 10
Brest-Litovsk, Treaty of 190
Brethren of the Free Spirit 82
Breton language 59
Bretton Woods Agreement 292
Bribes 115
Bride Price 170
British Columbia 32, 277
Brittany 62
Brooke, Edward 275
Brundtland, Gro Harlem 158
Brussels 212
Bryan, William Jennings 286
Bucharest, Treaty of 190
Buddhism 111–114
Buenos Aires 68
Bulgaria 12, 63, 90, 91, 176, 177, 192,
    223, 290
Bundesrat: Germany 217;
    Switzerland 157, 262
Bundestag, Germany 217, 255
Burgages 200
Burkina Faso 66, 226, 269
Burma 4, 22, 47, 50, 112, 161, 191, 192,
    226, 266, 278, 297
Burnside, Ambrose 33
Burundi 3, 271, 309
Bush, George 156, 183, 235
Bushmen 6
Byelorussia 62, 308

C

Caesar Augustus 15, 198

Caetano, Marcello 225
Cairo 122
Caitanya Mahaprabu 108
Calcutta 172
Calendars and holidays 117–119
California 13, 18, 28, 155, 220, 227,
    242, 245, 246, 270, 304, 316
Caligula 15
Calvin, John 82, 282
Cambodia 9, 46, 106, 161, 184, 267, 271
Cameroon 65
Canada 5, 18, 31, 59, 61, 66, 67, 210,
    212, 217, 218, 219, 220, 227, 231, 243,
    244, 263, 276, 277, 308
Canton 70
Canute, legendary king 323
Cape Town 6
Cape Verde 62, 301
Capitani Regenti 215
Capoid race 1
Caracas 172
Cardenas, Cuauhtemoc 229
Cardinals, College of 88
Carranza, Venustiano 184
Carthaginians 9
Cassandra, Princess of Troy 321, 324
Castro, Fidel 183, 224
Catalan Language 59
Catalonia 213
Catherine of Aragon 82
Catherine the Great 27
Caucasian languages 63
Caucasoid race 1
Ceausescu, Nicolae 224
Celtic language family 59
Celts 10
Censors (Roman) 197
Center Party (Germany) 247
Central African Republic 66, 185, 226, 269
Ceuta 182
Ceylon *see* Sri Lanka
Chad 7, 65, 185, 269
Chamorro, Violetta 162
Champa 8, 9
Ch'an Buddhism 113
Chandragupta Maurya 46
Charlemagne 16, 40, 153
Charles, Eugenia 162
Charles I, King of England 175
Charles V, Holy Roman Emperor 173
Charles VIII, King of France 175
Charles XII, King of Sweden 19
Chiang Kai Shek 52, 187

Chichen Itza 57
Child Marriage 170
Chile 5, 34, 57, 61, 66, 225, 235, 236, 248, 301
Ch'in dynasty 49
China 6, 9, 17, 28, 34, 37, 53, 48-52, 54, 55, 63, 64, 70, 71, 93, 112, 113, 115, 116, 129, 133, 161, 166, 171, 176, 179, 185, 186, 187, 188, 191, 224, 266, 295-297, 312
Chinese script 70, 71
Ch'ing dynasty 51
Chittagong Hill Tracts 272, 309
Chretien, Jean 277
Christian Democratic Party: Chile 235, 236; Germany 232, 255; Italy 230, 256; Switzerland 232, 262
Christian Science 83
Christianity, in general 80-84; Eastern Orthodox 89-91; Monophysite 92; Nestorian 92-93; Protestant 84-86; Roman Catholic 86-89
Chung Kuo 48
Churchill, Winston S. 25, 35, 291, 321
Cincinnati 251
Ciskei 179
Citizens, rights of 270-278
Clock time 119
Cloning 307
Closed Primary 242
Cochran, Barbara 120
Cold War 291, 292
Collor de Mello, Fernando 236
Cologne: Bishopric of 199; City of 24
Colombia 5, 232, 243, 301
Colorado, State of 316
Colorado Party (Uruguay) 232, 235
Columbus, Christopher 18
Comitia Centuriata 196, 197
Comitia Tributa 197
Commercial paper, origin of 281
Commons (Ecological sense) 318
Commons, House of: Canada 218, 231; Great Britain 200-202, 218, 231, 244, 250, 263
Communist Party: Albania 223; Bulgaria 223; China 224; Czechoslovakia 223; France 248; Germany 247, 261; Hungary 223; Italy 230, 256; Japan 251; Poland 223; Romania 224; Soviet 221-223; Switzerland 234; Vietnam 224; Yugoslavia 224

Community property 155
Concilium Plebis 197
Concubinage 164
Confederacy *see* Confederate States of America
Confederate States of America 178
Confucianism 143
Confucius 48, 115
Congo, People's Republic of 300
Congoid race 1
Congress of Vienna 28, 96, 192, 203, 209
Congress Party (India) 230, 233, 244
Conjugation of verbs 73
Connecticut 241
Consensual Democracy 234, 235
Conservative Jews 97, 98
Conservative Party: Canada 231, 233, 244, 263; Colombia 232, 233; Great Britain 231, 233, 244, 263; New York 243
Constantine I, Roman Emperor 80, 198
Constantine VI, Byzantine Emperor 153
Constantine XI, Byzantine Emperor 26
Constantinople 25, 26, 28, 41, 89, 90
Constitutional Amendments 220-221
Consuls (Roman) 197
Coolidge, Calvin 241
Copernicus, Nikolaus 17
Coptic Church 92
Corporative State (Italy) 290, 294
Cortez, Hernan 57
Costa Rica 5, 214, 301
Councillors, House of (Japan) 162, 218, 230
Counter-Reformation 87
Coventry 24
Creole languages 60
Cresson, Edith 158
Crete 279
Croatia 179, 190, 223, 308
Cromwell, Oliver 19, 175
Cross-Filing (in primaries) 242
Crusaders 17, 41, 95
Crusades 17
Cuauhtemoc 57
Cuba 32, 183, 184, 185, 186, 224, 225, 267, 270
Curacao 182
Curtesy 155
Cushitic languages 65
Cuzco 57
Cyprus 62, 63, 90, 91, 179
Cyrillic alphabet 70

Cyrus, King of Persia 39
Czechoslovakia 11, 59, 63, 177, 179, 184, 188, 211, 212, 223, 252, 290, 290, 295, 318

D

Da Gama, Vasco 18
Dahomey, Kingdom of 56
Daimyo 129
Dalai Lama 112
Damascus 40
Danes 10
Dar ul-Harb 100
Dar ul-Islam 100, 170
Darius III, King of Persia 39
Dark Age 16, 324
Darwin, Charles 21
Davis, Jefferson 36
Debernard, Danielle 120
Deborah, Israelite judge 151
Declension of nouns and adjectives 73, 74
de Gaulle, Charles 221, 233
de Klerk, Frederick 229
Delaware 67
Democracy as government form 194
Democracy and Authoritarianism 235–237
Democratic Party: Australia 250; U.S. 228, 230, 231, 233, 235, 237, 241–243, 245, 246, 248, 249, 261, 262; Denmark 182, 190, 214, 221, 232, 263
Dependencies and Colonies 181–182
Deputies, Chamber of: Argentina 251; Brazil 257; Italy 230, 256; Mexico 217, 228, 256; Spain 251
de Saxe, Marshal 19
Detroit 38
Devanagari script 70
Dewey, Thomas E. 241
Dharma 106
D'Hondt Proportional Representation 252
Dhul-al-Hijja 118
Dialects 66–69
Diaspora 94
Diaz, Bartholomew 18
Diaz, Porfirio 183
Dictator (Roman) 197, 198
Dictatorships: Military 225–226; Modern 226–227; Personalist Civilian 226; Totalitarian 221–224; Traditional 224–225

Diocletian 15, 198, 280
Direct Legislation 218–219
Direct Primary 241–243
Discrimination, racial and ethnic 273–278
District of Columbia 177, 231, 278
Djibouti 299
Dmitri Donskoi, Prince of Moscow 4
Docetists 80
Doe, Samuel 226, 309
Doenitz, Grand-Admiral Karl 191
Doge (Venice) 205
Doi, Takako 163
Dole, Elizabeth 156
Dominica 5, 162
Dominican Republic 5, 34, 225, 301
Donatists 80
Dower 155
Dowry 170
Dravidian: languages 64; peoples 7, 45
Dreikonigstag 118
Dresden 36
Dress 137, 138
Drew, Timothy 105
Druzes 104
Durga 107

E

East Timor, Republic of 178, 271
Easter Island 66
Eating habits 135, 136
Ebionites 80
Economic Systems: Afro-Asian non–Islamic 300–301; Ancient European 279–280; Chinese 295–297; Eighteenth Century European 284; Islamic 298–300; Japanese 297–298; Latin American 302; Medieval European 280–282; Nineteenth Century Western 284–288; Renaissance European 282–283; Soviet 290, 294–295; Twentieth Century Capitalist 288–290, 291–294
Ecosystems 321, 322
Ecuador 5, 57, 301
Eddy, Mary Baker 83
Edison, Thomas A. 34
Education: American and European compared 122–125; Japanese 125–126; Soviet 126; Third World 126
Edward I, King of England 95
Edward III, King of England 175
Edward IV, King of England 174

Eeds 99
Egypt 9, 14, 39, 40, 44, 69, 81, 92, 133, 159, 168, 171, 227, 299
Eighteenth-Century Government: England 199–202; France 203–204; Netherlands 204–205; Poland 206–207; Prussia 202–203; Switzerland 206; Venice 205–206
Eisenhower, Dwight 242
El Salvador 301
Eleanor of Aquitain 153, 154
Elizabeth, Czarina of Russia 27
Elizabeth I, Queen of England 154
Elizabeth II, Queen of England 213
Endogamous Cultures 170
England 10, 66, 154, 174, 175, 198, 199–202, 213, 245, 282, 283, 284
Entropy 323
Equatorial Guinea 226, 272
Eritrea 273
Eskimo-Aleut Languages 66
Estates-General: of France 203, 204; of the Dutch Republic 204, 205
Estonia 29, 63, 178, 189, 222, 275, 308
Ethiopia 2, 4, 56, 65, 81, 92, 184, 224, 273, 278, 301, 308
Eugene, Prince of Savoy 19
European Community 25, 157, 158, 231, 293, 308
European State System, origin of 173–176
Exogamous Cultures 170
Eyadema, Gnassinghe 225

F

Face, loss of 144
Falasha 96
Falkland Islands 158, 181
Falwell, Jerry 85
Family 147–150
Faroe Islands 182
Fascist Party (Italy) 233, 256
Fassnacht 118
Fatima, daughter of Mohammed 101
Federal Nations 210–212
Female circumcision 168
Ferdinand of Hapsburg 175
Ferdinand, King of Spain 9, 95
Ferraro, Geraldine 156, 158
Feudalism 16
Fiji 3
Finland 29, 59, 61, 62, 178

Finnbogadottir, Vigdis 158
First Past the Post 243
First Vatican Council 87
Fiver Shi'a 103
Flemish language 59
Flitterwochen 165
Florence 199
Florida 13, 18, 58, 67, 270, 275
Foot binding 168
Foreign Corrupt Practices Act (US) 135
Forty-shilling Freeholders 200
Four Noble Truths 111
Fourth Crusade 89
France 12, 16, 40, 59, 63, 67, 154, 173, 175, 186, 189, 190, 192, 198, 203–204, 209, 210, 215, 217, 218, 219, 220, 233, 239, 240, 247, 248, 266, 267, 276, 284, 287, 288, 290, 291, 294, 302, 318
Franco-Prussian War 288
Frankfurt-am-Main, Free City of 188, 199, 209
Franz Ferdinand, Austrian crown prince 22
Frederick II, King of Prussia 19, 35, 202
Frederick V, Duke of the Palatinate 175
Free Democratic Party (Germany) 255
Freeman 200
FRELIMO (Front for the Liberation of Mozambique) 185
French Guiana 181
French Polynesia 182, 308
Freud, Sigmund 21, 123
Freudianism 35, 123, 148
Fribourg 276
Frisian Language 60
Friulian Language 60
Frondizi, Arturo 236
Fujiwara family 53
Fukien 11, 64
Funan 8
Future Trends: Culture 303; Economic Systems 309–312; Family, Marriage, Gender, Children 305–308; Human Rights 309; Language 303–304; Racial Mingling 302–303; Religion 304–305; States and Governments 308–309

G

Galician Language 60
Galileo Galilei 17
Gandhi: Indira 109, 160, 230; Mohandas (Mahatma) 47; Rajiv 110

Gastarbeiter 268, 302
Gaugamela, Battle of 39
Gautama Siddartha (the Buddha) 45, 111
Gender in language 76, 77
Geneva: Canton of 234, 275; Republic of 188, 206
Genghis Khan 25, 50
Genoa 199
Genocide 270–272
George III, King of England 199, 201
Georgia: American state 36, 67, 242; Soviet republic 63, 178, 222, 308
Germanic languages 2, 61
Germany 1, 10, 11, 22–24, 35, 59, 60, 68, 85, 86, 87, 96, 147, 176, 179, 183, 186, 187, 190, 191, 192, 198, 199, 209, 211, 212, 215, 216, 217, 219, 220, 221, 223, 232, 233, 239, 240, 247, 252, 255, 261, 264, 268, 269, 276, 286, 287, 288, 289, 291, 293, 295, 302, 303, 318
Geronimo 58
Gerrymandering 245–247
Ghana 66, 225, 226, 227, 269
Gharar 300
Gibraltar 181
Giro d'Italia 141
Glarus 206
Gnostics 80, 82, 84, 110
Gobind Singh, Guru 109
Gohonzon 114
Golden Freedom 207
Golden Temple of Amritsar 109, 272
Gongyo 114
Good Hope, Cape of 18
Gorbachev, Mikhail 30, 38, 90, 129, 221, 222, 223, 251, 252, 274, 290, 294, 309
Gordon, General Charles "Chinese" 102
Governments, Recognition of 182–185
Granada 9
Grand Pensionary of Holland 205
Grant, Ulysses S. 33, 34, 35
Graubunden 62, 206, 276
Graue Alltag 165
Great Britain 60, 85, 86, 114, 119, 157, 158, 188, 190, 220, 233, 234, 238, 239, 240, 244, 265, 286, 288, 289, 291, 293, 303, 318
Great Schism 16, 173
Greece 10, 14, 62, 89, 91, 176, 179, 190, 210, 217, 225

Greek Alphabet 70
Green Party: Australia 250; Germany 255; Great Britain 231
Greenland 66, 182
Greenwich Mean Time 119
Gregorian Calendar 117, 118
Grenada 5, 36, 185
Group Marriage 163
Guadeloupe 5, 182
Guam 34, 66, 181
Guanabara 231
Guarani Language 59
Guatemala 5, 36, 57, 185, 301
Guderian, Heinz 24
Guinea 301
Guinea-Bissau 62
Guinevere, Queen of Britain 153, 165
Gunpowder 17
Gupta Empire 46
Gurmukhi Script 70
Guru Granth Sahib 109
Gustavus Adolphus, King of Sweden 19, 22
Gustavus III, King of Sweden 199
Guyana 301
Gwalior 160

H

Hadrian 15
Hagenbach-Bischoff Proportional Representation 254
Haiti 5, 34, 61, 162, 226, 270
Hajj 99
Hakim, Sultan of Egypt 104
Hamburg 24, 188, 199
Han Dynasty 49
Hangul Script 71
Hannover, Kingdom of 188
Hanseatic League 199
Hapsburg, House of 173, 175
Haram 300
Harappa 45
Hare Krishna 107
Hare Proportional Representation 257–259
Harijan 129
Haroun al-Raschid 40
Hashishim 104
Hasidic Jews (Hasidim) 97
Hassan, son of Ali 101
Hassan Sabah 104
Havel, Vaclav 223

Index

Hawaii 7, 34, 66, 187, 275, 297
Haya de la Torre, Raul 233
Hayakawa, Dr. S. I. 275
Hebrew alphabet 70
Heidelberg 175
Henry II, King of England 154
Henry IV, King of England 174
Henry VI, King of England 174
Henry VII, King of England 174
Henry VIII, King of England 82
Hera 151
Hesse-Cassel 188
Hesse-Nassau 188
Hezbollah 103
High German *see* Hochdeutsch
Hillel, Rabbi 94
Hills, Carla 156
Hinayana Buddhism 112
Hindu religion 11, 106–108
Hiragana script 71
Hirohito, Emperor of Japan 116
Hiroshima 36
Hispaniola 5
Hitler, Adolf 11, 23, 24, 34, 96,
    183, 188, 191, 221, 233, 269, 291,
    321
Ho Chi Minh 133
Hochdeutsch 68, 72
Hojo Regency 53
Holland 204–205
Hollywood 38
Holocaust 10, 96
Holy Grail 153
Honduras 301
Hong Kong 47, 51, 181, 192, 268, 297,
    301, 309
Hottentots 6
House of Representatives: Australia 217,
    249; Japan 217, 230, 251; Ohio 246,
    250, 259, 260; United States 216, 217,
    246, 259, 263
Huerta, Victoriano 183
Hulagu Khan 104
Human limitations 318–324
Humphrey, Hubert 241
Hundred Years' War 154, 175
Hungary 4, 41, 63, 177, 184, 209, 223,
    256, 291, 294, 295
Huns 4
Hus, John 82
Hussein, King of Jordan 269
Hussein, son of Ali 101
Hussein, Saddam 37, 133, 192

Hussites 82, 282
Hyderabad 189

I

I Ching 48
Ibadis 104
Iceland 132, 158, 216
Id al-Adha 118
Ideographic writing 70
Illia, Arturo 236
Illinois 67
Imam 102
Inacto da Silva, Luis 151
Inanna 151
Incas 18, 57
India 3, 7, 9, 11, 17, 18, 22, 39, 40,
    45–48, 50, 59, 63, 92, 104, 106–111,
    123, 160, 168, 169, 189, 211, 212, 216,
    217, 230, 244, 272, 300
Indiana 58, 67, 241, 246
Indo-European language family 61
Indonesia 1, 2, 46, 50, 64, 106, 162, 169,
    178, 191, 192, 226, 227, 271, 283, 296,
    298
Industrial Revolution, the 19, 20, 95,
    164, 165
Inflected languages 73–75
Iran 3, 9, 14, 15, 28, 36, 39, 40, 41, 44,
    45, 63, 93, 100, 102, 105, 107, 110,
    159, 180, 185, 227, 274, 298, 299
Iran-Iraq War 44, 45, 192
Iraq 37, 43, 44, 63, 69, 93, 96, 101, 133,
    180, 185, 227, 298, 299, 309
Ireland 62, 216, 217, 250, 257, 259
Irene, Byzantine Empress 153
Irish Gaelic Language 60
Iroquois Confederacy 57, 162
Isabella, Queen of Spain 9, 95, 155
Isandhlwana, Battle of 56
Iseult 153, 165
Ishtar 151
Isis 151
ISKCON *see* Hare Krishna
Islam 9, 17, 98–100; Shi'ite
    (Shi'a) 102–105; Sunni 100–102
Islamic Banking 300
Ismailis 103, 104
Israel 44, 63, 80, 94, 96, 97, 104, 158,
    180, 192, 215, 216, 217, 232, 233, 254,
    257, 261, 264, 269
Istanbul 28, 41, 89, 97
Italy 41, 59, 62, 87, 176, 210, 216,

218, 219, 220, 221, 230, 233, 235, 256, 263, 267, 276, 283, 290, 294
Ivan I "Kalilta," Prince of Moscow 26
Ivan III, Prince of Moscow 26
Ivan IV, "the Terrible," Czar of Russia 26, 95
Ivory Coast 301

J

Jackson, Andrew 239, 241
Jagellonian dynasty 207
Jainism 108
Jamaica 5, 33, 301
James II, King of England 199
Janata Party (India) 230
Janissaries 41
Japan 4, 11, 32, 49, 50, 52–55, 59, 72, 112, 113, 116, 121, 125, 126, 129, 130, 161, 166, 179, 185, 188, 191, 214, 217, 218, 221, 229, 235, 251, 268, 297, 298, 319
Jaruzelski, Wladyslaw 270
Java 50
Jehovah's Witnesses 83
Jerusalem 17, 41, 43, 89, 90
Jezebel, Queen of Israel 151
Jimmu Tenno 52
Jingo, Empress of Japan 161
Joan of Arc 154
Jodo Chinshu Buddhism 113
John I, King of England 154
John VIII, Pope 152
John XXIII, Pope 87, 88
John Paul II, Pope 88
Johnson, Prince 226
Jordan 43, 214, 269, 299
Judaism 94–98
Judicial Power 219–220
Julian Calendar 117, 118
Julius Caesar 10
Justicialist Party (Argentina) 227, 237
Justinian, Byzantine Emperor 153

K

Kaliningrad 10
Kami 116
Kamikaze 53, 55
Kanji 71

Kansas 156
Karelo-Finnish Republic 63
Karma 106, 107, 108, 145, 168, 323
Kassebaum, Nancy 156
Katakana Script 71
Kazan, Emirate of 26
Kefauver, Estes 241
Kemal, Mustapha "Ataturk" 180, 237
Kentucky 67
Kenya 2, 4, 65, 130
Kerala 92
Kerbala, Battle of 101
Kerekou, Mathieu 225
Khaddafi, Muammar 7, 44, 159, 227
Khamenei, Ayatollah Ali 103, 227
Khan, Ghulem Izhek 237
Khartoum, siege of 102
Khazar Empire, Khazars 94, 95
Khmer Rouge 271
Khoisanian Languages 65
Khomeini, Ayatollah Ruhollah 103, 105, 111, 227
Khrushchev, Nikita 221
Kibbutzim 158
Kiev 25, 27
Kievan Rus 25, 27
Kikuyu (Kenyan tribe) 130
Kilwa 56
Kim Il Sung 133, 191, 224
Kinship group 147
Kitchener, General 102
Knesset 215, 257, 264
Knights of Malta 181
Knox, John 82
Koan 113
Koenigsberg 10
Komeito 114
Kongo 56
Kopp, Elizabeth 157, 262
Korea 37, 49, 52, 53, 54, 71, 112, 161, 171, 185, 186, 188, 191, 192, 224, 298, 301
Korean War 37, 185, 186, 191
Kosovo 62, 274
Krishna 107, 108
Kshatriya 129
Kublai Khan 50
Kuhhandel 265
Kulaks 271
Kulikovo, Battle of 4, 26
Kung Fu Tse *see* Confucius
Kurdistan 180

Kuwait 13, 37, 44, 185, 298, 299, 302, 309
Ky, Nguyen Cao 133

L

Labor Party: Australia 247, 249, 250; Great Britain 231, 244, 245, 263; Israel 264; Malta 259; Norway 232
Ladakh 8
Ladin Language 60
Lagos 172
Lakshmi 107
Lancelot 153, 165
Landesgemeinde 219
Langue d'Oc 59
Langue d'Oil 59
Lao Tse 115
Laos 8, 268
Las Navas de Tolosa, Battle of 9
Latin Alphabet 69
Latvia 29, 178, 189, 222, 275, 308
Lausanne, Treaty of 180
Law, John 284
Learning Languages 74–77
Lebanon 63, 104, 269, 299
Leeuwenhoek, Anton 17
Lefebvre, Archbishop Marcel 88
Legislative Caucus 241
Legislatures 216–218
Leipzig, Battle of 20
Lenin, Vladimir 23, 29, 34, 184, 290
Leo IV, Byzantine Emperor 153
Leo XIII, Pope 87
Lesotho 65
Lhasa 112
Liberal Party: Australia 249, 250; Canada 231, 233, 263; Colombia 233; New York 243; Switzerland 234
Liberal Democratic Party: Great Britain 231; Japan 114, 161, 229, 233, 251
Liberal-Social Democratic Alliance (Great Britain) 231, 245
Liberation Theology 88
Liberia 65, 309
Liberum Veto 207
Libro de Oro 205
Libya 7, 44, 100, 159, 227, 299
Liechtenstein 61, 177, 240
Liegnitz, Battle of 4
Likud (Israel) 264
Limited Vote 251
Lincoln, Abraham 33, 285

Lisbon 68
Lithuania 27, 29, 158, 178, 189, 222, 275, 308
Little Big Horn, Battle of 58
Logging, ecological effects of 315, 316
Lok Sabha (India) 230
London 24, 119, 283, 284
Lords, House of 200, 217
Los Angeles 313
Louis VII, King of France 153
Louis XIV, King of France 35, 154, 203
Louis XV, King of France 203
Louis XVI, King of France 203, 204, 284
Louisiana 33, 155, 242, 249, 284
Louisiana Company 284
Low German see Plattdeutsch
Lubeck 24, 199
Lucerne 206
Lucifer 110
Ludendorff, Erich 22
Luo (Kenyan tribe) 130
Luther, Martin 68, 82, 323
Luxembourg 61, 217, 257
Lwow (Lvov) 10
Lycurgus 279

M

Macao 51, 182
MacArthur, General Douglas 191
Macchiavelli, Nicolo 173
Macchu Picchu 57
McClellan, George B. 33
Macedonia 14, 62
Madagascar 4, 66, 225
Madeira Islands 182
Madero, Francisco 183
Madrid 68
Maginot Line 23
Magna Charta 154
Magyars 16
Mahabharata 45
Mahadevi 107
Mahakala 107
Mahavira 108, 111
Mahayana Buddhism 113
Mahdi 102
Mahmud of Ghazni 46
Maine 67
Mainz, Bishopric of 199
Majoritarian Democracy 234, 235
Makarios, Archbishop 91
Malabar Christians 92

Malagasy *see* Madagascar
Malawi 65, 269
Malaya *see* Malaysia
Malayo-Polynesian Languages 64
Malaysia 8, 47, 50, 177, 192, 211, 216, 269, 278, 297, 298
Mali: Empire of 56; Republic of 65, 269, 299
Malindi 56
Malta 63, 181, 217, 247, 260
Mamelukes 41
Manchukuo 179, 191
Manchuria 179, 191
Mandarinate 129
Mandate of Heaven 49, 51, 296
Mani 110
Manichaenism 110
Manzikert, Battle of 9
Mao Tse Tung 11, 129, 133, 221, 297
Marathon, Battle of 14
Marcionites 80
Marco Polo 17
Marcos, Ferdinand 183
Marcus Aurelius 15
Mardi Gras 118
Maria Theresa, Empress of Austria 155
Marie Antoinette, Queen of France 175
Market Socialism (Yugoslavia) 295
Marquesas Islands 163
Marriage and Children 162–172
Martel, Charles 40
Martinique 5, 182
Marx, Karl 21, 287
Marxism 287, 288
Mary, mother of Jesus Christ 152
Mary I, Queen of England 154
Maryland 67, 156
Massachusetts 67, 83, 275
Matura 124
Mauretania 6, 63, 178, 269, 299
Maurya Empire 46
Maximilian, Duke of Bavaria 175
May Day 118
Mayan Indians 57
MDB (Brazilian Democratic Movement) 231
Mecca 98, 119
Mecklenburg 199
Medieval Government 198–199
Meir, Golda 158
Melanesians 4, 7
Melilla 182
Menen, Carlos 227

Mengistu, Haile Mariam 92, 273, 309
Mennonites 83
Mercantilism 283, 284
Meroe 56
Mesopotamia 14
Messiah 97
Mestizos 5
Methodism 83
Mexican War 32, 189
Mexico 18, 32, 57, 61, 66, 171, 183, 184, 189, 211, 212, 215, 216, 217, 218, 228, 229, 243, 256, 283, 301
Mexico City 68, 172, 189, 313
Miami 13
Micronesians 4, 7
Midway, Battle of 55
Mikoyan, Anastas 274
Mikulski, Barbara 156
Milan 199
Minerva 181
Ming dynasty 50
Mining, ecological harm done by 316
Minnesota 227
Mirza Ali Mohammed 105
Mirza Husain Ali 105
Mississippi 228
Missouri 67, 220
Miterrand, Francois 294
Mithras 151
Mixed Government 195
Mobutu Sese Seko 225
Mofford, Rose 156
Mohammed 9, 39
Mohammed Ahmed 102
Mohammed al-Muntazar 102
Mohammed Reza Shah Pahlavi 44, 45
Mohenjo-Daro 45
Mohi, Battle of 4
Moldavia 222, 275
Mombasa 56
Mon-Khmer Languages 64
Monaco 177
Monarchy 193, 213, 214
Mongolia 6, 65, 112
Mongoloid race 1
Mongols 4, 7
Monogamy 162 et seq.
Monophysites 81, 92
Monroe Doctrine 32
Montenegro 176, 177
Montezuma 57
Montreal 277
The Moral Majority 85

Mormonism 83
Morocco 9, 18, 43, 63, 65, 69, 96, 178, 182, 214, 267, 299
Moscow 25, 26, 28, 30, 89, 290, 294
Mossadegh, Mohammed 44, 185
Mozambique 61, 184, 185, 224, 269, 301
MPLA (Popular Movement for the Liberation of Angola) 184
Muawiya 101
Mulroney, Brian 277
Munda languages 64
Murphy's Law 320
Musaveni, Yoweri 272
Mussolini, Benito 17, 23, 56, 87, 221, 233, 290, 294
Myanmar *see* Burma

N

Nagasaki 36, 54
Nam Viet 8
Names *see* Personal Names
Namibia 61, 66
Nanking 191
Nanosecond 120
Naples, Kingdom of 175
Napoleon III 209
Narva, Battle of 27
Nasser, Gamal Abdel 44, 103, 227
Natal 6
National Assembly: Burma 161; France 218, 247, 248
National League for Democracy (Burma) 161
National Party (Australia) 247, 249, 250
National Republican Party (Switzerland) 233
National Socialist German Workers' Party 233, 261
Nationalist Party: Germany 247; Malta 259; South Africa 229, 245
Nationality 266
Nationalrat (Switzerland) 217, 255
Naturaja 107
Nauru 177
Nebraska 156, 227
Nebuchadnezzar 94
Negotiating with foreigners 78, 79
Negritos 2
Nestorius 92, 93
Netherlands 12, 60, 72, 82, 86, 87, 174, 177, 182, 190, 199, 204–205, 214, 217,

232, 235, 252, 254, 263, 283, 290
Netherlands Antilles 308
Neuchatel 206
Nevsky, Prince Alexander 25
New Britain 66
New Brunswick 278
New Caledonia 182, 308
New Democratic Party (Canada) 231
New Economic Policy 290
New Hampshire 67
New Mexico 58, 275
New Orleans 118, 267
New York: City of 67, 258; State of 67, 83, 241, 243
New Zealand 1, 3, 7, 66, 67, 182, 217
Newfoundland 67, 182
Nguema, Francisco Macias 226, 272
Nicaea, Council of 81
Nicaragua 162, 183, 224, 225
Nichiren Shoshu Buddhism 113
Niger 65, 269, 299
Niger-Congo languages 65
Nigeria 56, 65, 67, 178, 211, 215, 225, 237, 269, 276
Nilo-Saharan languages 65
Nineveh 39
Nirvana 46, 106, 113, 145, 323
Nkrumah, Kwame 227
Noble Eightfold Path 111
Noise Pollution 313, 314
Nomenklatura 129, 312
Nominating Convention 241, 242
Noriega, Manuel 185, 225
Normans 10
North Carolina 67, 228
North Kibris, Republic of 179
North Korea *see* Korea
North Yemen *see* Yemen
Northern Caroline Islands 181
Northern Ireland 67
Norway 157, 158, 177, 182, 190, 214, 218, 220, 232, 235, 264
Nova Scotia 278
Novgorod 25
Nuclear Pollution 314, 315
Number in languages 77, 78
Nuremberg, Free City of 199

O

Obote, Milton 226, 272
Occitan language 59

O'Connor, Sandra Day 156
Octavian *see* Caesar Augustus
Ogadai, Khan of the Mongols 4
Ogaden 273
Ohio 246, 250, 259
Oman 104, 214, 299
Omdurman, Battle of 102
On 145
Ontario 212, 277, 278
OPEC (Organization of Petroleum
  Exporting Countries) 100
Open Primary 242
Orange Free State 6, 188
Orleans 154
Ormuzd 110
Orr, Kay 156
Ortega, Daniel 224
Orthodox Jews 97
Osceola 58
Ostracism 196
Otto I, Holy Roman Emperor 16
Ottoman Turks 41
Oxford University 125

P

Pakistan 11, 45, 47, 48, 177, 189, 237,
  269, 274, 299
Palatinate, Duchy of the 175
Palenque 57
Paleo-Asiatic languages 65
Palestine 11, 17, 39, 40, 43, 94, 96, 180,
  308
Palimony 164
Panama 34, 36, 225, 301
Papua New Guinea 66
Papuan languages 66
Papuans 3, 7
Paraguay 59, 66, 225, 226, 301
Paris 86, 118, 284, 288, 313
Parlement of Paris 203
Parliamentary Government 215–216
Parsees 110, 111
Parthenogenesis 307
Parti Quebecois 231
Particratie 264
Partitioned Countries 185–187
Party Discipline 237–238
Party Systems: Multi-Party 232; No-
  Party 227; One-Party 227–230;
  Two-Party 230–232
Parvati 107
Pascal-Trouillot, Ertha 162

Passport 266
Pasupati 107
Paterfamilias 151
Patrilocal Cultures 169
Patronymic 130–133
Paul the Apostle 80, 94, 152
Paul, Ron 309
Peking: City of 70, 187; Treaty of 51
Pelagian 22, 35, 36
Pelagius 15, 91
Peloponnesian War 14, 279
Pennsylvania 58, 83
Pentecost 86
People's Action Party (Singapore) 228,
  244
Pericles 196
Perón, Eva 162
Perón, Isabel 162, 236
Perón, Juan Domingo 227, 233, 236
Perónista Party (Argentina) 233
Perry, Matthew C. 54
Persia *see* Iran
Persians 14
Personal Names 130–133
Peru 18, 57, 59, 66, 225, 233, 248, 301
Petain, Marshal Henri Philippe 190
Peter "the Great," Czar of Russia 27
Pesticides 316, 317
Petrodollars 43, 44
Philip, King of Macedonia 14
Philip II, King of Spain 174
Philippines 1, 2, 54, 64, 183, 191, 296,
  298
Photosynthesis 316
Pidgin languages 60
Pilsudski, Josef 179
Pinochet, Augusto 225, 235
Pius IX, Pope 87
Pizarro, Francisco 57
Plato 193
Plattdeutsch 68
Poland 2, 10, 26, 27, 28, 29, 88, 89, 95,
  177, 179, 187, 188, 190, 198, 199,
  206–207, 210, 223, 248, 269, 291, 294,
  295, 318
Political Parties, Nature of 232–234
Polity 194
Pollution Control, cost of 317, 318
Poltava, Battle of 27
Polyandry 163
Polygamy 83, 163
Polygyny 163, 168, 169
Polynesians 3, 7

Pontiac 58
Pope 16, 302
Popular Front 290
Porcupine Dilemma 306
Portugal 18, 40, 60, 174, 175, 178, 210, 216, 225, 248
Postwar Restorations 192
Pot, Pol 270
Potwalloper Franchise 201
Praetors (Roman) 197
Predestination 283
Preferential Voting 249, 250
Presidential Government 214–215
PRI (Party of Revolutionary Institutions, Mexico) 228, 243, 256
Priam, King of Troy 324
Progressive Conservative Party *see* Conservative Party, Canada
Progressive Party (U.S.) 233
Proletariat 287
Protestant Reformation 16
Proudhon, Jacques 21
Provencal language 59
Prunskiene, Kazimiera 158
Prussia 187, 188, 190, 202–203, 209
Pskov 26
Pu Yi, Henry 191
Puerto Rico 181, 278, 302
Pygmies 2

Q

Qatar 214, 298
Qom 103
Quaestors (Roman) 197
Quakers 83
Quasi-Federal Nations 213
Quebec 61, 68, 212, 231, 277, 308
Quechua language 57
Queensland 247
Qu'ran 100, 101

R

Racial Frontiers, Pre-1492 4, 5
Radical Party: Argentina 237; Switzerland 232, 233, 262
Rafsanjani, Hashemi 227
Rama 107
Ramadan 99, 119
Ramayana 45
Rawlings, Jerry 226
Reagan, Ronald 309

Realschule 123, 124
Reconstructionist Jews 97
Reformed Jews 97
Reichstag (German) 252, 258, 261
Reincarnation *see* Transmigration of Souls
Religious Party (Israel) 233
RENAMO (Mozambique National Resistance Organization) 185
Representatives, House of *see* House of Representatives
Republican Party (U.S.) 228, 230, 231, 235, 237, 241–243, 245, 246, 261, 262
Rerum Novarum 87
Reza Khan, Shah of Iran 44
Rhee, Syngman 191
Rhode Island 67, 83
Rhodes 181
Rhodesia, Republic of 179
Riba 299, 300
Richard I, King of England 154
Richard II, King of England 174
Richard III, King of England 174
Richards, Ann 156
Rig Veda 45
Rightly-guided Caliphs 101
Rinzai Buddhism 113
Rio de Janeiro 68, 118, 172
Rio de Oro 178
Robertson, Pat 85
Roh Tae Woo 133
Roman Empire 279, 280
Roman Numerals 71
Roman Republic 196–198
Romance languages 2, 61
Romania 61, 62, 91, 176, 177, 190, 224, 274, 291
Romanov dynasty 27
Romantic Love 165
Romanus Argyrus, Byzantine Emperor 153
Rome, City of 14, 15, 40
Rommel, Erwin 24
Roosevelt, Theodore 233, 286
Rosh Hashanah 118
Rotten boroughs 200
Rotterdam 24
Royal Canadian Mounted Police 212
Run-Off 248, 249
Rurik 25
Russia 2, 20, 25–31, 54, 89, 90, 95, 96, 187, 188, 190, 287, 288
Russian Civil War 29, 55

Russian Republic (of USSR) 222, 274
Russo-Japanese War 29
Russo-Turkish War of 1877–78 28, 90
Rwanda 3, 271, 309
Ryazan 25, 26

S

Sabutai, Prince of the Mongols 4, 25
Sadat, Anwar al 133
Saddam Hussein 37, 227, 309
Saenz-Pena Law 251
Saharan Arab Democratic Republic 178
Saigon 9
St. Berchtold's Day 118
St. Gall(en) 68, 206
St. Lague Proportional Representation 253
St. Nicholas's Day 118
St. Petersburg 27, 34
St. Pierre and Miquelon 182
St. Stephen's Day 118
Saipan 7
Sakti 107
Salamis, Battle of 14
Salic Law 153, 155
Salinas de Gortari, Carlos 228
Salinization of soil 316
Salzburg 68
Samsara 106, 108, 113
Samskara 106
Samurai 129
San Francisco 28
San Marino 177, 215, 216
Sandinista Movement 224
Santa Anna, Antonio Lopez de 189
Sao Paulo 172
Sarajevo 90
Sassanid dynasty (Persian) 39, 40
Satan 110
Sati 168
Satori 111, 113
Satyagraha 47
Saudi Arabia 13, 37, 100, 167, 214, 227, 266, 268, 298, 300
Savimbi, Jonas 184
Sawm 99
Schevarnadze, Edward 274
Schwyz 118, 206
Schwyzerduutsch 68
Scientific Socialism 287
Scot-and-Lot Franchise 200
Scotland 62, 67, 82, 213, 233, 245, 308

Scots Gaelic Language 60
Scottish Nationalist Party 233
Sealand 180
Sebastian, King of Portugal 174
Second Ballot 247, 248
Sejm 207
Sejmiks 207
Selah 99
Seljuk Turks 41
Seminole Indians 58
Semitic languages 63
Senate: Australia 217, 218, 257;
   Belgium 217; Brazil 217; Califor-
   nia 246; Canada 217; France 217, 218;
   Ireland 217; Italy 218; Mexico 218,
   229; Rome 197; Spain 251; United
   States 216, 218; Venic 205
Senegal 6, 66
Sephardic Jews (Sephardim) 95
Sepoy Rebellion 47, 160
Septuagint 94
Serbia 62, 90, 176, 177, 188, 223, 274
Seven Deadly Sins 281, 282
Sevener Shi'a 103, 104
Seventh Day Adventists 83
Sevres, Treaty of 180
Sexual Revolution 306
Shankara, Thomas 226
Shehada 99
Shema 94
Shimabara Peninsula 54
Shinto 116
Shiva 107
Shogunate 53, 54
Shona (Zimbabwean tribe) 130
Siddhartha Gautama 111
Sierra Leone 65
Simpatico 134
Singapore 8, 59, 121, 161, 177, 217, 228, 244, 298, 301
Sinkiang 63
Sino-Japanese War 188
Sino-Tibetan languages 64
Sioux Indians 58
Sitting Bull 58
Six Day War 103
Slavic languages 2, 62
Slovakia 179, 188
Slovenia 62
Smith, Adam 21, 32, 382, 384, 309
Smith, Alfred E. 85
Smith, Ian 179
Smith, Joseph 83

Social Credit Party (Canada) 231
Social Democratic Party: Austria 232,
    235; Germany 232, 247, 255; Great
    Britain 231; Sweden 232;
    Switzerland 232, 262
Social Gospel 85
Social Hierarchy 127–130
Socialist Party: Italy 230; Japan 163
Socrates 196
Soka Gakkai 114
Sol Invictus 151
Solid Waste 315
Solidarity 223
Solzhenitsyn, Alexander 321
Somalia 2, 65, 225, 273, 299
Somoza, Anastasio 183
Songhai, Empire of 56
Soto Buddhism 113
South Africa, Republic of 2, 6, 65, 67,
    188, 229, 245, 274
South Carolina 33, 67, 228
South Tyrol 213
Soviet Elections 251, 252
Soviet Union 10, 52, 61, 63, 65, 70, 72,
    89, 126, 128, 129, 159, 172, 180, 184,
    185, 189, 211, 212, 220, 221, 222, 251,
    252, 266, 271, 274, 275, 290, 291,
    294, 295, 314, 318, 319
Spain 9, 18, 32, 40, 59, 63, 82, 95, 99,
    121, 174, 175, 182, 198, 209, 210, 214,
    219, 225, 251, 252, 272, 283, 290
Spanish-American War 34
Spanish Civil War 182, 290
Sparta 14, 196, 279
Spitzbergen 182
Sputnik 30
Sri Lanka 8, 50, 272, 283, 300
Stadhouder (Dutch) 204
Stalin, Josef 23, 29, 63, 189, 221, 271,
    274, 290, 291, 321
Standerat (Switzerland) 217, 218
States, Recognition of 176–181
Stich, Otto 262
Stonehenge 10
Stroessner, Alfredo 225
Sudan 7, 63, 102, 273, 299, 309
Sudetenland 11, 269
Sudra 129
Sufis 104, 105
Suharto, General 226
Sui dynasty 49
Sukarno, Achmed 227
Suleiman "the Magnificent," Sultan of

Turkey 42
Sumatra 50
Sun Tsu 49, 52
Sung dynasty 50
Supreme Soviet 221
Suriname 6, 301
Suttee 168
Svalbard 182
Sviatoslav, Prince of Rus 95
Swaziland 214
Sweden 59, 157, 177, 198, 214, 220, 232,
    235, 264, 302
Swiss German Dialect 68
Swiss People's Party 232, 262
Switzerland 12, 34, 59, 62, 72, 86, 88,
    123, 124, 128, 157, 158, 199, 206, 212,
    215, 216, 217, 218, 219, 220, 232, 233,
    234, 238, 240, 247, 254, 255, 257,
    259, 260, 262, 263, 268, 270, 275,
    276
Sykes-Picot Agreement 43
Syllabus of Errors 87
Syracuse 14
Syria 17, 39, 40, 43, 44, 63, 93, 104,
    133, 180, 227

T

Taborites 282
Tadzhik Republic (USSR) 63
Tagsatzung 206
Tahiti 7
Taipei 187
Taiwan 11, 64, 121, 161, 187, 298, 301
Tamils 8
T'ang Dynasty 49
Tanganyika 7, 213
Tantric Buddhism 112
Tanzania 7, 40, 66, 213, 228, 301
Tao Te Ching 115
Taoism 115, 116
Taranto 41
Tasmania 259
Taylor, Charles 226
Taylor, Frederick J. 120
Tecumseh 58
Tejada, Lidia Gueiler 162
Tell-el-Kebir, Battle of 43
Tenochtitlan 57
Test-tube babies 307
Texas 33, 67, 155, 156, 187, 242, 248,
    249, 250, 304, 316
Thailand 64, 214, 298

Thatcher, Margaret 158, 293
Theodora, Byzantine Empress 153
Theodora, wife of Justinian 153
Theravada Buddhism 112, 145
Thirty Years War 175
Three Kings Day 118
Thuggee 107
Tiahuanaco 57
Tibet 52, 112, 163
Ticino 206, 275, 276
Time Attitudes 119–121
Time of Troubles, Russian 27
Timur-i-Leng (Tamerlane) 46
Tippecanoe, Battle of 58
Tips 135
Togo 66, 225
Tokugawa Iyeyasu 53, 133
Tokugawa Shogunate 53, 54, 297
Tokyo: City of 36, 313; University of 126
Tonga 181, 214
Tordesillas, Treaty of 18
Tour de France 141
Tour de Suisse 141
Tours, Battle of 40
Toxic wastes 314
Transit visa 267
Transkei 179
Transmigration of Souls 106
Transvaal 6, 188
Transylvania 63, 274
Tribunes (Roman) 197
Trier, Bishopric of 199
Trinidad and Tobago 6, 301
Tristan 153, 165
Troy 14
Trujillo, Rafael Leonidas 225
Tsushima, Battle of 54
Tunisia 43, 159, 171, 299
Tupamaro 235
Turenne, Marshal 19
Turkey 9, 10, 43, 62, 63, 176, 179, 180,
   190, 216, 237, 269, 270, 299
Tuvalu 177
Tver 25, 26
Twelver Shi'a 102
Tyler, Wat 282
Tyranny 194
Tzu Hsi 161

U

Uchtenhagen, Liliane 262
Uganda 65, 185, 225, 226, 272

Ukraine 62, 89, 222, 271
Umar 101
Umayyad dynasty 40, 101
UNITA (National Union for the Total
   Independence of Angola) 184
Unitarian Universalists 83
Unitary Nations 210
United Arab Emirates 13, 211, 214, 216,
   298
United Kingdom 12, 213, 215, 219, 231,
   250
United Party (South Africa) 245
United States 12, 13, 18, 31–38, 52, 61,
   66, 67, 83, 84, 114, 119, 177, 181,
   183–187, 189, 190, 193, 209, 210, 212,
   214, 216, 218, 219, 220, 228, 230, 231,
   233, 235, 237, 238, 239–247, 248,
   249, 251, 258, 259, 260, 261, 263,
   265, 266, 267, 270, 275, 278, 284,
   285, 286, 288, 289, 291, 292, 293,
   298, 301, 302, 303, 304, 308, 309,
   312, 314
UNR (Union for the New Republic,
   France) 233
Unterwalden 118
Untouchable 129, 130
Urban II, Pope 17
Uri 118, 206
Uruguay 5, 215, 225, 232, 235, 301
Utah 83
Uthman 101
Utopia 302
Utopian Socialism 287
Uzbekistan 275

V

Vaisya 129
Val d'Aosta 213
Valais 68, 276
Valparaiso 34
Values 138–146
van Buren, Martin 285
van Leiden, Jan 282
Vanished Cultures of the Past 55–58
Vargas, Getulio 236
Vatican I 87
Vatican II 88
Vatican City 86, 87, 177
Vaud 206
Venezuela 5, 211, 215, 243, 244, 301
Venice, Republic of 174, 199, 205–206
Vermont 156

Vienna 34, 41, 42, 96
Vietnam 8, 9, 161, 185, 188, 192, 224, 267, 268, 298
Vietnam War 186, 192, 292
Vijayanagar 46
Vikings 10, 16
Virginia 67, 228
Visa 266
Vishnu 107, 108
Visigoths 9
Vladimir 25, 26
Vladivostok 51
Vojvodina 63, 274
von Hindenburg, Paul 22, 183
von Manstein, Erich 24
von Schleicher, Kurt 183
Vorarlberg 68
Voting Rights 239–240

W

Wald, Patricia M. 156
Waldensians 282
Wales 10, 62, 233, 245
Wallace, George C. 233
Wang An Shih 296
Wang Mang 296
Warsaw: City of 24; Grand Duchy of 207
Washington, George 30, 193
Washington: City of 32; State of 242
Water Pollution 313
Wehrmacht 23
Welsh language 60
Welsh Nationalist Party 233
Wesley, John 83
Western Samoa 214
Whitney, Eli 32
Wilder, L. Douglas 275
William I of Orange 205
William III, King of England 199
William IV of Orange 205
William V of Orange 205
Wilson, Woodrow 183, 286
Woman's place 150–162
World League of American Football 141
World War I 22, 23, 29, 34, 35, 90, 176, 188, 210, 280, 288, 289
World War II 23, 24, 29, 35, 176, 188, 189, 210, 290, 297
Worldwide Church of God 84
Writing Systems 69–72
Wroclaw 10
Wuerttemberg 199

X

Xerxes, King of Persia 15

Y

Yahweh 151
Yamamoto, Isoroku 133
Yang di Pertuan Agong 216
Yaqui Indians 57
Yazid 101
Yeltsin, Boris 223
Yemen 96, 103, 224, 299
Yi Sun 53
Yom Kippur War 158
Yrigoyen, Ypolito 236
Yuan Dynasty 49
Yugoslavia 62, 70, 82, 177, 188, 210, 211, 212, 215, 216, 223, 295

Z

Zaidi Islam 103
Zaire 2, 65, 225, 269
Zakah 99
Zakat 100
Zambia 65, 130, 228, 269, 301
Zanzibar 7, 56, 213
Zarathustra (Zoroaster) 110, 111
Zazen 113
Zealand 204
Zen Buddhism 111
Zeus 151
Zevi, Shabbatai 130
Zhivkov, Todor 12, 223
Zia, Begum Khalida 159
Zia ul-Haq, Mohammed 226, 237
Zimbabwe: Great 56; Republic of 130, 179, 269
Zoroastrianism 9, 110, 111
Zwingli, Huldreich 82
Zulus 6, 56
Zurich 68, 72, 255, 275
Zvareva, Natalia 142, 143

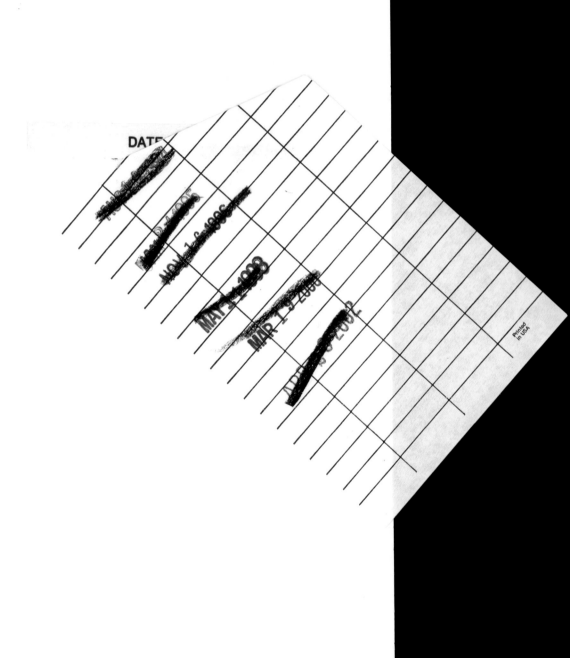

DATE